AMERICAN TRAVELLERS IN LIVERPOOL

American Travellers in Liverpool

Edited by David Seed

LIVERPOOL UNIVERSITY PRESS

First published 2008 by
Liverpool University Press
4 Cambridge Street
Liverpool L69 7ZU

British Library Cataloguing-in-Publication data
A British Library CIP record is available

ISBN 978–1–84631–129–1 limp

Typeset by Carnegie Book Production Limited
Printed and bound by Bell and Bain Ltd, Glasgow

Contents

Introduction

IN 1882 THE TRAVELLER Joel Cook declared: 'At Liverpool most American travellers begin their view of England.'[1] Throughout the nineteenth century it was the first port of call for most American travellers arriving in England. Following the end of the Napoleonic wars in 1815, regular transatlantic voyages were introduced, mostly from New York and Boston. Initially these voyages were hazardous and time-consuming, often taking as long as two weeks. The introduction of steamships in 1838 reduced the time of travel but did not remove the element of danger. During the winter of 1858–59 Sarah Parker Remond had such a terrifying voyage when her ship became coated in ice that she was taken ill and on her arrival in Liverpool had to recover at a friend's before she could start a lecture tour. By mid-century the Black Ball, Cunard, Guion and Inman lines were all serving the transatlantic routes to Liverpool. Every aspect of travel had its element of national competitiveness and these voyages were no exception. In 1853 the American journalist Matthew F. Ward declared smugly: 'The truth must be told, the British steamships have been beaten, and the most rapid passages ever achieved between the Old and New World have been accomplished by the American steamships.'[2]

The literary historian Robert E. Spiller has shown that, although there were American visitors to England in the eighteenth century – Quaker travellers, painters, students – it was not until the late 1810s that travel literature began to emerge as a popular genre. A number of factors combined to bring this about. Despite the brief war between Britain and the USA in 1812, by the end of that decade, Spiller argues, the United States had become accepted as a nation by Britain. In 1816 a regular passenger

---

1 Joel Cook, *England, Picturesque and Descriptive* (Philadelphia: Porter & Coates, 1882), and at http://ia30012.us.archive.org/0/items/england00cookuoft/england00cookuoft_djvu.txt/

2 Matthew F. Ward, *English Items; or, Microscopic Views of England and Englishmen* (New York: Appleton, 1853), and at http://ia30132.us.archive.org/3/items/englishitems00wardrich/ englishitems00wardrich_djvu.txt/

service was established between New York and Liverpool, facilitating that voyage.³ And also, as Americans became accustomed to their status as an independent nation, they became drawn to the Old Country and throughout the nineteenth century travel writing remained one of the most prolific and popular forms of literature in the USA.⁴ The sheer number of these accounts reflects a radical change in travel habits. Where the Grand Tour to western and southern Europe used to be the privilege of wealthy gentlemen, travel to Europe, the Holy Land and even farther afield now became accessible to thousands.

An early American guidebook, *The Tourist in Europe* (1838), declared, 'You may easily see Liverpool and its lions in a couple of days or less', but this dismissive attitude was not typical of American reactions to the city.⁵ Nor did their descriptions resemble guidebooks, although the docks and public buildings became standard features. The vast majority of these accounts were directed at an American readership and therefore were particularly conscious of national expectations in travellers. The Baltimore editor Charles C. Fulton's title for his description of a tour of Britain and the Continent could stand as a subtitle for the present volume. *Europe Viewed through American Spectacles* (1874) made the intention of the book clear: 'It contains precisely such facts about Europe, and the social life and peculiarities of the people of most of the Continental nations, as all Americans ought to know, which they desire to know, and which are usually ignored in similar books of travel.'⁶ Not all works were so straightforwardly informational. Some accounts were in the form of letters home, some dispatches to newspapers, and some were private journals, presumably only intended for family consumption. But all were American and, as such, all the accounts selected here negotiated national differences. Their characteristic rhetoric is comparative and the traveller's presumptions of social norms are constantly being put under pressure. For instance, Charles Fulton was full of admiration for Liverpool's commercial energy but at the same time, like Emerson before him, astonished by

---

3   Robert E. Spiller, *The American in England During the First Half Century of Independence* (Philadelphia: Porcupine Press, 1976), chap. 1, pp. 133–34, 346. Spiller's account remains one of the most useful discussions of this literature.

4   The most comprehensive listing of this literature remains Harold F. Smith's *American Travellers Abroad: A Bibliography of Accounts Published Before 1900*, 2ⁿᵈ edition (Lanham, MD: Scarecrow Press, 1999).

5   Quoted in William C. Gilman, *Melville's Early Life and 'Redburn'* (New York: New York University Press, 1951), p. 336.

6   Charles Carroll Fulton, *Europe Viewed through American Spectacles* (Philadelphia: J. B. Lippincott, 1874), p. 3, and at http://ia350636.us.archive.org/0/items/furopeviewedthrooofultrich/ furopeviewedthrooofultrich_djvu.txt/

how brazen the city prostitutes were. Emerson confined his astonishment to private conversation and his journal; Fulton at least writes it into his published description of the city. Samuel S. Cox's first impression of the city was one of bewilderment, recording that 'every object, even the go-carts, strike a stranger queerly at first'. Not least, there were the conventions of tipping servants, which were complicated, as there was a whole tariff depending on the servants' roles, but essential. The hapless traveller who, when surrounded by locals on the dockside offering to carry his luggage as happened to Frederick Law Olmsted, said he would take his bags himself, would be told that a gentleman didn't do that. A whole social code had to be learnt, including that of dress. In hotels the presumption would be that you ate alone; in America company would be the norm. And all the time we witness travellers' attempts to explain difference in terms of national characteristics. Emerson thought that the massive architecture of the Liverpool docks reflected a general 'solidity' in the nation; John Audubon was reduced to depression by the sombreness of an English Christmas. Indeed, the journalist Horace Greeley found the English to be so 'grave' that he diagnosed a national aversion to enjoyment. Whatever the differences, at least the two countries shared a common language. Or did they? Writing from Liverpool in 1867, the newspaper editor John Forney recognized that it was a delight to hear the speech of an 'accomplished English gentleman or lady', but complained that 'the lingual intercourse between the working people of England is so uncouth and barbaric as to sound more like the vernacular of Indian tribes'.[7] Throughout these extracts Americans constantly register their rather puzzled sense that England was both familiar and foreign, somehow the same and yet different.

First impressions might disorient visitors or engage them if they were favourably surprised. After being spoken to abruptly by a ship's master in Liverpool, Dr. Heman Humphrey recorded in his journal: 'I am sorry to find, that the English are an exceedingly *quarrelsome* people.'[8] Similarly, Henry B. McLellan, in Britain to pursue his studies, took a dim view of the Liverpool customs house where he was not only forced to rub shoulders with 'menials' but was also confronted by an official winking at him with an outstretched hand ready for his 'sweetener'. Among the most striking reactions was the comparison by N. P. Willis, Harriet Beecher Stowe and others that Liverpool resembled New York or, in other words, was like a displaced American city. In her journal of 1863, the Canadian Elizabeth

---

7 John W. Forney, *Letters from Europe* (1867), quoted in Henry Steele Commager, ed., *Britain Through American Eyes* (London: The Bodley Head, 1974), p. 397.
8 During a visit of 1835, quoted in Spiller, *The American in England*, p. 244.

A. Forbes admitted that 'Liverpool is very unlike my preconceived idea of the great commercial city; I had fancied it dirty, dingy, crowded and uninteresting. But my notions have been corrected, no very unusual occurrence. The solid masonry of the long miles of docks is in striking contrast to our dirty piers, and our landing upon the clean pavement of the wharf was as quiet as a walk in a country town.'9 In contrast, Louisa May Alcott passed through Liverpool in 1865 as travelling companion to an invalid lady, evidently without forming a very favourable impression of the place. Three years later a character in *Little Women* (1868–69) wrote: 'We only stopped at Liverpool a few hours. It's a dirty, noisy place, and I was glad to leave it.'10 In the 1850s William Wells Brown saw Liverpool as a city built for the future, whereas at the end of the century Helen Holt Jackson declared: 'Liverpool looked very old and musty, as if it had been finished centuries ago and put away.'11 Clean, dirty; new, old. Clearly general impressions of Liverpool varied enormously, depending on the expectations of visitors and their willingness to revise their preconceptions once they saw the city.

During his 1835 journey to England the French traveller Alexis de Tocqueville noted that Liverpool was 'destined to become the centre of English trade' and the same perception informed many Americans' reactions to the city.12 In fact, whether there was more to Liverpool than commerce became a recurring question. The first travellers to leave records of their visits were commercial and therefore stressed features such as road-building and of course the docks, which appear in every account. Their extent, size and the sheer variety of maritime traffic are standard highlights of descriptions of Liverpool throughout the century. Benjamin Silliman's descriptions from the 1810s are given in some detail because he establishes the main sights within the city that will become obligatory viewing for subsequent visitors: the Athenaeum, the Lyceum, the School for the Blind, and the Quarry, among other places. The last of these was converted into St James's Cemetery, which was consecrated in 1829. The windmills mentioned by early visitors were also soon to disappear as the city extended outwards from the 1820s. Silliman pays so much attention to these public

---

9 Elizabeth A. Forbes, *A Woman's First Impressions of Europe. Wayside Sketches Made during a Short Tour in the Year 1863* (New York: Derby & Miller, 1865) and at http://www.archive.org/details/womansfirstooforbrich/

10 Louisa May Alcott, *Little Women* (New York: Norton, 2004), p. 246.

11 William Wells Brown, *Three Years in Europe*; Helen Holt Jackson, *Bits of Travel* (1872), at

http://www.archive.org/details/bitsoftraveloojackiala/

12 Alexis de Tocqueville, *Journeys to England and Ireland* (Garden City, NY: Anchor, 1968), p. 99.

buildings because they reflect the civic energy of the city and importantly balance its commerce with its cultural facilities.

Silliman sets a trend in regard to two other aspects, both predictable. The traveller's first experience of Liverpool was passing through a customs check and all the signs are that 'contributions' were expected if luggage was going to be cleared promptly. To judge from the different accounts in this volume, tobacco was the favourite commodity for smuggling, hence the customs officers' careful search of ships' holds as well as luggage. Lastly, Americans' experience of Liverpool hotels was unavoidable, although once again impressions varied widely. Some travellers, such as Silliman, were bemused by the practices of the hotel staff and the elaborate rituals of taking tea or being shown to their rooms. N. P. Willis recorded that he had stayed in the worst hotel in the world, though his was a minority view. Praise was the norm, for the American Hotel, the Northwestern, and the Adelphi, which became the top hotel in the latter half of the century. Coincidentally, Elizabeth Forbes and Helen Holt Jackson both stayed in the Washington, which was just off St George's Square. Forbes simply describes it as an 'elegant hotel', whereas Jackson, with a more satirical turn of mind, joked about its large stained-glass effigy of Washington inside the entrance, commenting: 'I suppose it is intended as a delicate bait for Americans.' If it is, it doesn't work in her case, triggering laughter instead of a patriotic frisson.

Zachariah Allen's *The Practical Tourist* (1832) lives up to its title with a vengeance in directing the visitor to pay attention to the grime of the city. For most tourists dirt was just dirt; Wilbur Fisk described Liverpool simply as 'sombre and gloomy' and left it at that. But Allen wants to know what produces the dirt and pronounces the culprit to be the coal fires that are burnt throughout the city. Similarly, he notes the widespread use of gas lighting in Liverpool, which again marks progress but at the same time fills the city with a sulphurous smell. Allen's earnest fascination with road-surfacing and industrial processes such as the manufacture of iron chains makes his descriptions of the city refreshingly different from the more conventional surveys of Liverpool landmarks.

Allen's approach could not contrast more strongly with that promoted by the first famous literary visitor to Liverpool – Washington Irving. When Irving sailed to Liverpool in 1815 he came for commercial reasons, to help the family business there; but his record of that visit in *The Sketch Book of Geoffrey Crayon* (1819–20) gives us no indication of this fact. Instead Irving excludes all commercial motivation to present a version of himself as a tourist in search of the picturesque, who will provide the reader with sketches of Britain, i.e. lightly dashed-off impressions. His portrait of Roscoe includes a little topography but is mainly concerned with creating the image of a cultured gentleman to offset Liverpool's reputation for commerce. Throughout *The Sketch Book* Irving is responding to England as a storied land charged with literary associations, and that is an approach shared by a whole line of writers after Irving. Travelling to England is represented as a kind of return, a reunion with a shared culture. When the philosopher and educator Thomas Cogswell Upham first arrived in England, he recorded: 'I felt, on stepping for the first time on the soil of England, like the man who returns, after many years' absence, to his father's home.'[13] In the same spirit Nathaniel Hawthorne gave the title *Our Old Home* to his 1863 volume of English sketches. These sentiments were echoed by Harriet Beecher Stowe and many other American visitors. The Ohio newspaper editor Samuel S. Cox matched up the first person to speak to him in Liverpool with *Oliver Twist*, and the move was typical of many travellers enjoying what they thought was the realization of images of England they had drawn. The expert on these reactions was Henry James, who examined this mindset in his famous 1871 story 'A Passionate Pilgrim', where the narrator reflects: 'The latent preparedness of the American mind for even the most delectable features of English life is a fact which I never fairly probed to the depths.'[14] Throughout his life James cherished the first evening in 1869 that he spent in the Adelphi Hotel, which symbolized his adult entry into Europe. Foster Rhea Dulles sums up this predisposition as follows: 'The spirit in which these travellers sought out Europe was nostalgic and sentimental. Theirs was a romantic return to the past, a devoted search for the wellsprings of their own culture.'[15] Surprisingly, despite the growth in transatlantic travel, it rarely figured substantially in American fiction, with the honourable exception of Herman Melville's *Redburn* (1849), as we shall see. Cultural contrasts through voyages figure in W. D. Howells' *The Lady of the Aroostook* (1879), and Stephen Crane's *Active Service* (1899) uses a voyage to Liverpool to dramatize the opposing pulls of love and professional duty in a journalist setting off to cover a war in Europe. Finally, Willa Cather's first novel, *Alexander's Bridge* (1912), draws on her experiences of transatlantic travel a few years earlier.

---

13   Thomas Cogswell Upham, *Letters Aesthetic, Social and Moral, Written from Europe, Egypt, and Palestine* (Philadelphia: H. Longstreth, 1857), pp. 23–24. As we might expect, there were also dissenting voices. Nathaniel H. Carter recorded that on landfall at Liverpool 'there was no kneeling to kiss the parent earth' (quoted in Spiller, *The American in England*, p. 356). Carter's view was in the minority.

14   Maqbool Aziz, ed., *The Tales of Henry James. Volume 2: 1870–1874* (Oxford: Clarendon Press, 1978), p. 42.

15   Foster Rhea Dulles, *Americans Abroad: Two Centuries of European Travel* (Ann Arbor: University of Michigan Press, 1964), p. 31.

Melville's novel *Redburn* is an unusual case within this volume because it combines his memories of sailing to the port some ten years earlier with elements taken from an older guidebook to the city, *The Picture of Liverpool*, which Redburn's father has in his library. The novel is unusual in sacrificing plot to uniquely detailed descriptions of Liverpool in the early decades of the century. Redburn himself resembles a parody tourist, trekking round the city with his 'prosy old guide-book' in his hands, a guidebook that Melville did not hesitate to draw on for some of his descriptions. Redburn, like the later heroes of Henry James and Mark Twain, is an innocent abroad constantly being subjected to solicitations from beggars and constantly bewildered by the teeming street life around the docks. In that respect the novel makes a very good corrective to those accounts that only highlight the picturesque. Melville does for Liverpool what Dickens was doing for London in evoking a labyrinth of side streets and cellars where the poor live.

It is essential to remember that Henry James's enjoyment of the Adelphi was offset by a professional purpose: to develop his career as a writer. A similar urgency informed the arrival in 1826 of the naturalist John James Audubon, who was developing his techniques of painting birds. Forming a close friendship with the Rathbone family, he organized exhibitions of his works before moving on to Edinburgh, where he found an engraver who made possible his famous *Birds of America*. Like Harriet Beecher Stowe after him, Audubon became a celebrity, something he played to in his dress by promoting the image of an exotic backwoodsman. Later, in the 1870s, the painter James Whistler became closely associated with Liverpool through his patron, the shipowner Frederick Leyland. Not only did he suggest the term 'nocturne' for Whistler's experiments with night scenes, but he also rented Speke Hall, which became one of the main subjects for Whistler's painting of this period.

The other well-known American writer to take up residence in Liverpool was Nathaniel Hawthorne, who served as American Consul from 1853 to 1857. The Liverpool Consulate was established in 1790 with the appointment of James Maury, who stayed in office until 1829. Maury was a friend alike to Thomas Jefferson and William Roscoe, acting as president of the American Chamber of Commerce in Liverpool. Given the importance of commercial and political links between Liverpool and the USA, Hawthorne's appointment was a prestigious one, a fact of which he was well aware. In his account of his consular duties in *Our Old Home*, he recorded his sense of being in the 'gateway between the Old World and the New'. As befits a cultural diplomat, Hawthorne published little about Liverpool during his lifetime. Our main sources of information about his period in the city are two memoirs by his son and his English notebooks, which were published posthumously. From these we learn that one of Hawthorne's favourite activities was to stroll around the city, 'always finding himself among the poor and their dwellings'.[16] Whether we call this social voyeurism or not, Hawthorne gives us a fascinating series of Dickensian pictures of Liverpool street life at mid-century. Beggars seem to be everywhere, but Hawthorne comments interestingly on their general tolerance by the public. He shows a Dickensian relish for grotesquely vivid figures, especially when describing Liverpool women, and here Hawthorne's diplomacy collapses. Attending a soirée at the Town Hall, he gets distracted by the appearance of the women present, whom he writes off as 'gross, gross, gross'.[17] Otherwise we are given detailed vignettes of the Mersey ferries (for most of his period Hawthorne lived in Rock Park), the Necropolis, the West Derby Workhouse, itinerant musicians and a host of other city scenes. Although he reportedly liked to visit English graveyards to see if he could find traces of lost ancestors, Hawthorne was never a naïve 'passionate pilgrim'. He was enough of a realist to be fascinated by the way things were in a modern metropolis and was constantly bemused by the ease of social contact induced by the English class system.

Paradoxical as it may seem, Liverpool was at the same time a key port in the slave trade and an important centre for abolition. As more and more former slaves arrived in the city from America, from the 1830s onwards, the USA's cherished image of itself as a refuge for the persecuted became reversed. One such arrival was that of William Wells Brown, author of the first play and novel by an African American, who reflected as he strolled about the city, 'I am truly free'. The memoir prefacing his subsequent memoir, *Three Years in Europe* (1852), pointed out the irony: 'In the nineteenth century the victims of the oppressions of the American Republic find freedom and social equality upon the shores of monarchical England. Liverpool, which seventy years back was so steeped in the guilt of negro slavery that Paine expressed his surprise that God did not sweep it from the face of the earth, is now to the hunted negro the Plymouth Rock of Old England.'[18] Now the New World had become the persecutor and the Old World the refuge. Landfall at Liverpool for these travellers took on a special symbolism.

---

16 Julian Hawthorne, *Hawthorne and His Circle* (1903), chap. 6 at http://www.gutenberg.org/dirs/etext04/hcirc10.txt/

17 Nathaniel Hawthorne, *The English Notebooks*, ed. Randall Stewart (New York: Modern Language Association of America; London: Oxford University Press, 1941), p. 88.

18 William Wells Brown, *Three Years in Europe; or, Places I Have Seen and People I Have Met* (London: Charles Gilpin, 1852) and at http://docsouth.unc.edu/neh/brown52/brown52.html

Until the American Civil War, African Americans came to Liverpool to pursue different aims all connected with the pursuit of freedom. They might want to continue the campaign for abolition and towards this end they usually came armed with letters of introduction to sympathizers in the city. Often they began lecture tours around Britain to inform the public at first hand about the abuses of slavery; or they may have published their memoirs, many of which first appeared as booklets printed in Britain; or again, they may have simply wished to start a new life. Sarah Remond, for instance, lectured around the country and then trained as a doctor in Italy, never to return to the United States. The pieces relating to abolition collected in this volume therefore tend not to describe Liverpool. They show no interest in the scenic, but pay more attention to differences in racial attitudes between that city and what they had grown accustomed to in America. Frederick Douglass even discovered that racism persisted in the accommodation offered on the transatlantic voyages. For these visitors Liverpool above all offered a forum for the publicization and free discussion of slavery. In other words, Liverpool helped liberate their voices and it is particularly interesting to note in the records of their lectures the lively and usually positive responses of their audiences.

The campaign for abolition overlapped with missionary activity, evangelism, and the coming of African American culture to Victorian England. In the 1840s a minstrel group and the dancer William Henry Lane ('Juba') toured England. A performance in Liverpool by Juba was enthusiastically reported in 1848: 'Whilst his feet still seem upon the ground, he contrives to beat distinctly through all the variations of a popular and fashionable tune.'[19] The Georgia Slave Troupe gave a number of performances in the 1860s and the following decade the Jubilee Singers gave concerts in the Philharmonic Hall. Apart from these performances, the addresses on slavery had a strong religious, even evangelical dimension. Amanda Berry Smith was an important figure in this connection. Born a slave, she turned to evangelism in the 1870s and pursued missionary activities in Africa as well as speaking in cities such as Liverpool. Then, towards the end of the nineteenth century, the economist and reformer Henry George came to Liverpool, partly to investigate the poverty of the city and as a step in a campaign for the rights of landed tenants in Ireland and Scotland. He adopted the rhetoric of the abolitionists in attacking the abuses of the large estates.

In fact Liverpool hosted social reformers and lecturers throughout the nineteenth century. Emerson delivered lectures in his Great Men series during his 1847–48 tour, though he decided quickly that he had had

---

19   *Liverpool Journal*, 11 November 1848.

enough of Liverpool. This was not the case with Harriet Beecher Stowe, who visited the city soon after the publication of *Uncle Tom's Cabin* in 1851. Riding high on her success, she was welcomed as a celebrity and invited to give a number of talks on slavery. Her letters describing this tour of Britain and the Continent, *Sunny Memories of Foreign Lands* (1854), really straddle two genres: the report on lectures and the travelogue. As her title suggests, it was a very benign record, which paid tribute to the hospitality of the Croppers (a Quaker family active in the abolitionist cause) and of Liverpool generally. Where Stowe expressed her delight over the picturesque Dingle and Speke Hall, other visitors were far more critical. Margaret Fuller was outraged by the signs of class in Liverpool society and Horace Greeley decided that the English were a cold and stuffy lot. Both writers were in effect giving reports on Britain rather than travel narratives, and at the turn of the century the feminist writer Charlotte Perkins Gilman gave a number of talks on social reform in Liverpool.

During the American Civil War the position of Liverpool as a centre for representing American interests was compromised by the break between North and South, though the city retained its commercial importance. In *Gone with the Wind* the blockade runner Rhett Butler keeps some of his funds and most of his cotton in Liverpool. There was a widespread conviction that Liverpool was broadly sympathetic to the Confederacy, but the situation was more complex than that. When the New England minister Henry Ward Beecher gave a talk in 1863 stressing the shared interests of Britain and the Union, there seem to have been only a relatively small number of hecklers opposing him; and when Laird Brothers were building a Confederate battleship in their yard, some of the workers sympathetic to the Northern cause were giving information to the US Consul Thomas H. Dudley. Dudley was well aware of the threat to Union interests posed by this secret shipbuilding and organized a whole network of sympathizers and informers in the city. Dudley's opposite number was the Confederate agent James Dunwody Bulloch, who later published a detailed account of his activities in Liverpool. After the war he remained in the city, taking out British citizenship. Less known is the fact that, after the treason case against him collapsed, the leader of the Confederacy Jefferson Davis came to Liverpool in July 1868 with the intention of setting up a commission house for cotton and tobacco. In the event his plan fell through and he returned to America.

The Civil War period politicized all American visits to Liverpool because of the rival claims of the Confederacy and the Union. Even when there was no explicit political agenda, however, American travellers were acting as the ambassadors of their national culture. The encounter in these visits between New World and Old was a two-way process. While travellers were reporting on English customs and practices, their interactions with different sections of the Liverpool populace were introducing American culture to the locals. Thus Audubon's negotiations to exhibit his paintings were popularizing imagery of the American wilderness. Emerson's lectures were introducing his own brand of Transcendentalism to Liverpool audiences and the campaign of African American addresses on slavery was giving first-hand accounts of that system to listeners who probably had only a vague sense of its abuses. These lecture formed part of a broader introduction of African American culture to Liverpool, which started in the 1840s with the arrival of the first minstrel groups, followed in 1866 by Sam Hague's Georgia Slave Troupe and in 1873 by the Fisk Jubilee Singers.

This period is marked by the emergence of early signs of celebrity culture: wherever Harriet Beecher Stowe went in the 1850s she drew large audiences; in the 1870s the evangelist Dwight Lyman Moody returned to clamouring newsmen in the USA after drawing huge attendances for his meetings in Liverpool and elsewhere. Apart from the musical shows noted above, George Catlin's 'exhibitions' of Native Americans appeared in Liverpool in the 1840s. In 1844 the supreme American showman P. T. Barnum sailed to Liverpool with Charles Stratton, known as 'General Tom Thumb'. Although his intention had been to head directly for London, he explains in his memoirs: 'My letters of introduction speedily brought me into friendly relations with many excellent families and I was induced to hire a hall and present the General to the public, for a short season, in Liverpool.'[20] Barnum returned to Liverpool in 1857, again with General Tom Thumb and also with the precocious actress Cordelia Howard, who had achieved success by playing Little Eva in the dramatization of *Uncle Tom's Cabin*. An important event in the history of sport relations between the two countries took place on 30 July 1874 when the Philadelphia Athletic and Boston Red Stockings played a baseball match on Liverpool Cricket Ground at Edge Hill. Later, in 1891, Buffalo Bill's Wild West Show performed in Newsham Park. The *Liverpool Mercury* reported enthusiastically that it presented 'a piece of the Wild West bodily transported to our midst'.[21] All these events, together

---

20 P. T. Barnum, *Struggles and Triumphs; or, Forty Years' Recollections*, ed. Carl Bode (Harmondsworth: Penguin, 1981), p. 146. On both visits Barnum stayed in the Waterloo Hotel.

21 *The Graphic* reported on this match ('The American Baseball Players') on 15 August 1874. Philadelphia beat Boston by 14–11. The *Liverpool Mercury* quoted in Robert H. Rydell and Rob Kroes, *Buffalo Bill in Bologna: The Americanization of the World, 1869–1922* (Chicago: University of Chicago Press, 2005), p. 116.

with the less dramatic opening in 1909 of the first Woolworths '3d and 6d store' in Liverpool, signalled the arrival of American culture in the city and in Britain generally, a process that is still continuing to this day.[22]

---

22 The Woolworths stores opened on 5 November 1909 in Church Street and Williamson Street. They were an instant success, especially their refreshment rooms, which served free tea on the opening day.

List of Illustrations

1

Commercial, Diplomatic
and Scientific Travellers

T HE FIRST TRAVELLERS to record their visits to Liverpool did so
mainly from business motives, as during the second half of the
eighteenth century the town was evolving into a major commercial port.
Samuel Curwen (1715–1802) was one of the first to leave an account
of the fledgling city. He was a leading merchant in Salem and described
himself as a 'loyalist', an awkward label to adopt during the period that
the USA achieved independence. Curwen stayed in Liverpool briefly on
his way to a tour of Britain and Europe, and his account in a private
journal sets a keynote for subsequent descriptions of the city in stressing
the pace of commercial activity, especially in the docks. The Old Dock
(or Town Dock) extended into the centre of the city and was closed in
1825 and filled in 1826. The battery on which Curwen comments would
have been that constructed on a piece of land set apart for the purpose by
an order of 1761.

June 1780

At half past 10 o'clock reshipped ourselves on board same barge,
and in two good hours returned back from whence we took
departure. On arrival finding a chaise to set off, no passenger
therein, an easy fare of 4/– [four shillings] to Liverpool, and the
distance of 20 miles we again diverged from our right lined course
to Manchester, and struck off for that town. Returning back
through Warrington proceeded to Prescott at 10 miles distance,
where taking a relay made no abode longer than necessity obliged.
This town is noted for coal pits and watch movements. With
former Liverpool is principally supplied by wagons, the road, going
and coming being filled with them to our no small annoyance.
    From hence thither road is level and pleasant almost, if not
wholly, paved both in Carr and footway, at 6 o'clock entered

the City so celebrated for its mercantile character. Houses are
by a great majority in middling and lower style, few, very few
comparatively rise above that mark. Streets long narrow and
crooked, and dirty in an eminent degree. Choosing a small
abode here we scarce saw a well-dressed person, nor half a dozen
gentlemen. Few of the shops have the appearance to be seen in
all other great Towns, dress and looks more like inhabitants of
Wapping, Shadwell, Rotherhithe [dockland areas of London] than
in neighbourhood of Exchange or London anywhere above Tower.
The whole complexion nautical and so infinitely below all our
expectations that naught but the thoughts of the few hours we
had to pass here rendered it tolerable. The Docks, however, are
stupendously grand. The inner, or that called Town dock lying
almost in the centre of it, and is filled with innumerable vessels
exhibiting a forest of masts. Beside this are 3 or 4 very large
ones, all containing great numbers of vessels, lying in front of
city, communicating with each other by flood gates, intermixed
with dry ones for benefit of repairing. The lower or new one, of
greatest extent has a fine wide Quay on its outer seaboard side,
an agreeable walk, lined with trees on either hand. Below this
in river is now building, almost finished, a circular battery with
embrasures for more than 30 Cannon of 32, 24 and 18 pounders.
Parade and barracks are now in hand and when completed, will
provide a charming walk and prospect to inhabitants if allowed.

> Andrew Oliver, ed., *The Journal of Samuel Curwen, Loyalist*
> (Cambridge, MA: Harvard University Press, 1972).

Benjamin Silliman (1779–1864) studied law but became the most
distinguished chemist in America. He was appointed professor of chemistry
at Yale in 1802, and in 1805 came to Britain partly to pursue studies at
the University of Edinburgh and partly to buy scientific equipment and
books. The Olympic Circus had opened in 1805 in Christian Street. The
Liverpool Arms Hotel in Castle Street was the most prestigious hotel in
town until the building of the Adelphi Hotel. The subtitles below are
Silliman's own.

With my fellow passengers I took lodgings at a splendid hotel, the
Liverpool Arms.

CIRCUS

In the evening we went to the Circus, where equestrian feats, rope dancing, tumbling and pantomime formed the entertainment.

I shall occasionally attend the theatres, for public amusements furnish the most decisive criterion of national taste. And no contemptible one of the state of public morals, and of the dignity or degradation of the public mind; for when men go to be amused, they will demand such things as they really delight in.

The Circus was crowded; we were late, and being perfectly unknown, went into the gallery, as every other part of the house was full.

We were surrounded by those, whose deportment sufficiently indicated to what class of society they belonged, while they exhibited a spectacle of effrontery to which it would not be easy to find a parallel.

The feats performed were truly astonishing, and demonstrated the wonderful force and accuracy of muscular movement of which the human frame is capable.

There were two pantomimes.

The subject of the first was rustic love;—of the second, the story of Oscar and Malvina, from Ossian [cycle of Scottish heroic poems supposedly translated by James Macpherson].—But pantomime is altogether unnatural. In real life men never converse in this way, unless they are deaf and dumb, and such people are certainly the best actors in pantomime. It may be said that it affords room for the display of much ingenuity, in expressing a whole narration or drama without words;—this is true; but the drama would be far more interesting if expressed in words, and every one who has seen a pantomime must have felt a degree of impatience, and even *anger*, at the very incompetent, although ingenious, efforts which a performer in pantomime makes, to bring forth an idea, which a little plain talking would at once express, with force and beauty.

CUSTOM-HOUSE

[The Custom-House Silliman describes predates the domed building in Castle Street, which was built on the site of the Old Dock and opened in 1826.]

May 4.—The embarrassments created by revenue laws, and the formalities which most civilized nations observe, on admitting a stranger to enter their dominations, are among the unpleasant things which a traveller must encounter. Our share of vexation has not been very great, and yet some things have occurred which one would wish to avoid.

After our baggage had been landed, under the eye of a custom-house officer, and deposited in the public warehouse, it became necessary for us to reclaim it, that is to say, in plain English, to pay a douceur ['sweetener'] to the examining officer, to expedite its liberation, and not to molest us by rigorous examination of our parcels.

Being confident that I had no articles which could justly be charged with a duty, I felt strongly disposed to resist the oppressive demand of a contribution, for a mere discharge, or rather for a *neglect* of official duty. But, being informed that the thing was indispensable, unless I would submit to have my baggage delayed several days, with very circumstance of vexation and embarrassment, which experienced ingenuity could invent, I at length concluded to pay the tribute. But, I remarked to the person who had given me this information (an Englishman) that I supposed the money must be offered to some of those ragged fellows who act as tide waiters, and not to those *well-dressed* men about the custom-house. He replied, with a smile, that those were the men who *ultimately* received the money. Accordingly, among all the passengers of the *Ontario*, a sum was made up which, we supposed would cause *Justice* (a power whom allegory has ever represented as blind) to become still blinder than before. Nor were we disappointed; you can hardly imagine the effect of our douceur, for it would be harsh to call it a bribe. The *well-dressed* man, who ought to have inspected every thing in person, stood aloof, affecting to be engaged in conversation with other people, while a beggarly fellow received the money. We surrendered our keys, when he opened our trunks, and without taking up a single article, said that we had behaved like gentlemen, and that every thing was perfectly correct. He then closed our trunks, and returned the keys. Had they searched effectually, they would have found a quantity of costly goods, which, as they had not been entered, it was their duty to seize, and, indeed, their suspicions might well have been excited by the uncommon size of some of the trunks. [...]

My baggage being cleared, I next presented myself to the collector in person, who made out duplicate manifests of my name, age, place of birth and residence, profession, and business in England, together with a description of my person, and a list of those to whom I am known in Liverpool. I wrote my name on both papers, and he retains one, and I keep the other. With this instrument I am next to wait on the Major, to take further steps, *to ensure the safety of his Majesty's person and government during my residence in England.*

AMERICAN HOTEL

[Located in Wapping near the main docks. It was described in 1808 as a 'very large and handsome building, originally intended for, and chiefly frequented by the masters of ships in the American trade'. The national motto *e pluribus unum* ('out of many, one') was placed on the great seal of America in 1782, as was the symbol of the American Bald Eagle.]

I dined today at a house erected and kept for the accommodation of the multitude of Americans who resort to this port. The words AMERICAN HOTEL are written over the door, which is ornamented with the American Eagle, and the national motto, 'e pluribus unum.'

This parade of America insignia is not addressed, without effect, to the national vanity of our countrymen. They crowd to this house in great numbers. The inscription over the door arrests every American eye;—the national eagle excites patriotic sympathies, and those who cannot construe the motto, hope it means *good living.* And it must be confessed that this construction, although not very literal, is, in point of fact, substantially correct. The table is abundant and cheap, and although the house is not, perhaps, the most genteel, the strong temptation of national society, when held out to beings so gregarious as our countrymen, is generally successful; and, at the daily ordinary, a kind of Congress of the American States in convened, where, if they choose, they may rail with impunity at the country on whose productions they are feasting, nor fear a military arrest, before the next dinner.

LITERARY INSTITUTIONS

[James Maury served as the first American consul in Liverpool, 1790–1829, and also as chairman of the American Chamber of Commerce in the city. The Athenaeum and Lyceum are commented on below. The Union News

Room was opened in 1801, the year of union between England and Ireland,
hence its name. It was located in Duke Street and contained a large coffee
room for reading the newspapers.]

[5 May]

The politeness of Mr Maury, the American Consul, procured
us access to the ATHENÆUM and LYCEUM, two literary
institutions of very recent origin; and another gentleman
introduced us at a third, called the UNION, whose plan is
extremely similar to that of the other two. During my stay in
Liverpool I have the liberty of visiting these institutions, under
certain very reasonable restrictions.

In a city so commercial as Liverpool, these establishments must
be considered as highly honourable to the intelligence and taste of
the individuals, who have created and patronised them.

Each of them has an elegant structure of free stone, containing
a library of various literature and science, and a large coffee room,
where all the newspapers and literary journals of note are placed
daily upon the tables, for the free perusal of subscribers and of
such friends as they introduce.

To a stranger these places are highly interesting, as affording,
at a glance, a view of the most important occurrences of the
country, and to the citizens they are not less useful and agreeable;
for, the mere man of business finds here the best means of
information, and the man of literature can retire in quiet to the
library, where the librarian attends to hand down any volume that
is wanted.

Between institutions so similar, it is very natural, and doubtless
it is best, that there should be a spirit of rivalry. I know not how
much is to be imputed to this, but I heard it contended that
the library of the Athenæum is much superior to those of the
other two. This appears not improbable, for the library of the
Athenæum was selected by Mr Roscoe and Dr Currie.

Such institutions as these would be highly useful in America,
and most of our large commercial towns are rich enough to found
and sustain them.* Independently of the rational amusement which
they afford, they give a useful direction to the public taste, and
allure it from objects which are either frivolous or noxious.

* Boston, in the establishment of an Athenæum upon the plan
  of that at Liverpool, has had the honour of creating the first

institution of this kind in America, and, from the acquisitions already made, as well as from the well-known intelligence and liberality of the people of Boston, there is reason to expect that it will do much credit to this country (1809) [Silliman's note]

AN ENGLISH BREAKFAST

I have been present this morning at an English Breakfast. The lady of the house had been several years in America, and still retained so much partiality for the country, that my reception was such as to make me feel that I was at home in England.

Mrs.— pleasantly remarked that I had not been used to such frugal breakfasts in America, and indeed it must be confessed, that to a northern American, who is accustomed to see animal food on the table in the morning, an English breakfast presents no very promising prospect. It usually consists of tea and a little bread and butter. A boiled egg is sometimes added after morning exercise, and very rarely, a thin slice of ham. If an American is surprised at the frugality of an English breakfast, an Englishman is astonished at seeing beef steaks, or fish, and perhaps bottled cider on the America table at the same meal.★

★ I am sensible, however, that these habits are wearing away in our larger towns, and it is becoming *unpolite* to eat much animal food in the morning; but they are still unimpaired in the country [Silliman's note].

MUSEUM

[Bullock's Museum was located in Church Street.]

Liverpool has a small museum, which I visited this morning. It is not extensive, but is well worth seeing, especially on account of a collection of ancient armour, such as was worn from the time of the conqueror down to the period of Elizabeth. This is a remnant of an age, which though barbarous, and, on the whole, wretched, is connected with so much heroic grandeur, that every authentic vestige of it must excite a strong interest, especially in one whose country has never been the theatre of a similar state of things. The knights, when equipped for battle, were so completely encased in iron, that it is not easy to conceive how they could move joint or limb, or even sustain the enormous weight of their

armour, nor can one be surprised that an overthrow was so much
dreaded, since it must have been an arduous task to rise under
the rigidness of such a prison. But these were men whose limbs
had not been enervated by luxury; and the elegant decorations
and effeminate softness of many modern soldiers would have been
their jest and scorn. There was one singular suit of armour; or,
perhaps, it should rather be called a robe, for it was such in fact,
being a complete net work of small chains, so linked in every
direction, that it formed an iron vesture, which might be put on
and made to enclose the person completely, while it would leave
the limbs the liberty of free motion, and defend them from the
effect of cutting instruments, although not from contusions.

A fine panorama of Ramsgate with the embarkation of troops,
gave me a few minutes of pleasant entertainment, on my way to
visit.

[The Panorama was a round building adjacent to the Lyceum in Bold Street,
opened for the purpose of showing circular paintings, then in fashion.]

THE ASYLUM OF THE BLIND

[See notes below, under Ballard.]

In this institution the incurably blind are received, protected, and
instructed in such arts as they are capable of learning. The object
is to afford them the means of subsistence by personal industry,
and of amusement under the gloom of perpetual darkness. The
arts, in the practice of which I saw them engaged, were of course
such as required no uncommon accuracy, and whose operations
can be conducted by the touch; such as knitting, weaving, and
winding thread, among the women, and making baskets and
cords among the men. Their productions were much better than
one would imagine it possible they should be, did not experience
prove that the loss of one sense causes so active a cultivation of
the rest, that they become more perfect than before. How else can
we account for the acuteness of hearing which enabled a particular
blind man, by means of the echo produced by his whistling, to
decide when he was approaching any object of some magnitude,
or, for the delicacy of touch which led the blind Mr. Jay★ to
discover, by feeling, the place where the two pieces of an ancient
mahogany table were joined, which multitudes, for a succession of

years, although in possession of all their senses, had sought in vain to detect.

In the institution of which I am speaking, those who have a taste for it, learn music both instrumental and vocal, that they may be able to obtain their bread by performing in churches.

When I entered, two blind boys were playing on the organ and piano, and, at my request, a choir of both sexes performed a piece—the dying Christian's address to his soul,—which they sung to the organ. This production, in itself very solemn and interesting, was rendered doubly so by the associated effect produced by the *sightless* choir who performed it, with much apparent feeling. Printed papers were distributed about the rooms, containing religious songs appropriate to the situation of the blind and holding forth to them such consolations as must be peculiarly dear to those for whom the sun rises in vain. There was, however, in most of them, an air of cheerfulness which served to enliven a scene otherwise very gloomy. The charity urn at the door contained this simple inscription, which must produce a stronger effect on every mind than the most laboured address to the feelings:

> 'Remember the poor blind!'

These are the institutions which do honour to mankind, and show the active efficacy of Christian benevolence.

A SLAVE SHIP

The friend who had brought me to this interesting place, went with me to a large guinea ship, a thing which I had always wished to see, with a curiosity like that which would have led me to the Bastille. We descended into the hold, and examined the cells where human beings are confined, under circumstances which equally disgust decency and shock humanity. But I will not enlarge on a subject which, though trite, is awfully involved in guilt and infamy. *Our* country, so nobly jealous of its own liberties, stands disgraced in the eyes of mankind, and condemned at the bar of heaven, for being at once active in carrying on this monstrous traffic, and prompt to receive every cargo of imported Africans. I did not come to England to see guinea ships because there were none in America, but accident had never thrown one in my way before. Liverpool is *deep, very deep* in the guilt of slave-trade. It is now pursued with more eagerness then ever,

and multitudes are, at this moment, rioting on the wealth which
has been gained by the stripes, the groans, the tears, the blood of
Africans.

There will be a day when these things shall be told in heaven!

★ Brother of John Jay, Esq. late Governor of New-York, and envoy
extraordinary to England in the year 1794 [Silliman's note]

SKETCH OF LIVERPOOL

Under the guidance of Mr Wells, an English gentleman who
had visited America, I have been to the Exchange, the great
scene of the commercial transactions of the second trading town
in the British dominions. The Exchange stands at the head of
the handsomest street in Liverpool, and has strong claims to be
considered an elegant building. It is, however, much too small
for the commerce of the place, and for this reason they are now
making an extensive addition to it. We ascended to the top of the
building, where we had a good view of the town.

It extends between two and three miles along the eastern bank
of the Mersey. The country rises as it recedes from the river, so
that a part of the town is built on the declivity of the hill. The
streets contiguous to the river, which are principally on level
ground, are narrow and dirty; they are crowded with carts and
people, and in some of them the ware-houses are carried up
to a very great height. The streets on the slope of the hill are
sufficiently wide, clean, and handsome, but the houses, although
substantial and highly comfortable, are generally inelegant in their
exterior appearance. They are constructed with bricks of a dusky
yellow colour, obscured by the dust and smoke of coal, the bricks
are not polished, but have a degree of roughness, which makes
the town appear somewhat rude, and we look in vain for the
highly finished surface which is presented by the finest houses of
New-York, Philadelphia, and Boston, to which towns Liverpool is
inferior in the beauty of its private building. The public buildings
are, however, with few exceptions, elegant. They are constructed
of hewn sand stone, furnished by a quarry immediately contiguous
to the town. There are several handsome churches, some of which
have lofty spires on stone, and there is a magnificent one, with a
vast dome, modelled and named after St Paul's at London.

Liverpool is said to contain about 80,000 inhabitants, who
are almost exclusively employed in commerce, and the various

businesses immediately connected with it; for, although the town is not destitute of manufactures, most of these articles which are sold in America under the general name of Liverpool wares, are brought to this port from Staffordshire, and other interior counties.

On the hill back of the town are a number of beautiful situations. There is, on the highest part of the hill, a place called the Mount, where there is a public garden, with serpentine gravel walks, and in front of the garden is a wide gravelled area, used as a promenade, which commands a fine view of the city, the river, the opposite county of Cheshire, and the distant mountains of Wales. The city is surrounded by lofty wind-mills, which are among the first objects that strike a stranger coming in from sea. On the hills are a multitude of signal poles;—each principal merchant has one, by which a ship's name is announced some hours before she arrives in the river. There is a very great number of vessels, and among these the American flag is very frequent. The American trade to this port is probably greater than to all the other ports of Britain; it has become highly important to the merchants of Liverpool, and of this they are sufficiently aware.

The port is difficult of access. The tides rise from 12 to 30 feet, and, at low water, a great part of the road is bare. The currents are therefore very rapid, and it is only at rising water that ships can get in; there are besides, so many shoals and sand banks, that even then, it requires all the skill of the pilot to bring a vessel up to the town.

When a ship comes round Holyhead, and a gale immediately succeeds, blowing in towards the shore, she is in danger of being lost. These circumstances form the principal defence of the town against an attack by sea and are much more important to its security, than a battery of heavy cannon at the lower part of the town, and a large guard ship which is moored in the channel. Although stationed there ostensibly for the defence of the town, the most interesting object to the government is to afford a floating prison for the reception of impressed seamen. There are press gangs now about Liverpool, and impressments daily happen. I saw a sailor dragged off, a few evenings since, he was walking with one who appeared to be a woman of the town, and he of course was considered as a proper object of impressment; for it is the uniform practice of the press gangs to take all whom they find in such society, and all who are engaged in night brawls and drunken revels, not that the press gangs have any *peculiar solicitude* for the preservation of *good morals*, but because such things afford somewhat of a pretext for a practice which violates equally the laws of natural liberty, and the principles of English freedom. I grant it is necessary, but it is still grossly unjust, and were consistency regarded when it interferes with national policy, the English courts of justice would grant prompt and full redress. No doubt every country has a full right to the services of its citizens, but this right should be enforced according to some principle of impartial selection, which would place every man under the same degree of liability. England would rise in arms, should the military impress for the army citizens of every rank, from the fields, the streets, and the public roads; but one particular class of men seem to be abandoned by society, and relinquished to perpetual imprisonment, and a slavery, which though honourable, cuts them off from most things which men hold dear.

In Liverpool, as might be expected, American sailors are often impressed, but they usually get clear if they have protections, which are here more regarded than at sea. The press gangs have a rendezvous on shore, to which they bring their victims as fast they find them; they have no secrecy about the matter, for the place is rendered conspicuous by a large naval flag hung out at a window. One would suppose that popular vengeance would be excited by this triumphant display of the effrontery of power trampling on personal liberty, but, I believe the rendezvous is not often attacked, although it probably would be, were it not for the strong protection of government.

THE DOCKS

The ships are not here, as with us, stationed along the wharves, for at low water the foundations of these structures are in view, and ships, moored by their sides, would be left on the bare sand twice in twenty-four hours, with no small exposure to injury from the rapid influx and retreat of the water, and the great rise and fall which the ship must sustain by such powerful tides as flow in this channel.

To obviate these, and other inconveniences, the ships are hauled into docks, where they lie in perfect security.

These docks, of which there are six wet, besides several dry ones, are among the principal curiosities of the place.

In order to their construction, a large area on the bank of the river is excavated to a sufficient depth, but digging. It has a rectangular form, and is enclosed by very deep, wide, and strong walls of massy hewn stone, sunk below the bottom of the cavity; and rising to the surface of the ground. There is an opening into the basin sufficiently wide to admit one ship at a time. This opening is closed by gates, which are hinged upon opposite sides of the canal, and, when shut, they meet at an angle sufficiently acute to enable them to sustain the pressure of the water, in the basin. In short, they are constructed just as locks are in canals. They open inward, and their operation is very intelligible.

When the tide rises so as to bring the water in the river to the same level with that in the basin, the gates either open of their own accord, or easily yield to a moderate power exerted upon them. The water then flows indiscriminately in the river and basin, and it is at that time, or near it, that ships must pass in or out; for when the tide turns, the current, now setting outwards, closes the gates;—the water in the basin is retained, and the channel leading to it becomes entirely dry. The ships in the dock remain afloat, and the gates sustain the enormous weight of twenty feet of water. Great firmness is therefore necessary in the structure of the walls and of every part. When there is too much water in the docks, the excess is let out by means of vent holds, and it is obvious that the whole can be drawn off in this manner when it is necessary. The top of the gates is formed into a foot bridge, and a bridge for carts is thrown over the canal, somewhat nearer the outer basin. By means of machinery this last bridge is swung off to one side, when ships are to pass.

No small inconvenience is sustained by ships in getting into or out of dock; they are sometimes obliged to wait several days either for the spring tides or for their turns. The *Ontario* will have to wait ten days from the time of her arrival, as she draws too much water for the ordinary tides, and must therefore wait for the next spring tide. Common ships can enter now, but the *Ontario* is the largest American ship in the Liverpool trade. Much delay is said to be occasioned at the king's and queen's docks, by the captious and tyrannical disposition of the dock master. Last winter, an American captain, pretending to shake hands with this dock master, and, at the same time, affecting to stumble over something, pulled him off, along with himself in the water. He did not value a fall of 10 feet, with some chance of drowning, compared with the pleasure of taking this kind of vengeance on a man who was cordially hated by all the American masters of ships.

The dry docks are intended solely for the purpose of repairing the ship's bottom. They are nothing more than long and deep canals, whose sides are formed into sloping steps, like stairs, and as the object is to exclude the water, the gates open outwards. When a ship is to be admitted, the gates are thrown open at low water, and she comes in with the flood. The dock is wide enough to hold only one ship in its breadth, but it is so long, that several can come in, in succession. After they have arrived at their places, they are moored, and when the tide retires, they are left dry, resting upon the bottom of the dock, and sustained in a perpendicular position by means of props. The gates being closed at low water, the next tide is excluded, and thus the workmen are admitted with safety and convenience quite down to the keel.

The same bridges are used here as across the entrance of the wet docks.

The channel of the river Mersey affords safe anchorage for ships of any burthen.

In Liverpool the proportion of women is much greater than of men, especially in the lower orders of society. The men of this grade are usually in the army or navy, and multitudes of the females are maintained by their vices.

* The *Ontario* never returned to America. In getting out of dock, she struck the ground; the tide left her on the sand, and being heavily laden, she broke by her own weight, and the tide flowed into her. After being detained several months, and repaired at an enormous expense, she put on sea, and was never heard of any more [Silliman's note]

ENGLISH DINNERS

I dined today in Birchfield, a beautiful seat in the suburbs of Liverpool, formerly the residence of Mr Roscoe. The house is surrounded by highly improved grounds, ornamented with gravel walks, winding with easy turns among groves and green fields, for the verdure has now become general in this part of England. Mr E—, the possessor of this mansion, has been recently elected a bailiff of Liverpool, and, on this occasion, gave a kind of official dinner to the major, the aldermen, the town clerk, and other officers of the city. A previous introduction to their host, gave me the honour of dining with these gentlemen, and several others of the first citizens. There were two gentlemen at table, who, when the income tax was laid, gave in their incomes at twenty thousand pounds sterling, or almost ninety thousand dollars.

Our table was loaded with luxuries and splendidly furnished. The arrangements however differed very little from those which are usual at the tables of people of fortune in America. There was one custom which was wholly new to me. The gentlemen challenged each other to drink ale, just as did one, every where else, with wine, at the same time wishing health; this was merely introductory to the drinking of wine.*

The beef was not superior to the best in our markets; the apples were hard and insipid, having somewhat the taste of raw turnips, and there was no article better than the correspondence productions of America, except the ale.

[...]

I have the honour of an introduction to Mr Roscoe on my first arrival in Liverpool, and his son had the goodness to conduct me today to Allerton Hall, his father's seat, five or six miles from town. On our way we visited the Botanical Garden, an institution which Mr Roscoe and Dr Currie set on foot about three years since. Under their patronage it has flourished rapidly, and is now a fine establishment. It occupies five statute acres; the ground appears to be well adapted to the purpose, there is a pond and a portion of marshy land in the middle of the garden for such plants as require a wet soil or constant immersion; the hot-houses are extensive and handsome, and exhibit a great variety of exotics, while the whole garden is a place of great beauty.

Our road to Allerton Hall was through a most delightful country. The river Mersey was on our right, and the fields sloped with gentle declivity to its banks. The county of Cheshire was extensively in view over the river, and beyond that, Wales with its rude mountains.

Allerton Hall is a stone building which has an air of grandeur; it stands at a considerable distance from the road, in the midst of beautiful grounds, and appears every way fitted to be the residence of its present distinguished possessor. Mr Roscoe was, (as I am informed,) bred to the bar, but being disgusted with the profession, he turned his attention to literature. He is now connected in business with an extensive banking-house in Liverpool, and retired to this place that he might have more leisure for indulging in his favourite pursuits. His house is filled with statues, busts, and pictures, principally Italian, and in his study, he is surrounded by the figures of the men, who are the subjects of his history of Lorenzo, and of Leo X. Of the latter work, not yet given to the world, he showed me a copy, and pointed out the beauty of the plates executed from designs on wood.

Mr Roscoe's person is tall, his figure is graceful, his countenance intelligent, his expression mild, and his features what would generally be called handsome. He is now in middle life, and is possessed of a private character of distinguished excellence. From him I received every attention which was consistent with the obligations of politeness to a considerable number of gentlemen assembled at his table. Some of them were men of literature, and one in particular was said to be engaged in a biographical work upon one of the distinguished literary men of the period of Lorenzo, for, Mr Roscoe has diffused around him a general taste for Italian literature. In such a circle it was unpleasant to find literature excluded in favour of those personal and local topics, which, as only neighbours and friends can understand, such only should participate. I was particularly solicitous to hear Mr R. speak upon his favourite subject, the revival of arts and literature in Italy, but the conversation took a turn which precluded every thing of this nature, till a call to the drawing room cut it short and left Mr Roscoe at liberty, for a few minutes, to satisfy my curiosity. At an early hour in the evening I returned to Liverpool.

★ I never observed this practice at any other place in England, and therefore presume it was a local custom [Silliman's note]

A TRANSPORT SHIP

I found some amusement yesterday in witnessing the embarkation of a regiment of cavalry. The horses were hoisted in by means of a canvas bag which was made to surround the body of the animal, and tied with ropes over the back. To these ropes a tackle was fastened, and the horses were thus raised from the ground. When they first felt the lifting, they flounced and kicked violently, but the instant their feet were cleared of the ground, they became perfectly still as if dead, and hung dangling in the air, till they were gently lowered into the hold next the keel. There they stand in double rows, with their heads to a common manger, erected over the keep. In such a situation they must suffer greatly from the confined air.

The soldiers, with their wives and children (for some of them usually have families) are all crowded together between decks, immediately above the horses, and only a limited number are allowed to come on deck at once.

A QUARRY

After enjoying with a companion the fine views from the mount, and the delightful retreat in the gardens behind it, I was forcibly struck yesterday, with the sight of a vast quarry on the hill contiguous to Liverpool. By constant hewing, it has now become a regular pit, probably 60 or 70 feet deep, and it may be 50 rods long and 30 rods wide. Its walls are formed as if it had been designed for some vast cellar, they are very smooth and perpendicular. Carts go to the very bottom of this quarry by means of an easy descent cut through the solid rock; this passage is arched, for a considerable distance, and therefore carts coming out of it seem as if emerging from the ground.

The rock is a yellow sand stone, and, when first obtained, is very soft, so as readily to yield to iron tools, and is thus easily wrought into any form; but, after a short exposure to the air or immersion in the water, it hardens and continues to acquire firmness. This makes it peculiarly fit for the construction of wharves and docks, which, with many of the public buildings here, are formed of it. In the quarry the stone lies in strata, which are much broken and crumbled, for 10 or 12 feet from the surface, but become very regular at greater depths.

This quarry is said to be the *Hoboken*★ of Liverpool, where the young *men of spirit* come to partake in the fashionable pastime of shooting at each other for, *duelling*, the opprobrium of America, is also the disgrace of England.

After coming up from the quarry, we walked six or seven miles in the country around Liverpool. We were delighted with many beautiful country retreats at Edge Hill and Everton, eminences lying northeast of Liverpool.

The grounds are universally laid out with great neatness, and amidst the bright verdure of groves and grass, the eye is agreeably relieved by the smoothness and light colour of serpentine gravel walks.

The western side of Everton Hill, sloping to the river, presented us with green fields of great beauty, surrounded by green hedges, and exhibiting all that neatness for which English grounds are so much celebrated.

I expect much gratification from the picturesque scenery of England, as I am about to travel through the country at a season when it is beginning to assume its most beautiful appearance.

[St Domingo House, Everton, the home of the Duke of Gloucester.]

St. Domingo, a seat of the Prince of Gloucester, the King's nephew, limited our excursion. It has an appearance of grandeur and rural magnificence. The Prince of Gloucester is much a favourite in Liverpool. I saw an image of him as large as the life, placed beneath the bowsprit of a slave ship, by way of honouring his highness.

* A celebrated duelling ground on the Jersey shore, opposite to New-York [Silliman's note]

AN ENGLISH HOTEL

The Liverpool Arms is the resort of the nobility and gentry, as well as of men of business, and is, I presume a fair specimen of this kind of establishment in England. The house is very extensive and its apartments are furnished in a superior style. Over the door are the arms of the city of Liverpool, and the hotel certainly does not dishonour these insignia. One room is considered as common, and, for occupying that, no particular charge is made. Besides this, there are several parlours, where any one who chooses it may be as completely retired as in a private house, his food being served up for him without the danger of intrusion. Such a parlour our little party from the *Ontario* has occupied since we have been in Liverpool. But a separate charge at the rate of a guinea a week is made for this room.

Even the bed rooms are elegantly furnished, and the beds are perfectly clean, as is the whole house; all the accommodations necessary for dressing completely are furnished in the bed room, and a system of bells, extending to every part of this vast house, brings a servant instantly even to the third or fourth storey.

Indeed, every possible accommodation is furnished at the shortest notice, and with the utmost civility of manners on the part of the servants. A stranger may select, from a very ample bill of fare, such articles as he chooses, and he may have, in every instance, a separate table for himself. It is always expected that he will call for wine at dinner;—no complaints will be made if he omits it, but, the *oblique* looks of the waiter, when he carries away the unsoiled wine glass, sufficiently indicate in what estimation the gentility of the guest is held. In short, in such a hotel as that which I am now describing, almost every comfort of domestic life may be obtained.

But for all this there is a price. I cannot say however that the charges are very extravagant, considering the immense taxation of this country. The bed is one shilling and six pence a night. A common breakfast of tea or coffee, with toast and an egg, will not exceed one shilling and eight pence,*—tea at evening is about the same, but the dinner is much more expensive. If it consists of two dishes, it will cost five shillings, with a frugal dessert. A separate charge is made for almost every thing; a glass of beer will cost eight pence, and a bottle of Sherry wine six or seven shillings; a bottle of Port fives shillings, and one of Madeira nine or ten. In England the breakfast, and tea at evening, are considered as trivial meals, while dinner is a matter of great import, and therefore it is much more expensive than both meals, for supper is perfectly optional, it is very genteel to eat it, although it is not ungenteel to go without. But this list of charges by no means comprehends all. The servants at the public houses in England are paid by the guests, and not by their employers. They not only receive no wages, but many of them pay a premium for their places; that is, the masters of the hotels farm out to their servants the privilege of levying contributions, and the consideration is, their service At out hotel the chief waiter assured us that he paid one hundred pounds per annum for his place, besides paying two under waiters, and finding all the clothes' brushes, and some other etceteras of the house. He had, moreover, if we might credit his story, a wife and five children to support. The head waiters are commonly young men of genteel appearance, and often dress as well as gentlemen.

The servants whom it is indispensable to pay in every public house are, the waiter, who has three pence a meal; the chamber-maid, who has six pence for every night that you lodge in the house; and the shoe-black, who is very appropriately called *boots*, and receives two pence or three pence for every pair of shoes and boots which he brushes. Besides these, the stranger who comes with horses pays six pence a night to the ostler, and the porter demands six pence for carrying in the baggage, and the same sum for bringing it out. The rates which I have stated are the lowest which one can possibly pay with decency. It is usual to go little beyond them, and the man who pays most liberally is, you know,

in all countries, considered by this class of people as the most of a
gentleman.

These demands it is impossible to evade or repel; they are as
regularly brought forward as the bill itself; and a departing guest
is attended by the whole retinue of servants, who are officious to
render services which he does not want, and should he be in a fit
of mental absence, he will certainly be reminded that the waiter,
the chamber-maid, the boots, and perhaps the ostler and porter,
are not to be forgotten.

These customs, while they cannot be considered as honourable
to the national manners, and are very troublesome to travellers,
who are every where pestered with a swarm of expectants, are
however productive of some very useful consequences. The
servants, looking for their reward from the guest, are attentive to
all his wishes, and assiduous to promote his comfort; their service
is *cheerfully* rendered, and not with that *sullen salvo for personal
dignity*, which we so often see in America. In England, the servant
is contented with his condition; he does not aim at any thing
higher, while in America a person of this description will usually
behave in such a manner as to evince that he regards you as
being no better than himself. This inconvenience arises, however,
from the multiplied resources and superior condition of the lower
orders in America, and although one would wish to alter their
deportment, still, as a patriot, he would not choose to remove the
cause.

Being about to leave Liverpool, I have paid my bill, and after
giving the waiter his due, I asked him whether that was as much
as he usually received?—he replied, that it was what *mere travellers*
paid him, but that *American gentlemen* usually paid very liberally.

> Benjamin Silliman, *A Journal of Travels in England, Holland,
> and Scotland* (1812). Silliman returned to Europe in 1851
> and published *A Visit to Europe in 1851* in 1854.

Joseph Ballard (1789–1877), a merchant from Boston, was frank in his
account (*England in 1815*) of why he came to Liverpool, stating: 'Business
was my only object in visiting England.' It was a sign of the troubled times
that his ship was stopped by gunboats and boarded, and Ballard's account
has the added interest of describing travel by stagecoach, a means soon to
become a thing of the past once the railways were built. Ballard stayed

at the Liverpool Arms, the same hotel as that used by Silliman, which he employed as a base for observing Liverpool and the surrounding district before setting off for visits to London and the northern cities. Ballard was fascinated, or rather, horrified by business practices such as the employment of young children in the factories, and he recorded in graphic detail the Saturday-night binges of the Warrington factory workers.

[The Athenaeum was built in the 1790s with William Roscoe as Vice-President: see next chapter. The Liverpool School of Instruction for the Indigent Blind was founded in 1791 by Edward Rushton, a merchant sailor who had lost his sight. It was initially in Commutation, moving in 1800 to a purpose-built school in London Road. From 1805 onwards, regular hours were devoted to singing during which the school was opened to the public, partly as a fund-raising strategy. The first raised type used at the Liverpool School was that of James Hartley Frere in 1838 and the Braille system was not devised until 1828, so the book Ballard saw must have used an earlier form.]

Liverpool possesses an Athenaeum which contains a very large collection of books in every department of literature. There was one book I saw which I thought a great curiosity. It was for teaching the blind, the letters being raised so as to be felt by them. I could not distinguish them by feeling, but suppose a blind person could, as the sense of feeling is with them more acute. I was extremely fortunate in my visit to the blind asylum as I found the objects of its charity were engaged in singing. It was extremely solemn. I had never witnessed a scene more so. Twenty-five blind men, women, girls and boys composed the choir. They were singing anthems. The female voices were uncommonly fine-toned. There were many spectators present among whom I observed a man with a small blind lad (I presume his son) who he had brought for the purpose of being admitted. During the singing the father appeared to be very much affected and 'the big tears chased each other down his cheeks.' In the hall are tablets whereon are inscribed the names of the donors to this establishment and in every room is a money box with 'pray remember the poor blind' written upon it. I was witness to one blind person's walking alone across the yard, going up stairs, and seating himself to work at a loom. This he did as readily as if he were blessed with sight. One of the rooms is appropriated as a sales-room where baskets, rugs etc are shown. This admirable institution is certainly an honour to humanity!

[The Theatre Royal in Williamson Square was the first purpose-built theatre in the city, although others had been in existence since the sixteenth century. It was opened in 1772 and enlarged in 1803. Its actors included Julius Brutus Booth, who emigrated to the USA in 1821 and whose youngest son assassinated President Lincoln. St James's Walk was an elevated promenade constructed near the city quarry, which supplied material for the original dock walls.]

In company with Mr. M. I went to the Liverpool Theatre. It is a neat building but the performers were miserable. Many of the streets and squares in Liverpool are spacious and handsome. St. James' Walk is a fine promenade. At the back of it is a public garden laid out in a tasteful manner. From the terrace is a commanding view of the town and Cheshire shore, with the shipping lying in the river. The stone quarry is very near here. The entrance is through a subterraneous passage 60 yards in length, hewn through solid stone. All the stones necessary for the formation of the docks are taken from this place. The stone resembles the Connecticut red stone: it is quite liable to crumble into sand, but I am informed that the water hardens it. The trade to Liverpool is immense. A multitude of ships are now in the river waiting for a berth in the dock, which they can only gain by some other vessel's going to sea. The large warehouses near the docks, rising thirteen stories in height, and the bustle and noise in the streets show to the stranger that here 'commerce is busy with her ten thousand wheels.'

[The Herculaneum Pottery was founded in 1796 on the riverside edge of Toxteth Park, a little upriver from the Brunswick Dock. In its heyday from 1806 to 1821 it was producing fine porcelain comparable to that from Staffordshire. The factory closed in 1840.]

This morning went to the Herculaneum Pottery, a short distance from town. Here both common and fine wares are manufactured. These works employ about two hundred persons, men, women and children. Having an introduction from a gentleman at Liverpool to the intendant of the place, I received every possible attention in viewing the processes of the work. Some of the china was quite elegant. There were a great many very genteel looking men and women at work drawing the landscapes upon the china; many women were also engaged in laborious work, much more suitable for men, such as beating heavy lumps of clay, etc. etc.

It is however quite the custom in Great Britain to make the fair sex bear at least one-half the burden of life, but I have frequently thought, when I have seen them ploughing, digging and reaping, that they have had the greatest part. On your entrance to the works you are presented with a card whereon is a request that you will not give the workmen any money, but if you are disposed, that you many contribute an offering to a fund appropriated to the instruction of the children of the workmen and to the relief of the sick. This is a praiseworthy regulation and should be adopted by every factory to which curiosity leads visitants, as the workmen always expect some little present which is almost invariably applied to furnish drinks.

Joseph Ballard, *England in 1815 as Seen by a Young Boston Merchant* (1913).

James Buchanan (1791–1868) was to become President of the United States in 1857. In 1832 he was appointed American Ambassador to Russia and passed through Liverpool to take up this office. He sailed on the *Silas Richards*, landing on 3 May and going straight to the Adelphi Hotel. That evening he attended a dinner for the captain at *The Star and Garter*, where the American Consul and the banker William Brown were present. The following day he was shown the sights of the city:

Mr. Brown of Liverpool took me about in his carriage and showed me the town of Liverpool. The appearance of the people, their manners and language are so similar to those of New York that I could scarcely realize I was in England. The bricks of which the houses are built when new have a dirty yellow appearance and the coal dust soon gives them a darker hue. This imparts a gloomy appearance to the town and deprives it of that light and cheerful hue which we experience in Philadelphia and New York. It is a place of great wealth and vast commerce, although the approach to it is tedious and difficult and altogether impracticable at low tide. The Mersey is but a small river compared with those in America. Its docks are admirable and very extensive, covering a space actually under water of between eighty and ninety English acres. The cemetery is well worthy of observation. Mr. Barry and myself dined with Mr. Brown at his country house about three miles from Liverpool. It is beautifully situated, the grounds around it highly improved, and both its external and internal appearance prove the wealth and the taste of its opulent and hospitable owner. Francis B. Ogden, Esq., the American consul, and several other gentlemen were of the party. We spent a very pleasant afternoon and evening.

During our stay at Liverpool we received many attentions [...] I could not help observing at this place what a strong impression the successful operations of our Government had produced on the minds of Englishmen. Our national character now stands high, notwithstanding the efforts which have been made to traduce it.

John Basset Moore, ed., *The Works of James Buchanan Volume II: 1830–1836* (1908).

Zachariah Allen (1795–1882) was an American manufacturer and inventor. Trained as a lawyer, he went into textiles and also devoted much of his activity to improving looms and other industrial devices. His 1832 volume, *The Practical Tourist*, lives up to its title in drawing the reader's attention to the state of the roads, drawbacks to gas lighting, and coal consumption; in other words, exactly the things that tourists in search of the picturesque would blank out of their accounts. Which traveller these days would make a beeline to an iron chain factory? Allen's descriptions of Liverpool marked the first step in his survey of national industry; he was clearly looking out for developments that he might use at home. His fascination with procedures did not blind him to the hidden purposes within them, such as the customs officers' expectation of 'fees'.

The baggage of passengers is taken from the ship to the custom-house for examination. Here, the traveller in England commences upon the system of fees, or gratuities, which continues to annoy him at every stage of his progress. Having, as I had supposed, no article in my trunks subject to duty, I felt no hesitation in exposing them to the most thorough examination. Unnecessary delays, it soon became apparent, were resorted to by the custom-house officer, when he found that no fees were tendered. His hands performed their functions as if they were benumbed, and he continued to draw one fresh cravat after another, with its struggling and resisting folds entangled in the mazes of surrounding linen, from the depths of each trunk to the broad glare of daylight. A small pocket bible of American print proved the only stumbling block, by which the progress of the examination was arrested. Finding that he had seized upon it, and that he was about to place it in the scales, to assess a duty on each ounce of its weight, and that he would probably consume the whole morning in continuing to search among the troubled apparel for some further prize, I slipped into his unoccupied hand a half crown. Instantly, his other hand was withdrawn from the depths of the portmanteau, to which it had again penetrated in an exploring expedition, with as much speed as if it had touched a torpedo concealed there; or rather as if one hand had known what the other had done. The suspicious bible, rescued from the scales, which were left empty to perform their vibrations in the thin air, was immediately replaced by him beneath the closing lid; and the lock snapped as the iron bolt was thrown into its place by the key applied in his now vigorously moving hand. The electrical effect seemed to produce its most powerful action on the pliable joint of the hips, which unites the nether and the upper limbs. Throwing forward his body with a circular movement this pivot, like the shutting blade on the handle of a penknife, he extended even his neck and head horizontally to form a right angle with his rigidly perpendicular legs. Whilst I was regarding with admiration the magical effect of the fee, and saw the hairy crown of his head pointed at me, and parallel with it an extended hand holding the key of the trunk, his voice reached my ears repeating in accents as soft as those a lover addresses to his mistress—"all is right." At the door I found my first friend, the tide waiter, who had escorted the portmanteau to the custom-house. He had remained there in attendance to watch for its departure, apparently loth to be separated from it without receiving some trifle by way of remembrance, observing as an apology, that his salary was so very small, that he should fail of obtaining a decent living, unless he recruited his finances by perquisites.

There is a great difference in this respect between the custom-house officers of Liverpool and those of New York. The latter receive a more liberal pay, equal to about three dollars a day, as a compensation. They consequently find, that with common chances, they can make more profit from the regular emoluments of their office, than from pursuing a corrupt course. The obliging exertions of the tide waiters are rather retarded than expedited, when passengers, habituated to the drill of European custom-houses, extend toward them the customary largess. That American custom-house officers, however, are all immaculate, far be it from me to insinuate.

The great amount of business transacted at the Liverpool custom-house may be the apology for the hurried manner of administering oaths, which is fitted to destroy all respect for their sanctity. When the invoices are handed to the officers to be attested, a murmuring sound is heard. The only audible words I could understand were the terminating ones, 'so help you God; kiss the book.' In the same breath the stated fee is demanded. The bible, which is handed out to be kissed by way of sealing the oath, is so soiled and greasy from being frequently touched by unclean fingers, that it has become too revolting an object to be pressed to the lips. A clerk, long habituated to administering these oaths, it is related, was seized with a fever; and whilst he lay in a delirious state, for two or three days he kept continually repeating in his accustomed manner, as fast as he could in the same breath, 'So help you God, kiss the book, give me a shilling'.

On my way to Waterloo hotel in Liverpool [adjacent to the Lyceum at the bottom of Bold Street] I soon forgot that I was in a foreign country, the dress and languages of all around me being so nearly similar to those observable in New-York. The houses and streets, as well as the people who throng them, bear also a remarkable resemblance in general appearance, to those of the principal cities of the United States. The only striking difference appears in the uniform dingy colour of the exterior walls of the buildings, which are darkened with the sooty particles of the smoke of the bituminous coal. The clear bright colours of fresh paint, which impart an air of neatness to the ranges of houses in most of the American cities, are no where discernible in the cities of England. The vast consumption of bituminous coal fills the atmosphere with heavy smoke, which settles down upon the adjacent streets, and coming in contact with the surfaces of the large rough bricks, stains them of an uniform dusky hue, and throws a sombre shade over the long ranges of contiguous houses and stores. The chimneys of the furnaces of the steam engines are exceedingly lofty, and form conspicuous objects, with their summits of red brick rising above the surrounding house tops. They are built thus high for the purpose of quickening the ascending draft of air, to render the combustion of the fuel on the grates more perfect, and to discharge the imperfectly consumed portions of the fuel, which escape in the form of smoke, aloft amid the upper currents of wind, that bear them off from above the city, and dissipate them in the atmosphere. In hazy weather, these furnace-chimneys, notwithstanding their elevation, frequently become nuisances to the neighbourhood in which they are located. The smoke from them obscures the light of day, and fills the air with those little pear-shaped particles of soot, which floating about like motes, lodge upon the white linen cravat or shirt collar, and spread instantly, on being rubbed, into stains of an inky blackness. A change of linen may become necessary two or three times a day during this peculiar state of the smoky atmosphere. The vocation of a laundress, in a country where bituminous coal is the common fuel, is an employment of no inconsiderable extent and activity.

[Allen goes on to praise the construction of roads according to the McAdam method.]

After establishing myself at the hotel, my attention was directed to observing the customs which prevail in the administration of the civil affairs of eating and drinking, in order to conform myself to the usual modes of living adopted by English travellers in their own country. In practising some parts of the internal economy of an English hotel, an American feels a little awkward. A breakfast, a dinner, and even tea or supper, are matters of serious consideration, and are not here precipitately shared by the hungry guest with only the trouble of drawing his chair to a well spread table, on equal terms with some scores of fellow-lodgers, as is commonly the case at the hotels in the United States. At some of the minor inns, the commercial gentlemen or travellers, as they are emphatically called, or travelling agents for the sale of various manufactures, as they might more definitely be termed, dine together at a common table. But at the hotels and large inns, each individual or distinct party of gentlemen take seats at separate little boxes or tables, arranged in order around a hall or coffee-room, and partake of their breakfasts or dinners in a solitary, unsocial manner. After having taken a seat at a table at the hour most convenient or agreeable, should you not have left an order for the specific articles for dinner, you have gravely to consider the bill of fare handed you, and to select what will best suit your palate. The bread and potatoes are always furnished; but all the viands which you may order to be placed on the table, are specifically charged. A landlord's account of a few weeks board, when made out at large, swells with a daily growth to a frightful size—The numerous items darken the whole surface of a fair sheet of paper with all the daily details of gastronomic performances upon roast beef, fish and pastry—even including the almonds and raisins, and fruit of the dessert. Some study is required to plan out a dinner, and arithmetical powers must be exercised in settling for it.

Commencing with the morning of the first day of my arrival, I seated myself at my solitary breakfast table, and summoned the waiter before me to receive orders for my morning meal. Having determined upon the selection of tea, as my usual favourite beverage, the waiter presented, instead of the infusion already prepared as I expected, an empty teapot, freshly rinsed with hot water, and a small catty box stored with several varieties of the Chinese herb. Having always been in the habit of receiving a steaming cup under happier auspices, with the honour of the tea table dispensed by fairer hands than my own, I was totally unprepared for the sudden apparition of an empty teapot with its yawning mouth opened wide before me, to be replenished according to my own taste. The process of making a palatable cup of tea, it is well known, requires some little share of the practical skill of a good house-wife, to apportion the requisite quantity of the herb to the water in which it is to be infused. Conscious of my deficiency of skill in this matter, and ashamed to acknowledge it, lest I should excite the smiles of those who were enviably sipping the well prepared contents of their cups around me, and loth at the same time to manifest so much apparent fickleness of purpose as to order coffee, (which is always ready prepared, and is for this reason, as I afterwards discovered, commonly ordered by Americans, novices in this art like myself,) I hesitated, until quickened to a decision by the appearance of the waiter; who continued to stand like some haunting spectre, presenting the still gaping mouth of the teapot extended at arm's length in front of me. Thus driven to desperation, I extracted with scrupulous nicety a small portion of the contents of one of the catty boxes, and discharged the few shrivelled leaves into the receptacle extended to receive them. On perceiving the scanty measure dealt out by me, the waiter shook the teapot, and looked into its obscure cavity, to assure himself that he did not labour under an optical delusion; and then again at me with a significant smile. He however filled the vessel with boiling water from the spout of the brightly scoured copper tea kettle, which usually in winter occupies a corner of the grate, simmering and emitting vapour, and ready at hand for all emergencies, whether it maybe to temper the morning beverage, or evening dram of whisky punch or toddy. Whilst the tea is steeping, the waiter places before you the usual breakfast of an Englishman—a roll of bread, or dry toast and muffins, some eggs, and butter, together with the sugar bowl and milk pot. Whilst these preparations are making, you have leisure to dispatch the perusal of the morning papers, which form an indispensable accompaniment of the breakfast table. Thinking more of the result of my first essay, than of the contents of the papers before me, I watched with intense interest the first gush from the inverted beak. It was truly dismaying to behold the bright limpid stream of boiling water make its exit, almost as colourless as it entered. On a second trial, I proceeded with a bolder, and more unsparing hand, and was scarcely more gratified than by the first experiment. The white porcelain cup was now contrasted with the deep amber colour of the fluid poured into it, the concentrated strength of which might have disturbed even the nerves of a giant. This cup-full was also rejected, and a third experiment rendered me forever master of the art and mystery of the due preparation of a cup of tea.

There appears to be one peculiarity in tea drinking as practised in England, which is little regarded in the United States. It is common to mix the green and black teas together, to combine their flavours in the same savoury cup.

Whilst engaged in delivering some letters, I stopped at an extensive chain cable manufactory, the smoky precincts of which presented to view the appearance of the very workshop of Vulcan, with numerous glowing forges arranged in lines, and excited by the asthmatic heaving: of resounding bellows; the expiring, moaning blasts of which were mingled with the sounds of the strokes of hammers on the ringing anvils. The first process in the manufacture of chain cables is the application of a huge pair of shears, to cut the bars of iron into pieces of a uniform length, suitable for the links. These pieces of iron are bent, like osier twigs, by a powerful machine, to the proper form for making links. After each link is welded, the surface is rendered smooth by smaller hammers and swedges. One of the most interesting processes performed here is that for proving the strength of the great chain cables, after they are completed. The chains, which are to be subjected to proof, are extended on a massy frame, or table, sixty or seventy feet long. Strong cast iron cog-wheels and pinions are arranged in succession with a combination of levers, to produce the necessary force for the tension and proof of the strength of the chain. The power is applied to the chain until it sustains the stress with which it is required to be loaded, which is indicated by the lifting of the weight hung on the long extended arm of the last of the train of levers, like the weight on a steelyard. These weights are, of course, regulated by the size of the iron of which the links are composed. Some of the great chains for merchant vessels are subjected to a tension sufficient to lift forty tons or more; and whilst subjected to this stress each link is submitted to the shock of a blow from a hammer, as a severe test to cause it to yield at once, or to discover any latent flaw it may contain.

[...]

One of my Liverpool friends conducted me over the various apartments of the Liverpool Exchange, which is a magnificent edifice of hewn stone. Here the merchants usually assemble about two o'clock, when the buzz of business is heard, like the whispering sound of the leaves of a forest stirred by an autumnal wind. The Liverpool Exchange is said to be a more splendid building than any other of the kind in Europe.

The Town Hall, fronting the Exchange, is fitted up as if designed for festal purposes and dances, rather than for the accommodation of citizens convened for political purposes. If the feasts of the magistrates of Liverpool correspond in splendour with the costly furniture of their saloons, they must still maintain unimpaired the credit of being the veritable 'well fed English aldermen,'—a description almost identified with the names of turtle soup and John Bull.

On a conspicuous pedestal in the centre of the area, in front of the Town Hall, is a monument erected to Lord Nelson. It is not one of those plain monumental structures, which modestly depend for the interest they excite in the spectator on 'the magic of a name' inscribed on their imperishable tablet; but owing to the patriotic zeal or false taste of some artist or committee, it is encumbered by ornamental groups of statues. A bronze figure of the idolized hero appears on the pedestal, in the attitude of receiving from another figure, representing Victory, four naval or rostral crowns; whilst almost at the same instant the bony fingers of a skeleton figure, representing Death, appear extended from beneath a shroud to touch the heart of the hero, to stop the pulsations of life at the moment of his being crowned by Victory, and whilst flushed by success. The foot of Nelson rests upon the body of a dead foe, which serves as a sort of stepping stone, upon which the conqueror elevates himself to receive his rostral honours from the friendly hand of Victory. The whole group, when viewed together, is neither agreeable to the eye, nor calculated to excite pleasing emotions in the spectator. A hero trampling on a prostrate foe is an unmanly spectacle. To behold him in the act of aspiring and reaching forward for the laurels of victory, mounted on the lifeless body of his fallen enemy, divests those very laurels of their magic charms. The poet who has a true taste, always conceals the scene of triumph, which in this instance is brought forward by the sculptor as a prominent object of consideration to awaken the recollection of the blood of fellow-men, profusely shed on the field of battle to swell the conqueror's fame. This part of the group, it might well have been the study of the artist to have carefully kept out of sight, when he aimed to exalt the merit of the mere warrior, or advance the ideal standard or the estimation of military glory. In addition to the exhibition of bad taste already described, this monument 'lifts its head and lies,' like its taller brother erected in London to commemorate the great fire, ascribed by its lettered tablet to the Catholics. An American, when he views on the four sides of the pedestal, four sculptured figures, emblematical of the four quarters of the globe, Europe, Asia, Africa, and America, all writhing in chains and subjection at the feet of Nelson, is disposed to question the presumption of the artist, who has humbled America in chains as a fallen adversary, and has thus sacrificed truth at the shrine of national vanity. When, it may be asked, was America subdued or humbled, by the arm of this naval commander?

The streets of Liverpool are lighted by gas, which is also introduced into the shops and houses by small pipes, that are conducted over the various apartments. For lighting close rooms, the fetid odour attending the combustion of coal gas has been found disagreeable. In the shops containing a glittering army of silver ware, the portion of sulphuretted hydrogen, that escapes from the gas pipes unconsumed, pervades the air and penetrates every case, coating the purest silver with a black crust, as if alloyed with lead. Even the complexions of the fair, rendered artificially white by certain pigments or cosmetics, are immediately attacked by this gas, which combines with the metallic oxide forming the basis of the paint. The snowy tints of the skin, under the effects of the gas, become gradually darker, like the dusky twilight stealing over the firmament, until an European might be mistaken for an Ethiopian beauty. One is rendered sensible of approaching the gas works, by

the effluvium or peculiar odour of the products of the distillation
of the coal, which is here so offensive as to have become a subject
of complaint to all the neighbourhood, according to the statement
of one of the workmen. To carry off the disagreeable odours and
to discharge them in the air with as little annoyance as possible
to the disquieted neighbours, the chimneys are built so lofty as
to rival the spire of a church, being about 150 feet high. They are
conspicuous land marks for directing the stranger in his rambles
over the city. The formation of coal gas is effected in a simple
manner, by placing bituminous coal in cast iron retorts, or air-
tight hollow vessels of this metal, and subjecting it to a strong
heat in a furnace. Oil, rosin, wood, and indeed almost every
substance which yields flame during combustion, may be used to
create inflammable gas. The coal, when thus heated in red hot
iron retorts, parts with the inflammable gas, which rising in the
form of smoke is conducted by pipes to a vessel of lime water,
through which it passes in ascending bubbles, to become purified
by it; after which it continues to pass on through pipes until it
enters an immense sheet-iron gas vessel, of the capacious size of the
hold of a ship, suspended like an inverted tumbler over a cistern
of water; and so accurately balanced by ropes passing over pulleys
and connected weights, as to rise in the water, whilst the gas passes
into it, and renders it more buoyant, and also to descend when
the gas passes off into the pipes for distribution. A very ingenious
contrivance is employed to measure the quantity of gas produced
each day, and the quantity that the inhabitants of each house
consume. A small machine resembling a little water wheel, with
floats fitted to move around in a tight metallic case, is connected
with the current of gas passing through the pipes. In its passage the
gas drives before it the floats, causing the wheel to turn regularly,
as if a stream of water were acting upon it. At every revolution of
this wheel, a certain quantity of gas is enclosed between each of
the floats. The number of revolutions of the wheel is indicated by a
train of cog wheels, like that of clock work; and the hand or index
moving around the dial plate, also resembling that of an ordinary
clock, points out at once on inspection the quantity of gas that has
passed through the machine.
[…]
The Botanic Garden, into which the stranger is commonly
introduced, at this early season before the vernal equinox, appears
clad in the sober livery of winter; and only in the green houses
is perceptible the fresh verdure of anticipated spring. The surface

of the ground, tilled the past season, appears here covered with a moss or mould, indicating the excess of moisture which prevails in this climate.

Zachariah Allen, *The Practical Tourist, or Sketches of the State of the Useful Arts, and of Society, Scenery, &c. &c.* [1832] (New York: Arno Press, 1972).

2

Passionate Pilgrims

O NE OF THE MOST COMMON METAPHORS used by American
tourists in the nineteenth century was to compare their visits to
Britain and the Continent to a pilgrimage, an analogy that invests travel
with a special solemnity and that combines sightseeing with paying tribute
to a shared cultural past. **Washington Irving** (1783–1859) was one of the
first American authors to define what we now think of as a tourist circuit.
His miscellany *The Sketch Book* became widely popular for its presentation
of the benign leisurely traveller always on the lookout for the picturesque.
Irving helped to form the tradition of American tourists reading Britain
through its literary associations and is one of the very few authors in this
collection to address an English readership. His anecdote of the ill sailor
reflects Irving's preference for moving stories that have implications of
pathos for himself. In fact, far from being a 'stranger in the land', Irving
already had family connections in the city; indeed, in June 1817 Irving
made an excursion by steamboat to Runcorn with his brother. Ostensibly
sailing on the *Mexico* to help with the family hardware business, which
had a branch in Liverpool, Irving's 1815 voyage was motivated as much by
a desire to see the armies that had brought about Napoleon's defeat. After
touring England, Irving made unsuccessful attempts to salvage the finances
of the failing family business, while his real interests lay in developing his
literary career through *The Sketch Book* which, as can be seen from the
following excerpts, presented brief impressions of English life.

The Voyage

It was a fine sunny morning when the thrilling cry of 'land!' was
given from the mast-head. None but those who have experienced
it can form an idea of the delicious throng of sensations which rush
into an American's bosom, when he first comes in sight of Europe.
There is a volume of associations with the very name. It is the land
of promise, teeming with everything of which his childhood has
heard, or on which his studious years have pondered.

From that time, until the moment of arrival, it was all feverish excitement. The ships of war, that prowled like guardian giants along the coast; the headlands of Ireland, stretching out into the channel; the Welsh mountains towering into the clouds;—all were objects of intense interest. As we sailed up the Mersey, I reconnoitred the shores with a telescope. My eye dwelt with delight on neat cottages, with their trim shrubberies and green grass-plots. I saw the mouldering ruin of an abbey overrun with ivy, and the taper spire of a village church rising from the brow of a neighbouring hill;—all were characteristic of England.

The tide and wind were so favourable, that the ship was enabled to come at once to her pier. It was thronged with people; some idle lookers-on; others, eager expectants of friends or relations. I could distinguish the merchant to whom the ship was consigned. I knew him by his calculating brow and restless air. His hands were thrust into his pockets; he was whistling thoughtfully, and walking to and fro, a small space having been accorded him by the crowd, in deference to his temporary importance. There were repeated cheerings and salutations interchanged between the shore and the ship, as friends happened to recognize each other. I particularly noticed one young woman of humble dress, but interesting demeanour. She was leaning forward from among the crowd; her eye hurried over the ship as it neared the shore, to catch some wished-for countenance. She seemed disappointed and sad; when I heard a faint voice call her name.—It was from a poor sailor who had been ill all the voyage, and had excited the sympathy of every one on board. When the weather was fine, his messmates had spread a mattress for him on deck in the shade, but of late his illness had so increased that he had taken to his hammock, and only breathed a wish that he might see his wife before he died. He had been helped on deck as we came up the river, and was now leaning against the shrouds, with a countenance so wasted, so pale, so ghastly, that it was no wonder even the eye of affection did not recognize him. But at the sound of his voice, her eye darted on his features: it read, at once, a whole volume of sorrow; she clasped her hands, uttered a faint shriek, and stood wringing them in silent agony.

All now was hurry and bustle. The meetings of acquaintances— the greetings of friends—the consultations of men of business. I alone was solitary and idle. I had no friend to meet, no cheering to receive. I stepped upon the land of my forefathers—but felt that I was a stranger in the land.

William Roscoe (1753–1831) was a lawyer, historian, abolitionist and MP for Liverpool. In 1797 he co-authored a proposal to establish a 'library and news-room' to be called the Athenaeum. The news-room was opened in 1799, the library the following year, and the Athenaeum became an obligatory place to visit for American travellers. It subsequently inspired the foundation of the Boston Athenaeum in 1807. Roscoe was a partner in a banking concern that had financial difficulties in 1860, when Roscoe had to sell his collection of books and paintings, finally being declared bankrupt in 1820. The house Irving refers to is Allerton Hall in south Liverpool, Roscoe's residence from 1798 to 1816. Although Irving met Roscoe, he did not know him and in his reverential sketch composes an image of a meditative and solitary thinker whose very countenance commands respect and who stands impressively apart from the workings of commerce in the city.

Roscoe

One of the first places to which a stranger is taken in Liverpool is the Athenaeum. It is established on a liberal and judicious plan; it contains a good library, and spacious reading-room, and is the great literary resort of the place. Go there at what hour you may, you are sure to find it filled with grave-looking personages, deeply absorbed in the study of newspapers.

As I was once visiting this haunt of the learned, my attention was attracted to a person just entering the room. He was advanced in life, tall, and of a form that might once have been commanding, but it was a little bowed by time—perhaps by care. He had a noble Roman style of countenance; a head that would have pleased a painter; and though some slight furrows on his brow showed that wasting thought had been busy there, yet his eye beamed with the fire of a poetic soul. There was something in his whole appearance that indicated a being of a different order from the bustling race round him.

I inquired his name, and was informed that it was ROSCOE [Irving's capitals]. I drew back with an involuntary feeling of veneration. This, then, was an author of celebrity; this was one of those men whose voices have gone forth to the ends of the earth; with whose minds I have communed even in the solitudes of America. Accustomed, as we are in our country, to know European writers only by their works, we cannot conceive of them, as of other men, engrossed by trivial or sordid pursuits, and jostling with the crowd of common minds in the dusty paths of life. They pass before our imaginations like superior beings, radiant with the emanations of their genius, and surrounded by a halo of literary glory.

To find, therefore, the elegant historian of the Medici mingling among the busy sons of traffic, at first shocked my poetical ideas; but it is from the very circumstances and situation in which he has been placed, that Mr. Roscoe derives his highest claims to admiration. It is interesting to notice how some minds seem almost to create themselves, springing up under every disadvantage, and working their solitary but irresistible way through a thousand obstacles. Nature seems to delight in disappointing the assiduities of art, with which it would rear legitimate dullness to maturity; and to glory in the vigour and luxuriance of her chance productions. She scatters the seeds of genius to the winds, and though some may perish among the stony places of the world, and some be choked, by the thorns and brambles of early adversity, yet others will now and then strike root even in the clefts of the rock, struggle bravely up into sunshine, and spread over their sterile birthplace all the beauties of vegetation.

Such has been the case with Mr. Roscoe. Born in a place apparently ungenial to the growth of literary talent—in the very market-place of trade; without fortune, family connections, or patronage; self-prompted, self-sustained, and almost self-taught, he has conquered every obstacle, achieved his way to eminence, and, having become one of the ornaments of the nation, has turned the whole force of his talents and influence to advance and embellish his native town.

Indeed, it is this last trait in his character which has given him the greatest interest in my eyes, and induced me particularly to point him out to my countrymen. Eminent as are his literary merits, he is but one among the many distinguished authors of this intellectual nation. They, however, in general, live but for their own fame, or their own pleasures. Their private history presents no lesson to the world, or, perhaps, a humiliating one of human frailty or inconsistency. At best, they are prone to steal away from the bustle and commonplace of busy existence; to indulge in the selfishness of lettered ease; and to revel in scenes of mental, but exclusive enjoyment.

Mr. Roscoe, on the contrary, has claimed none of the accorded privileges of talent. He has shut himself up in no

garden of thought, nor elysium of fancy; but has gone forth into
the highways and thoroughfares of life, he has planted bowers
by the wayside, for the refreshment of the pilgrim and the
sojourner, and has opened pure fountains, where the labouring
man may turn aside from the dust and heat of the day, and drink
of the living streams of knowledge. There is a 'daily beauty in
his life,' on which mankind may meditate, and grow better. It
exhibits no lofty and almost useless, because inimitable, example
of excellence; but presents a picture of active, yet simple and
imitable virtues, which are within every man's reach, but which,
unfortunately, are not exercised by many, or this world would be
a paradise.

But his private life is peculiarly worthy the attention of the
citizens of our young and busy country, where literature and the
elegant arts must grow up side by side with the coarser plants
of daily necessity; and must depend for their culture, not on
the exclusive devotion of time and wealth; nor the quickening
rays of titled patronage; but on hours and seasons snatched from
the purest of worldly interests, by intelligent and public-spirited
individuals.

He has shown how much may be done for a place in hours of
leisure by one master-spirit, and how completely it can give its
own impress to surrounding objects. Like his own Lorenzo de'
Medici, on whom he seems to have fixed his eye, as on a pure
model of antiquity, he has interwoven the history of his life with
the history of his native town, and has made the foundations
of his fame the monuments of his virtues. Wherever you go,
in Liverpool, you perceive traces of his footsteps in all that is
elegant and liberal. He found the tide of wealth flowing merely
in the channels of traffic; he has diverted from it invigorating
rills to refresh the garden of literature. By his own example and
constant exertions, he has effected that union of commerce and
the intellectual pursuits, so eloquently recommended in one of
his latest writings; [*Address on the opening of the Liverpool
Institution: Irving's note] and has practically proved how
beautifully they may be brought to harmonize, and to benefit each
other. The noble institutions for literary and scientific purposes,
which reflect such credit on Liverpool, and are giving such an
impulse to the public mind, have mostly been originated, and
have all been effectively promoted, by Mr. Roscoe; and when we
consider the rapidly increasing opulence and magnitude of that
town, which promises to vie in commercial importance with the

metropolis, it will be perceived that in awakening an ambition of mental improvement among its inhabitants, he has effected a great benefit to the cause of British literature.

In America, we know Mr. Roscoe only as the author; in Liverpool he is spoken of as the banker; and I was told of his having been unfortunate in business. I could not pity him, as I heard some rich men do. I considered him far above the reach of pity. Those who live only for the world, and in the world, may be cast down by the frowns of adversity; but a man like Roscoe is not to be overcome by the reverses of fortune. They do but drive him in upon the resources of his own mind, to the superior society of his own thoughts; which the best of men are apt sometimes to neglect, and to roam abroad in search of less worthy associates. He is independent of the world around him. He lives with antiquity, and with posterity: with antiquity, in the sweet communion of studious retirement; and with posterity, in the generous aspirings after future renown. The solitude of such a mind is its state of highest enjoyment. It is then visited by those elevated meditations which are the proper aliment of noble souls, and are, like manna, sent from heaven, in the wilderness of this world.

While my feelings were yet alive on the subject, it was my fortune to light on further traces of Mr. Roscoe. I was riding out with a gentleman, to view the environs of Liverpool, when he turned off, through a gate, into some ornamented grounds. After riding a short distance, we came to a spacious mansion of freestone, built in the Grecian style. It was not in the purest style, yet it had an air of elegance, and the situation was delightful. A fine lawn sloped away from it, studded with clumps of trees, so disposed as to break a soft fertile country into a variety of landscapes. The Mersey was seen winding a broad quiet sheet of water through an expanse of green meadow land, while the Welsh mountains, blended with clouds, and melting into distance, bordered the horizon.

This was Roscoe's favourite residence during the days of his prosperity. It had been the seat of elegant hospitality and literary retirement. The house was now silent and deserted. I saw the windows of the study, which looked out upon the soft scenery I have mentioned. The windows were closed—the library was gone. Two or three ill-favoured beings were loitering about the place, whom my fancy pictured into retainers of the law. It was like visiting some classic fountain, that had once welled its pure waters in a sacred shade, but finding it dry and dusty, with the lizard and the toad brooding over the shattered marbles.

I inquired after the fate of Mr. Roscoe's library, which had consisted of scarce and foreign books, from many of which he had drawn the materials for his Italian histories. It had passed under the hammer of the auctioneer, and was dispersed about the country. The good people of the vicinity thronged like wreckers to get some part of the noble vessel that had been driven on shore. Did such a scene admit of ludicrous associations, we might imagine something whimsical in this strange irruption in the regions of learning. Pigmies rummaging the armoury of a giant, and contending for the possession of weapons which they could not wield. We might picture to ourselves some knot of speculators, debating with calculating brow over the quaint binding and illuminated margin of an obsolete author; of the air of intense, but baffled sagacity, with which some successful purchaser attempted to dive into the black-letter bargain he had secured.

It is a beautiful incident in the story of Mr. Roscoe's misfortunes, and one which cannot fail to interest the studious mind, that the parting with his books seems to have touched upon his tenderest feelings, and to have been the only circumstance that could provoke the notice of his muse. The scholar only knows how dear these silent, yet eloquent, companions of pure thoughts and innocent hours become in the season of adversity. When all that is worldly turns to dross around us, these only retain their steady value. When friends grow cold, and the converse of intimates languishes into vapid civility and commonplace, these only continue the unaltered countenance of happier days, and cheer us with that true friendship which never deceived hope, nor deserted sorrow.

I do not wish to censure; but, surely, if the people of Liverpool had been properly sensible of what was due to Mr. Roscoe and themselves, his library would never have been sold. Good worldly reasons may, doubtless, be given for the circumstance, which it would be difficult to combat with others that might seem merely fanciful; but it certainly appears to me such an opportunity as seldom occurs, of cheering a noble mind struggling under misfortunes by one of the most delicate, but most expressive tokens of public sympathy. It is difficult, however, to estimate a man of genius properly who is daily before our eyes. He becomes mingled and confounded with other men. His great qualities lose their novelty; we become too familiar with the common materials which form the basis even of the loftiest character. Some of Mr. Roscoe's townsmen may regard him merely as a man of business; others, as a politician; all find him engaged like themselves in ordinary occupations, and surpassed, perhaps, by themselves on some points of worldly wisdom. Even that amiable and unostentatious simplicity of character, which gives the nameless grace to real excellence, may cause him to be undervalued by some coarse minds, who do not know that true worth is always void of glare and pretension. But the man of letters, who speaks of Liverpool, speaks of it as the residence of Roscoe.—The intelligent traveller who visits it inquires where Roscoe is to be seen. He is the literary landmark of the place, indicating its existence to the distant scholar.—He is like Pompey's column at Alexandria, towering alone in classic dignity.

Washington Irving, *The Sketch Book of Geoffrey Crayon, Gent* (1819–20).

Nathaniel Parker Willis (1806–67), a literary dilettante, was the heir to Irving in continuing his practice of producing light sketches from his experiences of travel. *Pencillings by the Way* (1835) was the product of a tour of the Continent he made as foreign editor and correspondent for the *New York Mirror*. Unusually, Willis reached Liverpool by land from Scotland, via Carlisle and Manchester. Although his accommodation evidently left a lot to be desired, he also turned his irony against his compatriots.

There are good inns, I believe, at Liverpool; but the coach put me down at the dirtiest and worst specimen of a public-house that I have encountered in England. As I was to stay but a night, I overcame the prejudice of a first *coup-d'oeil* [glance], and made the best of a dinner in the coffee-room. It was crowded with people – principally merchants, I presumed; and the dinner-hour having barely passed, most of them were sitting over their wine and toddy at the small tables, discussing prices, or reading the newspapers. Near me were two young men, whose faces I thought familiar to me, and, with a second look, I resolved them into two of my countrymen, who, I found out presently by their conversation, were eating their first dinner in England. They were gentlemanlike young men, of good education, and I pleased myself with looking about and imagining the comparison they would draw, with their own country fresh in their recollection, between it and this. I could not help feeling how erroneous, in this case, would be a first impression. The gloomy coffee-room, the hurried and uncivil waiters, the atrocious cookery, the bad air, greasy tables, filthy carpet, and unsocial company – and one of the most popular and crowded inns of the first commercial town in England! My neighbours themselves, too, afforded me some little speculation. They were a fair specimen of the young men of our country, and after several years' exclusive conversance with other nations, I was curious to compare an untravelled American with the Europeans around me. I was struck with the exceeding *ambitiousness* of their style of conversation. Dr. Pangloss [a tutor in Voltaire's *Candide*] himself would have given them a degree. They called nothing by its week-day name, and avoided with a singular pertinacity exactly that upon which the modern English are as pertinaciously bent – a concise homeliness of phraseology. They were dressed much better than the people about them, (who were apparently in the same sphere of life) and had, on the whole, a superior air – owing possibly to the custom prevalent in America, of giving young men a university education before they enter into trade. Like myself, too, they had not yet learned the English accomplishment of total unconsciousness of the presence of others. When not conversing they did not study profoundly the grain of the mahogany, nor gaze with solemn earnestness into the bottom of their wine-glasses, nor peruse with the absorbed fixedness of Belshazzar, the figures on the wall [the Babylonian king described in Daniel 5:1–4, who holds a feast and then sees a mysterious message being written on the wall]. They looked about them with undisguised curiosity, ordered a great deal more wine than they wanted (*very* American that!), and were totally without the self-complacent, self-amused, sober-felicity air which John Bull assumes after his cheese in the coffee-room.

I did not introduce myself to my countrymen, for an American is the last person in the world with whom one should depart from the ordinary rules of society. Having no fixed rank, either in their own or a foreign country, they construe all uncommon civility into either a freedom, or a desire to patronize, and the last is the unpardonable sin. They called, after a while, for a 'mint julep' [drink made from mint, bourbon, sugar and water] (unknown in England), for slippers (rather an unusual call also – gentlemen usually wearing their own), and seemed very much surprised, on asking for candles, at being ushered to bed by the chambermaid.

I passed the next morning in walking about Liverpool. It is singularly like New York in its general air, and quite like it in the character of its population. I presume I must have met many of my countrymen, for there were some who passed me in the street, whom I could have sworn to. In a walk to the American consul's (to whose polite kindness I, as well as all my compatriots, have been very much indebted), I was lucky enough to see a New York packet drive into the harbour under full sail – as gallant a sight as you would wish to see. It was blowing rather stiffly, and she ran up to her anchorage like a bird, and, taking in her canvass with the speed of a man-of-war, was lying in a few moments with her head to the tide, as neat and tranquil as if she had slept for the last month at her moorings. I could feel in the air that came ashore from her that I had letters on board.

Anxious to get on to Cheshire, where, as they say of the mails, I had been *due* some days, and very anxious to get rid of the perfume of beer, beef-steaks, and bad soap, with which I had become impregnated at the inn, I got embarked in an omnibus at noon, and was taken to the Railway. I was just in time; and down we dived into the long tunnel, emerging from the darkness at a pace that made my hair sensibly tighten and hold on with apprehension. Thirty miles in the hour is pleasant going, when one is a little accustomed to it. It gives one such a contempt for time and distance. The whizzing past of the return-trains, going in the other direction with the same velocity, – making you recoil in one second, and a mile off the next, was the only thing which after a few minutes I did not take to very kindly.

N. P. Willis, *Pencillings by the Way* (1835), Vol. 3, Letter 32.

Willis expected a better experience in the Adelphi Hotel, especially in his comparison with the Astor House Hotel in Broadway, which was at the time considered the finest in New York. Like many American visitors, he apparently failed to pick up the signals for payment from the staff.

The Adelphi is the Astor House of Liverpool, a very large and showy hotel near the terminus of the railway. We were shown into rather a magnificent parlour on our arrival; and very hungry with rail-roading since six in the morning, we ordered dinner at their earliest convenience. It came after a full hour, and we sat down to four superb silver covers, anticipating a meal corresponding to the stout person and pompous manners of the fattest waiter I have seen

in my travels. The grand cover was removed with a flourish and disclosed divers small bits of second-hand beef steak, toasted brown and warped at the corners by a second fire, and on the removal of the other three silver pagodas, our eyes were gratified by a dish of peas that had been once used for green soup, three similarly toasted and warped mutton chops, and three potatoes. Quite incredulous of the cook's intentions, I ventured to suggest to the waiter that he had probably mistaken the tray and brought us the dinner of some sportsman's respectable brace of pointers; but on being assured that there were no dogs in the cellar, I sent word to the master of the house that we had rather a preference for a dinner new and hot, and would wait till he could provide it. Half an hour more brought up the landlord's apologies and a fresh and hot beef-steak, followed by a tough-crusted apple-pie, custard, and cheese and with a bottle of Moselle, which was good, we finished our dinner at one of the most expensive and showy hotels in England. The manners and fare at the American hotels being always described as exponents of civilisation by English travellers, I shall be excused for giving a counter-picture of one of the most boasted of their own.
[…]
My chamber is a large and well-furnished room, with windows looking out on the area shut in by the wings of the house; and I must make you still more contented at the Astor, by describing what is going on below at this moment. It is half-past eight, and a Sunday morning. All the bells of the house, it seems to me, are ringing, most of them very impatiently, and in the area before the kitchen windows are six or eight idle waiters, and four or five female scullions, playing, quarrelling, scolding, and screaming; the language of both men and women more profane and indecent than any thing I have ever before chanced to hear, and every word audible in every room in this quarter of the hotel. This has been going on since six this morning; and I seriously declare I do not think I ever heard as much indecent conversation in my life as for three mortal hours must have 'murdered sleep' for every lady and gentleman lodged on the rear side of the 'crack hotel' of Liverpool.

Sick of the scene described above, I went out just now to take a turn or two in my slippers in the long entry. Up and down, giving me a most appealing stare whenever we met, dawdled also the fat waiter who served up the cold victuals of yesterday. He evidently had some errand with me, but what I did not immediately fathom. At last he approached

'You a got your things, sir?'

'What things?'

'The stick and umbrella, I carried to your bed-room, sir.'

'Yes, thank you,' and I resumed my walk.

The waiter resumed his, and presently approached again.

'You a don't intend to use the parlour again, sir?'

'No: I have explained to the master of the house that I shall breakfast in the coffee-room.'

And again I walked on.

My friend began again at the next turn.

'You a pay for those ladies dinner yourself, sir?'

'Yes.' I walked on once more.

Once more approaches my fat incubus, and with a twirl of the towel in his hand looks as if he would fain be delivered of something.

'Why the devil am I badgered in this way?'

I stormed out at last, losing patience at his stammering hesitation, and making a move to get round the fat obstruction and pursue my walk.

'Will you a remember the waiter, if you please, sir?'

'Oh! I was not aware that I was to pay the waiter at every meal. I generally do it when I leave the house. Perhaps you'll be kind enough to let me finish my walk, and trust me till to-morrow morning?'

P.S. Evening in the coffee-room. They say the best beginning in love is a decided aversion, and badly as I began at Liverpool, I shall always have a tender recollection of it for the admirable and unequalled luxury of its baths. A long and beautiful Grecian building crests the head of George's Pier, built by the Corporation of Liverpool, and devoted exclusively to salt-water baths. I walked down in the twilight to enjoy this refreshing luxury, and it being Sunday evening, I was shown into the ladies' end of the building. The room where I waited till the bath was prepared was a lofty and finely proportioned apartment, elegantly furnished, and lined with superbly bound books and pictures, the tables covered with engravings, and the whole thing looked like a central apartment in a nobleman's residence. A boy showed me presently into a small drawing-room, to which was attached a bath closet, the two rooms lined, boudoir fashion, with chintz, a clock over the bath, a nice carpet and stove, in short, every luxury possible to such an establishment. I asked the boy if the gentlemen's baths were as elegant as these. 'Oh yes,' he said; 'there are two splendid pictures

of Niagara Falls and Catskill.' 'Who painted them?' 'Mr. Wall.'
'And whose are they?' 'They belong to our father, sir!' I made
up my mind that 'our father' was a man of taste and a credit to
Liverpool.

N. P. Willis, Loiterings of Travel (1840), Vol. 3.

Bayard Taylor (1825–78) achieved considerable success with his books
of travel to Egypt, Central Africa, India and other countries. In 1844
he started a tour of Europe by sailing to Liverpool on the packet ship
Oxford, describing his arrival below. The fruit of this tour was *Views A-Foot*
(1846), which appeared with a preface by N. P. Willis. After his arrival in
Liverpool, Taylor sailed immediately for Ireland and eventually returned
to America from London.

> In the afternoon we passed the Isle of Man, having a beautiful
> view of the Calf, with a white stream tumbling down the rocks
> into the sea; and at night saw the sun set behind the mountains of
> Wales. About midnight, the pilot came on board, and soon after
> sunrise I saw the distant spires of Liverpool. The Welsh coast was
> studded with windmills, all in motion, and the harbour spotted
> with buoys, bells and floating lights. How delightful it was to
> behold the green trees on the banks of the Mersey, and to know
> that in a few hours we should be on land! About 11 o'clock we
> came to anchor in the channel of the Mersey, near the docks, and
> after much noise, bustle and confusion, were transferred, with our
> baggage, to a small steamboat, giving a parting cheer to the Iowas,
> who remained on board. On landing, I stood a moment to observe
> the scene. The baggage-wagons, drawn by horses, mules and
> donkeys, were extraordinary; men were going about crying 'the
> celebrated Tralorum gingerbread!' which they carried in baskets;
> and a boy in the University dress, with long blue gown and yellow
> knee-breeches, was running to the wharf to look at the Indians.
>   At last the carts were all loaded, the word was given to
> start, and then, what a scene ensued! Away went the mules, the
> horses and the donkeys; away ran men and women and children,
> carrying chairs and trunks, and boxes and bedding. The wind
> was blowing, and the dust whirled up as they dashed helter-
> skelter through the gate and started off on a hot race, down the
> dock to the depot. Two wagons came together, one of which

was overturned, scattering the broken boxes of a Scotch family over the pavement; but while the poor woman was crying over her loss, the tide swept on, scarcely taking time to glance at the mishap.

Our luggage was 'passed' with little trouble; the officer merely opening the trunks and pressing his hands on the top. Even some American reprints of English works which my companion carried, and feared would be taken from him, were passed over without a word. I was agreeably surprised at this, as from the accounts of some travellers, I had been led to fear horrible things of custom-houses. This over, we took a stroll about the city. I was first struck by seeing so many people walking in the middle of the streets, and so many gentlemen going about with pinks stuck in their button-holes. Then, the houses being all built of brown granite or dark brick, gives the town a sombre appearance, which the sunshine (when there is any) cannot dispel.

Bayard Taylor, *Views A-foot; or, Europe Seen with Knapsack and Staff* (1846).

The New England poet **William Cullen Bryant** (1794–1878) described his *Letters of a Traveller* (1850) frankly as 'occasional sketches', taken from his travels with the result that they lack any sense of an itinerary. The description of his voyage to Liverpool is preceded by an account of an excursion in New Hampshire.

I suppose a smoother passage was never made across the Atlantic, than ours in the good ship *Liverpool*. For two-thirds of the way, we slid along over a placid sea, before the gentlest zephyrs that ever swept the ocean, and when at length the winds became contrary, they only impeded our progress, without making it unpleasant. The *Liverpool* is one of the strongest, safest, and steadiest of the packet-ships; her commander prudent, skilful, always on the watch, and as it almost seemed to me, in every part of the vessel at once; the passengers were good-tempered and quiet, like the sea on which we were sailing; and with all these advantages in our favour, I was not disposed to repine that we were a week longer in crossing the Atlantic, than some vessels which left New York nearly the same time.

It was matter of rejoicing to all of us, however, when we saw the Irish coast like a faint cloud upon the horizon, and still

more were we delighted, when after beating about for several
days in what is called the Chops of the Channel, we beheld the
mountains of Wales. I could hardly believe that what I saw were
actually mountain summits, so dimly were their outlines defined
in the vapoury atmosphere of this region, the nearer and lower
steeps only being fully visible, and the higher and remoter ones
half lost in the haze. It seemed to me as if I were looking at the
reflection of mountains in a dull mirror, and I was ready to take
out my pocket-handkerchief to wipe the dust and smoke from
its surface. About thirty miles from *Liverpool* we took on board a
pilot, whose fair complexion, unbronzed by the sun, was remarked
by the ladies, and soon after a steamer arrived and took us in tow.
At twelve o'clock in the night, the Liverpool by the aid of the
high tide cleared the sand-bar at the mouth of the port, and was
dragged into the dock, and the next morning when I awoke, I
found myself in Liverpool in the midst of fog and rain.

'Liverpool,' said one of its inhabitants to me, 'is more like an
American than an English city; it is new, bustling, and prosperous.'
I saw some evidences of this after I had got my baggage through
the custom-house, which was attended with considerable delay, the
officers prying very closely into the contents of certain packages
which I was taking for friends of mine to their friends in England,
cutting the packthread, breaking the seals, and tearing the wrappers
without mercy. I saw the streets crowded with huge drays, carrying
merchandise to and fro, and admired the solid construction of the
docks, in which lay thousands of vessels from all parts of the globe.
The walls of these docks are built of large blocks of red sandstone,
with broad gateways opening to the river Mersey, and when the
tide is at its height, which I believe is about thirty feet from low
water, the gates are open, and vessels allowed to enter and depart.
When the tide begins to retire, the gates are closed, and the water
and the vessels locked in together. Along the river for miles, the
banks are flanked with this massive masonry, which in some places
I should judge to be nearly forty feet in height. Meantime the
town is spreading into the interior; new streets are opened; in one
field you may see the brickmakers occupied in their calling, and
in the opposite one the bricklayers building rows of houses. New
churches and new public buildings of various kinds are going up in
these neighbourhoods.

The streets which contain the shops have for the most part a
gay and showy appearance; the buildings are generally of stucco,
and show more of architectural decoration than in our cities. The

greater part of the houses, however, are built of brick which has a rough surface, and soon acquires in this climate a dark colour, giving a gloomy aspect to the streets. The public buildings, which are rather numerous, are of a drab-coloured freestone, and those which have been built for forty or fifty years, the Town Hall, for example, and some of the churches, appear almost of a sooty hue. I went through the rooms of the Town Hall and was shown the statue of Canning, by Chantry, an impressive work as it seemed to me. One of the rooms contains a portrait of him by Lawrence, looking very much like a feeble old gentleman whom I remember as not long since an appraiser in the New York custom-house. We were shown a lofty saloon in which the Common Council of Liverpool enjoy their dinners, and very good dinners the woman who showed us the rooms assured us they were. But the spirit of corporation reform has broken in upon the old order of things, and those good dinners which a year or two since were eaten weekly, are now eaten but once a fortnight, and money is saved.

I strolled to the Zoological Gardens, a very pretty little place, where a few acres of uneven surface have been ornamented with plantations of flowering shrubs, many of which are now in full bloom, artificial ponds of water, rocks, and bridges, and picturesque buildings for the animals. Winding roads are made through the green turf, which is now sprinkled with daisies. It seems to be a favourite place of resort for the people of the town. They were amused by the tricks of an elephant, the performances of a band of music, which among other airs sang and played 'Jim along Josey,' [a minstrel song popular in the 1840s] and the feats of a young fellow who gave an illustration of the centrifugal force by descending a *Montagne Russe* [a roller coaster] in a little car, which by the help of a spiral curve in the railway, was made to turn a somerset [somersault] in the middle of its passage, and brought him out at the end with his cap off, and his hair on end.

One of the most remarkable places in Liverpool, is St. James's Cemetery. In the midst of the populous and bustling city, is a chasm among the black rocks, with a narrow green level at the bottom. It is overlooked by a little chapel. You enter it by an arched passage cut through the living rock, which brings you by a steep descent to the narrow level of which I have spoken, where you find yourself among graves set with flowers and half concealed by shrubbery, while along the rocky sides of the hollow in which you stand, you see tombs or blank arches for tombs which are yet to be excavated. We found the thickets within and around this valley of the dead, musical with innumerable birds, which build here undisturbed. Among the monuments is one erected to Huskisson, a mausoleum with a glass door through which you see his statue from the chisel of Gibson. On returning by the passage through the rock, we found preparations making for a funeral service in the chapel, which we entered. Four men came staggering in under the weight of a huge coffin, accompanied by a clergyman of imposing stature, white hair, and florid complexion. Four other coffins were soon after brought in and placed in the church, attended by another clergyman of less pre-possessing appearance, who, to my disappointment, read the service. He did it in the most detestable manner, with much grimace, and with the addition of a supernumerary syllable after almost every word ending with a consonant. The clerk delivered the responses in such a mumbling tone, and with so much of the Lancashire dialect, as to be almost unintelligible. The other clergyman looked, I thought, as if, like myself, he was sorry to hear the beautiful funeral service of his church so profaned.

In a drive which we took into the country, we had occasion to admire the much talked of verdure and ornamental cultivation of England. Green hedges, rich fields of grass sprinkled with flowers, beautiful residences, were on every side, and the wheels of our carriage rolled over the smoothest roads in the world. The lawns before the houses are kept smoothly shaven, and carefully levelled by the roller. At one of these English houses, to which I was admitted by the hospitality of its opulent owner, I admired the variety of shrubs in full flower, which here grow in the open air, rhododendrons of various species, flushed with bloom, azaleas of different hues, one of which I recognized as American, and others of various families and names. In a neighbouring field stood a plot of rye-grass two feet in height, notwithstanding the season was yet so early; and a part of it had been already mown for the food of cattle. Yet the people here complain of their climate. 'You must get thick shoes and wrap yourself in flannel,' said one of them to me. 'The English climate makes us subject to frequent and severe colds, and here in Lancashire you have the worst climate of England, perpetually damp, with strong and chilly winds.'

It is true that I have found the climate miserably chilly since I landed, but I am told the season is a late one. The apple-trees are just in bloom, though there are but few of them to be seen, and the blossoms of the hawthorn are only just beginning to open. The foliage of some of the trees, rich as it is, bears the appearance in some places of having felt the late frosts, and certain kinds of trees are not yet in leaf.

[Prince's Park was developed by Richard Vaughan Yates, designed by Joseph Paxton (of Crystal Palace fame) and James Pennethorne, and was opened in 1842.]

Among the ornaments of Liverpool is the new park called Prince's Park, which a wealthy individual, Mr. Robert Yates, has purchased and laid out with a view of making it a place for private residences. It has a pretty little lake, plantations of trees and shrubs which have just begun to strike root, pleasant nooks and hollows, eminences which command extensive views, and the whole is traversed with roads which are never allowed to proceed from place to place in a straight line. The trees are too newly planted to allow me to call the place beautiful, but within a few years it will be eminently so.

William Cullen Bryant, *Letters of a Traveller; or, Notes of Things Seen in Europe and America* (1850), Letter 18.

Young Americans Abroad (1852) presents a new concept in travel narration. In 1851 the **Reverend John Overton Choules** took a group of male students to Britain and the Continent, sailing on the *Arctic*. The volume produced from this tour presents a series of letters from one student to another, thereby giving the convention of description through letters more authenticity. The series of city sights by now sounds familiar and concentrates on buildings and locations of interest. At the time of their visit, St George's Hall was nearing completion; it opened in 1854, designed initially to house music festivals. The comparison between the Liverpool Necropolis and Mount Auburn Cemetery in Boston is an even one, since both were among the first landscaped cemeteries of their time.

Dear Charley,
Well, we have fairly commenced our travel, and yet I can scarcely realize the fact that I am here in Old England, and that, for some months at least, I shall be away from home and the occupations of the school-room. The next day after landing we went to the

custom-house to see our fellow-passengers pass their effects, and really felt glad to think of our good fortune in landing every thing at night and direct from the ship. It was an exciting scene, and I was not a little amused to observe the anxiety of the gentlemen to save their cigars from the duty imposed, and which amounts to nine shillings sterling per pound. All sorts of contrivances were in vogue, and the experiences of men were various, the man with one hundred, perhaps, being brought up, while his neighbour with five hundred passed off successfully, and, as he cleared the building, seemed disposed to place his finger on the prominent feature of his face.

I quite like the appearance of Liverpool. After walking through the principal streets and making a general survey of the shops,— no one speaks of *store*,—I think I can testify to the extraordinary cleanness of the city, and the massiveness and grandeur of the public buildings.

Our attention was first directed to the cemetery which had been described, you remember, to us one evening in the study. It is on the confines of the city, and is made but of an old quarry. I liked it better than any cemetery I ever saw; it is unlike all I had seen, and, though comparatively small, is very picturesque, I may almost say romantic. The walls are lofty, and are devoted to spacious tombs, and the groundwork abounds in garden shrubbery and labyrinth. Some of the monuments are striking. The access to this resting-place is by a steep cut through the rock, and you pass under an archway of the most imposing character. At the entrance of the cemetery is a neat chapel, and the officiating minister has a dwelling-house near the gate.

I wish you could see a building now in progress, and which has taken twelve or fourteen years to erect, and from its appearance will not, I suppose, be finished in four or five more. It is called St. George's Hall. The intent is to furnish suitable accommodations for the various law courts, and also to contain the finest ball-room in Europe. It is in a commanding position. I know little of architecture, but this building strikes me as one of exquisite beauty. We obtained an order from the mayor to be shown over it and examine the works, and we enjoyed it very much. The great hall will be without a rival in England. The town hall is a noble edifice, and the people are quite proud of it. The interior is finely laid out, and has some spacious rooms for the civic revelries of the fathers of the town. The good woman who showed us round feels complacently enough as she explains the uses of the rooms. The ball-room is ninety feet by forty-six, and forty feet high. The dining and drawing-rooms are spacious apartments. On the grand staircase is a noble statue of George Canning, by Chantrey, whose beautiful one of Washington we have so often admired in the Boston State House. In the building are some good paintings of the late kings; one or two by Sir Thomas Lawrence. The Exchange is directly behind the hall, and contains in the centre a glorious bronze monument to Lord Nelson, the joint production of Wyat and Westmacott. Death is laying his hand upon the hero's heart, and Victory is placing a fourth crown on his sword. Ever since I read Southey's Life of Nelson, I have felt an interest in every thing relating to this great; yet imperfect man. You know that illustrated work on Nelson that we have so often looked at it contains a large engraving of this monument. As Yankee boys, we found our way to the top of the Exchange, to look at the cotton sales-room. This same room has more to do with our good friends at the south than any other in the world. The atmosphere would have been chilly to a Georgian planter, as cotton was down—down.

The Necropolis is a very spacious burying-place, open to all classes, and where persons can be interred with the use of any form desired. The gateway is of stone, and not unlike the granite one at Mount Auburn; and on one side is a chapel, and on the other a house for the register. Not far from this we came to the Zoölogical Gardens, kept in excellent order, and where is a good collection of animals, birds, &c. The Collegiate Institution is an imposing structure in the Tudor style.

St. George's Church, which stands at the head of Lord Street, occupies the position of the old castle, destroyed, I believe, more than one hundred and fifty years ago, and is a very graceful termination to one of the best business avenues of the city. Several of the churches and chapels are in good style. But one of the best buildings is—as it should be, in a city like this—the Sailor's Home, not far from the Custom House. This is a highly-ornamented house, and would adorn any city of the world.

[The Liverpool Custom House was built on the filled-in site of the Old Dock and opened in 1827. The floating landing stage described below was moored on the site of what is now the Pier Head.]

The Custom House is thought to be one of the finest buildings in the kingdom. It occupied ten years in its erection.

It is composed of three *façades*, from a rusticated pavement, each having a splendid portico of eight Ionic columns. The whole is surmounted by a dome, one hundred and thirty feet high, and the effect of the building is excellent. The glory of Liverpool is her docks, and a stranger is sure to be pointed to the great landing stage, an immense floating pier, which was moored into its present position on the 1st of June, 1847. This stage is five hundred and seven feet long, and over eighty feet wide. This mass of timber floats upon pontoons, which have to support more than two thousand tons. At each end is a light barge.

In the Clarence dock are to be found the Irish and coasting steamers, and to the north are the Trafalgar, Victoria, and Waterloo docks; the Prince's dock, and the Great Prince's dock basin. On the outside of all these is a fine parade, of about one half a mile, and which affords one of the most beautiful marine promenades in the world, and gives an interesting view of the Cheshire shore, opposite the city. The Prince's dock is five hundred yards long, and one hundred broad. Vessels, on arriving, discharge on the east side, and take in cargo on the west. Besides all these there is the Brunswick dock, Queen's dock, Duke's dock, Salthouse dock, &c.

The Royal Liverpool Institution is a great benefit to the inhabitants. It has a good library, fine collections of paintings, and a good museum of natural history. Many of these paintings belong to the early masters, and date even before the fifteenth century. We were interested to find here a complete set of casts of the Elgin marbles. The originals were the decorations of the Parthenon at Athens, and are now in the British Museum. As we shall spend some time in that collection, I say no more at present about these wonderful monuments of genius. The Athenæum and the Lyceum are both fine buildings, and each has a good library, lecture, and news rooms.

We were disappointed at finding the Rev. Dr. Raffles, the most eloquent preacher of the city, out of town. He was the successor of Spencer, who was drowned bathing in the Mersey, and his Life by Raffles is one of deep interest. The great historical name of Liverpool is William Roscoe, the author of the Lives of Leo X. and the Medici. I must not omit to tell you that, during our stay, the town was all alive with a regiment of lancers, just arrived from Ireland, on their way to London. They are indeed fine-looking fellows, and are mounted on capital horses. I have watched their evolutions in front of the Adelphi with much pleasure, and have been amused to notice a collection of the most wretched-looking boys I ever saw, brought together by the troops. There seems to me more pauperism this week, in Liverpool, than I ever saw in New York in my life.

Truly yours,
James.

Young Americans Abroad; or, Vacation in Europe: Travels in England, France, Holland, Belgium, Prussia and Switzerland (1852), Letter 3.

On the eve of departure a letter summed up the attitude of the British towards America as follows:

To-morrow we are to take our departure; and, though very glad to return home, yet I feel sorry at leaving a country where there is so much that is excellent and noble and beautiful. I have learnt, certainly, that England and America have too much in common to justify the indulgence of hatred and prejudice; and I find the tone of feeling here, among wise and good people, very kind towards America. I have rarely heard a reflection upon our country, excepting upon our slavery. That they *must talk* about; and they are a little like the man who, having just got rid of the irritable affection supposed to trouble the North Britons, could not for his life help speaking of sulphur. An Englishman is sure to tell you that he is free from this sin—yes, washed, but scarcely dry. [Letter 54]

Samuel S. Cox (1824–89) was a lawyer and newspaper editor at the time when he made his tour of Europe, but went on to become a congressman and diplomat. In his travel memoir *A Buckeye Abroad* (1852) – 'buckeye' being a slang term for a native of Ohio – he was well aware of writing within a tradition set by Washington Irving and liberally sprinkles literary allusions throughout his account. Despite a bout of sea-sickness, like Irving, Cox was overwhelmed with cultural associations as his boat neared land.

The Commercial Metropolis

Here we are upon substantial soil. Liverpool! How languidly the word melts in the mouth! My partiality for steamships and

big ponds could not restrain the outbreak of joy with which we
pressed the solid land. The effects too of our experience, though
sad at first, have resulted in a bound of animal spirits almost
inconsistent with sanity.

At the mouth of the Mersey we took a pilot aboard, and
with our 'starboard, sir,' 'port, sir,' and 'steady, sir,' we reached
Liverpool at 11 o'clock, upon the night of the 17th of May, 1851.
It was some recompense for missing the green, bright green banks
of the Mersey, with its cottages and residences, that we passed
up amid a galaxy of many-coloured lights, which, reflected upon
the water from Birkenhead on the one side, and Liverpool on
the other, almost transformed the scene into one of fairyland.
Our guns boomed; mails were taken; and after the custom-house
proceedings, by no means vexatious, we were permitted to land.
The first person that spoke to me was a little imp, modelled after
the exterior of Oliver Twist. A police officer touched him with a
baton. He was *non est* [disappeared] in a jiffy.

Our first impression of the population here was not very
favourable. True, we saw the fag-end of humanity in the shape of
beggars and loafers at the landing. We had no sooner taken up our
march to our hotel, preferring to feel the delight of a walk, after
so long a ride on the billows, than a fellow who said that he was
a servant at the Waterloo, offered himself as our pilot. I suspected
him, but thought that we would use him, as it was nearly two in
the morning. We had not gone far before we were saluted with,
'Which hotel, sir which hotel?'

'Waterloo!'

'Sorry very sorry can't accommodate you, sir – I'm boots at the
Waterloo, sir – all full, sir. Three ship-loads just arrived, sir – very
sorry – Victoria Hotel near by – few minutes walk, sir – own
sister of the Waterloo keeps it.'

He had said too much. We marched on, heartily laughing at
'Boots!' Saint Somebody's church illuminated the hour of two, and
it was nearly daylight – a phenomenon belonging to this northern
clime which considerably bewildered our Buckeye experience.
We found the Waterloo open, and the lady at the door with her
servants, ready to take down our names. I introduced our pilot as
their servant. They, of course, disclaimed his acquaintance. 'You
are a pretty specimen of human veracity.'

'Yes, sir, I am obliged to you, sir.'

'But I suppose we ought to pay you for your guidance?'

'Oh yes, please you, sir, you are very kind, sir.'

I gave him a shilling, with a caution about lying, which he, with a rub over his red nose, and a low bow, acknowledged.

We had scarcely appeared this morning at our window, when that extreme of English civilization called 'starvation' was seen in the shape of a young urchin, whether boy or girl I could not discern, for the dress consisted of only two rags. He stood bobbing his head and whining, while I sketched him. His counterfeit presentment followed us, as soon as we left the hotel to take a stroll; and the little gipsy had the same monotone of grief. He was joined by another; and thus marshalled, we had to pass the agony of some squares. It was not until a fretful threat to 'cut his weazand,' that he cut our company, which he did with the remark, 'they won't pay any more.'

How comfortably every thing is conducted in these English hotels. We have our own parlours, and our own meals. It looks so cosy to see our own good company presiding at the tea-urn, and dispensing the Johnsonian beverage.

Of course, the modes here strike us strangely. But as we started out to admire all that is admirable, we must commend the English mode of hotel keeping, with its private parlours and private meals.

Every object, even the go-carts, strike a stranger queerly at first. Omnibuses, with nobody inside, and crowded a-top, dash past our windows. Cabs as big as our carriages, like a streak of lightning, dash by with one horse. Horns musically quiver in the fresh morning air. The tall dark houses and clean white pave[ment]s of Liverpool surround us, while on every side green foliage and twittering birds betoken that love of rural life which the English bring even into their cities. One thing in-doors is noticeable. The sedulous zeal displayed in curtaining out heaven's sun light. It would seem that, with the prodigality of gloomy weather in this isle, as much of the light as possible would be admitted, more especially as a heavy window tax is assessed. But no such thing. Why? Is it a phase of that habitual exclusiveness and love of domestic ease which form so prominent a trait in the English character?

We have viewed the city. Its Corinthian elegance of architecture, illustrated especially in the Exchange; excellent police; above all, its magnificent docks, by which the shipping is brought into the city and preserved afloat, notwithstanding the tides bespeak for Liverpool the encomium of the traveller. There are two provisos. The first, beggars, I have named. The other is, the apparent sacrilegious treatment of the buried dead. Would you believe it?

The pave to several of the first churches here is over and upon the
tombstones of the buried. The inscriptions are being effaced by
the feet of the passenger. Nurses with children, men, women, and
boys, indiscriminately, tread over the ashes of the departed.

In our walk, we noticed Roscoe street – a reminder that
Liverpool was the home of the Historian of the Medici. It
recalled his splendid descriptions of that age, when Scholarship
and Art were beginning to burst the barriers of the dark ages,
to herald the new-born civilization which is ours to-day. It also
recalled Irving's elegant tribute to the merchant litterateur. You
remember how Irving first saw him, entering the Athenaeum,
with his venerable air a fine illustration of 'a chance production'
disappointing the assiduities of Art, and working out of the busy
mart of traffic the glory and the genius of the great Tuscan era.

Samuel S. Cox, *A Buckeye Abroad* (1852).

Henry Adams (1838–1918) was a member of the distinguished family
of diplomats and historians. Looking back on his life he records his first
voyage to Liverpool as a young adult, stressing the romantic excitement
at stepping ashore on a land full of literary memories. Adams came to
Liverpool again in 1861, accompanying his father Charles Francis Adams
who was taking up his post as ambassador in London. That same year
Henry Adams began a series of dispatches to American newspapers about
attitudes to the blockade of the South during the Civil War, for which he
visited Manchester. Once his identity as correspondent became known, he
was obliged to stop the series abruptly. In his autobiography he refers to
himself in the third person to convey the impact on him of forces such as
modern technology.

Whether the boy deserved such indulgence, or was worth it, he
knew no more than they, or than a professor at Harvard College
but whether worthy or not, he began his third or fourth attempt
at education in November, 1858, by sailing on the steamer *Persia*,
the pride of Captain Judkins and the Cunard Line; the newest,
largest and fastest steamship afloat [...] The ocean, the *Persia*,
Captain Judkins, and Mr. G. P. R. James [a popular English
novelist of the period], the most distinguished passenger, vanished
one Sunday morning in a furious gale in the Mersey, to make
place for the drearier picture of a Liverpool street as seen from the

Adelphi coffee-room in November murk, followed instantly by the passionate delights of Chester and the romance of red-sandstone architecture. Millions of Americans have felt this succession of emotions. Possibly very young and ingenuous tourists feel them still, but in days before tourists, when the romance was a reality, not a picture, they were overwhelming. When the boys went out to Eaton Hall, they were awed, as Thackeray or Dickens would have felt in the presence of a Duke. The very name of Grosvenor struck a note of grandeur. The long suite of lofty, gilded rooms with their gilded furniture; the portraits; the terraces; the gardens, the landscape; the sense of superiority in the England of the fifties, actually set the rich nobleman apart, above Americans and shopkeepers. Aristocracy was real. So was the England of Dickens. Oliver Twist and Little Nell lurked in every churchyard shadow, not as shadow but alive. Even Charles the First was not very shadowy, standing on the tower to see his army defeated. Nothing thereabouts had very much changed since he lost his battle and his head. An eighteenth-century American boy fresh from Boston naturally took it all for education, and was amused at this sort of lesson. At least he thought he felt it.

The Education of Henry Adams (1918).

The novelist **Henry James** (1843–1916) first sailed to England in July 1855 aboard the S.S. *Atlantic* of the Collins line, in transit to Geneva, then to Paris, after which his restless father in 1858 returned to America with his family. James next sailed for England as a young adult in 1869 on board the S.S. *China*, arriving in Liverpool and putting up at the Adelphi Hotel. He had planned to visit Chester the next day but overslept and instead took a slow train to London. James only wrote briefly about Liverpool, whereas he published a full-length essay on Chester, and only discussed the port within the context of his personal development. In the letter he wrote home under the first enthusiasm of his arrival in Liverpool, we can see James's tendency to read his English experiences through the nation's literature.

Liverpool Adelphi Hotel, 27 February 1869 [Letter to the James family: excerpt]
    So, in fine, here I am, in the reading room of this dingy and venerable inn, scribbling with this uncommonly bad quill pen.

In health and strength I'm literally immense – c'est le mot [that's
the word]. If you could appreciate the discomforts to which.
my tender frame has been exposed – (I mean in the way of not
sleeping, you know, and cuddling about for ten days on a tossing
deck with nothing worthy of the name of a seat within 3,000
miles) you would appreciate the merit of my being able to hold
up my head – much more brandish my fist at this rate. The
last 24 hours have been fraught with exertion and fatigue and
yet – in fact, I'm all right! As for Liverpool – que c'est bien la
Vieille Angleterre [it really is Old England]. The impressions of
my boyhood return from the past and swarm about my soul. On
finally getting in off the ship (we'd a terribly tedious time of it) I
proceeded hither in a hansom and lunched off a muffin and a cup
of tea in the coffee room of this mellow and musty hotel. I don't
think I ever enjoyed anything quite so much as waiting for these
refreshments and gazing without at the ancient and aristocratic
streets and within at the full dressed waiters. This afternoon, after
a short repose, I proceeded (this is for Willy) [his brother William]
to call on our friend Dr Inman who lives about 5 minutes off,
in a dim and smoky vista of a street and a house of black and
corrugated brick. To my great regret he was out of town and
won't be home till Monday. I don't think it worth while to wait
over for him; but I'll see how I feel. If I don't wait I shall leave
for London tomorrow by the ten o'clock train.- I enjoy these
first hours of landing most deeply. The sense of change novelty
antiquity and all the rest of it, lies with the most warm and
comfortable weight on my soul. I am very glad I came to England
first. I foresee a rich harvest of emotions.

The Complete Letters of Henry James, 1855–1872
(Lincoln, NE: University of Nebraska Press, 2006).

[Looking back on this experience some twenty years later for the American
Century Magazine, James measures its value in terms of 'Englishness' and
attempts to recompose those early impressions; like an old photograph,
1855 had faded from his memory. James's aesthetic relish of his meal in
the Adelphi Hotel combined personal nostalgia with a ritualistic sense of
initiation into England.]

There is a certain evening that I count as virtually a first
impression – the end of a wet, Black Sunday, twenty years ago,
about the first of March. There had been an earlier vision, but

it had turned to grey, like faded ink, and the occasion I speak
of was a fresh beginning [...] The sense of approach was already
almost intolerably strong at Liverpool, where, as I remember, the
perception of the English character of everything was as acute as
a surprise without a shock. It was expectation exquisitely gratified,
superabundantly confirmed. There was a kind of wonder, indeed,
that England should be as English as, for my entertainment, she
took the trouble to be; but the wonder would have been greater,
and all the pleasure absent, if the sensation had not been violent.
It seems to sit there again like a visiting presence of the old
coffee-room of the Adelphi Hotel the unextended (as it then was),
the unimproved, the unblushingly local Adelphi. Liverpool is not a
romantic city, but that smoky Saturday returns to me as a supreme
success, measured by its association with the kind of emotion in
the hope of which, for the most part, we betakes ourselves to far
countries.

It assumed this character at an early hour – or rather, indeed,
twenty-four hours before – with the sight, as one looked across
the wintry ocean, of the strange, dark, lonely freshness of the
coast of Ireland. Better still, before we could come up to the city,
were the black steamers knocking about in the yellow Mersey,
under a sky so low that they seemed to touch it with their
funnels, and in the thickest, windiest light. Spring was already
in the air, in the town; there was no rain, but there was still less
sun – one wondered what had become, on this side of the world,
of the big white splotch in the heavens; and the grey mildness,
shading away into black at every pretext, appeared in itself a
promise. This was how it hung about me, between the window
and the fire, in the coffee-room of the hotel – late in the morning
for breakfast, as we had been long disembarking. The other
passengers had dispersed, knowingly catching trains for London
(we had only been a handful); I had the place to myself, and I felt
as if I had an exclusive property in the impression. I prolonged
it, I sacrificed to it, and it is perfectly recoverable now, with the
very taste of the national muffin, the creak of the waiter's shoes as
he came and went (could anything be so English as his intensely
professional back? It revealed a country of tradition), and the rustle
of the newspaper I was too excited to read.

'London', *Century Magazine* (1888), collected in *English Hours* (1905)
and *Collected Travel Writings* (New York: Library of America, 1993).

James made a second attempt to recapture the excitement of landing in Liverpool in his third autobiographical volume *The Middle Years* (published one year after his death in 1917). Here he recalls the thrill of travelling to distant shores but also presents the experience as crucial to the development of his sensibility and to his perceptions of cultural connections. Once again, the national symbolism of his experience is paramount, but now as evidence of his hypersensitivity to appearances. James is now making such an obvious effort to compose his scene at the Adelphi that we begin to wonder what is truth and what is aesthetic licence. The specific details of what he saw and heard are filtered through his emphasis on the growing life of the mind, within which the episode takes on the importance of an initiation into the Old Country.

> The small hour was just that of my having landed at Liverpool
> in the gusty, cloudy, overwhelmingly English morning and
> pursued, with immediate intensities of appreciation, as I may
> call the muffled accompaniment for fear of almost indecently
> overnaming it, a course which had seated me at a late breakfast
> in the coffee-room of the old Adelphi Hotel ('Radley's', as I had
> to deplore its lately having ceased to be dubbed) and handed
> me over without a scruple to my fate. This doom of inordinate
> exposure to appearances, aspects, images, every protrusive item
> almost, in the great beheld sum of things, I regard in other
> words as having settled upon me once for all while I observed for
> instance that in England the plate of buttered muffin and its cover
> were sacredly set upon the slop-bowl after hot water had been
> ingenuously poured into the same, and had seen that circumstance
> in a perfect cloud of accompaniments. I must have had with my
> tea and my muffin a boiled egg or two and a dab of marmalade,
> but it was from a far other store of condiments I most liberally
> helped myself. I was lucidly aware of so gorging – esoterically, as
> it were, while I drew out the gustatory process; and I must have
> said in that lost reference to this scene of my dedication which I
> mentioned above that I was again and again in the aftertime to
> win back the homeliest notes of the impression, the damp and
> darksome light washed in from the steep, black, bricky street, the
> crackle of the strong draught of the British 'sea-coal' fire, much
> more confident of its function, I thought, than the fires I had left,
> the rustle of the thick, stiff, loudly unfolded and refolded *Times*,
> the incomparable truth to type of the waiter, truth to history,
> to literature, to poetry, to Dickens, to Thackeray, positively to
> Smollett and to Hogarth, to every connection that could help

me to appropriate him and his setting, an arrangement of things hanging together with a romantic rightness that had the force of a revelation.

Henry James, *The Middle Years* (1917).

The first impressions of **Mark Twain** (1835–1910) about Liverpool when he first visited the city in 1872 were more prosaic than Adams's or James's, and consisted of complaints that he could not find a sharp razor or shut out the noise of Lime Street from the Washington Hotel where he was staying. The following year he gave a 'lecture' on 'Our Fellow Savages of the Sandwich Islands' in Liverpool, the only one he delivered outside London. In the 1870s Twain planned a volume to be called *English Notes*, though this never materialized. On the eve of his return to America after his last visit to Britain, Twain was guest of honour at the Lord Mayor's Dinner in Liverpool on 10 July 1907 and in his speech paid tribute to English hospitality.

During my four weeks' sojourn in England I have had another lofty honour, a continuous honour, an honour which has flown serenely along, without halt or obstruction, though all these twenty-six days, a most moving and pulse-stirring honour – the heartfelt grip of the hand, and the welcome that does not descend from the pale-grey matter of the brain, but rushes up with the red blood from the heart.

3

Audubon and Catlin: Artists of the American Wilderness

J OHN JAMES AUDUBON (1785–1851), born in San Domingo (now Haiti) and resident in America from 1803, is remembered for his monumental volume of life-size prints, *Birds of America*. Rejecting orthodox education, he spent much of his time observing and then drawing the creatures of the American wild, combining the roles of hunter, naturalist and artist. When he sailed for England from New Orleans in 1826 he was taking a major step on the road to publishing his paintings and drawings. By then he had acquired the nickname 'American Woodsman' due to his long hair and buckskin clothes. Armed with letters of introduction, Audubon quickly befriended the Rathbones and the Roscoes, two leading Liverpool families, who helped him gain recognition for his artwork. He recorded his impressions in a journal addressed to his wife Lucy, which sheds unique light on Liverpool society of the 1820s.

[21 July 1826] When I landed it was raining. Yet the outward appearance of the city was agreeable. But no sooner had I entered it than the smoke from coal fires was so oppressive on my lungs that I could scarcely breathe. I felt the same affecting my eyes also. All was nearly new to me.

After a breakfast taken at an inn for two shillings sixpence, Mr. Swift accompanied me to the Exchange Building, to the counting-house of Gordon & Forstall. I was anxious to deliver the letters that I had for Mr. Gordon from Mr. Briggs. After a few moments Mr. Gordon made his appearance but did not recollect my countenance (although I am sure it has always been of the odd order) until I opened my lips to pronounce my name [...]

We took lodgings and board at the Commercial Inn not far from the Exchange Buildings. We were well fed and well attended, although, to my surprise altogether, so far by females, neatly dressed and tolerably modest.

[24 July 1826] I bustled about briskly, locking my trunk, took my cane, my hat, my gloves – all in a hurry – ran downstairs, swallowed my breakfast without mastication, and made as directly as a I could through the sinuous streets of Liverpool to No. 87 Duke Street, where the polite English gentleman Richard Rathbone resides. My locks flew freely from under my hat, and every *lady* that I met looked at them and then at me until – she could see no more.

The kind gentleman was not in. I almost ran to his counting-house at the salt dock, down Duke Street, &c., &c., &c. A full dozen clerks were at their separate desks. The ledgers, day books, &c., were all under full sail – royals, royals extra, [studding] sails, &c. An immense letter bag belonging to the packet that sailed this day for the shores where I hope thou art happy, Dearest Friend, was near the entrance. My name was taken to the special room of Mr. Rathbone, and in a moment I was met by one who acted towards me *as a brother ought to do!* How truly kind and really polite. *He* did not give *his card* to poor Audubon. He gave me the most polite invitation to call at *his house* at 2 [P.M.] that I ever received since I left America.

[25 July 1826] I waited fully dressed nearly fifteen minutes before the sweet lark, my *reveille matin*, had turned his head from [his] soft pillow towards the orb of Apollo. I waited anxiously. I felt gay and – no, not happy. But the sweet tingling melody of the lark helped my spirits much. Mr. Swift rose and dressed in a moment, and my black chalk once more touched the paper to animate it. Ah yes, I have drawn in England! Ah, how much more I have drawn in my America! I finished early, so much so, indeed, that when 7 struck my ear from the clock, we were on the pavement bound towards the West, to near thee a step.

Naked streets look dull. We soon returned and eat [sic] a bountiful repast. I issued forth again. My dear Lucy, I bought a beautiful watch for thee from Mr. Roskell & Son, Church Street, and one also for me from the same polite gentleman. Ten of the morning was positively past, and I felt much ashamed when, after reaching Dale Street, where our lodgings are, [I found] a note from Mr. Rathbone, for it had been there some time, waiting for me. I dreaded that this should be.

A hackney coach was produced in a moment, I entered it with my Portfolio Number Two, and ordered Dale Street quickly. The Rathbones were gone to Mr. Rathbone's mother. I inquired the way, but before my sentence was finished I saw their carriage turning back, making for me. And I had once more the pleasure of being near these kind persons. Their youngest sweet little son Basil looked at me, and I wished him well. Mr. James Pyke was introduced to me. We proceeded slowly and I thought of my situation in England, in the carriage of a man generous and noble of heart. [I myself was] dressed, although perhaps queerly to them, in clothing very different from the Indian garb which, with gun cocked, I dashed through the deep swamps of lower Louisiana after the Wood Ibises in the company of my good friend [Augustin] Bourgeat.

[...]

What sensations I had whilst I helped to untie the fastening of my [Birds] Folio Book! I knew, by all around me, that all was full of best taste and strong judgement, but I did not know if I would at all please. A small book was opened. I was panting like the winged pheasant that dreads the well taught friend of man that may perhaps prove him too weak to proceed in full sight of his learned eye.

Ah Lucy, these *friends* praised my Birds, and I felt the praise, yes breathed as if some celestial being succoured me in Elysium. Praises are of many kinds, but kindly praises are true, and these good friends praised me kindly!!!

[26 July 1826] It is half past 6. The coach is at 87 Duke Street. The coachman has rung the bell and my heart fails me. Now this is, very simply, very foolish. As yes, it is all this and more; it is a most painful action on my faculties.

I am in the corridor, my hat is taken civilly from my hand, and my name humbly requested. I am pointed the way above and – bear me on my legs – I am in the sitting-room of Mr. Rathbone. It was time I met his eye, his lively mien! What a relief it gave me[!]

[...] Mr. Roscoe came in, tall, with a good eye under a good eyebrow, all mildness. He shook hands with me [...] Dinner is announced. Mr. Rathbone locks his tutor in arm. Mr. Roscoe locks thy husband in arm. I saw not the remainder of this friendly procession.

[The dinner guests included James Maury, the American Consul. After dinner Roscoe examined Audubon's drawings and then invited him to visit his home in Lodge Lane the following day, which Audubon did. On

28 July Audubon again had dinner at the Rathbones. The following day he visited St John's Market, which had opened in 1822 and which was the subject of a painting by Samuel Austin. The building between Great Charlotte Street and Market Street had five avenues of shops and offices, and was lit by some 144 gas burners.]

[29 July 1826] I have not found the population of Liverpool as dense as I expected, and, except during the evenings (that do not commence before 8 at this season), I have not been at all annoyed by the elbowings of the greater numbers that I still remember having seen in my youth in the largest cities of France. Some shops here are beautifully supplied. They are generally lined with two sets of purchasers, mostly ladies, seated and choosing the articles wanted. I counted in one of these shops sixteen gentleman attendants behind the counters.

The new market is, in my opinion, an object worth the attention of all traveller strangers. It is thus far the finest I have ever seen. It is a large, high and long building divided into five spacious avenues, each containing their specific commodities. I saw here viands of all description – fish, vegetables, game, fruits both indigenous and imported from all quarters of the world, bird sellers with even little collections of stuffed specimens, cheese of enormous sizes, butter in full abundance – superior freshness and quality – along with immense crates of hen's eggs laying upon and between layers of oats-straw, imported from Ireland – twenty-five for one shilling. This market is so well lighted with gas that at 10 o'clock this evening I could plainly see the colours of the [irises] of living pigeons in cages.

The whole city is lighted with gas. Each shop has one of these brilliantly illuminating fires in each window and many about the room. Fine cambrics can be looked at by good judges.

[30 July 1826] I went to the Church of the Asylum of the Blind. I have just returned and I write because it is a pleasant Sunday altogether with me.

Follow Dale Street, northeast, all its length, keep inclining to the right until you come opposite the Islington Market and continue where you see the asylum itself. The church is there near you. Ascend a few steps of cut stones after passing the iron-barred gates, walk under the colonnade, pay whatever you pledge *over* a sixpence to either of the collectors at the inner door, and if you are *a man* pull off your hat. Then look at the large picture

of Christ freeing the blind. It is a copy of the great original,
'Charity'. Follow an assistant down the middle aisle. He opens
a pew and you sit on a clean, well-stuffed serge cushion, under
which [you] place your 'cover-head', and look around before
the service begins. The general structure is a well proportioned,
oblong square. A niche contains the picture of Christ. Ten light
columns support the flat ceiling imitation of marble. A fine organ
with brass barrels is placed over the entrance in a kind of upper
lobby that also contains the blind musicians. The windows are
large; the glass of each pane is ground rough [so as] not to distract
the mind by admitting [sight] of outward objects. Congregational
attendants gradually fill the whole. All is silent, yes silent.

The mind is filled with heavenly subjects and thoughts (I mean,
of course, the mind of non-sinners). The two pulpits garnished
with purple velvet seem to be all that is lukewarm here. Hark!!!!
Angelically the sound [in] imitation of music sublime and heavenly
glides into your whole composition, until, by the exertions of
accord, a general chorus is produced, imbibing an idea of the
sounds of the trumpets of Resurrection. My frame shakes; not with
fear, no, but with a wish that I might feel the sensation oftener.

The rites proceed, and divine female voices open an anthem
entrusted by the Creator to Hayden!! Oh celestial voices!!! No, it
is impossible for me to describe them. A good, excellent service
is mixed with this to entice the mind and imagination to refrain
from evil doings. Prayers are read and musically echoed by the
blind, and each person gently rises, walks out lightly, and not
until entirely out of the colonnade do you hear the sound of a
single voice.

I give it here, as my opinion or my best recollection, that I
never before this day saw *such devotion in a Church* [...] During this
morning I saw long files of youths of both sexes, marching the
streets on their return from devotion. Nothing except the tread of
the feet on the pavement could be heard.

[Audubon arranges for an exhibition of 235 of his drawings to be held at the
Royal Institution. The latter was opened in 1817 and one of its purposes,
according to the 1814 Plan, was to build up 'collections of books, specimens
of arts, natural history, etc.']

[31 July 1826] At 9 this morning I was quite busy, arranging
and disposing in sets my drawings to be fairly inspected by the
public, the connoisseurs, the critics. This last word has something

very savage in its nature, as well as in its orthography or its pronunciation. I know not why. Yet I know that I dread this very casting askance of a single eye of those dangerous personages of whom I have so much heard, but whom, fortunately, thus far, I have only met in scanty form, and of little value.

I drew my new watch and in five minutes, by its regular movements, it proved to be at the meridian. The doors of the Royal Institution were thrown open and the ladies flocked in; I, however, saw but one: Mrs. Rathbone. Then I was in view of the world. How many glances to meet – questions to answer and repeat! '*La, that's beautiful*', again and again repeated, made me wish to be in the forests of America, to be able myself to say at meeting a new specimen, '*Ah, how beautiful!!*' The time passed, however [the exhibition closed at 2.00 p.m.]

[1 August 1826] I immediately went to the Institution. [By] 12 the assemblage was great. I saw Dr. Traill [Thomas Stewart Traill, physician, naturalist, and Royal Institution officer] and many other persons of distinction. Several persons who, I believe, are attached to that Institution, wished that I should be remunerated by exhibiting for money and [also that] an offer of the room [be] proposed to me *gratis*. But my heart revolted at the thought, and although I am poor enough, God knows, I could not think of doing such a thing consistently, with the station I wish to preserve, one forwarded, I may say, from America, by letters of our most eminent men, to eminent and kind persons in this country, who have all received and honoured me highly by personal attentions. I could not, I repeat, think it consistent to become a mere *show man* and give up the title of *J. J. Audubon, Naturalist*.

[4 August 1826. Attendance continued to be buoyant at Audubon's exhibition. In the evening he visited the Rathbones' family home at Green Bank.]

I was conducted by the young son [Edward Roscoe] again, and was soon put on the road. We parted. The evening was calm and pleasant. As I advanced into the country, groups of persons, exercising leisurely, met me. Some turned their heads to remark *that 'original'*, me. However, I passed again under the avenue of trees leading to 'Green Bank' and gently knocked at one of the inner doors, my hat and cane in one hand. Between the raps I

gave I passed my handkerchief over my face to take away the
moisture occasioned by a brisk walk. I could easily hear the
mirth of many whom I supposed were on the green, fronting the
buildings. I rapped with stronger blows and the Mother Rathbone
met me with, 'Oh, I am glad to see you'.

I was not mistaken. The green was covered with beauty, good
sense, and pleasure. I was attracted mostly, however, by the sight
of ladies with bows and arrows, shooting at a target perhaps
twenty-five paces off.

Presently it grew darker. I was seated between the two
brothers Rathbone, sorry that my little friend Basil had retired
to repose. I would have liked to kiss him very much. The father
of Mrs. Rathbone asked many questions respecting the religious
inclinations and rites of Indians. We spoke a good deal about
American trees, things quite unknown here where there are none
larger than common Louisiana saplings.

[7 August 1826. During the exhibition.] My drawings have been
exhibited at the Royal Institution here, and 413 persons rushed
in, [in] two hours. My fame reached distant places so quickly that
[on] the third day persons of wealth arrived from Manchester to
view them. I have been presented to one of the noblest and oldest
peers of England, *Lord Stanley*. He, Lucy, knelt down on the rich
carpet to examine my style closely. This renowned scientific man
received me as if [he were] a school mate, shook hands with me
with the warmth of friendship, and wished me kindly to visit
him often in Grosvenor Street, London. I dined with him and he
spent five hours looking at my drawings, and said, 'Mr. Audubon,
I assure you this work of yours is unique, and deserves the
patronage of the Crown' [...] My style of drawing is so admired
here that many ladies of distinction have begged lessons of me. I
could get one guinea for an hour's attendance, [and] drive to and
fro in the employers' carriages. My drawing of the Dove is worth
25 guineas, as well as a dozen of eggs or, with you, sixpence.

[6 August 1826. By 5 August Audubon's exhibition had closed.]
When I arrived in this city I felt dejected, yes miserably so.
The uncertainty of being kindly received, of having my work
approved, were all acting on both my physical and mental powers.
I felt as if nutritive food within my sight was not to be touched.
Now how different my sensations! I am well received wherever
I am known. Every object known to me smiles as I meet it, and

my poor heart is at least relieved the great anxiety that has for
so many years agitated it, by [the feeling that] I have not worked
altogether in vain: that I may no longer be positively ashamed of
my pencil.

[The same day Audubon attended church and then went to visit
the Roscoes.] A great deal was said about Lord Stanley [another
naturalist and artist], his bird [drawings], and my Birds. I was
asked to imitate the Wild Turkey call, and I did, to the surprise
of all the circle. Hooted like a Barred Owl, and cooed like the
doves […] Lucy, remark my position. I sat, rather reclining, my
legs extended before me at the upper end of the room between
Mr. William Roscoe and his son Edward, facing the whole of
the amiable circle before me, and having to answer question after
question, as fast as I dare answer. Mrs. Edward Roscoe has rose
from her seat twenty times, to come and ask me questions about
my style of drawing.

[William Roscoe advises him not to exhibit without
remuneration.] A beautiful young lady, called here a *miss*, is at
my side, and asks with the volubility of youth and enthusiasm
many, many questions about America. But they all appear very
much surprised that I have no wonderful tale to relate; that, for
instance, *I*, so much in the woods, have not been devoured at
least six times by tigers, bears, wolves, foxes, or – a rat. No, I
never was troubled in the woods by any animals larger than ticks
and mosquitoes; and that is enough, is it not, Dearest Lucy?

[He adds comments on British manners.] The gentlemen are
– no, it is impossible to be more truly polite than they are. A
gentleman at church this morning who knew me for a stranger,
handed me book after book, the book that contained the hymns
then [being] sung. With the page open and with a gentle bow,
he pointed to the verse with a finger that was covered with a
beautiful white glove. Have I not reason to like England thus
far? Indeed I have.

[10 August 1826. After a rain spell.] The morning was beautiful,
clear, pleasant. I was on the mound betimes, and saw the city
plainly and the country beyond the Mersey quite plain also. When
first I left the Inn the watchmen watched me, and perhaps thought
that I was an owl caught out by the day, as I moved not like a
meteor but like a man either in a hurry, or a flurry, or crazy. The
fact is that I thought of nothing but the exhibition. Nothing else
could have entered my brains.

The wind mills are very different here from the few I have seen in America, and so are the watchmen. Both, I think, are taller and fuller about the waist. I do not like four square angles breaking on the foreground of a landscape, and yet I was forced twice today to submit to that mortification. But to counterpoise this, I had the satisfaction of sitting on the grass, to watch four truant boys rolling marbles with great spirit for a good full half hour. How they laughed, how briskly they moved, how much they brought from afar again my younger days. I would have liked them better still, at this innocent avocation, had they been decently clean, but they were not so, and I arose after giving them enough to purchase a shilling's worth of marbles.

[14 August 1826] Is it not very shocking that whilst, in England, all is hospitality within, all is aristocratic without, no one dares *trespass*, as it is called, one foot on the grass. *Signs of large dogs* are put up to [warn] that further you must not advance. Steel traps and spring guns are set to destroy you, should you prove foolhardy. And to finish our exercise we were forced to walk [single] file on the narrow portion of a wall, fearing the rebuke of the landlord around whose grounds we had a desire to ramble.

[17 August 1826. Encounter with a tobacco smuggler.] Let us return to the Mersey and look on the country in Wales, on the calm, serene sky, and listen to the voice of the Quail here so shy. Ah yes, walk with me on the tide-beaten beach, and watch the Solan Goose in search of a retreat from the cruel destroyer, Man.

Seest thou the smuggler, how he runs away? How little he suspects that Goldsmith's Burchell [a character in *The Vicar of Wakefield*] was after him! Yet I must acknowledge he made me pant before I reached him. I have regretted, all day, my adventure of this morning, and I am sorry to think now how cruel it was in me to frighten the poor fellow so. Lucy, I had my sword-cane, and the moment the stranger dropped his bag and ran from me, that moment I drew the dangerous blade and, crying unmercifully, '*Stop thief!*', made my way towards him in a style that I am sure he never had seen used by the gentlemen of the Customs that no doubt were rather drowsy. Poor fellow, had he known me as I know thee and as I am known to thee, his eyes would not have started from his head as they did, nor his heart have swelled with apprehension. There he was begging for mercy – said it was the first time, and only some rotten leaves of tobacco. I positively did wish he had had all that I once purchased for Richard Atkinson of Richmond. The boat that had landed him quite in my view fled by rowing off like cowards instead of landing and defending their companion who was no longer visible to the smugglers on board.

I was astonished at such conduct from Englishmen. I told this poor being to arise and bring the bag. He did so. No Lucy, much is said here about the abject state of slavery in our truly United States, but I never beheld there a thing shaped like a man so completely subdued by fear of punishment. He walked to the bag and brought it. I told him that a smuggler was an enemy to his country, and that he deserved severe punishment. (Recollect my sword was already to defend me.) He cried and said, 'Oh, for God's sake save me – take the tobacco'. Poor fellow, I never even smoked a single cigar, and that thou knowest well. I could stand this no longer. I was [in dread lest] some real officer of the Customs might appear and interfere in a very different manner. I told him to clean himself and to be careful he should never do such an outrage again. I had one of my pockets disagreeably laden with copper stuff that the shopkeepers give here and call pennies. I gave them all to him, told him to look at my face well, and go. He did look, Lucy, with eyes that I cannot describe or understand. He prayed aloud for my salvation and made for a thick hedge, where he disappeared from my view.

I looked on the river. The boat was out of my sight. I would say that this poor fellow had perhaps fifty or sixty pounds of fine Virginia clear-leaf tobacco in the bag and two pistols which he said were not loaded. Of this I am not quite sure. But cannons in the hands of he who fears either the laws of his country whilst acting against them, fears not God but fears men!

[20 August 1826. Early morning by the Mersey.] I was at the Mersey before sunrise, when Nature was as calm as if yet asleep. So calm was all about Nature herself the noise of the paddles of a steamboat running down the River Dee, then eight miles distant, could be heard distinctly. 'I know by the smoke that so gracefully curled' [ballad by Thomas Moore] that a steamboat was the cause producing the sound. This morning I was quite surprised to see persons out so early. I saw two men hunting with a dog, without guns. The dog was a shabby looking setter, but moved well. I thought the men [drew back] as I approached them, but they stood still and saw me go by. Another man was catching linnets with bird lime. Others were searching for clams and other

shell-fish along the shores. I also examined some large baskets
with mouths upstream to catch fish as the river flows to the sea.

[Audubon moved to the Rathbones' at Green Bank and began an oil
painting of the 'Wild Turkey Cock', which was presented to the Royal
Institution in gratitude for their 'many kind attentions' to him, and also
worked on a number of drawings. An oil painting of an 'Otter caught
in a Trap' was given to Mrs Rathbone. Early in September Audubon left
Liverpool for Manchester. On the road from Liverpool to Prescott he saw
the following. 10 September 1826.]

My astonishment was great and I was aroused from my sullenness
at the sight of a lad perhaps twelve years of age [who] ran swiftly
along the side of the coach and suddenly tumbled five or six times
repeatedly, heels over head, exhibiting this feat to procure a few
half pence. I amply rewarded him, and I was glad that my coppers
made their way from the passenger's pockets onto the top of the
ground, where they were picked up with alertness by the little
mendicant. Mr. Munro assured me that these boys are frequently
[seen], and that a letter thrown out of the coach with a few pence
is taken by them and conveyed to its directed office or house with
great security.

[Audubon mounted an exhibition in the Academy of Natural Sciences in
Manchester. By the end of September he had returned to Liverpool. While
there, he met the London bookseller H.G. Bohn, who advised Audubon
to issue a prospectus on his planned book and also to bear in mind its
size. Mrs Rathbone asked him to sketch the wild turkey for her, which
he proceeded to do.]

[3 October 1826. Visit to the Borough Jail in Great Howard Street, which
had been built in 1786. The treadmill discussed below was invented by the
engineer Sir William Cubitt and was introduced to Liverpool Prison in
1818. It resembled a paddle wheel, which inmates had to 'climb', initially
without any separators between them.]

I have been to the jail of Liverpool to-day, my Lucy, and will try
to give thee some partial description, both of its building and [the]
manners within. The situation is fine, placed at or near the mouth
of the estuary that here is called the River Mersey. From its walls
an extensive view of the Irish Channel may be had, drawing the
eye to the country and mountains of Wales. The area altogether

occupied by the institution consists of about eight acres, and the arrangements within the walls are – but permit me, I think a slight sketch will describe faster and better than my poor pen. [A pen-and-ink plan follows.]

Beside these marks, my Lucy, imagine the cells for sleeping, one to each individual female, but sometimes one to two or three males. *I did no ask why so.* There are large apartments for cooking, washing, &c., council rooms, store rooms, &c., &c. I end this with: the institution, as far as [its being] comfortable if [one is] at rest [is concerned], is fine. I will try, at least, to enter its meritorious intentions, [while confessing that] I consider the tread mill infamous. Conceive of a wild squirrel within a round wheel, moving himself without progress. The labour is too severe, and the true motive of correction destroyed, as there are no mental resources attached to this laborious engine of shame only, if viewed by strangers. Why should each individual not be taught different trades enabling them, when thrown again on the vile world, to support themselves more honestly, and save them from the temptations that, through necessity, they must ultimately resort to (knowing naught but walking up hill), and be dragged again and again to the tread mill's transportation or to despair? Trades would be more profitable to the institution, four-fold, than the mere grinding [of] flour that is done here, and the principle would be more honourable and more worthy [of] the true intentions of such a [place]. Thus I do condemn the tread mills not only as machines of labour without benefit either general or personal, but also as extremely prejudicial to health. Think of those poor miserable beings, obliged either to weigh heavily on one paddle or raise their own weight to the next, which is the same labour as walking up a steep hill constantly for four or six hours, or averaging five, whilst the man [doing this] might [instead] make a good pair of shoes, cut nails, be a hatter or watchmaker, or [work at] any other useful business.

The wheel is only six feet in diameter. Therefore the motion is accelerated, and each step must be performed in quick succession. And as I know that a quick, short step is more fatiguing than a long one and soon destroys the ultimate power of the general frame, I say it is conducive to destruction. The sallow, withered, emaciated, thin visages and bodies of the men at work proved this to my eyes as well as to my powers of calculation. The wheel forces thirty steps to a rotation, and, as I say, these are steps going up hill more than equal in length and labour to those on level ground. I will calculate them at two and a half feet for each, and as the wheel goes round once per minute I will call the single movement seventy-five feet, the hour, 4500, the labour 22500. This repeated twice a day gives 45000.

Lucy, the circulation of free air is wanted. Each man receives the breath of his neighbour in exchange for his [own], and, as this is accompanied by the most debased conversations, both the body and the mind suffer. I would write more, but I am not William Roscoe. Therefore I close the subject. I was sorry to find the female deportment [is] more difficult to manage than that of the men. And to give thee an idea of the force of habits kept in this place, suffice it so say that through the want of tobacco the *ladies* there smoke their *petticoats*. Yes, when I entered the rooms the smoke was [thick] and most disagreeably so. Each female hid the cause in her bosom. Lucy, did nature intend the female bosom [to be] the receptacle of a filthy pipe?

Alice Ford, ed., *The 1826 Journal of John James Audubon*
(Norman, OK: University of Oklahoma Press, 1967).

Leaving Liverpool once again, Audubon travelled back to Manchester and then on to Edinburgh, where he met the engraver William H. Lizars, who would undertake to reproduce his paintings. This was the crucial breakthrough for ensuring the composition of *Birds of America*, which was being set up during the 1830s. While this was happening Audubon made a number of return visits to Liverpool, retaining the friendships he had made there.

Where Audubon played to his image as a backwoodsman by wearing hunting clothes, **George Catlin** (1796–1872) was a more thoroughgoing showman in mounting his exhibitions of Native American life. In the 1830s he lived for a number of years with the indigenous tribes of the West and, like Audubon, capitalized on that interest by painting scenes of Indian life. In the autumn of 1839 Catlin brought his exhibition to England, though 'exhibition' describes only part of his activities. In addition to displaying his paintings and Native American artefacts, tribesmen in native dress would perform tableaux vivants and Catlin even brought with him two grizzly bears from the Rocky Mountains, to the consternation of his fellow passengers on the packet boat *Roscius* and the Liverpool customs officers.

His memoir of his European tour describes his arrival at Liverpool as follows:

On nearing the docks at Liverpool, not only all the passengers of the ship, but all the inhabitants of the hills and dales about, and the shores, were apprised of our approach to the harbour by the bellowing and howling of the grizzlies, who were undoubtedly excited to this sort of Te Deum for their safe deliverance and approach to terra firma, which they had got a sight (and probably a smell) of.

The arrival of the *Roscius* on that occasion was of course a conspicuous one, and well announced; and we entered the dock amidst an unusual uproar and crowd of spectators. After the usual manner, the passengers were soon ashore, and our luggage examined, leaving freight and grizzly bears on board, to be removed the next morning. From the moment of landing on the wharf to the Custom-house, and from that to the hotel where I took lodgings, I was obliged to ' fend off,' almost with foot and with fist, the ragamuffins who beset me on every side; and in front, in the rear, and on the right and the left, assailed me with importunities to be allowed to carry my luggage. In the medley of voices and confusion I could scarcely tell myself to which of these poor fellows I had committed my boxes; and no doubt this (to them) delightful confusion and uncertainty encouraged a number of them to keep close company with my luggage until it arrived at the Grecian Hotel. When it was all safely landed in the hall, I asked the lad who stood fore most and had brought my luggage in his cart, how much was to pay for bringing it up? 'Ho, Sir, hi leaves it to your generosity, Sir, has you are a gentleman, Sir; hit's been a werry eavy load, Sir.'

I was somewhat amused with the simple fellow's careless and easy manner, and handed him eighteen pence, thinking it a reasonable compensation for bringing two small trunks and a carpet-bag; but he instantly assumed a different aspect, and refused to take the money, saying that no gentleman would think of giving him less than half-a-crown for such a load as he had brought. I soon settled with and dismissed him by giving him two shillings; and as he departed, and I was about entering the coffee-room, another of his ragged fraternity touched my elbow, when I asked him what he wanted. 'Wo, Sir, your luggage there.' 'But I have paid for my luggage I paid the man you see going out there.' 'Yes, Sir; but then you sees, hi elped im put it hon;

hand I elped im along with it, hand it's werry ard, Sir, hif Ise
not to be paid has well as im.' I paid the poor fellow a sixpence
for his ingenuity; and as he left, a third one stepped up, of whom
I inquired, 'What do you want ?' 'Why, Sir, your luggage, you
know, there I am very sorry, Sir, to see you pay that worthless
rascal what's just going out there I am indeed sorry, Sir he did
nothing, but was hoi the time hin our way hit urts me, Sir, to see
a gentleman throw is money away upon sich vagabonds, for it's
hundoubtedly ard earned, like the few shillings we poor fellows
get.' 'Well, my good fellow, what do you want of me?' 'Ho, Sir,
hit's honly for the cart, Sir you will settle with me for the cart,
Sir, hif you please that first chap you paid ad my cart, hand I'll be
bound you ave paid im twice has much has you bought.' 'Well,
to make short', said I, 'here, take this sixpence for your cart, and
be off.' I was thus brief, for I saw two or three others edging and
siding up in the passage towards me, whom I recollected to have
seen escorting my luggage, and I retreated into the coffee-room
as suddenly as possible, and stated the case to one of the waiters,
who promised to manage the rest of the affair.

I was thus very comfortable for the night, having no further
annoyance or real excitement until the next morning after
breakfast, when it became necessary to disembark the grizzly
bears. My other heavy freight had gone to Her Majesty's
Custom-house, and all the passengers from the cabin and
steerage had gone to comfortable quarters, leaving the two
deck passengers, the grizzlies, in great impatience, and as yet
undisposed of. My man Daniel had been on the move at an early
hour, and had fortunately made an arrangement with a simple
and unsuspecting old lady in the absence of her 'good man,' to
allow the cage to be placed in a small yard adjoining her house,
and within the same inclosure, which had a substantial pavement
of round stones.

This arrangement for a few days promised to be an
advantageous one for each party. Daniel was to have free access
and egress for the purpose of giving them their food, and the
price proposed to the good woman was met as a liberal reward for
the reception of any living beings that she could imagine, however
large, that could come within her idea of the dimensions of a
cage. Daniel had told her that they were two huge bears; and in
his reply to inquiries, assured her that they were not harmless by
any means, but that the enormous strength of their cage prevented
them from doing any mischief.

The kind old lady agreed, for so much per day, to allow the cage to stand in her yard, by the side of her house, at least until her husband returned. With much excitement and some growling about the docks and the wharf, they were swung off from the vessel, and, being placed on a 'float,' were conveyed to, and quietly lodged and fed in, the retired yard of the good woman, when the gate was shut, and they fell into a long and profound sleep.

The grizzly bears being thus comfortably and safely quartered in the immediate charge of my man Daniel, who had taken an apartment near them, and my collection being lodged in the Custom-house, I started by the railway for London to effect the necessary arrangements for their next move. I had rested in and left Liverpool in the midst of rain, and fog, and mud, and seen little else of it.

[Catlin moved his exhibition to London and then was invited to return to Liverpool.]

Several months after this passed on in the usual routine of my business and amusements (my collection open during the days and my lectures and tableaux given at night) without incidents worth reciting, when I received an invitation from the Mechanics' Institute at Liverpool to unite my Indian collection to their biennial fair or exhibition, which was to be on a scale of great magnificence. They very liberally proposed to extend the dimensions of their buildings for the occasion, and I consented to join them with my whole collection for two months. My lease had expired at the Egyptian Hall [in Piccadilly, London], and my collection was soon on its way to Liverpool.

I was received with great kindness in that town, and my collection for the two months gained me great applause and some pecuniary benefit. During its stay there I kept several men in Indian costumes constantly in it, and twice a day gave a short lecture in the room, explaining the costumes and many of the leading traits of the Indian character, sung an Indian song, and gave the frightful war-whoop.

There were here, as in London, many pleasing incidents and events for which I cannot venture a leaf in this book, with the exception of one, which I cannot forbear to mention. During the last week of their noble exhibition, the children from all the charitable and other schools were admitted free, and in battalions

and phalanxes they were passed through my room, as many
hundreds at a time as could stand upon the floor, to hear the
lectures (shaped to suit their infant minds), and then the deafening
war-whoop raised by my men in Indian paint and Indian arms,
which drove many of the little creatures with alarm under the
tables and benches, from which they were pulled out by their feet;
and the list that we kept showed us the number of 22,000 of these
little urchins, who, free of expense, saw my collection, and having
heard me lecture, went home, sounding the war-whoop in various
parts of the town. [Vol. 1]

[Catlin moved on to London to begin a tour of England. He subsequently
returned to Liverpool with fourteen Iowa Indians. The group arrived in
the capital at night (so as not to alarm the Londoners) and one of the
tribesmen explained his alarm at travelling through the Liverpool railway
tunnel.]

'My Friends, We have come on your great medicine road, and it
pleased us very much. When we landed from our ship, we came
on your medicine road, and were told it would be very fine; but
when we started, we were all very much alarmed; we went in
the dark; we all went right down into the ground, under a high
mountain; we had heard that a part of the white people go into
the ground when they die, and some of them into the fire; we
saw some fire; there was a great hissing, and a great deal of smoke
coming out of this place [the tunnel out of Lime Street station],
and we could not get out; we were then somewhat afraid, my
friends and I began to sing our death-song; but when we had
commenced, our hearts were full of joy, we came out again in the
open air, and the country was very beautiful around us.' (How,
how, how! and great applause.)

[Catlin mounted exhibitions in the Dublin Rotunda. The troop then sailed
to Liverpool, where one member, No-hu-mun-ya aka Roman Nose, was
taken ill. He stayed behind while the others toured and he later died in
Liverpool.]

Our voyage across the Channel was easy and pleasant; and
amongst the numerous and fashionable people on board, poor
Jim had the mortification of trying to test the intrinsic value of
his numerous stock of Bibles by occasionally offering one that
he carried in his pouch. 'I no sell em they no like em,' was his

reply again; and he began to doubt the value of them, which he was greatly disappointed to find they had fixed much above their market-price.

On landing at the wharf in Liverpool the Indians recognised the spot where they first set their feet upon English soil, and they raised the yell (not unlike the war-whoop) which is given by war-parties when, returning from battle, they are able to see their own village. This gathered a great crowd in a few moments, that was exceedingly difficult to disperse, and it instilled new ambition and strength into the poor Roman Nose, who thought in his weakness that they were near home; but he rallied only to look out and realize that he was too far from his home ever to see it again.

Lodgings had been prepared for them, to which they immediately repaired; and, as their sinking companion was so rapidly declining, they were all in sadness, though they tried, poor fellows, to be gay and cheerful. Their exhibitions had been advertised to commence, and they proceeded with them. Before they commenced, however, a feast was made to thank the Great Spirit for having conducted them quite around England to the place from whence they started, and also for the benefit of the health of their fellow-warrior, the Roman Nose.

A council was also held, when Mr. Melody and I were called in, and by some it was proposed to start for home, and by others to go to Paris and see a King, as they had tried, but in vain, to see the Queen of England. A visit to Paris had been a favourite theme with them for some months past, and all at length joined in the wish to see the King and Queen of France. The most skilful physicians were called to attend the poor Roman Nose, and they advised us to place him in an hospital. He was consulted, and, wishing to go, was removed there, where the interpreter, Jeffrey, stayed, and every attention was paid him. A few nights of exhibitions in Liverpool finished our stay in that town and brought us to an engagement we had made, for four nights, in the Free Trade Hall in Manchester. [Vol. 2]

George Catlin, *Notes of Eight Years' Travels and Residence in Europe: With his North American Indian Collection* (1848).

4

Herman Melville: *Redburn*

THE NOVELIST **Herman Melville** (1819–91) sailed to Liverpool on the *S. Lawrence*, arriving in July 1839 and returning by the same boat the following September. Disturbed by his failure to achieve success with his fiction, on 5 June 1849 he wrote to his English publisher that he was composing a 'plain, straightforward, amusing narrative of personal experience – the son of a gentleman on his first voyage to sea as a sailor.' This planning bore fruit in his 1849 novel *Redburn, His First Voyage*. When the novel was published, the reviewers praised Melville's descriptive detail, especially in the Liverpool sections. Indeed, the reviewer for the London *Literary Gazette* remarked: 'The inhabitants of Liverpool will, we imagine, be surprised at some of the minute local revelations of an American visitor.' The fact remains that *Redburn* gives the most detailed account of Liverpool dockland life in nineteenth-century fiction. Melville was clearly capitalizing on the vogue for travel writing around the mid-century, because many of the descriptions have only an indirect relation to the plot of the novel. Redburn's boat remains in the dock for several weeks and Melville uses this as a pretext for describing the sights of the city. The very fact that he can do this suggests that he assumed there was an interested readership, especially in America, for these descriptions. He dedicated the novel to his elder brother Thomas, a sailor by profession, unlike Redburn (and presumably the young Herman), who is strictly an amateur.

[As the *Highlander* approaches Liverpool, Redburn's first impressions of the city are that it is less glamorous and more familiar than he expected: 'I beheld lofty ranges of dingy ware-houses, which seemed very deficient in the elements of the marvellous; and bore a most unexpected resemblance to the ware-houses along South Street in New York.' (Chapter 27). The boat moors in the Prince's Dock, opened in 1822, the largest of the docks. Once ashore, Redburn continues to try to reconcile the sights of Liverpool with his preconceptions of England.]

[Chapter 28: Prince's Dock and a sailor's boarding house.]

In the afternoon our pilot was all alive with his orders; we hove up the anchor, and after a deal of pulling, and hauling, and jamming against other ships, we wedged our way through a lock at high tide; and about dark, succeeded in working up to a berth in *Prince's Dock*. The hawsers and tow-lines being then coiled away, the crew were told to go ashore, select their boarding-house, and sit down to supper.

Here it must be mentioned, that owing to the strict but necessary regulations of the Liverpool docks, no fires of any kind are allowed on board the vessels within them; and hence, though the sailors are supposed to sleep in the forecastle, yet they must get their meals ashore, or live upon cold potatoes. To a ship, the American merchantmen adopt the former plan; the owners, of course, paying the landlord's bill; which, in a large crew remaining at Liverpool more than six weeks, as we of the *Highlander* did, forms no inconsiderable item in the expenses of the voyage. Other ships, however—the economical Dutch and Danish, for instance, and sometimes the prudent Scotch—feed their luckless tars in dock, with precisely the same fare which they give them at sea; taking their salt junk ashore to be cooked, which, indeed, is but scurvy sort of treatment, since it is very apt to induce the scurvy. A parsimonious proceeding like this is regarded with immeasurable disdain by the crews of the New York vessels, who, if their captains treated them after that fashion, would soon bolt and run.

It was quite dark, when we all sprang ashore; and, for the first time, I felt dusty particles of the renowned British soil penetrating into my eyes and lungs. As for *stepping* on it, that was out of the question, in the well-paved and flagged condition of the streets; and I did not have an opportunity to do so till some time afterward, when I got out into the country; and then, indeed, I saw England, and snuffed its immortal loam – but not till then.

Jackson led the van; and after stopping at a tavern, took us up this street, and down that, till at last he brought us to a narrow lane, filled with boarding-houses, spirit-vaults, and sailors. Here we stopped before the sign of a Baltimore Clipper, flanked on one side by a gilded bunch of grapes and a bottle, and on the other by the British Unicorn and American Eagle, lying down by each other, like the lion and lamb in the millennium.—A very judicious and tasty device, showing a delicate apprehension of the propriety of conciliating American sailors in an English boarding-house; and yet in no way derogating from the honour and dignity of England, but placing the two nations, indeed, upon a footing of perfect equality.

Near the unicorn was a very small animal, which at first I took for a young unicorn; but it looked more like a yearling lion. It was holding up one paw, as if it had a splinter in it; and on its head was a sort of basket-hilted, low-crowned hat, without a rim. I asked a sailor standing by, what this animal meant, when, looking at me with a grin, he answered, 'Why, youngster, don't you know what that means? It's a young jackass, limping off with a kedgeree pot of rice out of the cuddy.'

Though it was an English boarding-house, it was kept by a broken-down American mariner, one Danby, a dissolute, idle fellow, who had married a buxom English wife, and now lived upon her industry; for the lady, and not the sailor, proved to be the head of the establishment.

She was a hale, good-looking woman, about forty years old, and among the seamen went by the name of '*Handsome Mary.*' But though, from the dissipated character of her spouse, Mary had become the business personage of the house, bought the marketing, overlooked the tables, and conducted all the more important arrangements, yet she was by no means an Amazon to her husband, if she *did* play a masculine part in other matters. No; and the more is the pity, poor Mary seemed too much attached to Danby, to seek to rule him as a termagant. Often she went about her household concerns with the tears in her eyes, when, after a fit of intoxication, this brutal husband of hers had been beating her. The sailors took her part, and many a time volunteered to give him a thorough thrashing before her eyes; but Mary would beg them not to do so, as Danby would, no doubt, be a better boy next time.

[…]

Entering the sign of the Clipper, Jackson ushered us into a small room on one side, and shortly after, Handsome Mary waited upon us with a courtesy, and received the compliments of several old guests among our crew. She then disappeared to provide our supper. While my shipmates were now engaged in tippling, and talking with numerous old acquaintances of theirs in the neighbourhood, who thronged about the door, I remained alone in the little room, meditating profoundly upon the fact, that I was

now seated upon an English bench, under an English roof, in an
English tavern, forming an integral part of the English empire. It
was a staggering fact, but none the less true.

I examined the place attentively; it was a long, narrow, little
room, with one small arched window with red curtains, looking
out upon a smoky, untidy yard, bounded by a dingy brick-wall,
the top of which was horrible with pieces of broken old bottles,
stuck into mortar.

A dull lamp swung overhead, placed in a wooden ship
suspended from the ceiling. The walls were covered with a
paper, representing an endless succession of vessels of all nations
continually circumnavigating the apartment. By way of a pictorial
mainsail to one of these ships, a map was hung against it,
representing in faded colours the flags of all nations. From the
street came a confused uproar of ballad-singers, bawling women,
babies, and drunken sailors.

And this is England?

But where are the old abbeys, and the York Minsters, and the
lord mayors, and coronations, and the May-poles, and fox-hunters,
and Derby races, and the dukes and duchesses, and the Count
d'Orsays, which, from all my reading, I had been in the habit of
associating with England? Not the most distant glimpse of them
was to be seen.

[Chapter 29: Redburn reflects on the difficulty of understanding new
places. The routine of dock duty is established.]

The ship remained in Prince's Dock over six weeks; but as I do
not mean to present a diary of my stay there, I shall here
simply record the general tenor of the life led by our crew
during that interval; and will then proceed to note down, at
random, my own wanderings about town, and impressions of
things as they are recalled to me now, after the lapse of so
many years.

[...]

At daylight, all hands were called, and the decks were washed
down; then we had an hour to go ashore to breakfast; after which
we worked at the rigging, or picked oakum, or were set to some
employment or other, never mind how trivial, till twelve o'clock,
when we went to dinner. At half-past nine we resumed work;
and finally *knocked off* at four o'clock in the afternoon, unless
something particular was in hand. And after four o'clock, we

could go where we pleased, and were not required to be on board again till next morning at daylight.

As we had nothing to do with the cargo, of course, our duties were light enough; and the chief mate was often put to it to devise some employment for us.

We had no watches to stand, a ship-keeper, hired from shore, relieving us from that; and all the while the men's wages ran on, as at sea. Sundays we had to ourselves.

Thus, it will be seen, that the life led by sailors of American ships in Liverpool, is an exceedingly easy one, and abounding in leisure. They live ashore on the fat of the land; and after a little wholesome exercise in the morning, have the rest of the day to themselves.

Nevertheless, these Liverpool voyages, likewise those to London and Havre, are the least profitable that an improvident seaman can take. Because, in New York he receives his month's advance; in Liverpool, another; both of which, in most cases, quickly disappear; so that by the time his voyage terminates, he generally has but little coming to him; sometimes not a cent. Whereas, upon a long voyage, say to India or China, his wages accumulate; he has more inducements to economize, and far fewer motives to extravagance; and when he is paid off at last, he goes away jingling a quart measure of dollars.

Besides, of all sea-ports in the world, Liverpool, perhaps, most abounds in all the variety of land-sharks, land-rats, and other vermin, which make the hapless mariner their prey. In the shape of landlords, bar-keepers, clothiers, crimps [swindlers or members of press-gangs], and boarding-house loungers, the land-sharks devour him, limb by limb; while the land-rats and mice constantly nibble at his purse.

Other perils he runs, also, far worse; from the denizens of notorious Corinthian haunts [i.e. prostitutes] in the vicinity of the docks, which in depravity are not to be matched by any thing this side of the pit that is bottomless.

And yet, sailors love this Liverpool; and upon long voyages to distant parts of the globe, will be continually dilating upon its charms and attractions, and extolling it above all other seaports in the world. For in Liverpool they find their Paradise—not the well known street of that name—and one of them told me he would be content to lie in Prince's Dock till *he hove up anchor* for the world to come.

[Chapter 30: Guidebooks.]

Among the odd volumes in my father's library, was a collection
of old European and English guide-books, which he had bought
on his travels, a great many years ago. In my childhood, I went
through many courses of studying them, and never tired of gazing
at the numerous quaint embellishments and plates, and staring at
the strange title-pages, some of which I thought resembled the
mustached faces of foreigners.

[In his father's library Redburn has found a collection of old guidebooks,
including *The Picture of Liverpool; or, Stranger's Guide* (1805, enlarged, 1808).
For a discussion of Melville's use of this book, see article by Willard Thorp
in 'Further Reading'. Redburn's wanderings around Liverpool are much
more then sightseeing. They represent a pious attempt by him to retrace his
father's steps. Melville's own father had visited the city in 1811 and 1818 on
business. Redburn turns to *The Picture of Liverpool* and considers inserting
in his account a chapter from the guidebook, but decides against it because
he might be 'charged with swelling out my volume by plagiarizing from
a guide-book – the most vulgar and ignominious of thefts!' Nevertheless,
that is what he proceeds to do in adapting stories from *The Picture* for his
novel, and in the following chapter (31) he decides that he will explore
Liverpool using the 'prosy old guide-book'. The latter's aim was partly to
demonstrate the antiquity of Liverpool and partly to describe the views
that could be enjoyed there. A rare criticism of the place concerns the
vegetable market in Castle Street because it obstructs the view, whereas
Redburn has constant difficulties in visualizing whole scenes. His 'rambles'
represent attempts to make sense of Liverpool. His first aim is to locate
the hotel where his father stayed, namely 'Riddiough's Royal Hotel [*sic*],
at the bottom of Lord-street, where are accommodations for families of
the first rank' (p. 178). The guidebook recommends the stranger to use this
hotel for bearings in walking round Liverpool. Redburn naively expects
to 'survey' the town and take in the main sights. These include the Old
Dock (no longer in existence) and, along the waterfront, the Fort, where
we are told: 'A strong guard of soldiers is always kept there. It is open
for public recreation. The soldiers are commonly exercised and the guard
relieved, every evening' (p. 87). Once Redburn tries to find these sights,
the result is perplexing: Chapter 31.]

In short, when I considered that my own father had used this
very guide-book, and that thereby it had been thoroughly tested,
and its fidelity proved beyond a peradventure; I could not but

think that I was building myself up in an unerring knowledge of
Liverpool; especially as I had familiarized myself with the map,
and could turn sharp corners on it, with marvellous confidence
and celerity.

In imagination, as I lay in my berth on ship-board, I used
to take pleasant afternoon rambles through the town; down St.
James-street and up Great George's, stopping at various places
of interest and attraction. I began to think I had been born in
Liverpool, so familiar seemed all the features of the map. And
though some of the streets there depicted were thickly involved,
endlessly angular and crooked, like the map of Boston, in
Massachusetts, yet, I made no doubt, that I could march through
them in the darkest night, and even run for the most distant dock
upon a pressing emergency.

Dear delusion!

It never occurred to my boyish thoughts, that though a guide-
book, fifty years old, might have done good service in its day,
yet it would prove but a miserable cicerone to a modern. I little
imagined that the Liverpool my father saw, was another Liverpool
from that to which I, his son Wellingborough was sailing. No;
these things never obtruded; so accustomed had I been to associate
my old morocco guide-book with the town it described, that the
bare thought of there being any discrepancy, never entered my
mind.

While we lay in the Mersey, before entering the dock, I got
out my guide-book to see how the map would compare with the
identical place itself. But they bore not the slightest resemblance.
However, thinks I, this is owing to my taking a horizontal view,
instead of a bird's-eye survey. So, never mind old guide-book,
you, at least, are all right.

But my faith received a severe shock that same evening, when
the crew went ashore to supper, as I have previously related.

The men stopped at a curious old tavern, near the Prince's
Dock's walls; and having my guide-book in my pocket, I drew it
forth to compare notes, when I found, that precisely upon the spot
where I and my shipmates were standing, and a cherry-cheeked
bar-maid was filling their glasses, my infallible old Morocco, in
that very place, located a fort; adding, that it was well worth the
intelligent stranger's while to visit it for the purpose of beholding
the guard relieved in the evening.

This was a staggerer; for how could a tavern be mistaken for
a castle? and this was about the hour mentioned for the guard

to turn out; yet not a red coat was to be seen. But for all this, I could not, for one small discrepancy, condemn the old family servant who had so faithfully served my own father before me; and when I learned that this tavern went by the name of 'The Old Fort Tavern'; and when I was told that many of the old stones were yet in the walls, I almost completely exonerated my guide-book from the half-insinuated charge of misleading me.

The next day was Sunday, and I had it all to myself; and now, thought I, my guide-book and I shall have a famous ramble up street and down lane, even unto the furthest limits of this Liverpool.

I rose bright and early; from head to foot performed my ablutions 'with Eastern scrupulosity,' and I arrayed myself in my red shirt and shooting-jacket, and the sportsman's pantaloons; and crowned my entire man with the tarpaulin; so that from this curious combination of clothing, and particularly from my red shirt, I must have looked like a very strange compound indeed: three parts sportsman, and two soldier, to one of the sailor.

My shipmates, of course, made merry at my appearance; but I heeded them not; and after breakfast, jumped ashore, full of brilliant anticipations.

My gait was erect, and I was rather tall for my age; and that may have been the reason why, as I was rapidly walking along the dock, a drunken sailor passing, exclaimed, 'Eyes right! quick step there!'

Another fellow stopped me to know whether I was going fox-hunting; and one of the dock-police, stationed at the gates, after peeping out upon me from his sentry box, a snug little den, furnished with benches and newspapers, and hung round with storm jackets and oiled capes, issued forth in a great hurry, crossed my path as I was emerging into the street, and commanded me to halt! I obeyed; when scanning my appearance pertinaciously, he desired to know where I got that tarpaulin hat, not being able to account for the phenomenon of its roofing the head of a broken-down fox-hunter. But I pointed to my ship, which lay at no great distance; when remarking from my voice that I was a Yankee, this faithful functionary permitted me to pass.

It must be known that the police stationed at the gates of the docks are extremely observant of strangers going out; as many thefts are perpetrated on board the ships; and if they chance to see any thing suspicious, they probe into it without mercy. Thus, the old men who buy 'shakings,' and rubbish from vessels, must turn

their bags wrong side out before the police, ere they are allowed
to go outside the walls. And often they will search a suspicious
looking fellow's clothes, even if he be a very thin man, with
attenuated and almost imperceptible pockets.

But where was I going?

[Riddough's Royal Hotel had been converted into shops in 1839.]

I will tell. My intention was in the first place, to visit
Riddough's Hotel, where my father had stopped, more than
thirty years before: and then, with the map in my hand, follow
him through all the town, according to the dotted lines in the
diagram. For thus would I be performing a filial pilgrimage to
spots which would be hallowed in my eyes.

At last, when I found myself going down Old Hall-street
toward Lord-street, where the hotel was situated, according to my
authority; and when, taking out my map, I found that Old Hall-
street was marked there, through its whole extent with my father's
pen; a thousand fond, affectionate emotions rushed around my
heart.

Yes, in this very street, thought I, nay, on this very flagging my
father walked. Then I almost wept, when I looked down on my
sorry apparel, and marked how the people regarded me; the men
staring at so grotesque a young stranger, and the old ladies, in
beaver hats and ruffles, crossing the walk a little to shun me.
[...]
But dispelling these dismal reflections as well as I could, I pushed
on my way, till I got to Chapel-street, which I crossed; and
then, going under a cloister-like arch of stone, whose gloom
and narrowness delighted me, and filled my Yankee soul with
romantic thoughts of old Abbeys and Minsters, I emerged into the
fine quadrangle of the Merchants' Exchange.

There, leaning against the colonnade, I took out my map, and
traced my father right across Chapel-street, and actually through
the very arch at my back, into the paved square where I stood.

So vivid was now the impression of his having been here, and
so narrow the passage from which he had emerged, that I felt like
running on, and overtaking him around the Town Hall adjoining,
at the head of Castle-street. But I soon checked myself, when
remembering that he had gone whither no son's search could
find him in this world. And then I thought of all that must have
happened to him since he paced through that arch. What trials

and troubles he had encountered; how he had been shaken by
many storms of adversity, and at last died a bankrupt. I looked at
my own sorry garb, and had much ado to keep from tears.

But I rallied, and gazed round at the sculptured stonework, and
turned to my guide-book, and looked at the print of the spot. It
was correct to a pillar; but wanted the central ornament of the
quadrangle. This, however, was but a slight subsequent erection,
which ought not to militate against the general character of my
friend for comprehensiveness.

[Redburn finds himself in Exchange Flags where the Nelson monument
was standing. It commemorates Nelson's four main naval victories and was
erected in 1813.]

The ornament in question is a group of statuary in bronze,
elevated upon a marble pedestal and basement, representing
Lord Nelson expiring in the arms of Victory. One foot rests on
a rolling foe, and the other on a cannon. Victory is dropping
a wreath on the dying admiral's brow; while Death, under the
similitude of a hideous skeleton, is insinuating his bony hand
under the hero's robe, and groping after his heart. A very striking
design, and true to the imagination; I never could look at Death
without a shudder.

At uniform intervals round the base of the pedestal, four naked
figures in chains, somewhat larger than life, are seated in various
attitudes of humiliation and despair. One has his leg recklessly
thrown over his knee, and his head bowed over, as if he had
given up all hope of ever feeling better. Another has his head
buried in despondency, and no doubt looks mournfully out of his
eyes, but as his face was averted at the time, I could not catch the
expression. These woe-begone figures of captives are emblematic
of Nelson's principal victories; but I never could look at their
swarthy limbs and manacles, without being involuntarily reminded
of four African slaves in the market-place.

And my thoughts would revert to Virginia and Carolina;
and also to the historical fact, that the African slave-trade once
constituted the principal commerce of Liverpool; and that
the prosperity of the town was once supposed to have been
indissolubly linked to its prosecution. And I remembered that
my father had often spoken to gentlemen visiting our house in
New York, of the unhappiness that the discussion of the abolition
of this trade had occasioned in Liverpool; that the struggle

between sordid interest and humanity had made sad havoc at the fire-sides of the merchants; estranged sons from sires; and even separated husband from wife. And my thoughts reverted to my father's friend, the good and great Roscoe, the intrepid enemy of the trade; who in every way exerted his fine talents toward its suppression; writing a poem ('*the Wrongs of Africa*'), several pamphlets; and in his place in Parliament, he delivered a speech against it, which, as coming from a member for Liverpool, was supposed to have turned many votes, and had no small share in the triumph of sound policy and humanity that ensued.

How this group of statuary affected me, may be inferred from the fact, that I never went through Chapel-street without going through the little arch to look at it again. And there, night or day, I was sure to find Lord Nelson still falling back; Victory's wreath still hovering over his swordpoint; and Death grim and grasping as ever; while the four bronze captives still lamented their captivity.

Now, as I lingered about the railing of the statuary, on the Sunday I have mentioned, I noticed several persons going in and out of an apartment, opening from the basement under the colonnade; and, advancing, I perceived that this was a news-room, full of files of papers. My love of literature prompted me to open the door and step in; but a glance at my soiled shooting-jacket prompted a dignified looking personage to step up and shut the door in my face. I deliberated a minute what I should do to him; and at last resolutely determined to let him alone, and pass on; which I did; going down Castle-street (so called from a castle which once stood there, said my guide-book), and turning down into Lord.

Arrived at the foot of the latter street, I in vain looked round for the hotel. How serious a disappointment was this may well be imagined, when it is considered that I was all eagerness to behold the very house at which my father stopped; where he slept and dined, smoked his cigar, opened his letters, and read the papers. I inquired of some gentlemen and ladies where the missing hotel was; but they only stared and passed on; until I met a mechanic, apparently, who very civilly stopped to hear my questions and give me an answer.

'Riddough's Hotel?' said he, 'upon my word, I think I have heard of such a place; let me see—yes, yes—that was the hotel where my father broke his arm, helping to pull down the walls. My lad, you surely can't be inquiring for Riddough's Hotel! What do you want to find there?'

'Oh! nothing,' I replied, 'I am much obliged for your information'—and away I walked.

Then, indeed, a new light broke in upon me concerning my guide-book; and all my previous dim suspicions were almost confirmed. It was nearly half a century behind the age! and no more fit to guide me about the town, than the map of Pompeii.

It was a sad, a solemn, and a most melancholy thought. The book on which I had so much relied; the book in the old morocco cover; the book with the cocked-hat corners; the book full of fine old family associations; the book with seventeen plates, executed in the highest style of art; this precious book was next to useless. Yes, the thing that had guided the father, could not guide the son. And I sat down on a shop step, and gave loose to meditation.

Here, now, oh, Wellingborough, thought I, learn a lesson, and never forget it. This world, my boy, is a moving world; its Riddough's Hotels are forever being pulled down; it never stands still; and its sands are forever shifting. This very harbour of Liverpool is gradually filling up, they say; and who knows what your son (if you ever have one) may behold, when he comes to visit Liverpool, as long after you as you come after his grandfather. And, Wellingborough, as your father's guide-book is no guide for you, neither would yours (could you afford to buy a modern one to-day) be a true guide to those who come after you. Guide-books, Wellingborough, are the least reliable books in all literature; and nearly all literature, in one sense, is made up of guide-books. Old ones tell us the ways our fathers went, through the thoroughfares and courts of old; but how few of those former places can their posterity trace, amid avenues of modem erections; to how few is the old guide-book now a clew! Every age makes its own guidebooks, and the old ones are used for waste paper. But there is one Holy Guide-Book, Wellingborough, that will never lead you astray, if you but follow it aright; and some noble monuments that remain, though the pyramids crumble.

But though I rose from the door-step a sadder and a wiser boy, and though my guide-book had been stripped of its reputation for infallibility, I did not treat with contumely or disdain, those sacred pages which had once been a beacon to my sire.

[The guidebook describes the Old Dock as the 'first dock we meet with on the outset of our ramble' (p. 55) and as offering good views across the river.]

No.—Poor old guide-book, thought I, tenderly stroking its back, and smoothing the dog-ears with reverence; I will not use you with despite, old Morocco! and you will yet prove a trusty conductor through many old streets in the old parts of this town; even if you are at fault, now and then, concerning a Riddough's Hotel, or some other forgotten thing of the past. As I fondly glanced over the leaves, like one who loves more than he chides, my eye lighted upon a passage concerning 'The Old Dock,' which much aroused my curiosity. I determined to see the place without delay: and walking on, in what I presumed to be the right direction, at last found myself before a spacious and splendid pile of sculptured brown stone; and entering the porch, perceived from incontrovertible tokens that it must be the Custom-house. After admiring it awhile, I took out my guide-book again; and what was my amazement at discovering that, according to its authority, I was entirely mistaken with regard to this Custom-house; for precisely where I stood, 'The Old Dock' must be standing, and reading on concerning it, I met with this very apposite passage:— 'The first idea that strikes the stranger in coming to this dock, is the singularity of so great a number of ships afloat in the very heart of the town, without discovering any connection with the sea.'

Here, now, was a poser! Old Morocco confessed that there was a good deal of 'singularity' about the thing; nor did he pretend to deny that it was, without question, amazing, that this fabulous dock should seem to have no *connection with the sea!* However, the same author went on to say, that the '*astonished stranger must suspend his wonder for awhile, and turn to the left.*' But, right or left, no place answering to the description was to be seen.

This was too confounding altogether, and not to be easily accounted for, even by making ordinary allowances for the growth and general improvement of the town in the course of years. So, guide-book in hand, I accosted a policeman standing by, and begged him to tell me whether he was acquainted with any place in that neighbourhood called the '*Old Dock*.' The man looked at me wonderingly at first, and then seeing I was apparently sane, and quite civil into the bargain, he whipped his well-polished boot with his rattan, pulled up his silver-laced coat-collar, and initiated me into a knowledge of the following facts.

It seems that in this place originally stood the '*pool,*' from which the town borrows a part of its name, and which originally wound round the greater part of the old settlements; that this pool was made into the 'Old Dock,' for the benefit of the shipping; but that, years ago, it had been filled up, and furnished the site for the Custom-house before me.

I now eyed the spot with a feeling somewhat akin to the Eastern traveller standing on the brink of the Dead Sea. For here the doom of Gomorrah seemed reversed, and a lake had been converted into substantial stone and mortar.

Well, well, Wellingborough, thought I, you had better put the book into your pocket, and carry it home to the Society of Antiquaries; it is several thousand leagues and odd furlongs behind the march of improvement. Smell its old morocco binding, Wellingborough; does it not smell somewhat mummy-ish? Does it not remind you of Cheops and the Catacombs? I tell you it was written before the lost books of Livy, and is cousin-german to that irrecoverably departed volume, entitled, '*The Wars of the Lord*' quoted by Moses in the Pentateuch. Put it up, Wellingborough, put it up, my dear friend; and hereafter follow your nose throughout Liverpool; it will stick to you through thick and thin: and be your ship's mainmast and St. George's spire your landmarks.

No!—And again I rubbed its back softly, and gently adjusted a loose leaf: No, no, I'll not give you up yet. Forth, old Morocco! and lead me in sight of the venerable Abbey of Birkenhead; and let these eager eyes behold the mansion once occupied by the old earls of Derby!

For the book discoursed of both places, and told how the Abbey was on the Cheshire shore, full in view from a point on the Lancashire side, covered over with ivy, and brilliant with moss! And how the house of the noble Derby's was now a common jail of the town; and how that circumstance was full of suggestions, and pregnant with wisdom!

But, alas! I never saw the Abbey; at least none was in sight from the water: and as for the house of the earls, I never saw that.

Ah me, and ten times alas! am I to visit old England in vain? in the land of Thomas-a-Becket and stout John of Gaunt, not to catch the least glimpse of priory or castle? Is there nothing in all the British empire but these smoky ranges of old shops and warehouses? is Liverpool but a brick-kiln? Why, no buildings here look so ancient as the old gable-pointed mansion of my maternal grandfather at home, whose bricks were brought from Holland long before the revolutionary war! Tis a deceit—a gull—a sham—a hoax! This boasted England is no older than the State of New York: if it is, show me the proofs —point out the vouchers.

Where's the tower of Julius Caesar? Where's the Roman wall?
Show me Stonehenge!

But, Wellingborough, I remonstrated with myself, you are only
in Liverpool; the old monuments lie to the north, south, east, and
west of you; you are but a sailor-boy, and you can not expect to
be a great tourist, and visit the antiquities, in that preposterous
shooting-jacket of yours. Indeed, you can not, my boy.

True, true—that's it. I am not the traveller my father was. I am
only a common-carrier across the Atlantic.

After a weary day's walk, I at last arrived at the sign of the
Baltimore Clipper to supper; and Handsome Mary poured me
out a brimmer of tea, in which, for the time, I drowned all my
melancholy.

[Chapter 32: Prince's Dock.]

As the description of any one of these Liverpool docks will pretty
much answer for all, I will here endeavour to give some account
of Prince's Dock, where the *Highlander* rested after her passage
across the Atlantic.

This dock, of comparatively recent construction, is perhaps the
largest of all, and is well known to American sailors, from the
fact, that it is mostly frequented by the American shipping. Here
lie the noble New York packets, which at home are found at the
foot of Wall-Street; and here lie the Mobile and Savannah cotton
ships and traders.

This dock was built like the others, mostly upon the bed of
the river, the earth and rock having been laboriously scooped
out, and solidified again as materials for the quays and piers.
From the river, Prince's Dock is protected by a long pier of
masonry, surmounted by a massive wall; and on the side next the
town, it is bounded by similar walls, one of which runs along
a thoroughfare. The whole space thus inclosed forms an oblong,
and may, at a guess, be presumed to comprise about fifteen or
twenty acres; but as I had not the rod of a surveyor when I took
it in, I will not be certain.

The area of the dock itself, exclusive of the inclosed quays
surrounding it, may be estimated at, say, ten acres. Access to the
interior from the streets is had through several gateways; so that,
upon their being closed, the whole dock is shut up like a house.
From the river, the entrance is through a water-gate, and ingress
to ships is only to be had, when the level of the dock coincides

with that of the river; that is, about the time of high tide, as the level of the dock is always at that mark. So that when it is low tide in the river, the keels of the ships inclosed by the quays are elevated more than twenty feet above those of the vessels in the stream. This, of course, produces a striking effect to a stranger, to see hundreds of immense ships floating high aloft in the heart of a mass of masonry.

Prince's Dock is generally so filled with shipping, that the entrance of a new-comer is apt to occasion a universal stir among all the older occupants. The dock-masters, whose authority is declared by tin signs worn conspicuously over their hats, mount the poops and forecastles of the various vessels, and hail the surrounding strangers in all directions:—'*Highlander ahoy! Cast off your bowline, and sheer alongside the Neptune!*'—'*Neptune ahoy! get out a stern-line, and sheer alongside the Trident!*'—'*Trident ahoy! get out a bowline, and drop astern of the Undaunted!*' And so it runs round like a shock of electricity; touch one, and you touch all. This kind of work irritates and exasperates the sailors to the last degree; but it is only one of the unavoidable inconveniences of inclosed docks, which are outweighed by innumerable advantages.

Just without the water-gate, is a basin, always connecting with the open river, through a narrow entrance between pier-heads. This basin forms a sort of ante-chamber to the dock itself, where vessels lie waiting their turn to enter. During a storm, the necessity of this basin is obvious; for it would be impossible to '*dock*' a ship under full headway from a voyage across the ocean. From the turbulent waves, she first glides into the ante-chamber between the pier-heads and from thence into the docks.

Concerning the cost of the docks, I can only state, that the *King's Dock*, comprehending but a comparatively small area, was completed at an expense of some £20,000.

Our old ship-keeper, a Liverpool man by birth, who had long followed the seas, related a curious story concerning this dock. One of the ships which carried over troops from England to Ireland in King William's war, in 1688, entered the King's Dock on the first day of its being opened in 1788, after an interval of just one century. She was a dark little brig, called the *Port-a-Ferry*. And probably, as her timbers must have been frequently renewed in the course of a hundred years, the name alone could have been all that was left of her at the time. A paved area, very wide, is included within the walls; and along the edge of the quays are ranges of iron sheds, intended as a temporary shelter for the goods unladed from the shipping. Nothing can exceed the bustle and activity displayed along these quays during the day; bales, crates, boxes, and cases are being tumbled about by thousands of labourers; trucks are coming and going; dock-masters are shouting; sailors of all nations are singing out at their ropes; and all this commotion is greatly increased by the resoundings from the lofty walls that hem in the din.

[Chapter 33: Variety of shipping.]

Surrounded by its broad belt of masonry, each Liverpool dock is a walled town, full of life and commotion; or rather, it is a small archipelago, an epitome of the world, where all the nations of Christendom, and even those of Heathendom, are represented. For, in itself, each ship is an island, a floating colony of the tribe to which it belongs.

Here are brought together the remotest limits of the earth; and in the collective spars and timbers of these ships, all the forests of the globe are represented, as in a grand parliament of masts. Canada and New Zealand send their pines; America her live oak; India her teak; Norway her spruce; and the Right Honourable Mahogany, member for Honduras and Cam-peachy, is seen at his post by the wheel. Here, under the beneficent sway of the Genius of Commerce, all climes and countries embrace; and yard-arm touches yard-arm in brotherly love.

A Liverpool dock is a grand caravansary inn, and hotel, on the spacious and liberal plan of the *Astor House*. Here ships are lodged at a moderate charge, and payment is not demanded till the time of departure. Here they are comfortably housed and provided for; sheltered from all weathers and secured from all calamities. For I can hardly credit a story I have heard, that sometimes, in heavy gales, ships lying in the very middle of the docks have lost their top-gallant-masts. Whatever the toils and hardships encountered on the voyage, whether they come from Iceland or the coast of New Guinea, here their sufferings are ended, and they take their ease in their watery inn.

I know not how many hours I spent in gazing at the shipping in Prince's Dock, and speculating concerning their past voyages and future prospects in life. Some had just arrived from the most distant ports, worn, battered, and disabled; others were all a-taunt-o—spruce, gay, and brilliant, in readiness for sea.

Every day the *Highlander* had some new neighbour. A black brig from Glasgow, with its crew of sober Scotch caps, and its staid, thrifty-looking skipper, would be replaced by a jovial French hermaphrodite, its forecastle echoing with songs, and its quarter-deck elastic from much dancing.

On the other side, perhaps, a magnificent New York Liner, huge as a seventy-four, and suggesting the idea of a Mivart's or Delmonico's afloat [two New York hotels], would give way to a Sidney emigrant ship, receiving on board its live freight of shepherds from the Grampians, ere long to be tending their flocks on the hills and downs of New Holland.

I was particularly pleased and tickled, with a multitude of little salt-droghers, rigged like sloops, and not much bigger than a pilot-boat, but with broad bows painted black, and carrying red sails, which looked as if they had been pickled and stained in a tan-yard. These little fellows were continually coming in with their cargoes for ships bound to America; and lying, five or six together, alongside of those lofty Yankee hulls, resembled a parcel of red ants about the carcass of a black buffalo.

When loaded, these comical little craft are about level with the water; and frequently, when blowing fresh in the river, I have seen them flying through the foam with nothing visible but the mast and sail, and a man at the tiller; their entire cargo being snugly secured under hatches.

It was diverting to observe the self-importance of the skipper of any of these diminutive vessels. He would give himself all the airs of an admiral on a three-decker's poop; and no doubt, thought quite as much of himself. And why not? What could Caesar want more? Though his craft was none of the largest, it was subject to *him*; and though his crew might only consist of himself; yet if he governed it well, he achieved a triumph, which the moralists of all ages have set above the victories of Alexander.

These craft have each a little cabin, the prettiest, charming-est, most delightful little dog-hole in the world; not much bigger than an old-fashioned alcove for a bed. It is lighted by little round glasses placed in the deck; so that to the insider, the ceiling is like a small firmament twinkling with astral radiations. For tall men, nevertheless, the place is but ill-adapted; a sitting, or recumbent position being indispensable to an occupancy of the premises. Yet small, low, and narrow as the cabin is, somehow, it affords accommodations to the skipper and his family. Often, I used to watch the tidy good-wife, seated at

the open little scuttle, like a woman at a cottage door, engaged
in knitting socks for her husband; or perhaps, cutting his hair,
as he kneeled before her. And once, while marvelling how a
couple like this found room to turn in, below, I was amazed by
a noisy irruption of cherry-cheeked young tars from the scuttle,
whence they came rolling forth, like so many curly spaniels from
a kennel.

[Chapter 35: The floating chapel and dockland clergy.]

This was the hull of an old sloop-of-war, which had been
converted into a mariner's church. A house had been built upon
it, and a steeple took the place of a mast. There was a little
balcony near the base of the steeple, some twenty feet from the
water; where, on week-days, I used to see an old pensioner of
a tar, sitting on a camp-stool, reading his Bible. On Sundays he
hoisted the Bethel flag, and like the *muezzin* or cryer of prayers
on the top of a Turkish mosque, would call the strolling sailors to
their devotions; not officially, but on his own account; conjuring
them not to make fools of themselves, but muster round the
pulpit, as they did about the capstan on a man-of-war. This old
worthy was the sexton. I attended the chapel several times, and
found there a very orderly but small congregation. The first time
I went, the chaplain was discoursing on future punishments, and
making allusions to the Tartarean Lake; which, coupled with the
pitchy smell of the old hull, summoned up the most forcible image
of the thing which I ever experienced.

The floating chapels which are to be found in some of the
docks, form one of the means which have been tried to induce
the seamen visiting Liverpool to turn their thoughts toward
serious things. But as very few of them ever think of entering
these chapels, though they might pass them twenty times in the
day, some of the clergy, of a Sunday, address them in the open air,
from the corners of the quays, or wherever they can procure an
audience.

Whenever, in my Sunday strolls, I caught sight of one of
these congregations, I always made a point of joining it; and
would find myself surrounded by a motley crowd of seamen
from all quarters of the globe, and women, and lumpers, and
dock labourers of all sorts. Frequently the clergyman would
be standing upon an old cask, arrayed in full canonicals, as a
divine of the Church of England. Never have I heard religious

discourses better adapted to an audience of men, who, like sailors, are chiefly, if not only, to be moved by the plainest of precepts, and demonstrations of the misery of sin, as conclusive and undeniable as those of Euclid. No mere rhetoric avails with such men; fine periods are vanity. You can not touch them with tropes. They need to be pressed home by plain facts.

And such was generally the mode in which they were addressed by the clergy in question: who, taking familiar themes for their discourses, which were levelled right at the wants of their auditors, always succeeded in fastening their attention. In particular, the two great vices to which sailors are most addicted, and which they practice to the ruin of both body and soul; these things, were the most enlarged upon. And several times on the docks, I have seen a robed clergyman addressing a large audience of women collected from the notorious lanes and alleys in the neighbourhood.

[Chapter 36: The Church of St Nicholas. The Church of Our Lady and St Nicholas, near the Pier Head, is the Parish Church of Liverpool, also known as 'the sailors' church'. A new tower had been added in 1815; otherwise the church stood unchanged at that time. *The Picture of Liverpool* describes the lower public parts of the church as producing models of genteel piety in its visitors.]

The floating chapel recalls to mind the '*Old Church,*' well known to the seamen of many generations, who have visited Liverpool. It stands very near the docks, a venerable mass of brown stone, and by the town's people is called the Church of St. Nicholas. I believe it is the best preserved piece of antiquity in all Liverpool.

Before the town rose to any importance, it was the only place of worship on that side of the Mersey; and under the adjoining Parish of Walton was a *chapel-of-ease*; though from the straight backed pews, there could have been but little comfort taken in it.

In old times, there stood in front of the church a statue of St. Nicholas, the patron of mariners; to which all pious sailors made offerings, to induce his saintship to grant them short and prosperous voyages. In the tower is a fine chime of bells; and I well remember my delight at first hearing them on the first Sunday morning after our arrival in the dock. It seemed to carry an admonition with it; something like the premonition conveyed to young Whittington by Bow Bells. '*Wellingborough!*

Wellingborough! you must not forget to go to church, Wellingborough! Don't forget, Wellingborough! Wellingborough! don't forget.'

Thirty or forty years ago, these bells were rung upon the arrival of every Liverpool ship from a foreign voyage. How forcibly does this illustrate the increase of the commerce of the town! Were the same custom now observed, the bells would seldom have a chance to cease.

What seemed the most remarkable about this venerable old church, and what seemed the most barbarous, and grated upon the veneration with which I regarded this time-hallowed structure, was the condition of the grave-yard surrounding it. From its close vicinity to the haunts of the swarms of labourers about the docks, it is crossed and re-crossed by thoroughfares in all directions; and the tomb-stones, not being erect, but horizontal (indeed, they form a complete flagging to the spot), multitudes are constantly walking over the dead; their heels erasing the death's-heads and crossbones, the last mementos of the departed. At noon, when the lumpers employed in loading and unloading the shipping, retire for an hour to snatch a dinner, many of them resort to the grave-yard; and seating themselves upon a tomb-stone use the adjoining one for a table. Often, I saw men stretched out in a drunken sleep upon these slabs

[…]

In the basement of the church is a Dead House, like the Morgue in Paris, where the bodies of the drowned are exposed until claimed by their friends, or till buried at the public charge.

From the multitudes employed about the shipping, this dead-house has always more or less occupants. Whenever I passed up Chapel-street, I used to see a crowd gazing through the grim iron grating of the door, upon the faces of the drowned within. And once, when the door was opened, I saw a sailor stretched out, stark and stiff, with the sleeve of his frock rolled up, and showing his name and date of birth tattooed upon his arm. It was a sight full of suggestions; he seemed his own headstone.

I was told that standing rewards are offered for the recovery of persons falling into the docks; so much, if restored to life, and a less amount if irrecoverably drowned. Lured by this, several horrid old men and women are constantly prying about the docks, searching after bodies. I observed them principally early in the morning, when they issued from their dens, on the same principle that the rag-rakers, and rubbish-pickers in the streets, sally out bright and early; for then, the night-harvest has ripened.

[Chapter 37: Redburn encounters the worst case of poverty and starvation in the novel. Launcelott's Hey, long demolished, was a street near the Prince's Dock.]

In going to our boarding-house, the sign of the Baltimore Clipper, I generally passed through a narrow street called 'Launcelott's-Hey,' lined with dingy, prison-like cotton warehouses. In this street, or rather alley, you seldom see any one but a truck-man, or some solitary old warehouse-keeper, haunting his smoky den like a ghost.

Once, passing through this place, I heard a feeble wail, which seemed to come out of the earth. It was but a strip of crooked side-walk where I stood; the dingy wall was on every side, converting the mid-day into twilight; and not a soul was in sight. I started, and could almost have run, when I heard that dismal sound. It seemed the low, hopeless, endless wail of some one forever lost. At last I advanced to an opening which communicated downward with deep tiers of cellars beneath a crumbling old warehouse; and there, some fifteen feet below the walk, crouching in nameless squalor, with her head bowed over, was the figure of what had been a woman. Her blue arms folded to her livid bosom two shrunken things like children, that leaned toward her, one on each side. At first, I knew not whether they were alive or dead. They made no sign; they did not move or stir; but from the vault came that soul-sickening wail.

I made a noise with my foot, which, in the silence, echoed far and near; but there was no response. Louder still; when one of the children lifted its head, and cast upward a faint glance; then closed its eyes, and lay motionless. The woman also, now gazed up, and perceived me; but let fall her eye again. They were dumb and next to dead with want. How they had crawled into that den, I could not tell; but there they had crawled to die. At that moment I never thought of relieving them; for death was so stamped in their glazed and unimploring eyes, that I almost regarded them as already no more. I stood looking down on them, while my whole soul swelled within me; and I asked myself, What right had any body in the wide world to smile and be glad, when sights like this were to be seen? It was enough to turn the heart to gall; and make a man-hater of a Howard. For who were these ghosts that I saw? Were they not human beings? A woman and two girls? With eyes, and lips, and ears like any queen? with hearts which, though they did not bound with blood, yet beat with a dull, dead ache that was their life.

At last, I walked on toward an open lot in the alley, hoping to
meet there some ragged old women, whom I had daily noticed
groping amid foul rubbish for little particles of dirty cotton, which
they washed out and sold for a trifle.

I found them; and accosting one, I asked if she knew of the
persons I had just left. She replied, that she did not; nor did she
want to. I then asked another, a miserable, toothless old woman,
with a tattered strip of coarse baling stuff round her body.
Looking at me for an instant, she resumed her raking in the
rubbish, and said that she knew who it was that I spoke of; but
that she had no time to attend to beggars and their brats.

[Redburn takes the woman some bread, cheese, and water, though only
the girls take the food. Returning to the vault later, he finds that they
have disappeared without trace.]

[Chapter 38: Dock-wall beggars.]

As it is against the law to throw the least thing overboard, even
a rope yarn; and as this law is very different from similar laws in
New York, inasmuch as it is rigidly enforced by the dock-masters;
and, moreover, as after discharging a ship's cargo, a great deal of
dirt and worthless dunnage [loose material laid in a ship's hold; i.e.,
rubbish] remains in the hold, the amount of rubbish accumulated
in the appointed receptacles for depositing it within the walls is
extremely large, and is constantly receiving new accessions from
every vessel that unlades at the quays.

Standing over these noisome heaps, you will see scores of
tattered wretches, armed with old rakes and picking-irons,
turning over the dirt, and making as much of a rope-yarn as if
it were a skein of silk. Their findings, nevertheless, are but small;
for as it is one of the immemorial perquisites of the second mate
of a merchant ship to collect, and sell on his own account, all
the condemned 'old junk' of the vessel to which he belongs, he
generally takes good heed that in the buckets of rubbish carried
ashore, there shall be as few rope-yarns as possible.

In the same way, the cook preserves all the odds and ends of pork-
rinds and beef-fat, which he sells at considerable profit; upon a six
months' voyage frequently realizing thirty or forty dollars from the
sale, and in large ships, even more than that. It may easily be imagined,
then, how desperately driven to it must these rubbish-pickers be, to
ransack heaps of refuse which have been previously gleaned.

Nor must I omit to make mention of the singular beggary practiced in the streets frequented by sailors; and particularly to record the remarkable army of paupers that beset the docks at particular hours of the day.

At twelve o'clock the crews of hundreds and hundreds of ships issue in crowds from the dock gates to go to their dinner in the town. This hour is seized upon by multitudes of beggars to plant themselves against the outside of the walls, while others stand upon the curb-stone to excite the charity of the seamen. The first time that I passed through this long lane of pauperism, it seemed hard to believe that such an array of misery could be furnished by any town in the world.

Every variety of want and suffering here met the eye, and every vice showed here its victims. Nor were the marvellous and almost incredible shifts and stratagems of the professional beggars, wanting to finish this picture of all that is dishonourable to civilization and humanity.

Old women, rather mummies, drying up with slow starving and age; young girls, incurably sick, who ought to have been in the hospital; sturdy men, with the gallows in their eyes, and a whining lie in their mouths; young boys, hollow-eyed and decrepit; and puny mothers, holding up puny babes in the glare of the sun, formed the main features of the scene.

But these were diversified by instances of peculiar suffering, vice, or art in attracting charity, which, to me at least, who had never seen such things before, seemed to the last degree uncommon and monstrous.

I remember one cripple, a young man rather decently clad, who sat huddled up against the wall, holding a painted board on his knees. It was a picture intending to represent the man himself caught in the machinery of some factory, and whirled about among spindles and cogs, with his limbs mangled and bloody. This person said nothing, but sat silently exhibiting his board. Next him, leaning upright against the wall, was a tall, pallid man, with a white bandage round his brow, and his face cadaverous as a corpse. He, too, said nothing; but with one finger silently pointed down to the square of flagging at his feet, which was nicely swept, and stained blue, and bore this inscription in chalk:—

> 'I have had no food for three days;
> My wife and children are dying.'

Further on lay a man with one sleeve of his ragged coat

removed, showing an unsightly sore; and above it a label with some writing.

In some places, for the distance of many rods, the whole line of flagging immediately at the base of the wall, would be completely covered with inscriptions, the beggars standing over them in silence.

But as you passed along these horrible records, in an hour's time destined to be obliterated by the feet of thousands and thousands of wayfarers, you were not left unassailed by the clamorous petitions of the more urgent applicants for charity. They beset you on every hand; catching you by the coat; hanging on, and following you along; and, *for Heaven's sake*, and *for God's sake*, and *for Christ's sake*, beseeching of you but *one ha'penny*. If you so much as glanced your eye on one of them, even for an instant, it was perceived like lightning, and the person never left your side until you turned into another street, or satisfied his demands. Thus, at least, it was with the sailors; though I observed that the beggars treated the town's people differently.

I can not say that the seamen did much to relieve the destitution which three times every day was presented to their view. Perhaps habit had made them callous; but the truth might have been that very few of them had much money to give. Yet the beggars must have had some inducement to infest the dock walls as they did.

As an example of the caprice of sailors, and their sympathy with suffering among members of their own calling, I must mention the case of an old man, who every day, and all day long, through sunshine and rain, occupied a particular corner, where crowds of tars were always passing. He was an uncommonly large, plethoric man, with a wooden leg, and dressed in the nautical garb; his face was red and round; he was continually merry; and with his wooden stump thrust forth, so as almost to trip up the careless wayfarer, he sat upon a great pile of monkey jackets [waist-length jackets tapering to a point behind, worn by ships' officers], with a little depression in them between his knees, to receive the coppers thrown him. And plenty of pennies were tossed into his poor-box by the sailors, who always exchanged a pleasant word with the old man, and passed on, generally regardless of the neighbouring beggars.

The first morning I went ashore with my shipmates, some of them greeted him as an old acquaintance; for that corner he had occupied for many long years. He was an old man-of-war's man, who had lost his leg at the battle of Trafalgar; and singular to tell, he now exhibited his wooden one as a genuine specimen of the oak timbers of Nelson's ship, the *Victory*.

Among the paupers were several who wore old sailor hats and jackets, and claimed to be destitute tars; and on the strength of these pretensions demanded help from their brethren; but Jack would see through their disguise in a moment, and turn away, with no benediction.

As I daily passed through this lane of beggars, who thronged the docks as the Hebrew cripples did the Pool of Bethesda, and as I thought of my utter inability in any way to help them, I could not but offer up a prayer, that some angel might descend, and turn the waters of the docks into an elixir, that would heal all their woes, and make them, man and woman, healthy and whole as their ancestors, Adam and Eve, in the garden.

[Chapter 39: Street life.]

In the evening, especially when the sailors are gathered in great numbers, these streets present a most singular spectacle, the entire population of the vicinity being seemingly turned into them. Hand-organs, fiddles, and cymbals, plied by strolling musicians, mix with the songs of the seamen, the babble of women and children, and the groaning and whining of beggars. From the various boarding-houses, each distinguished by gilded emblems outside—an anchor, a crown, a ship, a windlass, or a dolphin—proceeds the noise of revelry and dancing; and from the open casements lean young girls and old women, chattering and laughing with the crowds in the middle of the street. Every moment strange greetings are exchanged between old sailors who chance to stumble upon a shipmate, last seen in Calcutta or Savannah; and the invariable courtesy that takes place upon these occasions, is to go to the next spirit-vault, and drink each other's health.

There are particular paupers who frequent particular sections of these streets, and who, I was told, resented the intrusion of mendicants from other parts of the town.

Chief among them was a white-haired old man, stone-blind; who was led up and down through the long tumult by a woman holding a little saucer to receive contributions. This old man sang, or rather chanted, certain words in a peculiarly long-drawn, guttural manner, throwing back his head, and turning up his sightless eyeballs to the sky. His chant was a lamentation upon his infirmity; and at the time it produced the same effect upon me, that my first reading of Milton's Invocation to the Sun did, years afterward. I can not recall it all; but it was something like this, drawn out in an endless groan—

'Here goes the blind old man; blind, blind, blind; no more will he see sun nor moon—no more see sun nor moon!' And thus would he pass through the middle of the street; the woman going on in advance, holding his hand, and dragging him through all obstructions; now and then leaving him standing, while she went among the crowd soliciting coppers.

But one of the most curious features of the scene is the number of sailor ballad-singers, who, after singing their verses, hand you a printed copy, and beg you to buy. One of these persons, dressed like a man-of-war's-man, I observed every day standing at a corner in the middle of the street. He had a full, noble voice, like a church-organ; and his notes rose high above the surrounding din. But the remarkable thing about this ballad-singer was one of his arms, which, while singing, he somehow swung vertically round and round in the air, as if it revolved on a pivot. The feat was unnaturally unaccountable; and he performed it with the view of attracting sympathy; since he said that in falling from a frigate's mast-head to the deck, he had met with an injury, which had resulted in making his wonderful arm what it was.

[Chapter 40: Customs officers and tobacco. *The Picture of Liverpool* highlights the tobacco warehouse of the King's Dock as a major feature.]

As soon as we came to anchor in the river, before reaching the dock, three Custom-house underlings boarded us, and coming down into the forecastle, ordered the men to produce all the tobacco they had. Accordingly several pounds were brought forth.

'Is that all?' asked the officers.

'All,' said the men.

'We will see,' returned the others.

And without more ado, they emptied the chests right and left; tossed over the bunks and made a thorough search of the premises; but discovered nothing. The sailors were then given to understand, that while the ship lay in dock, the tobacco must remain in the cabin, under custody of the chief mate, who every morning would dole out to them one plug per head, as a security against their carrying it ashore.

'Very good,' said the men.

But several of them had secret places in the ship, from whence they daily drew pound after pound of tobacco, which they smuggled ashore in the manner following.

When the crew went to meals, each man carried at least one plug in his pocket; *that* he had a right to; and as many more were hidden about his person as he dared. Among the great crowds pouring out of the dock-gates at such hours, of course these smugglers stood little chance of detection; although vigilant looking policemen were always standing by. And though these 'Charlies' might suppose there were tobacco smugglers passing; yet to hit the right man among such a throng, would be as hard, as to harpoon a speckled porpoise, one of ten thousand darting under a ship's bows.

Our forecastle was often visited by foreign sailors, who knowing we came from America, were anxious to purchase tobacco at a cheap rate; for in Liverpool it is about an American penny per pipe-full. Along the docks they sell an English pennyworth, put up in a little roll like confectioners' mottoes, with poetical lines, or instructive little moral precepts printed in red on the back.

[Chapter 40: Brunswick Dock. The dock had been opened in 1832.]

Brunswick Dock, to the west of Prince's, is one of the most interesting to be seen. Here lie the various black steamers (so unlike the American boats, since they have to navigate the boisterous Narrow Seas) plying to all parts of the three kingdoms. Here you see vast quantities of produce, imported from starving Ireland; here you see the decks turned into pens for oxen and sheep; and often, side by side with these inclosures, Irish deck-passengers, thick as they can stand, seemingly penned in just like the cattle. It was the beginning of July when the Highlander arrived in port; and the Irish labourers were daily coming over by thousands, to help harvest the English crops.

One morning, going into the town, I heard a tramp, as of a drove of buffaloes, behind me; and turning round, beheld the entire middle of the street filled by a great crowd of these men, who had just emerged from Brunswick Dock gates, arrayed in long-tailed coats of hoddin-gray [coarse, undyed material], corduroy knee-breeches, and shod with shoes that raised a mighty dust. Flourishing their Donnybrook shillelaghs [cudgels], they looked like an irruption of barbarians. They were marching straight out of town into the country; and perhaps out of consideration for the finances of the corporation, took the middle of the street, to save the side-walks.

[Chapter 41: Racial tolerance. The contrast between public behaviour in Liverpool and in the USA made a particularly striking impression on African American visitors.]

And here, I must not omit one thing, that struck me at the time. It was the absence of negroes; who in the large towns in the 'free states' of America, almost always form a considerable portion of the destitute. But in these streets, not a negro was to be seen. All were whites; and with the exception of the Irish, were natives of the soil: even Englishmen; as much Englishmen, as the dukes in the House of Lords. This conveyed a strange feeling: and more than any thing else, reminded me that I was not in my own land. For *there*, such a being as a native beggar is almost unknown; and to be a born American citizen seems a guarantee against pauperism; and this, perhaps, springs from the virtue of a vote.

Speaking of negroes, recalls the looks of interest with which negro-sailors are regarded when they walk the Liverpool streets. In Liverpool indeed the negro steps with a prouder pace, and lifts his head like a man; for here, no such exaggerated feeling exists in respect to him, as in America. Three or four times, I encountered our black steward, dressed very handsomely, and walking arm in arm with a good-looking English woman. In New York, such a couple would have been mobbed in three minutes; and the steward would have been lucky to escape with whole limbs. Owing to the friendly reception extended to them, and the unwonted immunities they enjoy in Liverpool, the black cooks and stewards of American ships are very much attached to the place and like to make voyages to it.

Being so young and inexperienced then, and unconsciously swayed in some degree by those local and social prejudices, that are the marring of most men, and from which, for the mass, there seems no possible escape; at first I was surprised that a coloured man should be treated as he is in this town; but a little reflection showed that, after all, it was but recognizing his claims to humanity and normal equality; so that, in some things, we Americans leave to other countries the carrying out of the principle that stands at the head of our Declaration of Independence.

[Chapter 41: Chartist agitation and the railway arch. The Chartist movement for working men's socio-economic reform had been started in 1836. A correspondent for the Liverpool *Mercury* of 5 July 1839 reported: 'A stripling, about eighteen years of age, has lately been lecturing, morning and afternoon, on the Sundays, on Chartism.']

Though I almost invariably attended church on Sunday mornings, yet the rest of the day I spent on my travels; and it was on one of these afternoon strolls, that on passing through St. George's-square, I found myself among a large crowd, gathered near the base of George the Fourth's equestrian statue.

The people were mostly mechanics and artisans in their holiday clothes; but mixed with them were a good many soldiers, in lean, lank, and dinnerless undresses, and sporting attenuated rattans. These troops belonged to the various regiments then in town. Police officers, also, were conspicuous in their uniforms. At first perfect silence and decorum prevailed.

Addressing this orderly throng was a pale, hollow-eyed young man, in a snuff-colored surtout, who looked worn with much watching, or much toil, or too little food. His features were good, his whole air was respectable, and there was no mistaking the fact, that he was strongly in earnest in what he was saying.

In his hand was a soiled, inflammatory-looking pamphlet, from which he frequently read; following up the quotations with nervous appeals to his hearers, a rolling of his eyes, and sometimes the most frantic gestures. I was not long within hearing of him, before I became aware that this youth was a Chartist.

Presently the crowd increased, and some commotion was raised, when I noticed the police officers augmenting in number; and by and by, they began to glide through the crowd, politely hinting at the propriety of dispersing. The first persons thus accosted were the soldiers, who accordingly sauntered off, switching their rattans, and admiring their high-polished shoes. It was plain that the Charter did not hang very heavy round their hearts. For the rest, they also gradually broke up; and at last I saw the speaker himself depart.

I do not know why, but I thought he must be some despairing elder son, supporting by hard toil his mother and sisters; for of such many political desperadoes are made.

[Redburn here stumbles across the famous Moorish arch, which forms the entrance to the railway tunnel at Edge Hill. The entrance was flanked by high pillars over the engines houses which would haul wagons through the tunnels from Wapping Dock and Lime Street. The Liverpool and Manchester Railway opened in 1830 and Lime Street Station in 1836.]

That same Sunday afternoon, I strolled toward the outskirts of the town, and attracted by the sight of two great Pompey's pillars, in the shape of black steeples, apparently rising directly from the soil, I approached them with much curiosity. But looking over a low parapet connecting them, what was my surprise to behold at my feet a smoky hollow in the ground, with rocky walls, and dark holes at one end, carrying out of view several lines of iron railways; while far beyond, straight out toward the open country, ran an endless railroad. Over the place, a handsome Moorish arch of stone was flung; and gradually, as I gazed upon it, and at the little side arches at the bottom of the hollow, there came over me an undefinable feeling, that I had previously seen the whole thing before. Yet how could that be? Certainly, I had never been in Liverpool before: but then, that Moorish arch! surely I remembered that very well. It was not till several months after reaching home in America, that my perplexity upon this matter was cleared away. In glancing over an old number of the Penny Magazine, there I saw a picture of the place to the life; and remembered having seen the same print years previous. It was a representation of the spot where the Manchester railroad enters the outskirts of the town.

[Chapter 42: A visit to the Lyceum. The Lyceum – the building still stands at the bottom of Bold Street – had been founded in 1802 as a gentleman's club. *The Picture of Liverpool* describes its coffee room, where newspapers can be read, and its 'very handsome circular library' (p. 150).]

I was strolling down Bold-street, I think it was, when I was struck by the sight of a brown stone building, very large and handsome. The windows were open, and there, nicely seated, with their comfortable legs crossed over their comfortable knees, I beheld several sedate, happy-looking old gentlemen reading the magazines and papers, and one had a fine gilded volume in his hand.
    Yes, this must be the Lyceum, thought I; let me see. So I whipped out my guide-book, and opened it at the proper place; and sure enough, the building before me corresponded stone for stone. I stood awhile on the opposite side of the street, gazing at

my picture, and then at its original; and often dwelling upon the pleasant gentlemen sitting at the open windows; till at last I felt an uncontrollable impulse to step in for a moment, and run over the news.

I'm a poor, friendless sailor-boy, thought I, and they can not object; especially as I am from a foreign land, and strangers ought to be treated with courtesy. I turned the matter over again, as I walked across the way; and with just a small tapping of a misgiving at my heart, I at last scraped my feet clean against the curb-stone, and taking off my hat while I was yet in the open air, slowly sauntered in.

But I had not got far into that large and lofty room, filled with many agreeable sights, when a crabbed old gentleman lifted up his eye from the *London Times*, which words I saw boldly printed on the back of the large sheet in his hand, and looking at me as if I were a strange dog with a muddy hide, that had stolen out of the gutter into this fine apartment, he shook his silver-headed cane at me fiercely, till the spectacles fell off his nose. Almost at the same moment, up stepped a terribly cross man, who looked as if he had a mustard plaster on his back, that was continually exasperating him; who throwing down some papers which he had been filing, took me by my innocent shoulders, and then, putting his foot against the broad part of my pantaloons, wheeled me right out into the street, and dropped me on the walk, without so much as offering an apology for the affront. I sprang after him, but in vain; the door was closed upon me.

These Englishmen have no manners, that's plain, thought I; and I trudged on down the street in a reverie.

After his sightseeing Redburn falls in with one Harry Bolton who takes him to London by train and initiates him into the mysteries of a gambling house. They return to Liverpool to find that the *Highlander* is about to sail with a cargo of emigrants. They both embark and Redburn returns to New York.

Herman Melville, *Redburn: His First Voyage. Being the Sailor-boy Confessions and Reminiscences of the Son-of-a-Gentleman in the Merchant Service* (1849).

5

Nathaniel Hawthorne, American Consul

THE NOVELIST AND SHORT STORY WRITER **Nathaniel Hawthorne** (1804–64) wrote a biography of his college friend Franklin Pierce in 1852. After his election Pierce offered Hawthorne the consulship at Liverpool which, though reluctant at first, he accepted. In July of the following year he sailed with his family on the Cunard liner *Niagara* to take up the post and he served as Consul until October 1857. Far from being a career politician, Hawthorne saw his consulship as an opportunity to observe an endless panorama of supplicants coming to his office, visitors whom he describes as the 'vagabond discontents' of many nations. His sketches in *Our Old Home* can thus be read as extended meditations on the respective characteristics of Britain and the USA. Distanced from America, he became unusually alert to his compatriots' urge to travel and also to what he called the 'peculiar insanity' of claiming to be the rightful heir of an English estate, the sort of fantastic conviction that Mark Twain described in *The American Claimant*. One woman, for instance, came to see him carrying documentary 'proof' that she really owned the entire business district of Liverpool. The one recurring mercantile issue concerned the problematic relations between American seamen and their officers, which Hawthorne regarded as such an important matter that he wrote to the State Department about it. Summing up the city, Hawthorne concluded: 'Liverpool, though not very delightful as a place of residence, is a most convenient and admirable point to get away from.' The American consulate at the time was located in the Washington Building off Brunswick Street. Hawthorne later assembled a series of sketches of his years in England, published as *Our Old Home* in 1863. The other sources for our information about his period in Liverpool are his English notebooks and two memoirs by his son Julian.

Consular Experiences

The Consulate of the United States, in my day, was located
in Washington Buildings (a shabby and smoke-stained edifice
of four stories high, thus illustriously named in honour of our
national establishment), at the lower corner of Brunswick Street,
contiguous to the Goree Arcade, and in the neighbourhood of
some of the oldest docks. This was by no means a polite or
elegant portion of England's great commercial city, nor were the
apartments of the American official so splendid as to indicate
the assumption of much consular pomp on his part. A narrow
and ill-lighted staircase gave access to an equally narrow and
ill-lighted passageway on the first floor, at the extremity of
which, surmounting a door-frame, appeared an exceedingly stiff
pictorial representation of the Goose and Gridiron, according
to the English idea of those ever-to-be-honoured symbols. The
staircase and passageway were often thronged, of a morning,
with a set of beggarly and piratical-looking scoundrels (I do
no wrong to our own countrymen in styling them so, for not
one in twenty was a genuine American), purporting to belong
to our mercantile marine, and chiefly composed of Liverpool
Blackballers and the scum of every maritime nation on earth;
such being the seamen by whose assistance we then disputed the
navigation of the world with England. These specimens of a most
unfortunate class of people were shipwrecked crews in quest of
bed, board, and clothing, invalids asking permits for the hospital,
bruised and bloody wretches complaining of ill-treatment by
their officers, drunkards, desperadoes, vagabonds, and cheats,
perplexingly intermingled with an uncertain proportion of
reasonably honest men. All of them (save here and there a poor
devil of a kidnapped landsman in his shore-going rags) wore red
flannel shirts, in which they had sweltered or shivered throughout
the voyage, and all required consular assistance in one form or
another.

Any respectable visitor, if he could make up his mind to elbow
a passage among these sea-monsters, was admitted into an outer
office, where he found more of the same species, explaining their
respective wants or grievances to the Vice-Consul and clerks,
while their shipmates awaited their turn outside the door. Passing
through this exterior court, the stranger was ushered into an inner
privacy, where sat the Consul himself, ready to give personal
attention to such peculiarly difficult and more important cases as

might demand the exercise of (what we will courteously suppose
to be) his own higher judicial or administrative sagacity.

It was an apartment of very moderate size, painted in imitation
of oak, and duskily lighted by two windows looking across a by-
street at the rough brick-side of an immense cotton warehouse,
a plainer and uglier structure than ever was built in America.
On the walls of the room hung a large map of the United States
(as they were, twenty years ago, but seem little likely to be,
twenty years hence), and a similar one of Great Britain, with
its territory so provokingly compact, that we may expect it to
sink sooner than sunder. Farther adornments were some rude
engravings of our naval victories in the War of 1812, together
with the Tennessee State House, and a Hudson River steamer, and
a coloured, life-size lithograph of General Taylor, with an honest
hideousness of aspect, occupying the place of honour above the
mantel-piece. On the top of a bookcase stood a fierce and terrible
bust of General Jackson, pilloried in a military collar which rose
above his ears, and frowning forth immitigably at any Englishman
who might happen to cross the threshold. I am afraid, however,
that the truculence of the old General's expression was utterly
thrown away on this stolid and obdurate race of men; for, when
they occasionally inquired whom this work of art represented,
I was mortified to find that the younger ones had never heard
of the battle of New Orleans, and that their elders had either
forgotten it altogether, or contrived to misremember, and twist it
wrong end foremost into something like an English victory. They
have caught from the old Romans (whom they resemble in so
many other characteristics) this excellent method of keeping the
national glory intact by sweeping all defeats and humiliations clean
out of their memory. Nevertheless, my patriotism forbade me to
take down either the bust, or the pictures, both because it seemed
no more than right that an American Consulate (being a little
patch of our nationality imbedded into the soil and institutions
of England) should fairly represent the American taste in the fine
arts, and because these decorations reminded me so delightfully of
an old-fashioned American barber's shop.
[...]

Sitting, as it were, in the gateway between the Old World and
the New, where the steamers and packets landed the greater part
of our wandering countrymen, and received them again when
their wanderings were done, I saw that no people on earth have
such vagabond habits as ourselves. The Continental races never

travel at all if they can help it; nor does an Englishman ever think of stirring abroad, unless he has the money to spare, or proposes to himself some definite advantage from the journey; but it seemed to me that nothing was more common than for a young American deliberately to spend all his resources in an aesthetic peregrination about Europe, returning with pockets nearly empty to begin the world in earnest. It happened, indeed, much oftener than was at all agreeable to myself, that their funds held out just long enough to bring them to the door of my Consulate, where they entered as if with an undeniable right to its shelter and protection, and required at my hands to be sent home again. In my first simplicity,—finding them gentlemanly in manners, passably educated, and only tempted a little beyond their means by a laudable desire of improving and refining themselves, or, perhaps for the sake of getting better artistic instruction in music, painting, or sculpture than our country could supply,—I sometimes took charge of them on my private responsibility, since our government gives itself no trouble about its stray children, except the seafaring class. But, after a few such experiments, discovering that none of these estimable and ingenuous young men, however trustworthy they might appear, ever dreamed of reimbursing the Consul, I deemed it expedient to take another course with them. Applying myself to some friendly shipmaster, I engaged homeward passages on their behalf, with the understanding that they were to make themselves serviceable on shipboard; and I remember several very pathetic appeals from painters and musicians, touching the damage which their artistic fingers were likely to incur from handling the ropes. But my observation of so many heavier troubles left me very little tenderness for their finger-ends. In time I grew to be reasonably hard-hearted, though it never was quite possible to leave a countryman with no shelter save an English poorhouse, when, as he invariably averred, he had only to set foot on his native soil to be possessed of ample funds. It was my ultimate conclusion, however, that American ingenuity may be pretty safely left to itself, and that, one way or another, a Yankee vagabond is certain to turn up at his own threshold, if he has any, without help of a Consul, and perhaps be taught a lesson of foresight that may profit him hereafter.

Hawthorne devoted one of his sketches to the social conditions of Liverpool, coyly leaving the city unnamed. Here he summarized his views of street life, the result of many walks around the city, and a visit to an alms-house.

This sketch together with 'Consular Experiences' gave Hawthorne an opportunity to indulge his Dickensian fascination with vivid, grotesquely detailed urban spectacles.

Outside Glimpses of English Poverty
[Dirt and gin-shops.]

Dirt, one would fancy, is plenty enough all over the world, being the symbolic accompaniment of the foul incrustation which began to settle over and bedim all earthly things as soon as Eve had bitten the apple; ever since which hapless epoch, her daughters have chiefly been engaged in a desperate and unavailing struggle to get rid of it. But the dirt of a poverty-stricken English street is a monstrosity unknown on our side of the Atlantic. It reigns supreme within its own limits, and is inconceivable everywhere beyond them. We enjoy the great advantage, that the brightness and dryness of our atmosphere keep everything clean that the sun shines upon, converting the larger portion of our impurities into transitory dust which the next wind can sweep away, in contrast with the damp, adhesive grime that incorporates itself with all surfaces (unless continually and painfully cleansed) in the chill moisture of the English air. Then the all-pervading smoke of the city, abundantly intermingled with the sable snow-flakes of bituminous coal, hovering overhead, descending, and alighting on pavements and rich architectural fronts, on the snowy muslin of the ladies, and the gentlemen's starched collars and shirt-bosoms, invests even the better streets in a half-mourning garb. It is beyond the resources of Wealth to keep the smut away from its premises or its own fingers' ends; and as for Poverty, it surrenders itself to the dark influence without a struggle. Along with disastrous circumstances, pinching need, adversity so lengthened out as to constitute the rule of life, there comes a certain chill depression of the spirits which seems especially to shudder at cold water. In view of so wretched a state of things, we accept the ancient Deluge not merely as an insulated phenomenon, but as a periodical necessity, and acknowledge that nothing less than such a general washing-day could suffice to cleanse the slovenly old world of its moral and material dirt.

Gin-shops, or what the English call spirit-vaults, are numerous in the vicinity of these poor streets, and are set off with the magnificence of gilded door-posts, tarnished by contact with the unclean customers who haunt there. Ragged children come thither with old shaving-mugs, or broken-nosed teapots, or any such makeshift receptacle, to get a little poison or madness for their parents, who deserve no better requital at their hands for having engendered them. Inconceivably sluttish women enter at noonday and stand at the counter among boon-companions of both sexes, stirring up misery and jollity in a bumper together, and quaffing off the mixture with a relish. As for the men, they lounge there continually, drinking till they are drunken,—drinking as long as they have a half-penny left, and then, as it seemed to me, waiting for a sixpenny miracle to be wrought in their pockets so as to enable them to be drunken again. Most of these establishments have a significant advertisement of 'Beds,' doubtless for the accommodation of their customers in the interval between one intoxication and the next. I never could find it in my heart, however, utterly to condemn these sad revellers, and should certainly wait till I had some better consolation to offer before depriving them of their dram of gin, though death itself were in the glass; for methought their poor souls needed such fiery stimulant to lift them a little way out of the smothering squalor of both their outward and interior life, giving them glimpses and suggestions, even if bewildering ones, of a spiritual existence that limited their present misery. The temperance-reformers unquestionably derive their commission from the Divine Beneficence, but have never been taken fully into its counsels. All may not be lost, though those good men fail.

[A beggar.]

On the other hand, there were some mendicants whose utmost efforts I even now felicitate myself on having withstood. Such was a phenomenon abridged of his lower half, who beset me for two or three years together, and, in spite of his deficiency of locomotive members, had some supernatural method of transporting himself (simultaneously, I believe) to all quarters of the city. He wore a sailor's jacket (possibly, because skirts would have been a superfluity to his figure), and had a remarkably broad-shouldered and muscular frame, surmounted by a large, fresh-coloured face, which was full of power and intelligence. His dress and linen were the perfection of neatness. Once a day, at least, wherever I went, I suddenly became aware of this trunk

of a man on the path before me, resting on his base, and looking
as if he had just sprouted out of the pavement, and would sink
into it again and reappear at some other spot the instant you left
him behind. The expression of his eye was perfectly respectful,
but terribly fixed, holding your own as by fascination, never
once winking, never wavering from its point-blank gaze right
into your face, till you were completely beyond the range of
his battery of one immense rifled cannon. This was his mode
of soliciting alms; and he reminded me of the old beggar who
appealed so touchingly to the charitable sympathies of Gil Blas
[hero of eighteenth-century French picaresque narrative], taking
aim at him from the roadside with a long-barrelled musket.
The intentness and directness of his silent appeal, his close and
unrelenting attack upon your individuality, respectful as it seemed,
was the very flower of insolence; or, if you give it a possibly truer
interpretation, it was the tyrannical effort of a man endowed with
great natural force of character to constrain your reluctant will
to his purpose. Apparently, he had staked his salvation upon the
ultimate success of a daily struggle between himself and me, the
triumph of which would compel me to become a tributary to the
hat that lay on the pavement beside him. Man or fiend, however,
there was a stubbornness in his intended victim which this massive
fragment of a mighty personality had not altogether reckoned
upon, and by its aid I was enabled to pass him at my customary
pace hundreds of times over, quietly meeting his terribly respectful
eye, and allowing him the fair chance which I felt to be his due,
to subjugate me, if he really had the strength for it. He never
succeeded, but, on the other hand, never gave up the contest;
and should I ever walk those streets again, I am certain that the
truncated tyrant will sprout up through the pavement and look
me fixedly in the eye, and perhaps get the victory.

[Visit to West Derby Union Workhouse, Mill Road in February 1856. An
inspection in 1866 described it as 'wholly insufficient for the wants of the
[West Derby Poor Law] union'.]

After making myself as familiar as I decently could with the poor
streets, I became curious to see what kind of a home was provided
for the inhabitants at the public expense, fearing that it must needs
be a most comfortless one, or else their choice (if choice it were)
of so miserable a life outside was truly difficult to account for.
Accordingly, I visited a great almshouse, and was glad to observe

how unexceptionably all the parts of the establishment were
carried on, and what an orderly life, full-fed, sufficiently reposeful,
and undisturbed by the arbitrary exercise of authority, seemed to
be led there. Possibly, indeed, it was that very orderliness, and
the cruel necessity of being neat and clean, and even the comfort
resulting from these and other Christian-like restraints and
regulations, that constituted the principal grievance on the part of
the poor, shiftless inmates, accustomed to a lifelong luxury of dirt
and harum-scarumness. The wild life of the streets has perhaps
as unforgettable a charm, to those who have once thoroughly
imbibed it, as the life of the forest or the prairie. But I conceive
rather that there must be insuperable difficulties, for the majority
of the poor, in the way of getting admittance to the almshouse,
than that a merely aesthetic preference for the street would incline
the pauper-class to fare scantily and precariously, and expose their
raggedness to the rain and snow, when such a hospitable door
stood wide open for their entrance. It might be that the roughest
and darkest side of the matter was not shown me, there being
persons of eminent station and of both sexes in the party which I
accompanied; and, of course, a properly trained public functionary
would have deemed it a monstrous rudeness, as well as a great
shame, to exhibit anything to people of rank that might too
painfully shock their sensibilities.

The women's ward was the portion of the establishment which
we especially examined. It could not be questioned that they
were treated with kindness as well as care. No doubt, as has been
already suggested, some of them felt the irksomeness of submission
to general rules of orderly behaviour, after being accustomed to
that perfect freedom from the minor proprieties, at least, which
is one of the compensations of absolutely hopeless poverty, or
of any circumstances that set us fairly below the decencies of
life. I asked the governor of the house whether he met with
any difficulty in keeping peace and order among his inmates;
and he informed me that his troubles among the women were
incomparably greater than with the men. They were freakish, and
apt to be quarrelsome, inclined to plague and pester one another
in ways that it was impossible to lay hold of, and to thwart his
own authority by the like intangible methods. He said this with
the utmost good-nature, and quite won my regard by so placidly
resigning himself to the inevitable necessity of letting the women
throw dust into his eyes. They certainly looked peaceable and
sisterly enough, as I saw them, though still it might be faintly

perceptible that some of them were consciously playing their parts
before the governor and his distinguished visitors.

All the children in this ward seemed to be invalids, and,
going up stairs, we found more of them in the same or a worse
condition than the little creature just described, with their mothers
(or more probably other women, for the infants were mostly
foundlings) in attendance as nurses. The matron of the ward, a
middle-aged woman, remarkably kind and motherly in aspect, was
walking to and fro across the chamber—on that weary journey
in which careful mothers and nurses travel so continually and so
far, and gain never a step of progress—with an unquiet baby in
her arms. She assured us that she enjoyed her occupation, being
exceedingly fond of children; and, in fact, the absence of timidity
in all the little people was a sufficient proof that they could have
had no experience of harsh treatment, though, on the other
hand, none of them appeared to be attracted to one individual
more than another. In this point they differed widely from the
poor child below stairs. They seemed to recognize a universal
motherhood in womankind, and cared not which individual
might be the mother of the moment. I found their tameness as
shocking as did Alexander Selkirk that of the brute subjects of his
else solitary kingdom. It was a sort of tame familiarity, a perfect
indifference to the approach of strangers, such as I never noticed
in other children. I accounted for it partly by their nerveless,
unstrung state of body, incapable of the quick thrills of delight
and fear which play upon the lively harp-strings of a healthy
child's nature, and partly by their woeful lack of acquaintance
with a private home, and their being therefore destitute of the
sweet home-bred shyness, which is like the sanctity of heaven
about a mother-petted child. Their condition was like that of
chickens hatched in an oven, and growing up without the especial
guardianship of a matron hen: both the chicken and the child,
methinks, must needs want something that is essential to their
respective characters.

Nathaniel Hawthorne, *Our Old Home: A Series of English Sketches* (1863).

While in Liverpool Hawthorne kept detailed accounts in his notebooks
of sights that had particularly impressed him – not always for the better.
These descriptions tended to be more frank than those he had prepared
for publication.

[8 August 1853: Mersey Ferry.]

Day before yesterday, I escorted my family to Rock Ferry, two miles either up or down the Mersey (and I really don't know which) by steamer, which runs every half-hour. There are other steamers going continually to Birkenhead and other landings and almost always a great many passengers on the transit. On this occasion the boat was crowded so as to afford scanty standing room; it being Saturday, and therefore a kind of gala-day. I think I have never seen a populace before coming to England; but this crowd afforded a specimen of one, both male and female. The women were the most remarkable; there is almost always something ladylike and delicate about an American woman; but in these, though they seemed not disreputable, there was a coarseness, a freedom, an—I don't know what—that was purely English. In fact, men and women do things that would at least make them ridiculous in America; they are not afraid to enjoy themselves in their own way, and have no pseudo gentility to support. Some girls danced upon the crowded deck, to the miserable music of a little fragment of a band, which goes up and down the river on each trip of the boat. Just before the termination of the voyage, a man goes round with a bugle turned wide and upward, to receive the half eleemosynary pence and half-pence of the passengers. I gave one of them, the other day, a silver four-pence; which fell into the vitals of the instrument, and compelled the man to take it to pieces. At Rock Ferry, there was a great throng, forming a scene not unlike one of our muster-days or Fourth of July; and there were bands of music, and banners, with small processions after them; and there [was] a school of charity-children, I believe, enjoying a festival; and there was a club of respectable persons playing at bowls on the bowling-green of the hotel; and there were children infants riding on donkeys, at a penny a ride, while their mothers walked alongside, to prevent a fall.

[Dinner with Mayor. In 1853 Hawthorne was invited to participate in the dinner given to the judges and grand jury during the assizes. He was very impressed by the unique status given to the judges.]

The dinner was at the Town-Hall; and the rooms, and the whole affair, were all in the most splendid style. Nothing struck me more than the footmen in the city-livery; they really looked more magnificent, in their gold-lace, and breeches, and white silk

stockings, than any officers of state whom I have ever seen. The
rooms were beautiful; gorgeously painted and gilded, gorgeously
lighted, gorgeously hung with paintings, gorgeously illuminated—
the plate gorgeous, the dinner gorgeous, in the English fashion.
As to the company, they had a kind of roughness, that seems to
be the characteristic of all Englishmen so far as I have yet seen
them;—elderly John Bulls—and there is hardly a less beautiful
object than the elderly John Bull, with his large body, protruding
paunch, short legs, and mottled, double-chinned, irregular-featured
aspect. They are men of the world, at home in society, easy in
their manners, but without refinement; nor are they especially
what one thinks of, under the appellation of gentleman.

     After the removal of the cloth, the Mayor gave various toasts,
prefacing each with some remarks—the first of course, the
Sovereign, after which 'God Save the Queen' was sung; and there
was something rather ludicrous in seeing the company stand up
and join in the chorus, their ample faces glowing with wine,
enthusiasm, perspiration, and loyalty. There certainly is a vein of
the ridiculous running through these people; nor does it take away
from their respectability. Afterwards the Bar, and various other
dignities and institutions were toasted; and by-and-by came a toast
to the United States and me as their representative. Hereupon,
either 'Hail Columbia' or 'Yankee Doodle,' or some other of our
national tunes (but Heaven knows which) was played; and at the
conclusion—being cornered, and with no alternative—I got upon
my legs and made a response. They received me and listened to
my nonsense with a good deal of rapping; and my speech seemed
to give great satisfaction. My chief difficulty lay in not knowing
how to pitch my voice to the size of the room; as for the matter,
it is not of the slightest consequence. Any body may make an
after-dinner speech, who will be content to talk onward without
saying anything. My speech was not more than two or three
inches long;—and considering that I did not know a soul there,
except the Mayor himself, and that I am wholly unpractised in
all sorts of oratory, and that I had nothing to say, it was quite
successful. I hardly thought it was in me; but being once on my
legs, I felt no embarrassment, and went through it as coolly as if I
were going to be hanged.

[Hawthorne's favourite leisure activity in Liverpool was strolling round
the city. The following street scenes of 1853 are typical, and also convey
Hawthorne's uneasy mixture of fascination and fear on these walks.]

Almost every day, I take walks about Liverpool; preferring the
darker and dingier streets, inhabited by the poorer classes. The
scenes there are very picturesque in their way; at every two or
three steps, a gin-shop; also filthy in clothes and person, ragged,
pale, often afflicted with humours; women, nursing their babies
at dirty bosoms; men haggard, drunken, care-worn, hopeless, but
with a kind of patience, as if all this were the rule of their life;
groups stand or sit talking together, around the door-steps, or in
the descent of a cellar; often a quarrel is going on in one group,
for which the next group cares little or nothing. Sometimes, a
decent woman may be seen sewing or knitting at the entrance
of her poor dwelling, a glance into which shows dismal poverty.
I never walk through these streets without feeling as if I should
catch some disease; but yet there is a strong interest in such walks;
and moreover there is a bustle, a sense of being in the midst of
life, and of having got hold of something real, which I do not
find in the better streets of the city. Doubtless, this noon-day and
open life of theirs is entirely the best aspect of their existence; and
if I were to see them within doors, at their meals, or in bed, it
would be unspeakably worse. They appear to wash their clothes
occasionally; for I have seen them hanging out to dry in the
street.

[The Liverpool Necropolis was founded in 1825 as Liverpool's first custom-
built non-denominational cemetery. It was located at Low Hill, Everton
(also known as Low Hill General Cemetery) and covered some four acres.
The Necropolis closed down in 1898, to be replaced by a public garden.
Hawthorne visited the cemetery in 1853 for the burial of a sailor from his
lodgings.]

The Necropolis is quite a handsome burial-place, shut in by high
walls, so overrun with shrubbery that no part of the brick or
stone is visible. Part of the space within is an ornamental garden,
with flowers and green turf; the rest is strewn with flat grave-
stones, and a few raised monuments; and straight avenues run
to-and-fro between. Captain Auld's grave was dug nine-feet deep;
it is his own for twelve months; but if his friends do not choose
to give him a stone, it will become a common grave at the end
of that time; and four or five more people may then be piled
upon him. Everybody seemed greatly to admire this grave; the
undertaker praised it, and also the dryness of its site, which he
took credit to himself for having chosen; the grave-digger, too,

was very proud of its depth and the neatness of his handiwork. The clergyman (who had marched in advance of us from the chapel) now took his stand at the head of the grave, and lifting his hat, proceeded with what remained of the service, while we stood bare-headed around. When he came to a particular part ('ashes to ashes, dust to dust,' I think) the undertaker lifted a handful of earth, and threw it rattling on the coffin; so did the landlady's son, and so did I.

After the funeral, the undertaker's friend (an elderly, coarse-looking man) looked around him, and remarked that the grass had never yet grown on the graves of the 'parties' who died in the cholera-year; but at this the undertaker laughed in scorn.

As we returned to the gate of the cemetery, the Sexton met us, and pointed to a small office, on entering which, we found the clergyman, who was waiting for his burial-fees. There was now a dispute between the clergyman and the undertaker; the former wishing to receive the whole amount for the gravestone, which the undertaker of course refused to pay. I explained how the matter stood; on which the clergyman acquiesced, civilly enough; but it was very queer to see the worldly, business-like way in which he entered into this squabble, so soon after burying poor Captain Auld.

[1853: Gala day.]

This (Saturday) being the gala-day of the manufacturing people about Liverpool, the steam boats to Rock Ferry were seasonably crowded with large parties of both sexes. They were accompanied with two numerous bands of music, in uniform; and these bands, before I left the hotel, were playing in competition and rivalry with each other, in the court-yard—loud, martial strains from shining brass-instruments. A prize is to be assigned to one or other of these bands; and I suppose this was a part of the competition. Meanwhile, the merry-making people, who thronged the court-yard, were quaffing coffee from blue earthen-mugs, which they brought with them—as likewise they brought the coffee, and had it made in the hotel.

It had poured with rain about the time of their arrival—notwithstanding which, they did not seem disheartened; for, of course, in this climate, it enters into all their calculations to be soaked through and through. By and by, the sun shone out; and it has continued to shine and shade, every ten minutes, ever since. All these people were decently dressed; the men generally in dark clothes, not so smartly as in America, on a festal day, but so as not to be greatly different as regards dress. They were paler, smaller, less wholesome looking, and less intelligent, and, I think, less noisy, than so many Yankees would have been. The women and girls differed much more from what our girls and women would be, on a pleasure excursion;—being so shabbily dressed, with no kind of smartness, no silks, nothing but cotton gowns, I believe, and ill-looking bonnets—which, however, was the only part of their attire that they seemed to care about guarding from the rain. As to their persons, they generally, I think, looked better developed and healthier than the men; but there was a woeful lack of beauty and grace—not a pretty girl among them—all coarse and vulgar. How different would this be in Yankee-land. Their bodies, it seems to me, are apt to be very lengthy, in proportion to their legs; in truth, this kind of make is rather characteristic of both sexes in England. The speech of these folks, in some instances, was so broad Lancashire that I could not well understand it.

[1853: Elderly beggar on ferry.]

I don't know any place that brings all classes into contiguity, on equal ground, so completely as the waiting-room at Rock Ferry, on these frosty days. The room is not more than eight feet square, with walls of stone, and wooden benches ranged round them; and an open stove in one corner, generally well furnished with coal. It is almost always crowded; and I rather suspect that many persons, who have no fireside elsewhere, creep in here and spend the most comfortable part of their day.

This morning, when I looked into the room, there were one or two gentlemen and other respectable persons, male and female; but in the best place, close to the fire, and crouching almost into it, was an elderly beggar—with the raggedest of overcoats, two great rents on the shoulders, disclosing the dingy lining, all bepatched with various stuff, covered with dirt; and on his shoes and trousers the mud of an interminable pilgrimage. Owing to the posture in which he sat, I could not see his face, but only the battered crown and rim of the very shabbiest hat that ever was. Regardless of the presence of women (which, indeed, Englishmen seldom do regard, when they wish to smoke) he was smoking a pipe of vile tobacco; but, after all, this was fortunate, because the man

himself was not personally fragrant. He was terribly squalid—
terribly—and when I had a glimpse at his face, it well befitted the
rest of his development; grizzled, wrinkled, weather-beaten, yet
sallow, down-looking with a watchful kind of eye, turning upon
everybody and everything, meeting the eyes of other people rather
boldly, yet soon shrinking away; —a long, thin nose, grey beard
of a week's growth, hair not much mixed with grey, but rusty
and lifeless. A miserable object; but it was curious to see how he
was not ashamed of himself, but seemed to feel that he was one
of the estates of the kingdom, and had as much right to live as
other men. He did just as he pleased, took the best place by the
fireside, nor would have cared though a nobleman were forced to
stand aside for him. When the steamer's bell rang, he shouldered
a large and heavy pack, and hobbled down the pier, leaning on
a crook-staff, and looking like a pilgrim with his burden of sin,
but certainly journeying to hell, instead of heaven. On board, he
looked round for the best position, at first stationing himself near
the boiler-pipe, but finding the deck damp under foot, went to
the cabin-door, and took his stand on the stairs, protected from
the wind, but very incommodiously to those who wished to pass.
All this was done without any bravado or forced impudence, but
in the most quiet way, merely because he was seeking his own
comfort, and considered that he had a right to seek it. It was
an Englishman's spirit; but, in our country, I imagine, a beggar
considers himself a kind of outlaw, and would hardly assume the
privileges of a man, in any place of public resort. Here, beggary is
a system, and beggars are a numerous class, and make themselves,
in a certain way, respected as such. Nobody evinced the slightest
disapprobation of this man's proceedings. In America, I think, we
should have seen many aristocratic airs, on such provocation; and
probably the ferry-people would have rudely thrust the beggar-
man aside;—giving him a shilling, however-which no Englishman
would ever think of doing. There would also have been a great
deal of fun made of this squalid and ragged figure; whereas,
nobody smiled at him, this morning, nor in any way evinced the
slightest disrespect. This is good; but it is the result of a state of
things by no means good.

[1854: Vagabond musicians.]

The vagabond musicians about town are very numerous and
miscellaneous. On board the steam-ferry boats, I think I have

heretofore spoken of them; they infest them from May to
November, for very little gain, apparently. A shilling a day, per
man, must be the extent of their emolument. It is rather sad to
see somewhat respectable looking old men engaged in this way,
with two or three younger associates. Their instruments look
terribly the worse for wear, and even my unmusical ear can
distinguish more discord than harmony. They appear to be a very
quiet and harmless people. Sometimes there is a woman playing
on a fiddle, with her husband playing a wind-instrument. There
is an old blind fiddler, too. The greatest nuisance on board of
these boats is a boy, playing an accordion. In the streets, it is
not unusual to find a band of half a dozen performers, or more,
who, without any provocation or reason whatever, sound their
brazen instruments, till the houses re-echo. Sometimes, one passes
a man who stands whistling a tune, most unweariably, though I
never saw anybody give him anything. Then there are the Italian
organ-grinders. The ballad-singers are the strangest, from the total
lack of any kind of music in their cracked voices. Sometimes,
you see a space cleared in the street, and a foreigner playing some
instrument, while a girl—weatherbeaten, tanned, freckled, and
wholly uncomely in face, and shabby in attire, dances some such
dances as you may have seen on the stage. The common people
look on, and never seem to criticize, or to treat any of these poor
devils unkindly or uncivilly; but I do not observe that they give
them anything.

[The Liverpool Zoological Gardens were founded in 1833 by Thomas
Atkins, the owner of a travelling menagerie, who bought disused clay-pits
and transformed them into a zoo housing elephants, bears, a rhinoceros,
and many other animals. When Hawthorne visited the Gardens with his
son in 1854, he noted the sheer range of exhibits and took advantage of the
photographer's booth to have a portrait taken of Julian. A daguerrotypist
plays a key role in Hawthorne's 1851 novel *The House of the Seven
Gables*.]

Visiting the Zoological gardens, the other day, with Julian, it
occurred to me what a fantastic kind of life a person connected
with them might be depicted as leading,—a child, for instance.
The grounds are very extensive, and include arrangements for
all kinds of exhibitions, calculated to attract the idle people of
a great city. In one enclosure a bear, who climbs a pole to get
cake and gingerbread from the spectators. Elsewhere, a circular

building, with compartments for lions, wolves, tigers, etc. In
another part of the garden, a colony of monkeys; the skeleton of
an elephant; birds, of all kinds. Swans, and various rare waterfowl,
swimming on a piece of water—which was green, by the by; and
when the fowls dived, they stirred up black mud. A stork was
parading along the margin, with melancholy strides of its long
legs, and came slowly towards us, as if for companionship. In one
apartment, was an obstreperously noisy society of parrots, macaws,
etc, most gorgeous and diversified of hue. These different colonies
of birds and beasts were scattered about in various parts of the
grounds; so that you came upon them unexpectedly. Also, there
was an archery-ground, a shooting ground, a swing, and other
such things. Also, a theatre, at which a rehearsal was going on—
we standing at one of the exterior doors, and looking towards the
dusky stage, where the company, in their ordinary dress, were
rehearsing something that had a good deal of dance and action
in it. In the open air, too, there was an arrangement of painted
scenery, representing a wide expanse of mountains, with a city
at their feet, and before it the sea, with actual water, and large
vessels upon it—the vessels having only the side that would be
presented towards the spectator; but the scenery was so good that,
at first casual glance, I almost mistook it for reality. There was
refreshment-room, with drinks, and cake and pastry, but, so far
as I saw no substantial victual. About in the centre of the garden,
there seemed be an actual, homely looking, small dwelling-house
or cottage, where perhaps the overlookers of the concern live.
Now, this might be wrought, in imaginative description, into a
pleasant sort of a fool's paradise, where sorts of unreal delights
should seem to cluster round some suitable personage; and it
would relieve, in a very odd and effective way, the stern realities
of life on the outside of the garden walls. I saw a little girl, simply
dressed, who seemed to have her habitat within the garden. There
was also a daguerreotypist, with his wife and family, carrying
on his business in a little shed or shanty, and perhaps having his
home in its inner-room. He seemed to be an honest, intelligent,
pleasant young man, and his wife a pleasant woman; and I got
Julian's daguerreotype, for three shillings, in a little brass frame.
In the description of the garden, the velvet-turf, of a charming
verdure, and the shrubbery, and shadowy walks under large trees,
and the slopes and inequalities of ground, must not be forgotten.
In one place, there was a maze and labyrinth, where perhaps a
person might wander a long while in vain endeavour to get out;

although, all the time, looking at the exterior garden over the low hedges that border the walks of the maze. And this is like the inappreciable difficulties that often beset us in life.

[26 September 1854: Town Hall soiree.]

On Saturday evening, my wife and I went to a soiree, given by the Mayor and Mrs. Lloyd at the Town Hall. It was quite brilliant; the public rooms being really magnificent; and adorned for the occasion with a large collection of pictures, belonging to Mr Naylor. They were mostly (I believe entirely) of modern artists, comprising some of Turner, Wilkie, Landseer, and others of the best English painters. Turner's seemed too airy to have been done by mortal hands.

The British scientific association being now in session here, many distinguished strangers were present. What chiefly struck me, however, was the lack of beauty in the women, and the horrible ugliness of not a few of them. I have heard a good deal of the tenacity with [which] English women retain their personal charms to a late period of life; but my experience is, that an English lady of forty or fifty is apt to become the most hideous animal that ever pretended to human shape. No caricature could do justice to some of their figures and features; so puffed out, so huge, so without limit, with such hanging dewlaps, and all manner of fleshly abomination—dressed, too, in a way to show all these points to the worst advantage, and walking about with entire self-satisfaction, unconscious of the wrong they are doing to one's idea of womanhood. They are gross, gross, gross. Who would not shrink from such a mother! Who would not abhor such a wife? I really pitied the respectable elderly gentlemen whom I saw walking about with such atrocities hanging on their arms— the grim, red-faced monsters! Surely, a man would be justified in murdering them—in taking a sharp knife and cutting away their mountainous flesh, until he had brought them into reasonable shape, as a sculptor seeks for the beautiful form of woman in a shapeless block of marble. The husband must feel that something alien has grown over and incrusted the slender creature whom he married, and that he is horribly wronged by having all this flabby flesh imposed upon him as his wife. 'Flesh of his flesh,' indeed! And this ugliness surely need not be, at least to such a dreadful extent; it must be, in great part, the penalty of a life of gross feeding—of much ale-guzzling and beef-eating. Nor is it possible to conceive of any delicacy and grace of soul existing within; or if there be such, the creature ought to be killed, in order to release the spirit so vilely imprisoned.

I really and truly believe that the entire body of American washerwomen would present more grace than the entire body of English ladies, were both to be shown up together. American women, of all ranks, when past their prime, generally look thin, worn, care-begone, as if they may have led a life of much trouble and few enjoyments; but English women look as if they had fed upon the fat of meat, and made themselves gross and earthy in all sorts of ways. As a point of taste, I prefer my own countrywomen; though it is a pity that we must choose between a greasy animal and an anxious skeleton.

[The Mersey Iron Foundry was founded by John Cragg and was located initially in Tithebarn Street. Hawthorne visited it in 1856.]

After lunch, we all got into an omnibus and went to the Mersey Iron Foundry, to see the biggest piece of ordnance in the world, which is there almost finished. The overseer of the works received us, and escorted us courteously throughout the establishment, which is very extensive, giving employment to a thousand men, what with night-work and day-work. The big gun is still on the axle, or turning-machine, by means of which it has been bored out. It is made entirely of wrought and welded iron, fifty tons of which were originally used; and the gun, in its present state, bored out and smoothed away, weighs nearly twenty-three tons. It has as yet no trunnions, and does not look much like a cannon, but only a huge iron cylinder, immensely solid, and with a bore so large that a young man of nineteen shoves himself into it, the whole length, with a light, in order to see whether it is duly smooth and regular. I suppose it will have a better effect, as to the impression of size, when it is finished, polished, mounted, and fully equipped, after the fashion of ordinary cannon. It is to throw a ball of three hundred pounds weight, five miles; and woe be to whatever ship or battlement shall bear the brunt.

After inspecting the gun, we went through other portions of the establishment, and saw iron in various stages of manufacture. I am not usually interested in manufacturing processes, being quite unable to understand them, at least in cotton-machinery, or the like; but here there were such exhibitions of mighty strength, both of men and machines, that I had a satisfaction in looking on. We

saw lumps of iron, intensely white hot, and all but in a melting
state, passed through rollers of various size and pressure, and
speedily converted into long bars, which came curling and waving
out of the rollers, like great red ribbons, or like fiery serpents
wriggling out of Tophet; and finally, straightened out, they were
laid to cool in heaps. Trip-hammers are very pleasant objects to
look at, working so massively as they do, and yet so accurately,
chewing up, as it were, the hot iron, and fashioning it into shape,
with a sort of mighty and gigantic gentleness in their mode of
action. What great things man has contrived, and is continually
performing! What a noble brute he is!

Also, I found much delight in looking at the molten iron,
boiling and bubbling in the furnace, and sometimes slopping over
when stirred by the attendant. There were numberless fires on
all sides, blinding us with their intense glow; and continually the
pounding strokes of huge hammers, some wielded by machinery,
others by human arms. I had a respect for these stalwart workmen,
who seemed to be near kindred of the machines amid which they
wrought—mighty men, sure enough, smiting stoutly, and looking
at the fierce eyes of the furnace fearlessly, and handing the iron
when it would have taken the skin off from ordinary fingers.
They looked strong, indeed, but pale; for the hot atmosphere, in
which they live, cannot but be deleterious, and I suppose their
very strength wears them quickly out. But I would rather live ten
years as an iron-smith than fifty as a tailor.

[1857: Foundation of the city library.]

In a little while, we formed ourselves into a procession, four in
a row, and set forth from the Town Hall through James-Street,
Church Street, Lord Street; Lime Street; all the way through a
line of policemen and a throng of people; and the windows were
alive with heads; and I never before was so conscious of a great
mass of humanity, though perhaps I may often have seen as great
a crowd. But a procession is the best point of view from which
to see the crowd that collects together. The day, too, was very
fine, even sunshiny, and the streets dry; a blessing which cannot
be overestimated, for we should have been in a strange pickle
for the banquet, had we been compelled to wade through the
ordinary mud of Liverpool. The procession itself could not have
been a very striking object. In America, it would have had a
hundred picturesque and perhaps ludicrous features; the symbols

of the different trades, banners with strange devices, flower-shows, children, volunteer soldiers, cavalcades, and every suitable and unsuitable contrivance; but we were merely a trail of ordinary-looking individuals, in great coats, and with precautionary umbrellas. The only characteristic or professional costumes, as far as I noticed, was that of the Bishop of Chester, in his flat cap and black silk gown, and that of Sir Henry Smith (the general of the District) in full uniform, with a star and half-a-dozen medals on his breast. Mr. Brown himself, the hero of the day, was the plainest, and simplest man of all; an exceedingly unpretending old gentleman in black, small, withered, white haired, pale, quiet, and respectable. I rather wondered why he chose to be the centre of all this ceremony, for he did not seem either particularly to enjoy it, or to be at all incommoded by it, as a more nervous and susceptible man might.

The site of the projected edifice is on one of the streets bordering on St. George's Hall; and when we came within the enclosure, the corner stone (a large square of red-free stone) was already suspended over its destined place. It had a brass-plate let into it, with an inscription, which perhaps will not be seen again till the present English type has grown as antique as black-letter. Two or three photographs were now taken of the site, the cornerstone, Mr. Brown, the distinguished guests, and the crowd at large; then ensued (or followed, I forget which) a prayer from the Bishop of Chester, and speeches from Mr. Holmes, Mr. Brown, Lord Stanley, Sir John Packington, Sir Henry Smith, and as many others as there was time for [...]

From the scene of the corner-stone, we went to St. George's Hall, where a drawing-room and dressing-room had been prepared for the principal guests [...] Mr. Brown now took me up into the gallery, which by this time was full of ladies; and thence we had a fine view of the noble hall, with the tables laid, in readiness for the banquet. I cannot conceive of anything finer than this hall; it needs nothing but painted windows to make it perfect, and those, I hope, it may have, one day or another.

At two o'clock, or a little after, we sat down to the banquet, which hardly justified that epithet, being only a cold collation, though sufficiently splendid in its way. In truth, it would have been impossible to provide a hot dinner for 900 people, in a place remote from kitchens. The principal table extended lengthwise of the hall; and was a little elevated above the other tables, which stretched across, about twenty in all. Before each guest, besides the bill of fare, was laid a programme of the expected toasts, among which appeared my own name, to be proposed by Mr. Monckton Milnes.

Nathaniel Hawthorne, *The English Notebooks* ed. Randall Stewart (Oxford: Modern Language Association/Oxford University Press, 1941).

Julian Hawthorne (1846–1934), the novelist's only son who subsequently became a writer too, is an important additional source of information on his family's years in Liverpool, combining first-hand impressions with summaries of his parents' views in his two memoirs, *Nathaniel Hawthorne and His Wife* (1884) and *Hawthorne and His Circle* (1903). The following passage describes the family's arrival in Liverpool.

On the 18th of July [1853], or thereabouts, the 'Niagara' came to anchor in the Mersey, and it was a day. Our first resting-place on English soil was at a hotel in one of the lower streets of the city [the Waterloo Hotel], gloomy, muddy, and grimy, but with the charm that belongs to the first experience of a foreign land. The most interesting objects to the children were, however, two or three gigantic turtles, lying half immersed in a large tank in the basement of the hotel; it did not seem credible that such creatures could be made into soup, which we were assured was their destiny. They were very different from the little creatures with variegated carapaces which we used to find in the Concord ditches at home. A few days later we left the hotel, and went to Mrs. Blodget's boarding-house, in Duke Street, unquestionably the most comfortable, reasonable, hospitable, and delightful boarding-house that ever existed before or since; nor has nature been able to afford such another boarding-house keeper as Mrs. Blodget, so kind, so hearty, so generous, so unobtrusive, so friendly, so motherly. Never, certainly, has the present writer consumed so much food (in proportion to his weight and size) or of better quality than it was his good fortune to do during his sojourn beneath this excellent lady's roof. She was stout and rotund of figure, rosy and smiling of countenance, with brown curls on each side of her face, a clean white cap, a black dress, and (for the most part) a white apron. She also wore spectacles. Her cuisine was superb; her servants perfectly disciplined; everything went with the regularity and certainty of the solar system; she loved all her boarders, and they all loved her. Her house was the rallying-point of the better class of American captains who made voyages to Liverpool; and to her care some good friend of Hawthorne recommended him. We stayed there only a month on this first occasion; but afterwards, when Mrs. Hawthorne and her daughters visited Portugal and Madeira, Hawthorne returned to Mrs. Blodget's with his son; and they lived there, in great comfort and plenty, the better part of a year.

[Lunchtimes.]

At one o'clock Hawthorne would sometimes put on his hat and take his son through one or two narrow back-streets to a certain baker's shop, where there was a lunch-counter at which one could stand and eat excellent bread and butter and cheese. Or, if the day were fine, and there were nothing going on at the office, they would go to the museum, or the Zoological Gardens, or to some other place of amusement; or take the ferry-boat and steam over to New Brighton, and stroll about on the beach. The last incident of the official day would be the entrance into the little office of old Mr. Pearce or young Mr. Wilding, with a paper full of coin, the proceeds of the day's labour. The gold and the silver Hawthorne would put in his pocket; but if there were any coppers, he would hand them over to the little boy, who used to wish that copper had been the only current coinage of the realm. Then they would walk home to Duke Street; or, after the final change of residence, go down to the steamboat landing, and get into the 'Bee' or the 'Wasp,' and be steam-paddled over to Rock Ferry, about two miles up the muddy river. On Sundays Mrs. Hawthorne, with the two elder children, would go to the Unitarian Chapel in Renshaw Street, and listen to eloquent sermons from the Rev. W. H. Channing, the American; but Hawthorne himself never attended church, that I remember.

Julian Hawthorne, *Nathaniel Hawthorne and His Wife* (1884).

The Hawthornes stayed briefly at the Waterloo Hotel, then in Mary Blodget's lodging-house in Duke Street before they rented a house in Rock Ferry, from which Hawthorne would commute by ferry. Later still, the family moved out to Southport. At the time of their stay, Rock Park was a prosperous area of Victorian villas within easy reach of the countryside, which was a further advantage for Hawthorne.

[Rock Park.]

Rock Park, as I remember it, was a damp, winding, verdurous
street, protected at each end by a small granite lodge, and studded
throughout its length with stuccoed villas. The villas were
mended-on to each other (as one of the children expressed it) two
and two; they had front yards filled with ornamental shrubbery,
and gardens at the back, an acre or two in extent; they were
fenced in with iron pickets, and there were gates to the driveways,
on which the children swung. Every normal child supposes that
gates are made for no other purpose. The trees were not large,
but there were many of them, and they were thick with leaves.
There was a damp, arboreal smell everywhere, mingled with
the finer perfume of flowers and of the hawthorns and yellow
laburnums. Flowers, especially purple English violets, grew
profusely in the gardens, and gooseberry-bushes, bearing immense
gooseberries such as our climate does not nourish. There were
also armies of garden—snails, handsome gasteropods, which were
of great interest to me; for I was entering, at this period, upon a
passionate pursuit of natural history. For many years I supposed
that the odour of the violets proceeded from snails, and to this
day I always associate snails with violets, or vice versa. Una, Rose,
and I were given each a section of a garden-bed for our own; I
cultivated mine so assiduously that it became quite a deep hole;
but I do not recall that anything ever grew in it. The soil was a
very rich loam, and ceaseless diligence must have been required in
me to keep it barren.
[...]
But it was a good and happy life in Rock Park, and I think
our father and mother enjoyed it almost as much as we children
did. They were meeting people many of whom were delightful
[...] and they were seeing towns and castles and places of historic
and picturesque interest; and my father was earning more money
than ever before, though less than a quarter as much as he would
have earned had not Congress, soon after his accession to office,
cut down the emoluments. This was England; the Old Home, and
the Old World, for the understanding of which they had prepared
themselves all their lives previous. My father once said, 'If
England were all the world, it would still have been worth while
for the Creator to have made it.' The children were radiantly
content with their lot; and it is on record that the little boy once
remarked, 'I don't remember when I came down from heaven;

but I'm glad I happened to tumble into so good a family.' The
same individual, rolling on the floor in excess of mirth over some
childish comicality, panted out, 'Oh, mamma, my ball of jolly is
so big I can't breathe!' The ball of jolly became a household word
for years thereafter. It was well nourished in those days.

Julian Hawthorne, *Hawthorne and His Circle* (1903), Chapter 7.

In October 1855 Hawthorne and Julian moved into Mary Blodget's boarding
house while the rest of the family sailed to Portugal. They were reunited
the following year.

It was observed a little way back that English boarding-houses
were much like other boarding-houses in the civilized world. The
rule is proved by the exception of Mrs. Blodget's establishment.
There never was such another; there never will be; it was unique.
It has vanished from earth long since; but if there were boarding-
houses in paradise, I should certainly expect it to be found again
there. Who was Mrs. Blodget? Save that she was a widow of the
British middle class, I doubt if any one of her boarders knew.
She had once been rich, and had lived at Gibraltar. I have often
meditated with fruitless longing about what manner of man Mr.
Blodget could have been. He must have been, like the Emperor
Titus, the delight of mankind in his day. He was a man, we
must surmise, whose charms and virtues were such that his wife,
having felt the bliss and privilege of knowing and living with
him, registered a vow over his bier that she would devote her
future career to the attempt to make others as happy as he had
made her; that she would serve others as faithfully and generously
as she had served him. It was a lofty and beautiful conception,
for she must have perceived that only in that way could she keep
his blessed spirit near her; that the little heaven she would make
in Duke Street, Liverpool, would attract him from the kindred
heaven above; that he would choose to hover, invisible, above her
plenteous table, inhaling the grateful aromas that arose from it as
from a savoury sacrifice, basking in the smiles and sympathizing
in the satisfaction of the fortunate guests, triumphing in their
recognition of his beloved consort as a queen among women. One
might almost fancy that the steam arising from the portly soup-
tureen assumed as it arose something suggesting a human form;
that from its airy and fragrant mistiness a shadowy countenance
beamed down upon the good lady in black, with the white cap,

who ladled out the delicious compound to her waiting devotees. The murmur of the tea-urn would seem to fashion itself into airy accents, syllabling, 'Mary, thy Blodget is here!' His genial spirit would preside over her labours in the kitchen, suggesting ever more delightsome dishes and delicate desserts. He would warn her against undesirable inmates and intractable servants, and would inspire her tradesmen to serve her with the choicest comestibles and to temper their bills to the unprotected widow. At night he would bless her lonely pillow with peace, and would gently rouse her in the morning to a new day of beneficences.

Mrs. Blodget was about five feet four inches high, and may have weighed twelve stone; into such limits were her virtues packed. She was perhaps in the neighbourhood of her fiftieth year; her dark hair was threaded with honourable gray. Her countenance was rotund and ruddy; it was the flower of kindness and hospitality in full bloom; but there was also power in the thick eyebrows and in the massy substance of the chin—of the chins, indeed, for here, as in other gifts, nature had been generous with her. There was shrewdness and discernment in the good-nature of her eyes; she knew human nature, although no one judged it with more charity than she. Her old men were her brothers, her young men were her sons, all children were her children. Solomon foresaw her in the most engaging of his Proverbs. Her maid-servants arose at six in the morning and called her blessed, for though her rule was strict it was just and loving. She was at once the mistress and the friend of her household; no Yankee captain so audacious that he ventured to oppose her law; no cynic so cold as not to be melted by her tenderness. She was clad always in black, with a white cap and ribbons, always spotless amid the grime of Liverpool; in her more active moments— though she was always active—she added a white apron to her attire. She was ever anywhere where she was needed; she was never anywhere where she could be dispensed with. Wherever she went she brought comfort and a cheerful but not restless animation. Her boarders were busy men, but it was always with an effort that they wrenched themselves from her breakfast-table, and they sat down to dinner as one man. She made them happy, but she would not spoil them. 'You're a pretty young man!' she said, severely, to complacent Mr. Crane, when, one morning, he came late to breakfast. 'I always knew that,' returned he, reaching self-satisfiedly for the toast-rack. 'Well, I'm sure your glass never told you so!' was the withering retort. Mr. Crane did not lift his

neck so high after that. The grin that went round the table was
too crushingly unanimous.

[...]

If the Blodget house, or houses, were unique, so were the
Yankee boarders. The race of our merchant-marine captains
disappeared with their ships, and they will return no more. The
loss is irretrievable, for in many respects they held the ideal of
patriotic and energetic Americanism higher than it is likely to go
again. When at sea, in command of and responsible for their ships
and cargoes, they were, no doubt, upon occasion, despots and
slave-drivers; but their crews were often recruited from among
the dregs of men of all nations, who would interpret kindness as
timidity and take an ell where you gave them an inch. No doubt,
too, there were incarnate devils among these captains—actual
monomaniacs of cruelty and viciousness—though none of these
were known at Mrs. Blodget's. Round her board sat men only of
the manliest sort. They had the handiness and versatility of the
sailor, wide and various knowledge of all quarters of the globe
and of types of mankind, though, to be sure, their investigations
did not proceed far beyond their ports, and you were sometimes
more astonished at what they did not know than at what they
did. They had the self-poise and self-confidence of men who day
by day and month by month hold their lives in their hands, and
are practised in finding a way out of danger and difficulty. They
had a code of good manners and polite behaviour which was not
highly refined, but contained the sound, essential elements of
courtesy; not expressed in fancy, but honest and solid. They had
great shrewdness, and were capable of really fine diplomacy, for
the school they attended demanded such proficiency. They had
a dry, chuckling humour; a homely philosophy, often mingled
with the queerest superstitions; a racy wit, smacking somewhat, of
course, of the quarter-deck, or even of the forecastle; a seemingly
incongruous sensibility, so that tears easily sprang to their eyes
if the right chord of pathos were touched; a disposition to wear
a high-coloured necktie and a broad, gold watch-chain, and
to observe a certain smartness in their boots and their general
shore rigging; a good appetite for good food, and not a little
discernment of what was good; a great and boy-like enjoyment
of primitive pleasures; a love of practical jokes and a hearty roar
of laughter for hearty fun; a self-respecting naturalness, which
made them gentlemen in substance if not in all technical details;
a pungent contempt for humbug and artifice, though they might

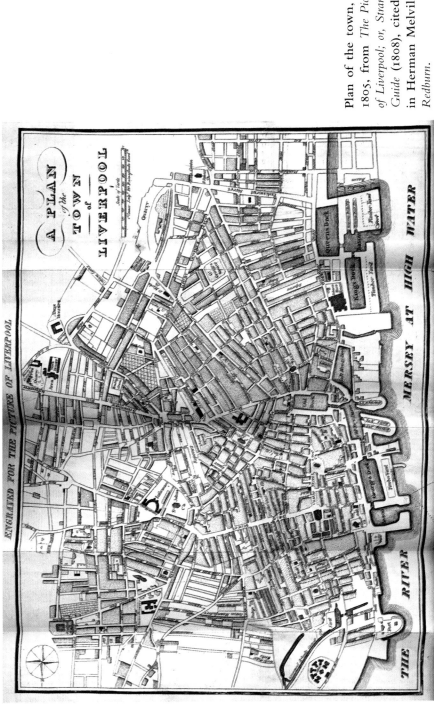

Plan of the town, 1805, from *The Picture of Liverpool; or, Stranger's Guide* (1808), cited in Herman Melville's *Redburn*.

SCHOOL FOR THE BLIND.

LYCEUM.

The School for the Blind and the Lyceum from *The Picture of Liverpool; or, Stranger's Guide* (1808), cited in Herman Melville's *Redburn*.

TO
GEORGE CASE, Esq.
THIS VIEW OF THE ATHENÆUM,
IS HUMBLY INSCRIBED, BY HIS OBEDIENT SERVANT,
T. TROUGHTON.

The Athenaeum on
its original site in
Church Street, 1810.

Allerton Hall, William Roscoe's former home, as it looks now.

John James Audubon, *Self Portrait*, 1826 (pencil on paper).
© University of Liverpool Art Gallery & Collections/
The Bridgeman Art Gallery.

The Old
Dock and
Custom
House
(1715).

Canning Dock
and the new
Custom House
(1839).

The Moorish Arch at Edge Hill on the Liverpool–Manchester railway,
and St James's cemetery.

The Wellington Monument,
from W.D. Howells, *Seven English Cities* (1909).

'To the Friends of Negro Emancipation'.
© National Maritime Museum, Greenwich, London (neg. no. PY7366)

Cammell Laird shipyard, 1857, by courtesy of Williamson Art Gallery, Birkenhead.

Cunard Line advertisement, from *Guide to Liverpool* (1902), and the departure of a Cunard ship.

The Liverpool landing stage, from *Guide to Liverpool* (1902).

ADELPHI HOTEL—ENTRANCE HALL.

ADELPHI HOTEL—" SEFTON " RESTAURANT.

ADELPHI HOTEL—SMOKING ROOM.

Adelphi Hotel, from *Guide to Liverpool* (1902).

A Woodside ferry-boat and a view of Lime Street,
from William H. Rideing, 'England's Great Sea-Port', *Harper's New
Monthly Magazine*, January 1879. Courtesy of Cornell University Library,
Making of America Digital Collection.

ST. GEORGE'S HALL, LIVERPOOL

St George's Hall,
from W.D. Howells,
Seven English Cities
(1909).

not mind a good, swaggering lie upon occasion; a robust sense of honour in all matters which were trusted to their honourable feeling; and, to make an end of this long catalogue, a practical command of language regarded as a means of expressing and communicating the essential core of thoughts, though the words might not always be discoverable in Johnson's dictionary or the grammatical constructions such as would be warranted by Lindley Murray [American grammarian of late eighteenth century]. They were, upon the average, good-looking, active, able men, and most of them were on the sunny side of forty. They were ready to converse on any subject, but if left to themselves they would choose topics proper to their calling – ships and shipwrecks, maritime usages of various countries, of laws of insurance, of sea-rights, of feats of seamanship, of luck and ill luck, and here and there a little politics of the old-fashioned, elementary sort. They boasted themselves and their country not a little, and criticised everybody else, and John Bull especially, very severely often, but almost always very acutely, too. They would play euchre and smoke cigars from nine o'clock till eleven, and would then go to bed and sleep till the breakfast-bell. Altogether, they were fine company, and they did me much good. Such were the captains of our merchant marine about the middle of the last century.
[...]

Without letting me feel that I was the object of special solicitude or watchfulness, my father knew all that I did, and saw to it that my time was decently occupied. In addition to the dancing-lessons already mentioned (in which I became brilliantly proficient, and achieved such feats in the way of polkas, mazurkas, hornpipes, and Scotch reels as filled my instructor and myself with pride)— in addition to this, I was closeted twice a week with a very serious and earnest drawing-master, who taught me with infinite conscientiousness, and sighed heavily over the efforts which I submitted to him. The captains, who were my champions and abettors in all things, might take in their large hands a drawing of mine and the copy by the master which had been my model, and say, one to the other, 'Well, now, I couldn't tell which was which—could you?' But the master could tell, and the certainty of it steeped his soul in constant gloom. I doubt if he recovered from the pangs I gave him. The fact was, I thought an hour of dancing with lovely Mary Warren was worth all the art in the world. Another instructor to whom I brought honour was thick-shouldered, portly, unctuous M. Huguenin, a Swiss, proprietor of the once-famous gymnasium which bore his name. He so anointed me with praise that I waxed indiscreet, and one day, as I was swinging on the rings, and he was pointing out to some prospective patrons my extraordinary merits, my grasp relaxed at the wrong moment and I came sailing earthward from on high. It seemed to me that, like Milton's Lucifer, 'from dawn to eve I fell,' M. Huguenin sprinting to intercept my fall; but I landed on a mat and was little the worse for it. I fear the prospective patrons were not persuaded, by my performance, of the expediency of gymnastic training. On the other hand, M. Huguenin managed to dispose to my father of one of his multum-in-parvo [Latin 'much in little'; probably in the sense of multi-purpose] exercising-machines, on the understanding that it was to be taken back at half-price on the expiration of our stay in Liverpool; but, when that time came, M. Huguenin failed to remember having been a party to any such understanding; so the big framework was boxed up, and finally was resurrected in Concord, where I laboured with it for seven or eight years more during my home-comings from Harvard.

Hawthorne and His Circle, Chapter 10.

Among the Americans the Hawthornes met in Liverpool was the family of **William Henry Channing** (1810–84), a leading Transcendentalist and Unitarian. Hawthorne knew Channing's uncle William Ellery Channing from his Concord days. William Henry Channing served as pastor of the Renshaw Street Unitarian chapel from 1854 to 1857, when he took over the Hope Street Unitarian chapel. He returned to the USA with his family in 1862 when the Civil War broke out. Julian took part in private theatricals at Mrs Blodget's.

In these avocations I was also companioned by Frank Channing, whose specialty was ornithology, and who was making a series of coloured portraits of the birds in the museum, very cleverly done.

Frank was the son of the Rev. William Henry Channing, who was pastor of a Unitarian church in Liverpool; he had brought his family to England at about the same time that we came. He was a nephew, I believe, of the William Ellery Channing who was one of the founders of American Unitarianism, and the brother, therefore, of the Ellery Channing of Concord. Frank inherited much of the talent of his family.

He was afterwards sent to Oxford, where he took the highest
honours. All intellectual operations came easy to him. He also
showed a strong proclivity to art, and he was wonderfully clever
in all kinds of fine handwork. He was at this time a tall and very
handsome boy, about two years my senior. He was, like myself,
fanatically patriotic, an American of Americans, and this brought
us together in a foreign land; but, aside from that, I have seldom
met a more fascinating companion. I followed him about with joy
and admiration. He used to make for me tiny little three-masted
ships, about six inches long, with all the rigging complete; they
were named after the famous American clippers of the day, and he
painted microscopic American flags to hoist over the taff-rail. He
tried to teach me how to paint in water-colours, but I responded
better to his eloquence regarding the future of our country. He
proved to me by a mathematical demonstration, which I accepted
without in the least understanding it, that in fifty years New York
would be larger and more populous than London at the end of the
same period. This brilliant boy seemed fitted for the highest career
in his native country; his father did not contemplate a permanent
stay in England, and in after years I used to look for his name in
our Senate, or among the occupants of the Supreme Bench.
[...]
Frank's father was a tall, intellectual, slender Yankee, endowed
with splendid natural gifts, which he had improved by assiduous
cultivation. In the pulpit he rose to an almost divine eloquence
and passion, and a light would shine over his face as if reflected
from the Holy Spirit itself. My father took a pew in his church,
and sent me to sit in it every Sunday; he never went himself.
He was resolved, I suppose, if there was any religion in me, to
afford it an opportunity to come out. Now, I had a religious
reverence for divine things, but no understanding whatever of
dogma of any sort. I never learned to repeat a creed, far less to
comprehend its significance. I was moved and charmed by Mr.
Channing's discourses, but I did not like to sit in the pew; I did
not like 'church.' I remember nothing of the purport of any of
those sermons; but, oddly enough, I do recall one preached by
a gentleman who united the profession of preacher with that of
medicine; he occupied Channing's pulpit on a certain occasion,
and preached on the text in John xix., 34: 'But one of the
soldiers with a spear pierced his side, and forthwith came thereout
blood and water.' The good doctor, drawing on his physiological
erudition, demonstrated at great length how it was possible that

blood should be mingled with the water, and showed at what precise point in Christ's body the spear must have entered. I seem to hear again his mellifluous voice, repeating at the close of each passage of his argument, 'And forthwith came thereout blood-AND WATER!' I did not approve of this sermon; I was not carried to heaven in the spirit by it, as by Channing's; but somehow it has stuck in my memory all these forty-eight years.

Hawthorne and His Circle, Chapter 10.

[A cricket match described in a letter by Sophia Hawthorne.]

The last thing that happened was Mr. Hawthorne's and my going to see a cricket match between Liverpool and Derbyshire. We sat in the carriage, and looked out upon a perfectly level plain of eight or nine acres, a smooth, sunny, velvet lawn. In the midst of it the two wickets were erected at the distance apart of twenty or thirty feet, each composed of three sticks, with another stick laid transversely. The cricketers were all dressed in pale buff wash-leather or felt doublet and hose, with boots of thick and buff leather in strips over the instep; and those who stood before each wicket with a bat in hand were guarded from the severe blows of the ball by a peculiar coat-of-mail reaching from the ankles above the knee. This shin-guard was made of buff leather, very much like a child's sun-bonnet; but instead of pasteboard sewed in, it is thickly padded with wool, and I do not know but a thin wooden board or whale-bone besides, making the limb look very clumsy. At each wicket stood, therefore, a well-padded man with a bat. Behind him and each wicket stood another man who threw the ball and tried to knock down the wicket, which the man with the bat was studious to prevent. In a vast circle from these four stood, I believe, eight men, at exact distances from one another, who were to catch the ball when a bat sent it off from either wicket. If the man with the bat was so fortunate as to drive it to a great distance, he and the other batman ran from one wicket to another; and just as many times as they could exchange places, so much the better for them, for each time counts one in the game. We alighted from the carriage, and went into the plain, and finally sat down under a tent, where were some ladies and gentlemen, or, more properly, respectable men and women; for in England there is great discrimination used in this nomenclature. If a batman hits the ball before it reaches the ground, and strikes it into the air, and it is caught by one of the outstanders, there is a loss. Once a young man who had been a bat-man and had failed to defend his wicket exclaimed near me, as an outstander caught the ball from the clouds, 'Ah, what a shame, and one of our own men too!' So it seemed that this man was obliged to play against himself in such circumstances. I was astonished, all the time, to see the want of animation in the players. They lounged along after the ball upon the ground, as if they were taking an evening stroll, with a sort of Oriental languor.

Nathaniel Hawthorne and His Wife, Vol. II, Chapter 2.

[In November 1856 Melville arrived in Liverpool on his way to the Levant and the Holy Land. Julian here quotes his father's impressions of that writer.]

At Southport the chief event of interest during the winter was a visit from Herman Melville, who turned up at Liverpool on his way to Constantinople, and whom Hawthorne brought out to spend a night or two with us. 'He looked much the same as he used to do; a little paler, perhaps, and a little sadder, and with his characteristic gravity and reserve of manner. I felt rather awkward at first, for this is the first time I have met him since my ineffectual attempt to get him a consular appointment from General Pierce, However, I failed only from real lack of power to serve him; so there was no reason to be ashamed, and we soon found ourselves on pretty much the former terms of sociability and confidence' [...] Melville made the rounds of Liverpool under the guidance of Henry Bright; and afterwards Hawthorne took him to Chester; and they parted the same evening, at a street corner, in the rainy evening. 'I saw him again on Monday, however. He said that he already felt much better than in America; but observed that he did not anticipate much pleasure in his rambles, for that the spirit of adventure is gone out of him.'

Nathaniel Hawthorne and His Wife, Vol. II, Chapter 4: 'Eighteen Months Before Rome'.

6

Social Observers

I N A SENSE ALL VISITORS to Liverpool were social observers, whether they were conscious of the fact or not. However, the examples presented so far have shown travellers with vested commercial or aesthetic purposes. Audubon combined naturalistic and artistic interests; and Melville presents the special case of an author transforming his memories of Liverpool into fiction. We turn now to American travellers who incorporate into their accounts an important element of social commentary. **Henry Blake McLellan** (1810–33) was a graduate of Harvard who was heading for Edinburgh University in 1831 to pursue his studies. He was collecting material for a study of England, but died prematurely before he could complete the project. The title of his *Journal of a Residence in Scotland* of 1834 does not prepare us for his detailed descriptions of servants and the poor of the city. In particular, he shows how class entered all social activities.

The day was delicious. A few white clouds only floated over the blue sky, casting their flying shade over the green fields and bright water. It seemed to lend a sweeter loveliness to the scene. In the midst of this transparent air there was a dense cloud. It rose up amongst a forest of masts, lines of houses, turrets, and steeples; it was the smoke, which like an evil spirit, hangs day and night over the great city of Liverpool.

A little black steamer now came briskly up to us. It was a custom-house boat. It received our letters and also the cabin passengers, and in a few minutes we were running rapidly by the docks, whose massive walls of stone shut up the shipping of this commercial metropolis. Here and there the large basins communicated by tide gates with the water of the river. The regular character of these docks, and the peculiar slope given to the yards of all the vessels which fill them, has an imposing appearance. You discover the extent of its commerce at a glance. Perhaps this unity made it appear to me more extensive than it

really was; for my impression was that the shipping in the harbour
at that time did not fall much short of that of New York and
Boston combined. I was disappointed with the appearance of the
stores along the docks. They were built of brick, but the brick
was not only irregular in shape when compared with ours, but its
face was rough and much soiled with dust and coal smoke. A dark
piazza ran along their front, the face of the buildings resting on
square pillars.

As far as we could see all was bustle. Heavy drays and large
wagons drawn by huge horses loaded with cotton, thundered
over the pavements; and a thousand blended sounds assailed our
ears as we reached our landing place. A grim crowd awaited us
there. Forty or fifty drivers held up their whip handles to engage
our attention. 'Coach, your honour,' 'Coach, sir,' were reiterated
by as many voices from persons whose dirty hands and faces
and ragged garb did not offer a flattering promise for the beauty
and cleanliness of their vehicles. Their claim to our notice was
disputed by about a hundred or two other persons ranging far
beneath them in personal cleanliness.

Such a set of characters were perhaps never collected in our
country. A dozen thrust themselves forward, 'Shall I carry
your baggage, your honour,' 'your umbrella'; 'Shall I show you
to the Adelphi, to the Mersey Hotel,' &c., cried others; here
were women ready to sell the 'gemmen' oranges, and here the
suspicious children of the wandering nation ready to buy 'old
clothes'; in all a motley group. This was not so painful. But
to regard the group of ragged, wretched, lame and miserable
creatures that had collected round us, as if we had been the last
resource upon which their hopes rested, this was enough to rend
one's heart. For such piteous tones and fearful accounts of their
famishing condition I never before heard faltered forth from the
tongues of human beings. It was the first phalanx of a class, that
I afterwards found eating the bread of bitterness in large numbers
through all the cities of Great Britain. Trained as our eyes are
to see only well-fed decent and comfortable persons, even in the
lowest rank in America, walking amongst the grim assemblage
of an English crowd, even what is really elegant and neat is for
a period almost unnoticed, until the first shock which so much
distress and poverty makes on the feelings has subsided. An
Englishman, so far as respects his enjoyment of what is beautiful,
is disciplined into an entire disregard for these elements, which
enter into the texture of their social system, to dim its glory. He

only sees what is splendid; all the meanness thrown over it by surrounding want, he is accustomed to disregard, as much as if it did not exist. If it was not so he would be continually miserable. But it stares an American in the face in every street. This dark veil hides for a period all the grandeur that stands towering up behind it. I found it precisely so in my case.

We succeeded in separating ourselves from nearly all the rabble that had at first surrounded us, though one or two of the more professional or more hungry beggars harassed our march through several of the shorter streets. Three things struck me, in particular, as soon as I entered Liverpool, viz: the large size and powerful appearance of the dray horses; the vast extent and prison-like aspect of the ware houses, and the convenience and stability of their docks. But while the ware houses were so immense, the streets were narrow and choked up; the side walks by men, women and children, nearly all of whom were clothed in wretched garments, whilst the pavement was thickly covered with carts and wagons heavily laden with cotton and merchandize. A narrow strip of sky gray with smoke shone dimly above, lighting up the street, it is true, but not with that transparent brightness which cheers even the purlieus of our towns. The shops in these streets had a contracted and indigent air. We decided to go to the 'Adelphi,' one of the best houses in Liverpool. On the way we passed through two handsome streets, much like parts of Broadway in New York, or Washington Street in Boston. In the coffee room I had the pleasure of meeting a gentleman, who had been a fellow student with me at Andover. There is no place where one is more independent than in an English hotel. If he has money enough he can command everything. We might have such houses if we desired them; perhaps they would be frequented and be profitable, but they are not suited to, at least they do not grow out of, our national character. They are the legitimate germ of English feeling. In England, condition, title and wealth are everything; character, person, humanity comparatively nothing. All yields to the dazzle of wealth and hereditary influence. This aristocracy predominates everywhere. Its spirit communicates itself to everything. See its genius in a Hotel. You are met at the door by the waiter. He measures at a glance your condition. He looks out to see whether you have come in your own carriage with livery, or post it in style. He watches the postilions to estimate the height of your dignity by the profoundness of their obeisance. And they do not leave the house till they have told him what

you have paid them, and all other things which they know about
you. In short he looks at the hack that you have come in; at the
silver you pay for it; at your baggage, dress, and deportment, and
scores you down accordingly; or, in the pithy language of an
Englishman, 'he sets you down as a porter, port wine and water,
or champagne customer at once, and treats you at that rate, until
you have fixed your own standard, by what you call for.' If you
do not immediately ask for the 'travellers' room,' or for the 'coffee
room,' he inquires, 'Will you see your chamber, sir.' The bell is
pulled; the chamber-maid appears, and you are conducted to an
apartment suited to their estimate of your rank. If you do not like
it, you are shown to another of higher price, and you are sure to
get a very complaisant smile from the chamber-maid if you move
like one that intends to pay well. They do not like too many
'thank you's,' thinking that when courtesy is too current, coin is
rare. And if you have many needs, coats to be dusted, shoes to
be cleaned, and trifles to be done, even if you pay no more for
it, it purchases their respect, and satisfies them that you intend
giving them their fees. Of such a person their opinion is, 'he's a
gentleman, he will pay for our services'.

The 'coffee room' is arranged in the same style. After seeing my
room I descended to it. It was a large and handsome apartment,
with about ten or twelve tables, capable of accommodating four
persons each; these were all covered with elegant white cloths,
with knives and silver forks and spoons. At some of them parties
of gentlemen were sitting, each group apparently as much alone
as if they only, occupied the room. At others was seen but a
single individual. I sat down at one of the tables. 'Waiter, I'll
thank you to bring me breakfast.' 'What will you have, sir?'
said he in reply; for the price of breakfast, and particularly other
meals, is regulated by what one calls for. If you say 'coffee and
rolls,' you pay forty cents; if you add 'eggs, or such meat as you
have prepared,' you are charged six cents more; if you call for
other things, you pay according to their relative value. There are
no fixed hours; come in when you may, and call for what you
choose, if it is to be obtained in the market, it is immediately
provided. You are perfectly independent; you may have all, if
you are rich enough to pay for all. There you sit alone; eat your
dinner, pick over your nuts and raisins, and read the newspapers;
no one thinks of you, speaks to you, or even looks at you. All
keep aloof. They don't know you. Perhaps you are lower in the
scale of importance than themselves. Such persons would of course

feel uncomfortable at Bunker's or the Tremont's elegant table, with
so many persons brought into juxtaposition with them, of whom
they were ignorant. They would esteem it almost the compromise
of their dignity to speak. It is not strange then that their public
room differs from ours. It is not a matter of caprice, but it arises
from the character of the people. It is a germ from the spirit of
their constitution. Both the English and Americans are generous
by nature; but English laws and institutions very naturally confine
their courtesy to the circle of their acquaintance; whilst ours, on
the contrary, give us a freedom of manner towards all men, which
no circumstances ever disturb.

The accommodations of the Adelphi were excellent; the tables
were laid with elegance, and the servants of the coffee room, or
waiters, as they are uniformly called, very attentive and respectful.
After breakfast I walked to the upper part of the town with
my American companion to visit the cemetery. The city in this
direction had more the air of Boston or New York than the
streets which I had hitherto seen. In general, however, the houses,
which were arranged like our own, in connected streets or retired
'courts' were not so elegant as the ranges which distinguish our
cities. They were not so much adorned by beautiful porticoes,
piazzas, and blinds as our habitations. Their brick was not so
smooth; it was rarely painted white, nor was it sustained on
granite bases, which is so common rather, so universal with us;
nor were the handles of the door and bell knobs so often plaited
with silver as is usual in our cities. Yet if in general the houses
through the city fell beneath our own in brightness and beauty,
nevertheless, it was the case that here and there, there were houses
of uncommon splendour, which would have surpassed our most
expensive buildings. I expected this. Wealth is monopolized by
the few; hence we find uncommon grandeur, then uncommon
plainness, then uncommon woe. There is not that beautiful
gradation of style which characterizes everything at home. You
would look, therefore, for shoeless beggars and brilliant equipages.
And you find them. Here comes a splendid carriage! How it
whirls along. It has four horses. Two 'jockeys' bestride them,
bobbing up and down as they kick and spur along at a furious
rate. These are a singular genus, much the same all over England.
They are accoutred with a round riding cap, short blue pea-
coat, tight buckskin breeches, white top-boots, spurs, and short
whip, and with a round red face, just suited to their habiliments.
The footman peered up proudly behind. He looks with elevated

disdain upon all beneath his conspicuous station; for lo! his gold
laced hat, his new blue coat profusely decorated with the same,
his red velvet breeches, his white silk stockings, his polished shoes,
and his unsullied wash-leather gloves, behold the man of place and
dignity ! It stopped at a splendid house which we were passing.
One 'jockey' sprung from his horse. The footman tripped down
from behind, and pulled the bell, and a kindred spirit opened the
door, bowing his powdered head most complacently. The carriage
door was opened, and a very beautiful, graceful, and elegantly
dressed young lady was handed out. She entered, and we passed
on, whilst the two lackeys exchanged compliments together on
the steps. We admired her fine colour and the elegant simplicity
of her dress. This seemed to me always the noble characteristic
of English ladies of the first rank. An elegant simplicity of taste.
Not so much of the French diversity of dress. Beauty is never so
attractive, as when simply, yet elegantly adorned; it shines like the
diamond out of the chaste gold which it decorates.
[...]
   The Cemetery, which we had now reached, occupied a very
favourable situation. It stood in the highest part of the city. It
is removed in a great degree from the business, bustle, dirt, and
wretchedness through which we had passed. The houses around
had a more cheering aspect. The air had a freer circulation,
and the brightness of the sunshine poured light over the scene.
Even the thunder of the agitated city was softened down by the
distance into a soothing hum. Here stood the receptacle of the
dead. It was enclosed by a low granite wall, surmounted by an
iron railing. Its gateways were in the Egyptian style. From the
exterior we discerned nothing else than a Grecian temple and a
beautiful porter's lodge, in excellent keeping with the genius of
the place. Along the borders, there were smooth gravel walks,
shaded by trees, and their sides, which were tastefully laid out,
adorned with flowers of sweetest hue. No one touches these.
Even the little children stooped down and gazed at them, and
left them uninjured. 'Oh ! how pretty,' said a sweet little child
near me, looking up in the face of her brother, who was a few
years older; 'Ma loved flowers so, too.' 'Yes,' said he, 'and pa says
that these are sacred to ma's memory.' And may they rest there
unharmed, thought I, beautiful and touching remembrancers
of the delicate being that once loved you! I did not pass away
without feeling an interest in this unknown grave and unknown
occupant. Her love for these beautiful plants indicated at least the

existence of one bond of sympathy between us. We stood near the temple. A deep excavation lay beneath us. It is cut through the solid rock. It is five hundred feet long, and fifty-two feet in depth. Inclined carriage roads twine round the sides, passing three successive galleries of catacombs before reaching the burial-place beneath, which is laid out in flower beds and shrubberies, from whose grateful shade the white marble funeral urns and columns rose with a sweet and chastened soberness. We descended. 'How suitable an entrance to the place,' said my companion, as we passed through a gallery cut in the solid rock, whose length had changed the intense light of day into the solemn obscurity of parting twilight. It ushered us once more into the light; but how changed! If there are flowers and shrubbery on one side of the carriage way, on the other are the silent mansions of the dead, hewn out of the massive rock. A flat marble slab in the lower part of the cemetery formed the inconspicuous monument of the illustrious Huskisson. The whole scene is deeply impressive. It is at once grand, simple, solemn, and beautiful. It was converted into its present character at an expense of one hundred thousand dollars. It was formerly a stone quarry, whose resources being nearly exhausted, it was very judiciously converted to its present purpose.

[McLellan then describes some of the public buildings and monuments.]

The old custom house into which I now entered in order to obtain my baggage was but a rude affair. It is a disagreeable matter to pass through the custom house in England. You have to do with menials. And these in England are too often a contemptible class. We have unfortunately formed our opinion of English men, manners, morals, generosity, and refinement from such characters, and by the order of travellers met with in the stages and public houses through the land. Nothing can be more incorrect and unjust. It is true that one meets with many uncultivated and rude men on the outward face of society; and he must therefore penetrate beyond it in order to discover generosity, as well as delicate feeling, and courteous manners. If he has once an introduction to good society, he enters a region entirely distinct from that which he had before trodden, distinguished by courtesy, cordiality of manner, and high and refined intelligence. Candour demands this early acknowledgment of a truth which I did not at this time distinctly apprehend. I trust that this circumstance

will not be lost sight of. It arises from the nature of their political
existence and explains the wide difference which exists in the
minds of travellers respecting the spirit of English society.

I could not possibly have entered a place where the standard of
character is lower than the room of bonds and baggage in which
I now stood. Two or three coarse looking fellows, like spiders in
a dusty web, hovered round to seize upon the strangers, who have
come as visitors to their island. One would suppose that the office
they hold would render them honest; or one would imagine, that
the honour of their country would make them civil and upright.
Not so. A man with a wooden leg hobbled up to me. As he took
the keys of my trunk and travelling bag he hemmed and shuffled
and gave a knowing wink, still keeping his hand wide open. 'I
believe it is all right, sir,' I said. He turned the key, opened the
trunk, and began to look over the things. It was quite a farce.
He scarce touched anything, but ever and anon gave me a gentle
touch with his wooden member by way of suggestion. Seeing that
I did not take the hint, he begins to pry into the trunk. There
were several books in it. He seizes upon these. 'Books, hem ! not
allowed, something to pay on these' another touch with the leg:
'large number, couldn't think of passing these.' The hint began
to take effect, his elbow was at work against my side and one
hand came down to receive 'a husher'; it was not worth disputing
about, so I put some silver into his hand. It rang over every nerve,
brightened up his eyes and wits to such an extent that he saw
at once that the books were 'too few to be worth naming,' &c.
However, before I left the room I had two or three tips on the
nose from the under-craft, with 'Hey ! all right, sir; all right, sir.'
One bolder than the rest pursued us into the street, and demanded
a shilling of us as a matter of right; 'for I ought to have been
employed as your porter; I do the waiting there, your honours,
and when the gentlemen doesn't hire me they pay me as though
they did, your honours.' 'If it is your right,' said my friend, 'you
had better pursue your right; otherwise, you had better be off.'
And he went growling away.
[...]

After a few days I decided to visit Manchester, on my route
to Scotland. But before leaving Liverpool, I must be indulged
with a few general remarks. An American who goes to Liverpool
expecting to discover beauty, brilliancy, and life impressed on
everything, will be disappointed. The importance of that city is
not to be estimated in any such way. It undoubtedly possesses

a vast amount of wealth. But this must be seen in its costly docks and extensive warehouses, in the canals, that glide with streams of silver into its deep treasure-houses; and in its pathway of iron, which seems beaten into greater stability by the unchecked course of its cars, freighted with the wealth of precious merchandize. Of its politeness and affability he must not take the first outward appearance as the measure. For behind the dark and unprepossessing features which strike him at first, he will find there, if he comes in contact with it, all the sweet courtesies which give a charm to life. Even the very persons whose constraint, under certain circumstances, was disagreeable to his feelings, under different circumstances, he may perhaps admire and love. I offer these remarks as the fruit rather of a second and third visit to Liverpool than as the offspring of my earliest impressions.

Henry B. McLellan, *Journal of a Residence in Scotland, and Tour through England, France, Germany, Switzerland and Italy* (1834).

The clergyman **Calvin Colton** (1789–1857) spent the years 1831–35 in England and recorded the great popularity of Dr Raffles, the famous minister of a city-centre chapel, whom he heard soon after landing in Liverpool.

At six o'clock I wended my way alone and unguided to Great George-street Chapel. As the hour of commencing worship was half after six, I was in season to obtain a good seat by the kind offices of a pew-opener. Soon, however, the people began to pour in, in dense columns, till I found myself, before the services commenced, standing in the aisle with a multitude of gentlemen, to accommodate the ladies. After remaining a little in this posture, I received a beck from a venerable gentleman near me, to take a seat in his pew, already crammed with a range of fine-looking young men and youth, who appeared as if they might be his twelve sons, and he the patriarch. 'Have you room, sir?' said I. 'O yes; come in.' On my right, half way along the pew, a full-souled-looking young man of twenty-five showed me much civility when I first sat down and during the service.

It was a grateful hour, and grateful every circumstance, after the scenes of a sea-voyage, and after such an unsabbath-like day, to find myself seated in a modest but spacious church, and one of a congregation of two thousand in a foreign land; to hear my native tongue in its purest forms; to have opened and read the same Bible, to listen to the same hymns and the same music, as in my own country; the dress and manners of the people the same, and with no circumstance to admonish me of a change of place from one part of the globe to another. It was like a dream; for that day three weeks (and far less time in seeming) I was worshipping with a Christian congregation in New-York.

At the appointed hour a clergyman ascended the pulpit, knelt, and offered his silent prayer a custom most befitting and impressive, but not practised in America, except by two denominations; and then opening the Bible, he read the twenty-fourth chapter of Matthew with great pertinency and pathos of expression, in silvery and subduing tones. From the first opening of his lips, he seemed moved from his inmost soul. I could have imagined, though ignorant of the cause, that the deep fountains of feeling were opened within him, and that some mighty sympathies were working there. And I thought, too, that the congregation were ready to be with him in feeling; but still I knew not the occasion. 'Is that Dr. Raffles?' said I in a whisper to the gentleman on my right, as the preacher began to read. 'Yes, sir,' was the answer. After the usual introductory services, and a prayer, which breathed the soul, and seemed communion with the skies, a fellowship with heaven, and fitted well to raise the heart that wished to be with God, the following text was announced: 'Therefore, be ye also ready; for in such an hour as ye think not the Son of Man cometh.'

Calvin Colton, *Four Years in Great Britain, 1831–1835* (1835).

Wilbur Fisk (1792–1839) was a New England Methodist minister and President of the Wesleyan University, Middletown Connecticut. He was very conscious of his moral purpose in visiting Europe in the 1830s and his cultural contrasts usually worked in America's favour. Like Henry McLellan, he found Liverpool's general appearance to be oppressive.

The general exterior of the city is sombre and gloomy. This is what is said of all English towns. The reason is, doubtless, that the smoke of the coal, here universally used for fuel and for manufacturing purposes, renders any attempt at external brightness and freshness altogether futile; and to this may be added the fact that the dampness of the climate operates powerfully upon paint and masonry, whether of stone or brick, to impart a dark and ancient appearance to the edifices. Hence this has become the English fashion, and now, therefore, the inhabitants would not have a fresh-looking edifice if they could; it would be out of taste. This, to one accustomed to the bright and fresh walls of an American city, has a most gloomy aspect, and I am not sure but it contributes something towards the low spirits of the inhabitants themselves. This must be greatly counteracted, however, by the increased comforts within; for, while Americans may have a livelier exterior to their dwellings, the English appear to have, in general, a greater share of interior accommodations and conveniences.

Wilbur Fisk, *Travels on the Continent of Europe* (1838).

The writer **Lydia Howard Sigourney** (1791–1865) gives a rare account of the Blue Coat Hospital in her 1842 travelogue. The institution was founded in 1708 for poor children and at the time of Sigourney's visit was still housed in premises in School Lane.

By Mr. Gair, formerly from Boston, who, with his lady, showed us great politeness and hospitality, we were taken to attend divine worship in the chapel of the Blue Coat Hospital. Two hundred and fifty boys, and one hundred girls, were assembled there, in the neat uniforms of the Institution. To our surprise, the whole service was performed by them. A boy of very grave deportment read the liturgy with solemn intonation, and the others distinctly responded. Another officiated as organist, and all joined zealously in the singing. Catechisms and portions of Scripture were recited by a selection of the scholars, and the exercises conducted and closed decorously.

The building appropriated to the Institution is spacious, and perfectly neat. In one apartment are portraits of its benefactors, among whom are some who were once pensioners of its bounty. The advantages for an extended education are not so great here as in the establishment for the Blue Coat Boys in London, which has produced some literary men of note. The Liverpool beneficiaries are prepared for the practical walks of life, and become apprentices to artisans or tradesmen. Before leaving, we were invited to see the children taking their Sunday supper. Each had on a wooden plate a huge mass of bread, with a modicum of cheese, and by its side a small cup of ale; all of which elements they were discussing with a visible relish. Their appearance was healthful, and their deportment quiet, and in perfect subordination. How blessed is that benevolence, which rescues the young from ignorance and poverty, and inspires them with motives to become useful here, and happy hereafter. It is peculiarly honourable, in a commercial city, to devote time and attention to these departments of philanthropy.

Lydia Howard Sigourney, *Pleasant Memories of Pleasant Lands* (1842).

The accounts given above have all been by prosperous middle-class travellers. **Lorenza Stevens Berbineau**'s travel diary of 1851 is unusual in being that of a domestic servant attending members of the Lowell family, who were making a tour from Boston to London and the Continent. Despite the class difference, she was evidently drawn to the same sights that have already been described.

[spelling standardized] July 20th. Rainy this morning a pilot came on board quite early we did not go into the dock a steamboat carried us to the wharf it look very pretty when we came in sight of Liverpool we arrived there about 2 o'clock we got into a carriage went to the Adelphi Hotel, kept by James Radley. The sides of the streets are paved and the centre is macadamised the cross walks are flag stone Mr Putnam and Mr Allen and Mrs Snodgrass families came to the hotel where we are we took clothing in carpet bags for the night the Custom-House officers came on board examined what things we took. We dined today at five o'clock I have just come in from a walk. One of my fellow passengers went with me Miss Clink we saw several fine buildings we walked in St James Cemetery fine-looking place we took tea half past eight. The room Edie and I have nice room a mahogany bedstead the posts are as high as the ceiling with red damask worsted curtains and the same at the windows.
July 21st. Pleasant went shopping bought small leather bag gave five and sixpence English money bought some ribbon 17 cents yard American money 62 cents they have some very nice shops.

Been packing for Chester left in Liverpool my carpet bag and Mrs Lowell's sea things Miss Clink gone to London today.

[The next day the family went to Chester.]

Lorenza Stevens Berbineau, *From Beacon Hill to the Crystal Palace: The 1851 Travel Diary of a Working-Class Woman* (Iowa City, IA: University of Iowa Press, 2002).

The novelist **Anne Bullard** (1808–96) sailed with **Henry Ward Beecher** on the *New World* to Liverpool in 1850. This was the first step in her tour of the Continent. Customs searches evidently could not dampen her enthusiasm at arriving.

Owing to the low tide, we were compelled to anchor out in the stream and here were visited by custom-house officers. The steerage was first examined, and one man was detected in stowing away large plugs of tobacco about his person. On examination fourteen large plugs were found upon him, and in his chest a bag of plugs was found, weighing a great many pounds. It was taken from him, and he held in arrest, liable to a fine of £100 or $500. The examination on board ship was very rigid. Several men with lanterns searched every state-room, although it was broad day-light; they looked under the berths, lifted up the mattresses, looked between the bed-clothes, and in every nook and corner. The baggage of the passengers, however, was reserved for inspection at the custom-house, but the ship was faithfully searched. At length, a steamer took us from the ship, and with three cheers, long and loud, which it seemed must startle old John Bull, we bade adieu to the *New World*, and turned our faces to the beautiful city of Liverpool, which loomed up to our view.

Anne Tuttle Jones Bullard, *Sights and Scenes in Europe* (1852).

Frederick Law Olmsted (1822–1903) was the founder of American landscape architecture and is commemorated in many parts of the USA for the parks he designed. In 1850 he went on a walking tour of England

and Wales with his compatriot Charles Loring Brace, and he devoted a substantial part of his *Walks and Talks of an American Farmer in England* (1852) to detailed descriptions of Merseyside and dedicated it in his preface to farmers and farmers' families. Olmsted had considerable experience of journalism, which fed his travel narratives of Texas (*A Journey through Texas*, 1857) and the slave states (*Journeys and Explorations in the Cotton Kingdom*, 1861). Olmsted's detailed attention to dress, street life, etc., nicely conveys the texture of Merseyside life at the time. He was so impressed by the layout of Birkenhead Park that he subsequently incorporated aspects into his own design for Central Park in New York later in the 1850s.

[Landfall and the docks.]

At five, in the rumble and roar of the town, our anchor dropped. The ship could not haul into the docks until midnight tide, and the steam-tug took us, who wished it, to the shore, landing us across the Dublin steamer at the Prince's Dock quay.

At the head of the gang-plank stood a policeman, easily recognised and familiar, thanks to Punch, who politely helped us to land, thus giving us immediate occasion to thank the government for its hospitality, and its regard for our safety and convenience. It was a real pleasure to stamp upon the neat, firm, solid mason-work of the dock, and we could not but be mindful of the shabby log-wharves we had stumbled over as we left New York. We were immediately beset by porters, not rudely, but with serious, anxious deference and care to keep a way open before us. I was assisting a lady, and carried her bag; a man followed me pertinaciously. 'I tell you I have no baggage,' said I. 'But, sir, this bag?' 'Oh, I can carry that.' 'Excuse me, sir; you must not, indeed; *gentlemen* never does so in *this country*.' After handing the lady into a hackney-coach, we walked on. The landing-place was spacious, not encumbered with small buildings or piles of freight, and though there was a little rain falling, there was a smooth, clean stone pavement, free from mud, to walk on. There was a slight smell of bituminous smoke in the air, not disagreeable, but, to me, highly pleasant. I snuffed it as if passing a field of new-mown hay—snuffed and pondered, and at last was brought to my mind the happy fireside of the friend, in the indistinct memory of which this peculiar odour of English coal had been gratefully associated.

Coming on shore with no luggage or any particular business to engage our attention, we plunged adventurously into the confused tide of life with which the busy streets were thronged, careless whither it floated us. Emerging from the crowd of porters, hackmen, policemen, and ragged Irish men and women on the dock, we entered the first street that opened before us. On the corner stood a church—not un-American in its appearance—and we passed without stopping to the next corner, where we paused to look at the dray-horses, immensely heavy and in elegant condition, fat and glossy, and docile and animated in their expression. They were harnessed, generally, in couples, one before another, to great, strong, low-hung carts, heavy enough alone to be a load for one of our cartmen's light horses. Catching the bustling spirit of the crowd, we walked on at a quick pace, looking at the faces of the men we met more than any thing else, until we came to a wall of hewn drab stone, some fifteen feet high, with a handsomely cut balustrade at the top. There was a large gateway in it, from which a policeman was driving away some children. People were going in and out, and we followed in to see what it was. Up stairs, we found ourselves on a broad terrace, with a handsome building, in Tuscan style, fronting upon it. Another policeman here informed us that it was a railway station. The door was opened as we approached it by a man in a simple uniform, who asked us where we were going. We answered flat we merely wished to look at the building. 'Walk in, gentlemen; you will best take the right-hand platform, and return by the other.' A train was backing in; a man in the same uniform stood in the rear car, and moved his hand round as if turning' an imaginary driving-wheel, the engine at the other end being governed by his motions:—forward—slower— slower—faster—slower—stop—back. The train stopped, the doors were unlocked by men in a more brilliant uniform, and there was a great rush of passengers to secure good seats. Women with bundles and band-boxes were shoved this way and that, as they struggled to hoist themselves into the doors; their parcels were knocked out of their hands, porters picked them up and threw them in, reckless where. So bewildered and flustered did they all seem to be, that we could not refrain from trying to assist them. There was nothing in the plan or fittings of the building that needs remark, and we soon returned to the terrace, where we remained some time observing the peculiarities of the houses and the people passing in the vicinity.

[…]

The broad promenade outside the dock walls was occupied by the police, stevedores, watermen, boarding-house keepers, and a crowd of women, waiting to help in the ships or to receive their crews when the tide should have risen enough to admit them. I was surprised at the quietness and decency of these 'sailors' wives,' as they called themselves; they were plainly and generally neatly dressed, and talked quietly and in kind tones to each other, and I heard no loud profanity or ribaldry at all. Whether this was owing to the presence of the police I cannot say, but I am sure it would be impossible to find, in America, vice, shame, and misery so entirely unassociated with drunkenness or excitement and riot. They were not as young as girls of the same sort in the streets of New York, and in the strong gas-light their faces seemed expressive of a quite different character; generally they were pensive and sad, but not ill-natured or stupid. It occurred to me that their degradation must have been reached in a different way, and had not brought with it that outcasting from all good which they would suffer with us. As they stood, companioned together with each other, but friendless, some with not even hats to protect them from the rain, others, with their gowns drawn up over their head, and others, two together, under a scanty shawl, it would have been difficult, I thought, for a woman, who is always found most unforgiving of her sister's sin, not to have been softened towards those abandoned thus to seek support of life that night. We could not but think the kind words with which the sailors recognised and greeted them, as the ships hauled near, were as much dictated by pity and sympathy as by any worse impulses. They said, 'If nobody else cares for you, we do.' If nobody else is waiting to welcome us, we know that you will be glad that we are coming to the land once more, so, cheer up, and we will help each other again to enjoy a short space of jollity, excitement, and forgetfulness.

[...]

Tired of waiting for the ship, and a good deal fatigued with our tramps on the pavements, about half-past twelve we went back into the town, and by the very obliging assistance of the policemen found lodgings in a 'Temperance Hotel,' still open at that late hour. We were a little surprised to find a number of men in the coffee-room drinking beer and smoking. The subject of their conversation was some project of an association of working-men to combine their savings, and make more profitable investment of them than could be made of the small amounts of each separately. There were late newspapers on the table, and we sat up some time longer to read them, but they were still at it,

puffing and drinking, and earnestly discussing how they could best
use their money, when we went up to bed. We had good beds in
pleasant rooms for which we paid twenty-five cents each.

[Buildings, streets, markets.]

The common building material here is a light, greyish-red brick.
Stone of different colours is used in about the same proportion
that it is in New York. The warehouses are generally higher than
the same class of buildings there, but the dwelling-houses lower,
seldom over three stories. The old houses, in narrow streets, are
generally small, and often picturesque from the carvings of time
upon them, or from the incongruous additions and improvements
that have been made to them at intervals. At the railway station
we noticed such differences in the windows of a two-story house
near us, as these. There were two below; one of these, being
a shop front, was entirely modern, with large panes of glass in
light wooden sashes. The other was of small panes, set in heavy
wood-work, such as you see in our oldest houses. One of the
upper windows had small square panes set in lead; those of the
other were *lozenge*-shaped, and in neither were they more than
three inches wide. The frames were much wider than they were
high, and they opened sideways. In the newer part of the city, the
fashionable quarter, there are a good many brick-walled houses
faced with *stucco*. Others are of Bath stone, and these are not
unfrequently *painted* over of the original colour of the stone. Bath
stone, which is the most common material of mason work, is a
fine-grained freestone, very easy to the chisel. It is furnished much
cheaper than our brown stone, so much so that there would be
a chance of exporting it to America with profit. There is a finer
sort of it, called by the masons Caen stone, which is brought from
Normandy. The colour of both is at first buff, but rapidly changes
to a dark brown. There are some buildings of red sandstone, of
a little lighter colour than that now so much used in New York.
In buildings mainly of brick, stone is used more considerably
than with us; and there are none of those equivocating, sanded-
wood parapets, porticos, steps, &c.; all is the *real grit*. The bricks
are mottled, half red and half greyish yellow; the effect, at a little
distance, being as I said a yellow or greyish red, much pleasanter
than the bright red colour of our Eastern brick. Every thing
out of doors here soon gets *toned down*, as the artists say, by the
smoke. Perhaps it is partly on this account that pure white paint is

never used; but the prevailing taste is evidently for darker colours than with us. The common hues of the furniture and fitting up of shops, for instance, is nearly as dark as old mahogany. This gives even the dram-shops such a rich, substantial look, that we can hardly recognise them as of the same species as our tawdry 'saloons', that are so painted, gilded, and bedizened to catch flies with their flare. There are no 'oyster cellars', but oysters 'raw and in the shell', are exposed in stands about the street, like those of our 'hot corn,' and apple women. Liquor shops, always with the ominous sign of '*Vaults*,' are very frequent, and often splendid. The tea and coffee shops are among the richest in the streets. The bakers' fronts are also generally showy, and there are a great many of them. It seems to be the general custom, for poor families at least, to make their own bread, and send it in to them to be baked. The first night we were ashore, we got some bread and butter, and American cheese, at a baker's, and saw in ten minutes a dozen loaves called for. They had sheet-iron checks, with numbers on them, which were given up on the presentation of a corresponding check, and, for a loaf of ten or twelve pounds, a penny our baking—in the same way that passengers' baggage is checked on our railroads.

Wood is used in the interior of houses more than I had imagined it would be. Its cost is high. I inquired the price of what looked like a common 'Albany board,' such as I buy in New York for sixteen cents; it was of the value of about thirty-five cents. The kitchens, as far as we have observed, are on the street floor, level with the living apartments. Coarse pottery and wicker-work utensils are more common than with us. Few of the houses in the town have trees about them. Occasionally an old mansion is set a little back, and has a little shrubby foliage in front of it—most commonly of elms dwarfed to the size and natural shape of a green-gage plum-tree. There are, though, in the better part of the town, some most charming public grounds. I have never seen any thing in America to compare with them.

[…]

I have been through two markets. One of them is an immensely large building, covering about two acres, right in the centre of the town; it is clean, light, and well ventilated. What a wonder it is that the people of New York will put up with such miserable, filthy, crowded hovels as their markets are! In this building there are over five hundred stalls and tables. It has its own superintendent of weights and measures, and a thorough

and constant police. There are twelve men whose employment is
to keep it clean. The garbage is passed readily through traps into
vaults below, from which it is removed at night. The rules for
those who use it, are excellent to secure healthy condition of food,
neatness, order, and fair play, and they are strictly enforced. To
my mind, this structure, and the arrangements connected with it,
is an honour to Liverpool, not second to her docks. And she has
three other large public markets, besides small ones for particular
purposes. The meat stalls are frequently owned by women, and,
except a better supply of birds and rabbits, did not offer any thing
different from those of our butchers. A part of the market seemed
to be occupied by country women for the sale of miscellaneous
wares.

The fish market was in another building, which was entirely
occupied by women, nice and neat, though skinning eels and
cleaning fish. The milk market also seemed to be altogether in
the hands of women. Milk is not peddled about as in New York,
but sold from cellar-shops. If one wants a cup of tea, our landlady
runs across the street for a penny-worth of it. 'From hand to
mouth' so, seems to be common with many things. The material
for our breakfast is mostly bought after we have ordered it. As
we did not mention what we would have till after the shops
were closed last night, we had to wait till nine o'clock for it this
morning. Business hours begin later than in America. I think the
market is not open till eight, which they speak of as 'very early.'
In this respect we have found no difficulty in accommodating
ourselves to English customs.

[Liverpool people and donkeys.]

After we had wandered for about an hour through the streets the
first afternoon we were ashore, I remarked that we had not yet
seen a single well-dressed man, not one person that in America
would have been described as 'of respectable appearance.' We were
astonished to observe with what an unmingled stream of poverty
the streets were swollen, and J. remarked that if what we had
seen was a fair indication of the general condition of the masses
here, he should hardly feel justified in dissuading them from
using violent and anarchical means to bring down to themselves
a share of the opportunities and comforts of those 'higher classes'
that seem to be so utterly separated from them. There are a great
many Irish in Liverpool, but the most that we had thus far seen

evidently were English, yet not English as we have known them. Instead of the stout, full-faced John Bulls, we had seen but few that were not thin, meagre, and pale. There was somewhat rarely an appearance of actual misery, but a stupid, hopeless, state-prison-for-life sort of expression. There were not unfrequently some exceptions to this, but these were men almost invariably in some uniform or livery, as railroad hands, servants, and soldiers.

The next morning, in the court-yard of the Exchange (the regular 'Change assemblage seemed to meet out of doors), we saw a large collection of the merchants. There was nothing to distinguish them from a company of a similar kind with us, beyond a general Englishness of features and an entire absence of all *oddities*—with astonishing beards and singularities of costume. One young man only wore small clothes and leggings, which would perhaps have disagreeably subjected him to be noticed with us. They were stouter than our merchants, and more chubby-faced, yet not looking in vigorous health. They were, on the whole, judging by a glance at their outsides, to be more respected than any lot of men of the same number that I ever saw together in Wall street. Many of them, and most of the well-dressed men that we have seen in the streets, have had a green leaf and simple posy in a button-hole of their coats.

The shopkeepers of the better class, or retail merchants, are exactly the same men, to all appearance, that stand behind the counters with us. *Merchant*, means only a wholesale dealer in England; retailers are *shopkeepers*. The word *store* is never applied to a building; but the building in which goods are stored is a *warehouse*.

Women are more employed in trade than with us; I have no doubt with every way great advantage. The women in the streets are more noticeably different from ours than the men. In general, they are very cheaply and coarsely clad. Many of the lower class have their outer garments ordinarily drawn up behind, in the scrubbing-floor fashion. Caps are universally worn, and being generally nice and white, they have a pleasant effect upon the face. The very poorest women look very miserably. We see bruised eyes not unfrequently, and there is evidently a good deal of hard drinking among them. They are larger and stouter, and have coarser features. There are neither as many pretty nor as many ugly faces as with us; indeed, there are very few remarkably ill favoured in that respect, and almost none strikingly handsome. The best Ewes we have seen were among the fish-stalls in market.

With scarcely an exception, the fish-women were very large and
tall, and though many of them were in the neighbourhood of
fifty, they had invariably full, bright, unwrinkled faces, beautiful
red cheeks, and a cheerful expression. English women, generally,
appear more bold and self-reliant, their *action* is more energetic,
and their carriage less graceful and drooping than ours. Those
well dressed that we have seen, while *shopping*, for instance, are
no exceptions. Those we have met to converse with are as modest
and complaisant as could be desired, yet speak with a marked
promptness and confidence which is animating and attractive. We
met a small company last night at the residence of a gentleman
to whom we had a letter, and spent the evening precisely as
we should at a small tea-party at home; we might easily have
imagined ourselves in New England. The gentlemen were no
way different, that we noticed, from cultivated men with us, and
the ladies only seemed rather more frank, hearty, and sincere-
natured than we should expect ours to be to strangers.★ There
was nothing in their dresses that I can think of as peculiar, yet a
general air, not American—a heavier look and more *crinkles*, and
darker and more mixed-up colours. We see many rather nice-
looking females, probably coming in from the country, driving
themselves about town as if they understood it, in jaunty-looking
chaises and spring-carts.

[...]

The children look really *punchy*. It strikes me the young ones
are dressed much older, while the young men are clothed much
more boyishly than in America. Quite large children, of both
sexes, are dressed exactly alike, and whether girls or boys (they
look between both), you cannot guess—girls with fur hats, such as
full-grown men wear, and boys in short dresses and pantalettes.

There are lots of the queerest little donkeys in the streets; some
of them would not weigh more than Nep (my Newfoundland
dog), and most of them are not as large as our two-year-old steers.
They are made to draw most enormous loads, I saw one tugging
a load of coal, on the top of which two stout Irishmen sat, and
stopped them to ask the weight. It was 1200 (besides themselves),
and the top of the donkey's back was just even with my waist,
The driver said he bought her five years ago for two pounds ($10),
and she was then called an old one. Here is one now coming
up the hill with a great load of furniture, a man on behind it,
and a boy on the shafts—a poor little rat of a thing, with the
meekest expression you can conceive of. It is just as much as he

can stagger along with, and the boy jumps off to relieve—no! the young satan has gone to his head and is cudgelling him. The poor little donkey winks and turns his head, and drops his ears, and nearly falls down. The boy stops (probably a policeman heaves in sight) and takes his seat on the shaft again, and the donkey reels on. The man aft has continued his smoking all the while, without taking any notice of the delay. As I write, there goes by another—a very handsome, large fat one, drawing a market cart, with a pretty country girl among the hampers driving.

* These ladies were Irish. The remark hardly applies to English ladies, certainly not unless you meet them domestically. The English in their homes, and the English 'in company,' are singularly opposite characters [Olmsted's note].

[Birkenhead Ferry.]

The ferry-boat by which we crossed to Birkenhead was very small and dingy. There was no protection from the weather on board of her, except a narrow, dark cabin under deck. There were uncushioned seats all around the outside, against the rail, and the rest of the deck was mostly filled up with freight, spars, &c. She had a bowsprit, and a beautiful light, rakish mast, and topmast fitted to carry a gaffsail. She was steered with a wheel in the stern. The pilot or master (a gentleman with a gold band on his hat and naval buttons), stood on the paddle-boxes to direct, and a boy stood over the engine to pass orders below. The engine was under deck, the tops of the cylinders only appearing above it. It was, however, entirely exposed to observation, and showed excellent workmanship, and was kept perfectly clean and highly polished. It was of entirely different construction from any American engine, having three oscillating cylinders. The 'hands' looked like regular tars, wearing tarpaulins, with the name of the boat in gilt letters on the ribbon, blue baize shirts, and broad-bottomed trousers hung tight on the hips. The boat came *alongside* the wharf, ran out her hawsers, and took in her passengers by a narrow gang-plank; and yet she makes her trip once in ten minutes. There would not be room enough on her decks for one of our Rockaways [four-wheeled carriage with two seats] to stand, and she seemed to have no idea of ferrying any thing but foot-passengers. What would the good people of Birkenhead think of a Fulton ferry-boat, with its long, light, and airy rooms, their floors level with the street, and broad carriage-roads from stem to stern, crossing and re-crossing without turning round, or ever a word of command, or a rope lifted from morning till evening and from evening till morning? The length of the ferry is about the same as the South Ferry of Brooklyn, and the fare one penny.

Right in the midst of the town, at the corner of a new brick house, we came upon an old pile of stone work. Old, indeed !—under the broken arch of a Gothic window, the rain-water had been so long trickling as to wear deep channels; cracking, crumbling, bending over with age, it seemed in many places as if the threatening mass had only been till now withheld from falling prostrate by the faithful ivy that clung to it, and clasped it tight with every fibre.

You cannot imagine the contrast to the hot, hurrying, noisy world without, that we found on entering the little enclosure of the old churchyard and abbey walls. It was all overshadowed with dense foliage, and only here and there through the leaves, or a shattered arch round which the ivy curled with enchanting grace, would there be a glimpse of the blue sky above. By listening, we could still hear the roar of wheels, rumbling of rail-cars, clanging of steamboat bells, and the shouts of jovial sea-captains, drinking gin and water in a neighbouring tea-garden, over which the American flag was flying. But within the walls there was no sound but the chirps of a wren, looking for her nest in a dark cranny; the hum of bees about an old hawthorn bush; the piping of a cricket under a gravestone, and our own footsteps echoed from mysterious crypts.

Our guide having pointed out to us the form of the ancient structure, and been requited for his trouble by seeing the pleasure he had given us, took his leave. We remained a long time, and enjoyed it as you may think.

Did you ever hear of Birkenhead Abbey? I never had before. It has no celebrity; but coming upon it so fresh from the land of youth, as we did, so unexpecting of any thing of the kind— though I have since seen far older ruins, and more renowned—I have never found any so impressively aged.

[Birkenhead Park had been designed by Joseph Paxton (who also designed the Crystal Palace) and opened in 1847, one of the first civic parks in the world. Olmsted's admiration for its landscaping is evident .]

The baker had begged of us not to leave Birkenhead without
seeing their *new park*, and at his suggestion we left our knapsacks
with him, and proceeded to it. As we approached the entrance,
we were met by women and girls, who, holding out a cup of
milk, asked us—'*Will you take a cup of milk, Sirs?—good, cool, sweet,
cow's milk, gentlemen, or right warm from the ass!*' And at the gate
was a herd of donkeys, same with cans of milk strapped to them,
others saddled and bridled, to be let for ladies and children to
ride.

The gateway, which is about a mile and a half from the ferry,
and quite back of the town, is a great, massive block of handsome
Ionic architecture, standing alone, and unsupported by any thing
else in the vicinity, and looking, as I think, heavy and awkward.
There is a sort of grandeur about it that the English are fond of,
but which, when it is entirely separate from all other architectural
constructions, always strikes me unpleasantly. It seems intended
as an impressive preface to a great display of art within; but here,
as well as at Eaton Park, and other places I have since seen, it
is not followed up with great things, the grounds immediately
within the grand entrance being very simple, and apparently rather
overlooked by the gardener. There is a large archway for carriages,
and two smaller ones for those on foot, and, on either side, and
over these, are rooms, which probably serve as inconvenient lodges
for the labourers. No porter appears, and the gates are freely open
to the public.

Walking a short distance up an avenue, we passed through
another light iron gate into a thick, luxuriant, and diversified
garden. Five minutes of admiration, and a few more spent in
studying the manner in which art had been employed to obtain
from nature so much beauty, and I was ready to admit that
in democratic America there was nothing to be thought of as
comparable with this People's Garden. Indeed, gardening, had here
reached a perfection that I had never before dreamed of. I cannot
undertake to describe the effect of so much taste and skill as had
evidently been employed; I will only tell you, that we passed
by winding paths, over acre's and acres, with a constant varying
surface, where on all sides were growing every variety of shrubs
and flowers, with more than natural grace, all set in borders of
greenest, closest turf, and all kept with most consummate neatness.
At a distance of a quarter of a mile from the gate, we came to an
open field of clean, bright, green-sward, closely mown, on which
a large tent was pitched, and a party of boys in one part, and a

party of gentlemen in another, were playing cricket. Beyond this
was a large meadow with rich groups of trees, under which a
flock of sheep were reposing, and girls and women with children,
were playing. While watching the cricketers, we were threatened
with a shower, and hastened back to look for shelter, which we
found in a pagoda, on an island approached by a Chinese bridge.
It was soon filled, as were the other ornamental buildings, by a
crowd of those who, like ourselves, had been overtaken in the
grounds by the rain; and I was glad to observe that the privileges
of the garden were enjoyed about equally by all classes. There
were some who were attended by servants, and sent at once for
their carriages, but a large proportion were of the common ranks,
and a few women with children, or suffering from ill health,
were evidently the wives of very humble labourers. There were
a number of strangers, and some we observed with note-books
and portfolios, that seemed to have come from a distance to study
from the garden. The summer-houses, lodges, bridges, &c., were
all well constructed, and of undecaying materials. One of the
bridges which we crossed was of our countryman, Remington's
patent [a form of bridge lattice], an extremely light and graceful
erection.

Frederick Law Olmsted, *Walks and Talks of an
American Farmer in England* (1852).

Randal William MacGavock (1826–63) was a member of one of the
leading families of Nashville, Tennessee. He was evidently unimpressed by
the hotels of Liverpool but fascinated by the city draught-horses.

The hotels here are called excellent, but really they are inferior
to our American hotels in every particular. They are nothing
more than large coffee-houses with lodging rooms attached. The
idea of one taking his meals all alone is rather anti-democratic
for Americans, and more particularly a Westerner. You go into
the coffee-room and call for what you wish, which is served up
in a few minutes by females, in large old-fashioned white caps,
which makes one feel like laughing more than eating. Nothing
has attracted my attention more than the draft-horses that I see
in the streets. Their size and capabilities are really wonderful;
as a general thing they are about sixteen hands high and in

proportion. They are in excellent order, and look as sleek as a
new hat. Yesterday I counted as many as thirty steam-pressed bales
of cotton on one wagon, and drawn by only two horses, which
would be considered a tremendous load on our turnpikes for a
team of six horses. Being rather curious, I stopped the driver and
inquired what he fed his horses with; and he told me that steamed
beans and corn were most widely used, but that every thing was
steamed.

Randal William MacGavock, *A Tennessean Abroad* (1854).

Daniel Clarke Eddy (1823–96), a Baptist minister from Lowell,
Massachusetts, recorded his impressions of religious practice while starting
a tour of the Continent in 1850. Although he was impressed by aspects of
the city, Eddy clearly had misgivings about Liverpool and in his *Europa*
(1859) gives one of the earliest descriptions of leaving Lime Street by train.
Eddy was the author of a number of advice volumes for young men and
women.

We soon passed the custom-house, had our baggage examined,
and were on our way to a hotel. Every thing was new and
strange. I expected to have seen a crowd of jostling hackmen,
a multitude of beggars, and a swarm of pickpockets, but was
agreeably disappointed in finding the streets as quiet as our own.
The police officers, with a neat distinguishing livery, ready to
bestow any attention, and the people free from that idle gaze with
which a person is received in an American city, if he chances to
arrive at an unusual hour, or in an incomely plight. As we moved
on, the corners of the streets were seen covered with notices of
religious meetings. The objectionable practice prevails all over
England, and clergymen, on Saturday, have large placards pasted
on the corner of the streets, and on public buildings, informing
the people of the hour and the subject on which they will
discourse. Some of these notices are several feet in length; and
are worded so as to draw attention. One was headed, 'POPERY
MISREPRESENTED AND REPRESENTED; or, *Which is
which*;' and below followed a notice that Rev. Mr. Somebody
would preach on Popery at a given hour.

After dinner, I went out to find a religious service. I went to
several chapels of our own denomination, but found them closed,

the prevailing custom being to hold service in the morning and
evening. St. David's Church I found open. It would seat more
than a thousand persons, and but twenty-four adults and thirty-
one children were present. An elderly man was preaching from
the words 'Wherefore gird up the loins of your mind', &c. The
discourse was sound in doctrine, ably written, but drawled and
jerked out in the most unpardonable manner. The children were at
play, and the adults were asleep. On the evening of the same day, I
wandered out to the church of the famous Hugh M'Neile, one of
the best pulpit orators I heard in England. His church is far away
from the noise and confusion of the city, in a beautiful park, and is
a costly and elegant Gothic structure. Though so far removed from
the mass of habitations and the crowded streets, it is always well
filled with an aristocratic audience. On the evening in question,
it was crowded. We entered after the service had commenced;
a song of praise was sweetly sounding through the aisles, and
echoing amid the arches overhead. As we passed up the aisle, we
were at once recognized as strangers, and several pew doors were
immediately thrown open to us—an instance of genuine politeness
seldom shown so promptly, and with such apparent cheerfulness, in
England or America. Dr. M'Neile is apparently about sixty years
of age, tall and dignified in his demeanour, erect and manly in
his bearing, having a countenance full of life, and an eye flashing
with the fires of genius and intellect. His tone is earnest, and his
enunciation clear and distinct. His hair is gray, bordering on snowy
whiteness, and is carefully arranged. His countenance is one of
the most expressive I have ever seen, and marks him as a man of
vigorous thought and energy. He has recently entered into the
arena of theological discussion, as an opponent of the church of
Rome; and few men in England are feared more by the pope and
his cardinals than Hugh M'Neile.

[He delivers a sermon.]

During the delivery of this discourse, the preacher stood with a
small Bible in his hand, and was unembarrassed with notes. The
sermon was ingenious rather than profound, impressive rather than
eloquent. It was followed by an extemporaneous prayer, offered
in a subdued and melting tone, and seemed full for the true and
unmistakable spirit of devotion.
[...]
Perhaps the stranger's attention is arrested, in an English town, by

nothing more than the heavy, massive, frowning appearance of the public and private buildings. The eye of an American, which has long gazed upon neat white dwellings and churches, enclosed in gardens of luxuriant freshness soon tires with the dull monotony of a city all built of brick and stone, blackened by age and storms, and begrimed with the smoke of the chimney and the dust of the furnace. The buildings in Liverpool all look as if built to last through time. They seem to defy the heat of summer and the blasts of winter—the assaults of time, and the ravages of fire and sword. Among the churches is one of cast iron; and another for the blind, in which the singing is done by, and the congregation composed chiefly of, the poor, unfortunate inmates of the blind asylum, a charity which adorns the city of Liverpool even more than its dock, or its commercial advantages.

[...]

After surveying Liverpool and its environs, we repaired, just at nightfall, to the railway station, to take the cars for Manchester. The depot formed a remarkable contrast with those in our own country. It was erected in 1837, at an immense expense, and is lighted from the roof. The stone front has thirty-six Corinthian columns and four large arched gateways, and stands out in its nobility, fit exterior of this great palace of transportation. On leaving the station, the train enters a long tunnel, dark as Egypt, and dreary as night. This tunnel is six thousand six hundred and ninety feet long, seventy-five feet wide, and fifty-one feet high, and passes directly under the city, while over it rise churches, houses, halls and places of trade and industry. He who had never rode in a rail-car would hardly be willing to begin by riding through the subterranean passage. The oppressive darkness, which be *felt;* the cold, damp chill, which pierces to the bones; the glaring lamp on the engine, and the screaming of the iron horse,—all render the five minutes spent under the streets and temples of the great mart of commerce most unpleasant and disagreeable.

On emerging from this dark passage, the traveller has opportunity to examine the car in which he rides, and the countenances of his fellow-passengers. The railway arrangements are very different in England from ours in America. There are three classes of cars, and for either of them the traveller purchases his ticket as he may choose. Having secured his ticket, he is sent into a room where he finds others who are to ride in the same class cars. If he be a third-class passenger, he does not see those who are to ride in the first and second-class cars. They too are shut up, to await the hour of starting. When this arrives, the first-class passengers are taken from the room where they have been held in durance, and seated in the cars, and the doors are closed, and, in some instances, locked. They the second-class passengers are seated, and at length the third. The cars are short, being only about eight feet long and six wide, and are frequently divided by a partition as high as the head of a person sitting. The first class are well arranged, well fitted, and comfortable; but the fare in them is so high, that few besides the nobility and the wealthy ride in them. The second class are destitute of cushions, and almost every other comfort. On the hard seat, with the straight back, the passenger is compelled to sit, with his feet covered up with boxes and baggage, gazing upon the placards which are pasted up on the sides and ends of the car. Generally these cars have two seats, each holding five persons—one half looking into the faces and trampling upon the feet of the other half. The window, or ventilator, as it should be called, is a small, square aperture in the door, like the window of a coach, and sometimes has a slide of glass, but more generally of wood, to keep out the rain. Smoking, snuff-taking, tobacco-chewing are all allowed; and these privileges are improved by the English generally. The last time I rode in the cars in England, I found myself in company with one Frenchman and his lady, two young men who were smoking the most abominable cigars, three apparently well-bred English ladies, and an Irish woman. The young men kept on smoking, the rain dashed against the window of the car, and compelled us to close it; and twice or thrice during the day, the Irish woman drew an onion of very respectable dimensions from her basket, and slicing it up with bread, devoured it eagerly, with as much apparent relish as if it were a finely-flavoured peach.

Daniel Clarke Eddy, *Europa; or, Scenes and Society in England, France, Italy, and Switzerland* (1859).

John Weiss Forney (1817–81) was editor of the *Philadelphia Press* and the *Washington Chronicle*. In 1867, when he made his voyage to Liverpool on the Royal Mail steamship *Scotia*, he was serving as the US Secretary of the Senate. His letters describing his travels use Philadelphia as a point of comparison, often to Liverpool's advantage, and offer unusual comments on paper money, the role of women, and the use of stone for building. He had some problems understanding Liverpool speech too.

Solidity is written everywhere; every thing seems built to last, from the immense docks themselves down to the burly frames of the men and the large feet of the women. Landing at the quay, after a tedious delay in the Mersey, while the custom-house officers were examining the baggage, I was very much edified at the curious sights and manners around me. The first was the absence of greenbacks and small paper currency, and the substitution, in counting money, of pounds, crowns, shillings, and pence, for dollars, half-dollars, quarters, ten, and five-cent pieces. Some very amusing mistakes were the result. It is a habit you so soon fall into, that I am more than ever anxious for the return of specie payments in the United States.

Reaching the Washington, in Liverpool, a pleasant but somewhat expensive hotel, I was startled to find the book- keeper and registrar a woman; and I noticed that women performed many of the offices that are monopolized by men in our country. In most of the hotels they act as clerks. On the subject of cabs and 'hansoms' I shall have something to say hereafter; but I cannot now forbear a note upon the extraordinary difference between this mode of transportation and that in the United States. You can ride miles for a shilling, (about twenty-five cents) and on Sunday three of us, Mr. Caldwell, of Philadelphia, Mr. Prescott Smith, of Maryland, and myself, rode about the town and environs for three hours and a half for about two dollars of our currency. In Philadelphia that excursion would have cost at least five, and, probably ten dollars. But the most curious of all the sights was St. John's market in Liverpool, on Saturday night; it was on Saturday, you will remember, that we landed. There is no better way to understand a people and a country, than to attend places in which they buy and sell the necessaries of life, generally the product of their own labour and soil. Although the surging mass in which I was tossed about spoke my own language, it was very difficult to realize it in the jargon that filled my ears, a patois in which the broad English and the broader Scotch, and the rapid Irish, were strangely commingled. The stalls literally overflowed with vegetables and meats of every description, and it was not difficult to understand English fruitfulness from these substantial proofs. Strange fish, called after strange names, were mingled with the

finest salmon I ever saw, and the mutton and beef only needed
the experiment upon them at my hotel to establish that they were
worthy of their fame. About midnight the market closed, the
great throng retiring in order, but amid shouts of laughter, before
the command of the uniformed and ubiquitous police. Once
more in the streets, I found a new feature of foreign life. Bands
of music were playing to delighted crowds; itinerant orators were
talking incomprehensible politics to absorbed listeners; soldiers
were countermarching; and gin-shops in a blaze of light! These
were novel scenes to me, and when I retired for the rest I needed
so much, you need not wonder if my sleep was visited by many
conflicting and illogical visions.
[...]
There are ten miles of these docks, seven miles on the Liverpool
and three on the Birkenhead side of the Mersey. They cost
more than one hundred millions of dollars. They are built
as if they were intended to endure as long as the Pyramids.
From this statement you can form some idea of the magnitude
of the commerce of this great port. It must not be forgotten
that while such accommodations are wholly needless at our
American ports, London and Liverpool would be nowhere as
commercial capitals without them. As I have said, every thing is
solid about Liverpool. The great docks, warehouses, counting-
houses, public buildings, and even the private houses, have a
sort of monumental air. Even the streets, clean and strong, as if
they had been laid by the same masons that built these stately
piles, are composed of the same material, a native stone found
in many parts of England. Soft and white when it is dug from
the earth, it grows hard and dark when it is exposed to the
mists of the sea, which hang like clouds over the British isles
through the best part of the year, making the atmosphere humid
and frequently shutting out the sun from the gaze of men.
Among the many things that attract the traveller is the almost
universal use to which this stone is applied, especially in modern
improvements. You find it in almost every town and village,
superseding the old buildings and composing the new. As the
English clay does not seem to make good brick, the value of this
material cannot be calculated. The magnificent railway stations
are chiefly built of it, and most of the new castles and mansions
of the nobility, together with the new public edifices. Although
it has a somewhat sombre air, yet, susceptible as it is of being
easily cut, shaped, and carved, it is at once ornate and useful.

The cleanliness of Liverpool is very remarkable, though, as I have heard, it is surpassed in this, as in all respects, by London. The heavy blocks with which the streets are built render it impossible for dirt to accumulate, and it is said that, however foul the day, the public thoroughfares are always decent.

John W. Forney, *Letters from Europe* (1867).

Charles C. Fulton (1816–83), editor of the *Baltimore American*, sailed to Bremen in the early 1870s, toured Europe and stopped in Liverpool on the last leg before his return voyage. The subtitles are Fulton's.

Aspect of Liverpool

We find Liverpool looking, if possible, more solid, more sombre, and more ponderous than it did twelve years ago. The same mammoth horses, with their elephantine legs and hoofs, seem to be drawing the same heavy loads of merchandise, and the same Irishmen seem to be urging them on. We observe, however, vast improvements in the business centres, in the construction of new and elegant establishments, which have taken the place of the antiquated structures of the past, whilst at every turn there are indications of the flood of wealth which commerce is pouring into its harbour.

City of Liverpool

Although the greatest commercial city in the world, it does not come up to the anticipations of the stranger in all those stirring, bustling scenes of activity which an American will look for as inseparable from the transactions of so vast a business. On approaching the city from the sea, the whole front presents a series of blank granite walls, tall warehouses, and yawning entrances to dock basins, over the top of which, and apparently in close contact with the chimneys of the houses, the topmasts of vessels can be discerned spread for many miles around. If the tide is low, the granite walls of the docks tower up thirty-five feet from the water, as the fluctuation of the tide here is never less than twenty feet, whilst the spring-tides vary from twenty-nine to thirty-three feet.

The warehouses fronting on the docks are generally of immense proportions, six or seven stories high, without any attempt at architectural display, but of solid and massive appearance, their brick fronts dingy and blackened, or sometimes coated with the dust from the many thousands of barrels of flour which are constantly being conveyed to and from their upper stories. With the exception of the public buildings, no money seems to have been expended in business sections for beautifying the city, strength and utility being the only objects aimed at. In proportion to the size of the city, which has nearly six hundred thousand inhabitants, the retail business seems to be very small, and is certainly not equal to that of Glasgow. In comparison with any of our large American cities, it would rate in this respect as a fourth-rate city, and we doubt if there are more than half as many such establishments as may be found in Baltimore.

Street Scenes

The drinking-houses and resorts for sailors along the front of the city, adjoining the docks, are very numerous, and, notwithstanding the vigilance of the police, it is not regarded as safe to visit that section of the city after gas-light. The streets swarm with the most brazen and vicious of a herd of courtesans that the world can produce, whose language and conduct in the streets would not be tolerated even in New York. Although they are numerous in all parts of the city, they seem to be under more rigorous police control elsewhere, and are not allowed to annoy or insult respectable people.

The Liverpool Docks

The shipping and trans-shipping of goods being mostly carried on within the walls of the dock-yards, the casual visitor sees nothing but a forest of masts as indicating the vastness of the commerce of Liverpool. Commerce does not show itself here as it does in our American cities, but is confined within prescribed limits and bounds. The cargo of a vessel arriving will often be taken to load another ready to depart, and not hauled and stored and rehauled, as in New York. The docks are all supplied with immense sheds, and many of them with large warehouses, in which goods are temporarily piled away under the control of the custom-house authorities. The immense products of the manufactories of

Manchester, only about thirty miles distant, are brought by rail
direct to the docks, and immediately placed in the holds of the
ships for which they are designed, the American merchants buying
direct from the factories, and naming the dock, vessel, and time
at which they are to be delivered in Liverpool for transportation
to America. Liverpool is thus rather a great mercantile depot than
such a magnificent commercial city as an American would expect
to find it.

The docks of Liverpool are undoubtedly fine specimens of
engineering. Their immense solidity is, however, a matter of
necessity, as the rushing tide of the Mersey, even in its calmest
moods, would quickly sweep away a structure of less massive
character. Each dock has a large basin in front, into which the
gates of the dock open, for the entrance or departure of vessels.
These gates can only be opened at high tide, and are closed as
soon as the water commences to fall, keeping one depth of water
always inside the docks, whilst that in the basin fluctuates twenty
feet with the tide of the river. The great weight of water, from
twenty to thirty feet deep, thus retained inside the docks, as will
readily be understood, requires the most massive masonry to
retain it within bounds.

[Fulton was particularly impressed by St George's Hall, which had been
built originally as a concert venue. It opened in 1854.]

St. George's Hall

The public buildings of Liverpool, although few in number, are
very extensive and grand specimens of architecture. The custom-
house is an immense white freestone building, surmounted by
a cupola and dome; the Exchange and City Hall are also very
imposing structures; but the pride and glory of Liverpool is 'St.
George's Hall,' which it seems was built with the determination
that it should exceed in size, architectural beauty, and grandeur
of design and finish, any other building in the United Kingdom,
excepting only the Houses of Parliament at London. It occupies
the centre of what seems to be a mound in the very heart of the
city, and approach it from any of the numerous streets converging
towards St. George's Square, and it looms up before the eye
in all its grand prominence. The building is constructed in the
Corinthian style of architecture. The eastern is four hundred and

twenty feet long, and has a columnar projecting centre, with depressed wings. Indeed, the building has really four fronts, each presenting striking architectural features. One end of the building is occupied by the Assize Courts, whilst the other contains concert-rooms, one of which is of immense proportions, fitted up and decorated in a style of magnificence seldom attempted in a hall for such purposes. The interior of this largest hall is one hundred and sixty-seven feet long by seventy-seven in breadth, with an altitude of eighty-two feet.

The grand organ in St. George's Hall is claimed to be the largest instrument in the world, costing about sixty thousand dollars. It is thirty-three feet in breadth and forty-two feet in height, and stands in a splendid gallery of a receding semi-circular form. We were present at a concert given on this grand instrument by a distinguished organist. The music comprised marches and overtures, and displayed the wonderful power and compass, as well as the sweetness of its tones, with fine effect. Concerts are given on this great organ every Wednesday and Saturday afternoon, when there are large audiences present, the charge for admission being sixpence.

Charles C. Fulton, *Europe viewed through American Spectacles* (1874).

Edward Sylvester Morse (1838–1925) was the son of a Calvinist cleric, who became one of America's leading naturalists, studying with Louis Agassiz at Harvard and publishing a number of books on zoology. Although he was more famous for his extended visits to Japan, in the 1880s he visited Europe twice, partly to attend scientific exhibitions. However, on his 1883 visit to Liverpool it was the people of the street that caught his attention and led him to record his impressions in his journal. The Salvation Army was an evangelical offshoot of Protestantism famous for its members' uniform and for their use of brass bands for their street meetings. Morse speculates fantastically on a different kind of evangelism led by key scientists such as Thomas Huxley, Richard Owen and John Tyndall, which overwhelms royalty and the established Church:

May 17, 1883, Liverpool … the dirty slovenly women on the street, big bare-footed girls selling papers, little beggar boys with matches, old women coming out of ginshops. Tonight I saw a detachment of the Salvation Army, a young man with a flag, red;

another with a bass drum; four young girls looking like factory girls, and one or two other young men marching down the street singing at the top of their lungs, followed by a ragged mob of males and females. Four horrid-looking wretches, men, marching in the ranks as scoffers. It was a pathetic, frightful delusion that animated them but to a thoughtful ignorant person, if ignorant persons can be thoughtful, a very impressive sight. The simple admission that it is God's work makes the whole thing so absurdly inadequate to what they intend to do. If God can do such things, what might be achieved if He ordered the royal family and all the Princes and Dukes to be seized with mania with a battalion of Bishops and regiments of vicars and curates parading with thundering chorus down the street, having Huxley, Owen, Tyndall and the rest in the brass band!

[The first museum in Liverpool opened in 1853, then relocated from Duke Street to purpose-built premises in William Brown Street in 1860. The Liverpool Lunatic Asylum was opened in 1792 on grounds adjoining the Liverpool Infirmary. The asylum and a new hospital, the Liverpool Royal Infirmary, were opened in 1851.]

May 18, 1883: Liverpool. Visited the Free Museum and found the whereabouts of Rev. W. W. Higgins with whom I corresponded nearly 30 years ago. Sent him shells and he sent me a large collection of English shells … Mr. Higgins came to the hotel and we spent an hour or two at the Museum. The collection indicates the intelligence and liberality of the Liverpool people. For the support of the Museum a tax of one penny on every pound of income is collected. At 4.30 Mr. Higgins took me to his house in the country about 10 miles from Liverpool; explained to me that he was a clergyman but of the broadest type, that he could not subscribe to the articles [the Thirty-Nine Articles of religion of the Anglican Church] without hypocrisy; he therefore chose a position in which he would not be bound and took the position at a Pauper Lunatic Asylum which he had occupied for 30 years.

[Morse sailed for Liverpool again in August 1887, recording the distressing signs of poverty in his journal.]

Great number of people out of employment, groups sitting on steps of public buildings or plodding along wearily and hopelessly. It is a curious fact that a man gets in a state of utter dejection

and despair. The squalor seems dreadful, after leaving America ...
Women barefooted ... , tramps, bummers and dissolute women
in clothing that once belonged to the upper classes. Fancy an
elaborate spring bonnet crushed and filthy on a frowzy head; or a
swallowtail coat, one tail missing, sodden with grease, on the back
of a dirty tramp ...

Respectable English society seems to care most for outward
demeanour of respectability, submission and piety. I saw a boy
on his knees, blacking a man's boot, a rent in the boy's trousers
exposing skin so dirty that at first I thought he had on grey
underdrawers. The man with one boot blacked ... and a policeman
stonily sending them away to some alley. Somewhat indignant at
this interference with the boy's occupation, I stepped up to the
policeman and asked if the boy had committed any offence ...
'Oh, no, sir; his trousers is torn, sir, and I sent him away'.

> Dorothy C. Wayman, *Edward Sylvester Morse: A Biography*
> (Cambridge, MA: Harvard University Press, 1942).

Later in the century **Joel Cook** (1842–1910) passed through Liverpool. Cook
was a Republican congressman and civic dignitary of Philadelphia, the city
of his birth. His attention was particularly caught by the developments in
the city's transport system, as was W. D. Howells' at the turn of the century
(see Chapter 10).

These docks are the great sight of the city, stretching along
the entire river front, crammed with the ships of all nations,
carrying every commercial flag; among the ensigns, however, the
American flag being a somewhat scarce article. Huge warehouses
line the quays. Steam railways have tracks all along the inside
edge, but locomotives do not draw the cars, this being done
by horses. The railway, however, is as convenient for freight
shipments as that along our Delaware front, though I did not
notice any sidings leading out on the piers alongside the ships.
The most extraordinary specimen of a street-car for passengers
I also saw running on this line, with broad wheels fitting the
rails, but capable of running off the track whenever the driver
wished to do so to get around the slowly travelling freight-cars.
Only these passenger cars, called, in the language of the town,
'trams,' were allowed to run on this dock-border railway. There

was another road alongside for ordinary wagons. Along these
docks merchandise of all sorts in vast amounts is stored and
being moved, the greater part of it apparently being American
products, such as provisions, grain, cheese, cotton, and lumber.
The excellent street pavements and the large breed of horses in
Liverpool enable teams to haul astonishing loads. There are plenty
of regular street passenger railways throughout the city, the tracks
being laid by the city corporation, and being of a pattern that
enables carriage-wheels to cross them and to turn out and in
without the wrenching process that tears the heart and shatters
the wheels whenever the attempt is made in Philadelphia to turn
out of the tracks. The rail is laid so that the top is even with
the pavement, and along the centre of the rail a narrow trench
is cut, just wide enough to admit the flanges of the car-wheels,
but not wide enough to let any carriage-wheel enter. Carriages,
therefore, pass over at all angles without any apparent strain or
even a jolt. Instead of the street railways controlling the city, as in
Philadelphia, in England the cities control the street railways. The
city corporation of Liverpool lays down all the lines according to
a given pattern for the street-car companies, and charges them the
expense. The cars are all two-storied, holding more on top than
inside, and are without platforms. The question that has never yet
been settled in Philadelphia, When is a streetcar full? is settled
in Liverpool by the legend painted plainly on every such vehicle
here, and announcing that it is full when it has eighteen inside
and twenty on top.

Joel Cook, *A Holiday Tour in Europe* (1889).

The Unitarian minister and writer **Edward Everett Hale** (1822–1909)
published a number of travel works including *Young Americans Abroad*
(1898), which is characterized by its light, humorous touch. The following
excerpts note the female management of hotels and the difficulties of the
pre-decimal English currency.

Travelling-bag in hand, which contained my entire wardrobe,
I now went in search of an hotel. The 'Angel Hotel' was soon
pointed out to me, and on entering it, I learned that several of
my fellow-passengers had already taken rooms there. It is entirely
under the control of ladies, being managed by a proprietress

and female clerks. The house is an excellent one, and the accommodations are excellent. It bears a very appropriate name. [...]
I had expected to see people dressed differently in Liverpool from what is customary in America. In this and a dozen other anticipations I was utterly disappointed. Thus I was surprised at every step, because I was not surprised.

It was a scourge of great grief to me that I could not indulge in refreshments on Sunday evening. A passenger after landing, is much like a patient after the fever has left him, he is hungry all the time. I had some American silver in my pocket, which I repeatedly offered to exchange for cakes, fruits and refreshments, at the numerous stores and stands which I passed, but no one was willing to invest in my stock of change. Thus I had to suffer both from hunger and thirst, because I did not have the right kind of money. On Monday I drew my cheque in English currency, and bought a suitable purse; but I was very awkward for a few days at counting money. England has the oddest and most irregular money table that I found from here to Egypt, except those of Holland and Germany.

Edward Everett Hale, *Young Americans Abroad* (1898).

7

African American Campaigners, Abolition and Evangelism

BECAUSE OF ITS MERCANTILE INVOLVEMENT in the eighteenth-century slave trade, Liverpool became known as the 'New Orleans of Great Britain' and was widely perceived to be sympathetic to the Confederacy during the American Civil War. However, there was another side to this coin. Writing in the American abolitionist *Liberty Bell* in 1849, Richard D. Webb paid tribute to figures like William Roscoe and the sailor-poet Edward Rushton, who did much to further opposition to slavery. Indeed, Liverpool was an important centre of abolitionist activity and offered fugitive slaves the security of a ready network of helpers in their pursuit of liberty. The Liverpool Society for Promoting the Abolition of Slavery had been active since the 1820s.

In 1811 the *Liverpool Mercury* ran the following article:

> On the first of the present month of August, 1811, a vessel arrived at Liverpool, with a cargo from Sierra Leone, the owner, master, mate, and whole crew of which are free Negroes. The master, who is also owner, is the son of an American Slave, and is said to be very well skilled both in trade and navigation, as well as to be of a very pious and moral character. It must have been a strange and animating spectacle to see this free and enlightened African entering, as an independent trader, with his black crew, into that port which was so lately the nidus [nerve centre] of the Slave Trade. – *Edinburgh Review*, August, 1811.
>
> *We are happy in having an opportunity of confirming the above account, and at the same time of laying before our readers an authentic memoir of Capt. Paul Cuffee [sic], the master and owner of the vessel above referred to, who sailed from this port on the 20th ult. with a licence from the British Government, to prosecute his intended voyage to Sierra Leone.*

The father of Paul Cuffee, was a native of Africa, whence he was
brought as a Slave into Massachusetts. – He was there purchased
by a person named Slocum, and remained in slavery a considerable
portion of his life.– He was named Cuffee, but as it is usual in
those parts took the name of Slocum, as expressing to whom
he belonged. Like many of his countrymen he possessed a mind
superior to his condition, and although he was diligent in the
business of his Master and faithful to his interest, yet by great
industry and economy he was enabled to purchase his personal
liberty.

At this time the remains of several Indian tribes, who originally
possessed the right of soil, resided in Massachusetts; Cuffee
became acquainted with a woman descended from one of those
tribes, named Ruth Moses, and married her. – He continued in
habits of industry and frugality, and soon afterwards purchased a
farm of 100 acres in Westport in Massachusetts. Cuffee and Ruth
has a family of ten children. – The three eldest sons, David,
Jonathan, and John are farmers in the neighbourhood of Westport,
filling respectable situations in society, and endowed with good
intellectual capacities. – They are all married, and have families to
whom they are giving good educations. Of six daughters four are
respectably married, while two remain single.

Paul was born on the Island of Cutterhunkker, one of the
Elizabeth Islands near New Bedford, in the year 1759; when he
was about 14 years of age his father died leaving a considerable
property in land, but which being at that time unproductive
afforded but little provision for his numerous family, and thus
the care of supporting his mother and sisters devolved upon his
brothers and himself.

At this time Paul conceived that commerce furnished to
industry more ample rewards than agriculture, and he was
conscious that he possessed qualities which under proper culture
would enable him to pursue commercial employments with
prospects of success; he therefore entered at the age of 16 as
a common hand on board of a vessel destined to the bay of
Mexico, on a Whaling voyage. His second voyage was to the
West Indies; but on his third he was captured by a British ship
during the American war about the year 1776: after three months
detention as a prisoner at New York, he was permitted to return
home to Westport, where owing to the unfortunate continuance
of hostilities he spent about 2 years in his agricultural pursuits.
During this interval Paul and his brother John Cuffee were called

on by the Collector of the district, in which they resided, for the payment of a personal tax. It appeared to them, that, by the laws of the constitution of Massachusetts, taxation and the whole rights of citizenship were untied. – If the laws demanded of them the payment of personal taxes, the same laws must necessarily and constitutionally invest them with the rights of representing, and being represented, in the state Legislature. But they had never been considered as entitled to the privilege of voting at Elections, nor of being elected to places of trust and honour. – Under these circumstances, they refused payment of the demands. – The Collector resorted to the force of the laws, and after many delays and vexations, Paul and his brother deemed it most prudent to silence the suit by payment of the demands. But they resolved, if it were possible, to obtain the rights which they believed to be connected with taxation.

The subject of this article was **Captain Paul Cuffe** (1759–1817), the freeborn son of African and Native American parents born on Chuttyhunk Island in Massachusetts. He developed an expanding mercantile network of trade with the Quakers among others, and himself joined that sect. Cuffe was an unusual figure at the beginning of the nineteenth century with his all-black crews and became known as the 'African Captain'. His Liverpool trade connections were with the pottery business of William and Richard Rathbone, but opposition to slavery was one of Cuffe's main concerns. Along with his prospering trade, he made a number of voyages to Sierra Leone where he helped freed African Americans to settle. After an invitation from British abolitionists to visit Liverpool, among other cities, during his voyage of 1811 from Philadelphia to Africa via Liverpool, he recorded in his log how a member of his crew had fallen foul of press gangs. The latter were active in some fifty ports around Britain, their aim being to coerce men into the navy. Their local base was called the Rendezvous. A foreigner might secure his release by having his Consul apply to the Admiralty. The pressing of Americans was one of the causes of the war between Britain and the USA in 1812.

[Spelling standardized] At 1PM saw a pilot boat toward the shore who fired her Pilot Signal gun. We hauled our wind for her and she keep for us. At 2PM we received a pilot who directed our course SE by E for Liverpool, at 10 PM hove to below the … at 2AM passed the rocks, at 3AM the custom-house boat came alongside. At 4AM hauled into dock. This day may be reckoned at 36 hours and called 6 day 12. Arrived safe, all well after a passage of 62 days.

This day soon after we got in the dock two of my men going out of the dock gate were met by the press gang and carried to the Rendezvous. The press gang then came onboard my vessel and let me know that they had two of my men, and overhauled the remainder of the crew among which they found Aaron Richards, an African that I had taken an apprentice in Africa to instruct in navigation. They claimed him as British subject and took him off. At 11 o'clock I went to the Rendezvous and got the two men first mentioned, but they would not let Aaron off. Attended to entry of the brig *Traveller* [Cuffe's ship]. Get through. Attended to getting Aaron's liberty, used every influence as I was capable of but all in vain. I then interceded with my friends but in vain.

My friends Richard Rathbone and Thomas Thompson were very anxious in assisting me to regain Aaron. We got the promise from the regulating officer that Aaron should not be sent from Liverpool. They wrote immediately to London for the liberation of Aaron with a petition to the Board of Admiralty.

I this day put up with Thomas Thompson and took first day meeting with them and feeling very anxious for Aaron's liberty. I took place in the stage for London, 10 in the evening we set forward for London. Arrived in London 3 day morning 6 o'clock, it making 32 hours, distance 208 miles.

> Rosalind Cobb Wiggins, *Captain Paul Cuffe's Logs and Letters,*
> *1808–1817* (Washington, DC: Howard University Press, 1996).

William Lloyd Garrison (1805–79) was one of the founders of the American Anti-Slavery Society and was a tireless campaigner for abolition, partly through his newspaper *The Liberator*. In 1833 he sailed to Liverpool on the *Hibernia* to raise funds for a 'manual labour school for coloured youth'. In the first of his letters to *The Liberator*, on 23 May 1833, he recorded his first positive impressions of England:

Although in a strange land, and for the first time a foreigner, I cannot but feel myself at home among a people whose cry is for universal freedom, who never speak in the cause of suffering humanity but with authority, who are doing so much in behalf of American emancipation, and whose voices have cheered my spirit even on the other side of the Atlantic.

In a letter the following day, Garrison noted that the British Press was full of discussion of abolition and in a letter of 27 May 1833 he reflected on the impossibility of living permanently in Liverpool. He had expected to meet his friend, the Quaker merchant John Cropper (who was to play host to Harriet Beecher Stowe in the 1850s) but instead met Cropper's brother-in-law, the sail-maker James Riley and other abolitionists in the city. Garrison gives us a glimpse of the activities of the Quakers in the cause of abolition.

> The population of Liverpool, including its suburbs, is about as large as that of New York. I have had but a cursory view of the place, and shall therefore avoid entering into the minute in my descriptions. Let this suffice: it is bustling, prosperous and great. I would not, however, choose it as a place of residence. It wears strictly a commercial aspect; and you well know there is nothing of trade or barter in my disposition [...] Hence, another place for me than Liverpool; and such a place I could easily find, in almost any direction, within a few miles of it – that is to say, if I were friendly to colonization. My excellent friend James Cropper has a delightful retreat, called *Dingle Bank*, which nature and art have embellished in the most attractive manner. This great and good man is now in London, but there has been no lack of hospitality toward me on the part of those whom he has left behind. I have also been very kindly entertained by James Riley, a worthy and much respected member of the Society of Friends.

Garrison passed through Liverpool again in 1840, on his way to the World's Anti-Slavery Convention in London as the delegate of the Massachusetts Anti-Slavery Society. Garrison's travelling companions included Charles Lenox Remond, the first African American lecturer for the Anti-Slavery Society. As the *Columbus* approached Liverpool, the pilot boat brought the latest issue of the *Liverpool Chronicle*, which carried the news of an attempted assassination of Queen Victoria. Garrison continues:

> When, on reading the account aloud at their request, I came to the statement that 'the prisoner's father was a mulatto, and his grandfather was a black', they yelled like so many fiends broke loose from the bottomless pit – (remember! They have been to

America, and have got the *virus* of slavery and prejudice infused into their veins!).

Walter M. Merrill, ed., *The Letters of William Lloyd Garrison*
(Cambridge, MA: Harvard University Press, 1971).

Throughout the 1840s and 1850s a considerable number of African American abolitionists visited Liverpool, partly to publish their own memoirs of slavery and partly to campaign against the 'Peculiar Institution'. England generally, and Liverpool specifically, offered them a refuge and a potential financial resource. **Moses Roper** (*c*.1815–*c*.1861) was one of the earliest to come to the city and in his narrative declared: 'My feelings when I first touched the shores of Britain were indescribable.' He arrived with letters of introduction to Dr Thomas Raffles, the minister of the Congregational church in Great George Street and spent his first night with a member of the church. His subsequent lecture schedule included addresses given in Liverpool (Myrtle Place, Pembroke Place, Pleasant Street and Sidney Place).

The free-born **Alexander Crummell** (1819–98), a leading proponent of settlement in Liberia, visited Liverpool in 1848–49 and during 1849 made ten appeals for funds at St Silas's church and elsewhere. He also spoke at St George's, Everton, soon after his arrival:

> On this occasion, great interest was evinced in hearing the Negro preacher. The church was crowded by a most respectable congregation to repletion—many parties being unable to obtain seats, and fain to stand at the entrances, and others obliged to retire, hopeless of even this last accommodation.
> All eyes were riveted on the preacher as he ascended the pulpit. He is a good-looking man, of small stature, of black complexion, and of an intelligent countenance. His voice is strong and manly; his articulation so clear, and his pronunciation of the English language so generally accurate, with, at the same time, a rapid flow of words and a modesty of bearing, that he immediately won the deep attention of his hearers; the first general feeling being that of astonishment [...]

The preacher (of whose address this is but an imperfect sketch) evidently made a strong impression upon his auditory, and a general whisper ran through the congregation, expressive of surprise at his attainments, and admiration of his Christian and philanthropic views. He spoke calmly, not vindictively, of the wrongs of his countrymen, and exhibited talents as a scholar and an orator in unobtrusive and neat figures of speech, which stamp him as a man of reading and intelligence. His manner is agreeable and energetic, and he is, assuredly, a living proof of the capability of the African race to be elevated to a high standard of intellectual and religious culture. The countenance of this Negro clergyman, though black, is described as interesting and well-formed, beaming with bright intelligence, and his expression free and manly; and, notwithstanding American prejudice, the Archbishops, Bishops, and Clergymen of Britain, acknowledge him as a brother and an equal. 'When I was in America,' says he, 'I THOUGHT I was a man;—in England I FEEL,—I KNOW that I am!'

Wilson Armistead, *A Tribute for the Negro* (1848).

The passage in 1850 of the Fugitive Slave Act meant that the Northern states were no longer safe. Landfall in Liverpool then took on a special symbolism as signalling the travellers' arrival in a free nation. In this respect America's cherished image as a land of the free was reversed and the Old World became the refuge from persecution. **William and Ellen Craft** declared that 'it was not until we stepped upon the shore at Liverpool that we were free from every slavish fear'; they landed in December 1850 and recorded the event in *Running a Thousand Miles for Freedom* (1860). Ellen was taken ill and convalesced in Liverpool at the house of the Rev. Francis Bishop. **James Watkins** (originally known as Sam Berry) was advised by friends to leave America, although he was living in a northern state, and accordingly he too set sail for Liverpool. Despite the signs of some infection from the 'leprosy' of slavery, landing filled him with joy:

The prospect of free soil, even though a long way off at this time, made me feel delighted, and when we entered the Mersey and came into the docks at Liverpool, I could not help shouting and leaping for joy, and I sung a song of liberty. Some of the bystanders and waiters on declared that a mad black man had just landed from an American ship. They little knew the emotions I was then the subject of. I cannot make them understood by any description; persons must be in similar circumstances to know what they are. To say that I was greatly excited is like saying nothing. My joy was unbounded.

I had now got fairly into England, and I began to feel more and more certain of the truth that I was now out of danger, as I mixed in English society,—I say '*English*,' for, during my stay in Liverpool, I had more than one proof, that the 'leprosy' had effected some on British soil, especially those who came much into contact with American merchants and captains, &c., and just as far as I found the pro-slavery feeling had been received, I considered these parties *un*-English. With the exception of these instances, I felt as though I had started a new life. The kind sympathy everywhere shown to me, and hearty reception I received from some of the best men in Liverpool, made me feel very happy.

> *Narrative of the Life of James Watkins, Formerly a 'Chattel'*
> *in Maryland, U.S.* (1852), Chapters 8 and 9.

Watkins, like many other visitors, records his gratitude for the hospitality shown him in Liverpool by, among others, Dr Thomas Raffles and John Cropper and family. There are many indications that these individuals had created a reception network to welcome all visitors engaged in the cause of abolition. Among the latter figures passing through Liverpool were Maria W. Chapman, William Lloyd Garrison and Henry C. Wright.

Watkins' reaction was shared by **Samuel Ringgold Ward** (1817–*c*.1866), who was born into slavery in Maryland, but escaped to the North and subsequently to Canada. Later becoming a Congregationalist minister, in 1853 he sailed on the Cunard liner *Europa* for England, then abuzz with *Uncle Tom's Cabin*, with the support of the Anti-Slavery Society of Canada, for whom he raised funds by lecturing in Britain. After 1855 he took up residence in Jamaica. His voyage to Liverpool revealed the same racism as Frederick Douglass experienced, when the ship authorities insisted that he should take his meals in his stateroom for fear of 'offending' the other (white American) passengers. As will be seen below, apart from an unwelcome experience with a local cabman, Ward's impressions of working-class dress and behaviour were positive indeed.

On Saturday, the last day of April, we saw land on the coast of Ireland. We then moved gracefully along the coast of Wales, telegraphed our approach at Holyhead, took a pilot early on Sunday morning, and, at eleven o'clock precisely, anchored in the Mersey, after a passage of ten days, fifteen hours, and fifteen minutes, mean time. I was in England—the England of my former reading, and my ardent admiration. I was at Liverpool—that Liverpool whose merchants, but sixty years before, had mobbed Clarkson [Thomas Clarkson, the English abolitionist] for prying into and exposing the secret inhumanities of their slave trade. I was in a land of freedom, of true equality. I did not feel as some blacks say they felt, upon landing—that I was, for the first time in my life, a man. No, I always felt that; however wronged, maltreated, outraged—still, a man. Indeed, the very bitterness of what I had suffered at home consisted chiefly in the consciousness I always carried with me of being an equal man to any of those who trampled upon me.

My first experience of English dealing was in being charged treble fare by a Liverpool cabman, a race with which I have had much to do since. Acting upon the advice given me by John Laidlaw, Esq., I went to Clayton Square, where I found good quarters at Mr. Brown's very genteel Temperance Hotel. The Rev. Dr. Willis had very kindly given me a note of introduction to the master of the Grecian Hotel; but I found no reason to desire a change, and therefore remained, while in Liverpool, where I first lodged.

Several things arrested my attention upon the first day of my being in England. One was, the comfort and cleanliness, not to say the elegance of appearance, presented by the working classes. I had always, in the United States, heard and read of the English working classes as being ground down to the very earth—as being far worse in their condition than the American slaves. Their circumstances, in the rural and the factory districts, I had always heard described as the most destitute. That they wrought for sixpence a day I had been informed by I know not how many Americans, who had visited England. How many times have I heard from the lips of American protectionists, and seen in the columns of their journals, statements such as this—'If we do not maintain a protection tariff, English manufacturers, who pay their operatives but sixpence a day, will flood our markets with their products, and the factory operative in America will, in consequence, be compelled to work for sixpence a day, as the English operative now does!' When I was an American protectionist, how I used to 'take up that parable,' and, believing it, repeat it! How others with me believed the same too often told falsehood! Here was before me, in Lancashire and her noble port—Lancashire, the head quarters of British, if not European, factory interest—almost a manufacturing kingdom in itself—a most abundant refutation of what, on this subject, I had nearly a thousand times heard, read, believed, and repeated.

But this was Sunday. The next day, having occasion to cross the Mersey, I saw nearly as many well-dressed working men, with their wives and sweethearts, enjoying the holiday of that Monday, as I had seen the day before. This led me, as I travelled further into the factory district, to make definite inquiries into the condition of the operatives; and, as I may not again recur to it, I will put down here, in few words, a sort of summary of the information I obtained. I learned—indeed, saw with my own eyes—that throughout Lancashire the young women in the factories dress as well as the young women I had seen at Lowell, Dover, Manchester, Nashua, and other manufacturing towns in New England.

Samuel Ringgold Ward, *Autobiography of a Fugitive Negro: His Anti-Slavery Labours in the United States, Canada and England* (1855).

William Wells Brown (1814–84), author of the first novel and play written by an African American, was born into slavery in Kentucky and published his memoir *The Narrative of William W. Brown, A Fugitive Slave* in 1847, which had a considerable influence on *Uncle Tom's Cabin*. He was commissioned by the American Peace Society to serve as their delegate to the Paris Peace Congress of 1849. He sailed for England in the Royal Mail Steamship *Canada* and describes his arrival in Liverpool below, stressing his feeling of release from the bonds of race prejudice. In a striking reversal of the usual contrast between the USA and Europe, he describes Liverpool as a new city of the future. Liverpool was Brown's first step on a tour of Britain and France, which he recorded in *Three Years in Europe* (1852) and *Sketches of Places and People Abroad* (1855).

The next morning I was up before the sun, and found that we were within a few miles of Liverpool. The taking of a pilot on board at eleven o'clock, warned us to prepare to quit our ocean palace and seek other quarters. At a little past three o'clock, the ship cast anchor, and we were all tumbled, bag and baggage, into a small steamer, and in a few moments were at the door of the

Custom-House. The passage had only been nine days and twenty-two hours, the quickest on record at that time, yet it was long enough. I waited nearly three hours before my name was called, and when it was, I unlocked my trunks and handed them over to one of the officers, whose dirty hands made no improvement on the work of the laundress. First one article was taken out, and then another, till an *Iron Collar* that had been worn by a female slave on the banks of the Mississippi, was hauled out, and this democratic instrument of torture became the centre of attraction; so much so, that instead of going on with the examination, all hands stopped to look at the 'Negro Collar.'

Several of my countrymen who were standing by, were not a little displeased at answers which I gave to questions on the subject of Slavery; but they held their peace. The interest created by the appearance of the Iron Collar, closed the examination of my luggage. As if afraid that they would find something more hideous, they put the Custom-House mark on each piece, and passed them out, and I was soon comfortably installed at Brown's Temperance Hotel, Clayton Square.

No person of my complexion can visit this country without being struck with the marked difference between the English and the Americans. The prejudice which I have experienced on all and every occasion in the United States, and to some extent on board the *Canada*, vanished as soon as I set foot on the soil of Britain. In America I had been bought and sold as a slave, in the Southern States. In the so-called free States, I had been treated as one born to occupy an inferior position,—in steamers, compelled to take my fare on the deck; in hotels, to take my meals in the kitchen; in coaches, to ride on the outside; in railways, to ride in the 'negro car;' and in churches, to sit in the 'negro pew.' But no sooner was I on British soil, than I was recognised as a man, and an equal. The very dogs in the streets appeared conscious of my manhood. Such is the difference, and such is the change that is brought about by a trip of nine days in an Atlantic steamer.

I was not more struck with the treatment of the people, than with the appearance of the great seaport of the world. The grey appearance of the stone piers and docks, the dark look of the magnificent warehouses, the substantial appearance of every thing around, causes one to think himself in a new world instead of the old. Every thing in Liverpool looks old, yet nothing is worn out. The beautiful villages on the opposite side of the river, in the vicinity of Birkenhead, together with the countless number of vessels in the river, and the great ships to be seen in the stream, give life and animation to the whole scene.

Every thing in and about Liverpool seems to be built for the future as well as the present. We had time to examine but few of the public buildings, the first of which was the Custom-House, an edifice that would be an ornament to any city in the world.

For the first time in my life, I can say 'I am truly free.' My old master may make his appearance here, with the Constitution of the United States in his pocket, the Fugitive Slave Law in one hand and the chains in the other, and claim me as his property, but all will avail him nothing. I can here stand and look the tyrant in the face, and tell him that I am his equal! England is, indeed, the 'land of the free, and the home of the brave.'

> *Three Years in Europe; or, Places I have Seen and*
> *People I Have Met* (1952) Letter 1.

[In the last line above, Brown displaces the American national anthem on to England.]

The word Englishman is but another name for an American, and the word American is but another name for an Englishman— England is the father, America the son. They have a common origin and identity of language; they hold the same religions and political opinions; they study the same histories, and have the same literature. Steam and mechanical ingenuity have brought the two countries within nine days sailing of each other. The Englishman on landing at New-York finds his new neighbours speaking the same language which he last heard on leaving Liverpool, and he sees the American in the same dress that he had been accustomed to look upon at home, and soon forgets that he is three thousand miles from his native land, and in another country. The American on landing at Liverpool, and taking a walk through the great commercial city, finding no difficulty in understanding the people, supposes himself still in New-York; and if there seems any doubt in his own mind, growing out of the fact that the people have a more healthy look, seem more polite, and that the buildings have a more substantial appearance than those he had formerly looked upon, he has only to imagine, as did Rip Van Winkle, that he has been asleep these hundred years.

> *Three Years in Europe*, Letter 21.

Frederick Douglass (1818–95) was the most famous of the African American campaigners to pass through Liverpool. Born into slavery in Maryland, he subsequently escaped to the North, taking up residence in New York. He became one of the best-known anti-slavery speakers and recorded his experiences in three autobiographies, the second of which is excerpted below. Sailing on the *Cambria* in August 1845, he encountered crude prejudice over his accommodation.

On applying for a passage to England, on board the *Cambria*, of the Cunard line, my friend, James N. Buffum, of Lynn, Massachusetts, was informed that I could not be received on board as a cabin passenger. American prejudice against colour triumphed over British liberality and civilization, and erected a colour test and condition for crossing the sea in the cabin of a British vessel. The insult was keenly felt by my white friends, but to me, it was common, expected, and therefore, a thing of no great consequence, whether I went in the cabin or in the steerage [...] My fellow-passengers not only visited me, but invited me to visit them, on the saloon deck. My visits there, however, were but seldom. I preferred to live within my privileges, and keep upon my own premises. I found this quite as much in accordance with good policy, as with my own feelings. The effect was, that with the majority of the passengers, all colour distinctions were flung to the winds, and I found myself treated with every mark of respect, from the beginning to the end of the voyage, except in a single instance; and in that, I came near being mobbed, for complying with an invitation given me by the passengers, and the captain of the *Cambria*, to deliver a lecture on slavery. Our New Orleans and Georgia passengers were pleased to regard my lecture as an insult offered to them, and swore I should not speak. They went so far as to threaten to throw me overboard, and but for the firmness of Captain Judkins, probably would have (under the inspiration of *slavery* and *brandy*) attempted to put their threats into execution. I have no space to describe this scene, although its tragic and comic peculiarities are well worth describing. An end was put to the *melee*, by the captain's calling the ship's company to put the salt water mobocrats in irons. At this determined order, the gentlemen of the lash scampered, and for the rest of the voyage conducted themselves very decorously.

[The incident drew public attention to Douglass's arrival. In a letter of
1 January 1846, addressed to Garrison's *The Liberator* and included in
his narrative, Douglass described the sequel after all the passengers had
landed.]

> The second day after my arrival at Liverpool, in company with
> my friend, Buffum, and several other friends, I went to Eaton
> Hall, the residence of the Marquis of Westminster, one of the
> most splendid buildings in England. On approaching the door,
> I found several of our American passengers, who came out
> with us in the *Cambria*, waiting for admission, as but one party
> was allowed in the house at a time. We all had to wait till the
> company within came out. And of all the faces, expressive of
> chagrin, those of the Americans were pre-eminent. They looked
> as sour as vinegar, and as bitter as gall, when they found I was to
> be admitted on equal terms with themselves. When the door was
> opened, I walked in, on an equal footing with my white fellow-
> citizens, and from all I could see, I had as much attention paid me
> by the servants that showed us through the house, as any with a
> paler skin. As I walked through the building, the statuary did not
> fall down, the pictures did not leap from their places, the doors
> did not refuse to open, and the servants did not say, '*We don't
> allow niggers in here!*'

> Frederick Douglass, *My Bondage and My Freedom* (1855),
> Chapter 24.

Prior to returning to America, Douglass gave a valedictory speech on 30
March 1847 in which he recalled his first impressions of Liverpool after
being accustomed to exclusion and insult in the USA.

> I came to this land – how greatly changed! Sir, the moment I
> stepped on the soil of England – the instant I landed on the quay
> at Liverpool – I beheld people as white as any I ever saw in the
> United States; as noble in their exterior, and surrounded by as
> much to commend them to admiration, as any to be found in
> the wide extent of America. But, instead of meeting the curled
> lip of scorn, and seeing the fire of hatred kindled in the eyes of
> Englishmen, all was blandness and kindness. I looked around in
> vain for expressions of insult. Yes, I looked around with wonder!
> For I hardly believed my own eyes. I searched scrutinizingly to
> find if I could perceive in the countenance of an Englishman any

disapprobation of me on account of my complexion. No; there was not one look of scorn or enmity. (Loud cheers.)

John Blassingame, ed., *The Frederick Douglass Papers. Series One: Speeches, Debates, and Interviews. Volume 2: 1847–54* (New Haven, CT: Yale University Press, 1979).

[When he was arranging his return voyage to America, Douglass encountered the same prejudice again.]

Proposing to leave England, and turning my face toward America, in the spring of 1847, I was met, on the threshold, with something which painfully reminded me of the kind of life which awaited me in my native land. For the first time in the many months spent abroad, I was met with proscription on account of my colour. A few weeks before departing from England, while in London, I was careful to purchase a ticket, and secure a berth for returning home, in the *Cambria*—the steamer in which I left the United States—paying therefore the round sum of forty pounds and nineteen shillings sterling. This was first cabin fare. But on going aboard the *Cambria*, I found that the Liverpool agent had ordered my berth to be given to another, and had forbidden my entering the saloon! This contemptible conduct met with stern rebuke from the British press. For, upon the point of leaving England, I took occasion to expose the disgusting tyranny, in the columns of the London *Times*. That journal, and other leading journals throughout the United Kingdom, held up the outrage to unmitigated condemnation. So good an opportunity for calling out a full expression of British sentiment on the subject, had not before occurred, and it was most fully embraced. The result was, that Mr. Cunard came out in a letter to the public journals, assuring them of his regret at the outrage, and promising that the like should never occur again on board his steamers; and the like, we believe, has never since occurred on board the steamships of the Cunard line.

It is not very pleasant to be made the subject of such insults; but if all such necessarily resulted as this one did, I should be very happy to bear, patiently, many more than I have borne, of the same sort. Albeit, the lash of proscription, to a man accustomed to equal social position, even for a time, as I was, has a sting for the soul hardly less severe than that which bites the flesh and draws the blood from the back of the plantation slave. It was rather hard, after having enjoyed nearly two years of equal social privileges in England, often dining with gentlemen of great literary, social, political, and religious eminence never, during the whole time, having met with a single word, look, or gesture, which gave me the slightest reason to think my colour was an offence to anybody—now to be cooped up in the stern of the 'Cambria', and denied the right to enter the saloon, lest my dark presence should be deemed an offence to some of my democratic fellow-passengers. The reader will easily imagine what must have been my feelings.

Frederick Douglass, *My Bondage and My Freedom* (1855), Chapter 24.

[The letter referred to by Douglass above was written from Brown's Temperance Hotel in Liverpool and sent to the editor of the London *Times* on 3 April 1847.]

Sir:

1   I take up my pen to lay before you a few facts respecting an unjust proscription to which I find myself subjected on board the steam-ship *Cambria*, to sail from this port at 10 o'clock to-morrow morning for Boston, United States.

2   On the 4th of March last, in company with Mr. George Moxhay, of the Hall of Commerce, London, I called upon Mr. Ford, the London agent of the Cunard line of steamers, for the purpose of securing a passage on board the steam-ship *Cambria* to Boston, United States. On inquiring the amount of the passage I was told 40*l.* 19*s.*; I inquired further, if a second class passage could be obtained. He answered no, there was but one fare, all distinctions having been abolished. I then gave to him 40*l.* 19*s.* and received from him in return a ticket entitling me to berth No. 72 on board the steam-ship *Cambria*, at the same time asking him if my colour would prove any barrier to my enjoying all the rights and privileges enjoyed by other passengers. He said "No." I then left the office, supposing all well, and thought nothing more of the matter until this morning, when in company with a few friends, agreeably to public notice, I went on board the *Cambria* with my luggage, and on inquiring for my berth, found, to my surprise and mortification, that it had been given to another passenger, and was told that the agent in London had acted without authority in selling me the ticket.

I expressed my surprise and disappointment to the captain, and inquired what I had better do in the matter. He suggested my accompanying him to the office of the agent in Water-street, Liverpool, for the purpose of ascertaining what could be done. On stating the fact of my having purchased the ticket of the London agent, Mr. M'Iver (the Liverpool agent) answered that the London agent, in selling me the ticket, had acted without authority, and that I should not go on board the ship unless I agreed to take my meals alone, not to mix with the saloon company, and to give up the berth for which I had paid. Being without legal remedy, and anxious to return to the United States, I have felt it due to my own rights as a man, as well as to the honour and dignity of the British public, to lay these facts before them, sincerely believing that the British public will pronounce a just verdict on such proceedings. I have travelled in this country 19 months, and have always enjoyed equal rights and privileges with other passengers, and it was not until I turned my face towards America that I met anything like proscription on account of my colour.

Yours respectfully,
Frederick Douglass

There was so much public indignation in England over Douglass's treatment that a public subscription raised £500, which was sent to him in America. Douglass's programme in Britain from 1845–47 was to deliver a series of talks on the evils of slavery. He gave one such talk at the Liverpool Concert Hall on 19 October 1846 accompanied by the Liverpool-born abolitionist George Thompson and William Lloyd Garrison. It was reported that 2,500 people attended. The excerpt conveys the enthusiastic responsiveness of this audience and also exemplifies Douglass's policy of appealing to the common humanity of his audience without drawing any national distinctions between Britain and the USA.

Slavery Exists Under the Eaves of the American Church

Frederick Douglass, who was received with vehement manifestations of applause[, spoke]. Delivered a long, powerful, and argumentative speech, which we regret we cannot give at length. After urging the peculiar rights of the black men and of slaves to speak out against slavery, and detailing some of its blasting influences upon men and society, he said the Americans set out in their charter of national independence, that they held these truths as self-evident—'that all men are created equal, and are endowed by their Creator with certain inalienable rights, among which are life, liberty, and the pursuit of happiness.'

And yet what was the commentary upon that declaration? That three millions of slaves—one-sixth of the entire population of the United States—were that night in chains, in fetters; stripped of their rights; herded together like brutes; without the institution of marriage amongst them; without the Bible, driven from time into eternity in the dark before the biting lash of their tyrannical slave-drivers. And this horrid crime was sanctioned and sanctified, sanctioned by the law, and sanctified by the religion of America. There was no such thing left as a rational heart to which a successful appeal might be made against it. He was, however, disposed to think that the work of abolition in the United States was to be carried on mainly by the people of this country.

He believed that, by speaking to America from this side of the Atlantic, they were doing more good than if they spoke to her in the immediate vicinity of slavery. Were he on his native soil that night he should not be able to meet with the sympathy and support of an audience; he would be mobbed as he had been-mobbed for daring to express his wrongs; for daring to show the scars on his back; for daring to tell them that he had four sisters and a brother still in slavery. For doing this he had been mobbed, beaten, stoned, and had had his right hand broken in Christian America, but in this country he could stand up and state his wrongs, receive the sympathies—(tremendous cheers) of a British audience; and have his denunciations of American slavery and slaveholders borne across the Atlantic, attended with the shouts of British Christians. (Cheers.)

But let it not be supposed that he was there for the purpose of stirring up anger against the United States. He had never done any such thing. He had always met too lively an indignation in the people of this country against slavery; and his only object was to enlist the Christian, moral, and religious influences of the world against it. It was by such means that he, and those with him, expected to put down slavery in America. They did not seek to put it down by physical force; their instrumentalities were such only as were sanctioned by the doctrines of Christianity, and such only as good men of all countries could commend. The people of

America might be able to drive the armies of England from their shores, should they go there; but there was an influence which might be exerted that they could not meet or overthrow-it was the power of truth, the power of love, the power of the pulpit, and the power of the press.

One Englishman standing up thoughtfully on this or the other side of the Atlantic, and proclaiming to the American clergy, and to the American slaveholders, his abhorrence of their crime, would do more to alarm their consciences and to disturb the American people than all the threats of war which might be uttered against them. They could not resist this; they would see the cancer that was eating into their vitals, and that all their vaunted independence was a lie. (Cheers.) They would see that their 4th of July orations were regarded on this side of the Atlantic as downright hypocrisies; they would see that all their pretensions to a love of God, while they hated the slave, was regarded as an absolute profanity; they would see that their boast of sending the Gospel to the heathen, while they withheld it from their slaves, was all marked down here as utter blasphemy. When they saw that they would not be able to lift up their heads among Christian nations, in consequence of the continuance of slavery, then they would abolish it.

If the hypocrisy of the American church was fully known to British Christians, they would as soon think of linking themselves to a pirate ship as to that church. But he would not believe that these men (the American delegates) had succeeded in separating the abolitionists of this country from the abolitionists of the United States, but that the churches of this country were yet prepared to say that they would have no union with slaveholders. (Cheers.)

Liverpool Mercury, 23 October 1846. Collected in John Blassingame, ed., *The Frederick Douglass Papers. Series One: Speeches, Debates, and Interviews. Volume 1: 1841–46* (New Haven, CT: Yale University Press, 1979).

Another famous speaker in the cause of abolition was **Sarah Parker Remond** (1826–94) from Salem, Massachusetts, a member of a family committed to the anti-slavery cause. Her brother Charles Lenox Remond was a prominent speaker for the American Anti-Slavery Society and the whole family participated in different abolitionist organizations. Sarah

Remond had attracted public attention by refusing to sit in the segregated section of a Boston opera house. She was such an effective speaker for the American Anti-Slavery Society that in December 1858 she was sent to Britain. Unwell from the voyage, she recuperated at the house of William Robson in Warrington and then began a lecture tour throughout Britain. She gave one of her talks in Liverpool on 21 January 1859, with William Henry Channing, the Unitarian clergyman who had been living in Liverpool since 1854. The following day the *Liverpool Mercury* reported on the event.

A Lady Lecturing on American Slavery

Miss Remond of Salem, Massachusetts, last night addressed the Tuckerman Institute, Bedford Street, an English audience, for the first time, upon the subject of American slavery. The Reverend W. H. Channing presided, and a crowded assembly greeted the lady with the utmost enthusiasm. The chairman briefly introduced her as one who, with her family, had long taken a deep and most active part in the abolition movement – as a countrywoman who had consecrated her best gifts to the cause of heroism and humanity, and he urged that as women, without at all feeling that they had sacrificed their womanhood, appeared on the public stage to rehearse a fictitious tragedy, there was no reason why a woman should not speak in public of a real tragedy, and on a subject upon which she so deeply felt. Miss Remond then proceeded to deliver her address; and though it occupied about an hour and a half in the delivery, she retained throughout the closest attention of her audience as she eloquently depicted the wrongs of the slave, dwelt in the most touching manner upon the social degradation of her sisters in slavery, expressed her unbounded indignation at the apathy which the professing Christians throughout the whole of the United States as a body manifested on the subject; and concluded with an earnest appeal for the moral and religious sympathy and influence of free England in the abolition movement. Miss Remond is an able advocate of the cause she has espoused; she speaks strongly because she no doubt feels strongly upon the subject on which she speaks, and is eloquent because she makes no effort to be so. She has a clear, musical voice, a distinct utterance, and – if it be not a needless remark of a lady – we may add she has at her command a great flow of language, for she speaks without any assistance from notes, and is never at a loss for words admirably calculated to express her sentiments. Her repeated quotations from the public addresses of American senators on the subject of slavery display a most retentive memory, whilst the whole of her address as plainly denotes that she has paid no little attention to general literature, and particularly to the poets of this and her native country. At the close, as frequently throughout her lecture, she was rapturously applauded, and on the motion of the Rev. S. A. Steinthal, seconded by Mr. Wilson, a cordial vote of thanks was unanimously passed to her, and she was requested to be the medium for conveying the sympathy of those present to the American abolitionists in the work in which they are engaged.

Liverpool Mercury, 22 January 1859.

[In 1866 Remond entered a hospital in Florence to study medicine. She never returned to America and spent the rest of her life in Italy.]

The African Missionaries

From the very beginning the anti-slavery movement had been in part a religious one and there was an ongoing controversy over whether to promote African settlement as against reform within the USA. With the emancipation of the slaves and the ending of the Civil War, missionary activity continued. African American song had been heard in Liverpool in July 1866, when Sam Hague's Georgia Slave Troupe of minstrel singers performed at the Theatre Royal in Williamson Square; several members of the troupe subsequently settled permanently in Liverpool. In April 1873 the Jubilee Singers landed in Liverpool to start an evangelical tour of Britain to raise funds for Fisk University, giving performances before the Earl of Shaftesbury and Queen Victoria. Wherever they appeared, they were greeted with large, enthusiastic audiences, particularly when they sang 'John Brown's Body', which was being converted from a political song into a spiritual. During their tour they gave concerts in the Philharmonic Hall and stayed (at preferential rates) in the Northwestern Hotel. The *Liverpool Daily Albion* reported of their first concert:

They had not sung a dozen notes when the audience knew that it was not to be disappointed. The marvellous quality of the voices, that strange sympathetic power, which is not the possession of an individual but the dower of a race, – which has often been described, but can only be known by hearing it, – at once arrested attention. On the whole the first concert of the Jubilee Minstrels must be pronounced a great treat and a genuine success.

> Quoted in Gustavus D. Pike, *The Singing Campaign for Twelve Thousand Pounds; or, The Jubilee Singers in Great Britain* (1874).

[Pike was the Jubilee Singers' manager. The Jubilees' tour was ending as that of Moody and Sankey (see below) was beginning.]

The Freedmen's Missions Aid Society: A Public Meeting in Liverpool (1878)

The American Missionary Association was founded in 1846 to promote African Americans' rights to full citizenship in the USA. It developed close links with the Congregational churches and founded Fisk University in 1866. It also promoted the Mendi (or Mende) Mission, established after the Amistad Incident of 1839, involving a group of West Africans who were kidnapped from Mendeland and sold into slavery in Cuba. When they were being transported from Cuba they seized their schooner, *La Amistad* ('friendship'), but they were in turn seized by the USS *Washington*. The trial of the Africans for murder became one of the most notorious cases involving slaves. After their acquittal, the Africans returned to their homeland in what is now Sierra Leone, where a mission was set up in their memory.

> On the evening of March the 8th, a large congregation came together in the Great George street church (formerly Dr. Raffles), to welcome to Liverpool four coloured missionaries, ex-slaves, from Fisk University, and also to bid them farewell on the eve of their departure; under the care of the American Missionary Association, for the Mendi Mission, on the west coast of Africa. The missionaries were very cordially greeted by many of the old, and also the new, friends of the African race.
>
> William Crosfield, J.P., a life-long friend of the oppressed race, presided. After an appropriate hymn, prayer was offered by the Rev. Stanley Rogers. Then the chairman said: 'It gives me great pleasure to preside at such a meeting of this society. These missionaries before you are the first-fruits from the Fisk University, which was established at Nashville, Tenn., for the education of those who were freed from slavery by the late Civil

War in America. And now, here they are ready for work in that
great mission field of Africa. It is a vast field. And it is to be
hoped that the British people will do their part in the aid of this
most important enterprise. Fisk University was introduced to the
English people a few years ago by the Jubilee Singers, who have
done wonders towards its support.' The chairman then turned and
added: 'We must not forget the wives of these young missionaries;
we must give them a shake of the hand, as a token of our interest
in them.

The Rev. Dr. O. H. White (one of the secretaries of the
Freedmens Aid Society), then gave an interesting statement of the
origin of the American Missionary Association, of its plan and
work for the African race, and of the formation of the Freedmens
Missions Aid Society, with the Earl of Shaftesbury as President,
to be auxiliary to the Association in New York. And he stated
that the united societies are now making a special effort to send
missionaries from among the freedmen to that dark and long-
plundered continent beyond the sea – Africans to teach and to
save Africans!

The Rev. Andrew Jackson, one of the missionaries, then spoke,
and gave a very interesting account of their call to the work, and
of the great increase of the missionary spirit in Fisk University
during the year, and of the great self-denial on the part of the
coloured parents and of pupils, that larger numbers may get an
education, and so be prepared for a greater usefulness among their
own benighted people.

The chairman then called on the Rev. Hugh Stowell Brown,
pastor for many years of the Myrtle Street Baptist Church. He
stated his great interest in the Jubilee Singers, and in the efforts
making to send the Gospel to that long-neglected Africa, which
is now so wonderfully opening up to trade and commerce, and
especially to Christianity. He expressed his strong hope that
these young missionaries would be brought safely to their field of
labour, and that they might be greatly successful in their work,
and that many more might follow their example, and go forth to
that great African field.

Rev. Albert Miller (a true type of the African race), then
addressed the meeting, with the warmth and glow peculiar to the
sable children of the summer and more genial climes. He spoke of
the depressed condition of his people in America, and of the need
on that dark continent, to which he and his associates were now
going, under the Divine lead. He expressed the desire of his heart

that all Christians should pray and give for the evangelization of
the benighted millions of Africa.

The Rev. Mr. Pearson, M.A., pastor of the church, next spoke,
in the most cordial manner, of his great pleasure in welcoming
these young missionaries and the freedmen's cause to that ancient
historic church. He commended the plan for sending educated
Africans to that great work to be done in those vast fields, which
have proved so fatal to Anglo-Saxon life. He said the British
people had special reasons for taking part with the American
people in this effort to redeem Africa from the darkness and doom
of the past centuries. If the work so well begun was followed up,
as it ought to be, the time was not distant when we should see far
better days for that dark continent with its millions of people.

In the absence of the Rev. Mr. Wech, M.A., who was expected
to speak, his Elder, John Patterson, Esq., was called to fill the
place. He spoke with the pith and pathos characteristic of those
from the Emerald Isle. He recalled a little of the past history of
Liverpool and contrasted it happily with the present state of things,
when so many, from the different denominations of the city, could
come together so harmoniously to greet the young missionaries
from Fisk University, on their way to the west coast of Africa to
teach the knowledge of the Gospel to the benighted of their race.

The Rev. Wardlaw Thompson, in a few words, cordially
commended the Freedmen's cause to the hearts and to the
pecuniary support of the friends of Africa. He then led the
congregation in an earnest prayer for the blessing of God upon the
missionaries, in their voyage to their distant home, and upon their
work for many years among their own people.

An appropriate hymn was then sung, and the services, which
had been highly satisfactory, were closed with the Benediction.

The American Missionary, 32:v (May 1878).

Liverpool continued to be an important centre for African missionary
activity. The Baptist ministers Thomas L. Johnson and James Newby both
stayed at Shalom House in Upper Parliament Street during the 1890s.
In the same decade **Amanda Berry Smith** (1837–1915), known as the
'Coloured Evangelist', visited Liverpool. She was a former slave who turned
to evangelizing in the 1860s. She joined the African Methodist Episcopalian
Church and in the late 1870s made her first voyage to England, returning in

1881, when she headed directly for a big evangelical meeting near Keswick. From there she moved on to India and Liberia, leaving Sierra Leone for England in 1890. On the voyage back to Liverpool she fell ill and the chapter of her autobiography about this experience describes how her illness posed a spiritual test for her, the different remedies suggested by friends, and the different cultural assumptions involved in her wearing plain Quaker clothes. Smith's account of her life is a spiritual autobiography that concentrates on the inner life and so excludes the circumstantial detail we have seen in other memoirs. The very simplicity with which she describes her passage through the Liverpool customs reflects her ignorance of these procedures.

[Chapter 19] When I got to Liverpool I knew nothing about the Custom House. All the ladies had gentlemen to look after their baggage, and as there is always a commotion when we get in, so I said, 'Lord, I have no one to look after my baggage or do anything for me, now help me and keep me quiet, and just help me through with everything.'

The good doctor seemed to take special pains to hinder me. He had a good deal of baggage to be examined, I had but one trunk, he had three officers. I waited; then I saw a chance, and I just spoke to one of the men, and pointed out my trunk; just then the good doctor stepped right in front of me, clapped the man on the arm, took him away so roughly, so I waited till all were pretty well through. The doctor got in his cab and was off. Then the man turned to me and said, 'Madame, this is your trunk?'

'Yes, sir,' I said.

'I suppose you have no tobacco nor cigars, nor books?'

'No, no,' was my reply.

'Well, all right, where do you want to go?'

'Lime Street Station, sir.'

He whistled for a cab, I locked my trunk, and a moment more I was off.

[Chapter 35] I did not go to any of my friends in Liverpool, or Southport, as they wanted I should do. I was so tired, and weak, and I thought of the care and anxiety I would be to them, and then the extra work for the servants—all this I thought of— though I never saw better principled servants in my life, than in England.

[...]

While on the steamer I had my first attack of 'la grippe.' I had not heard of it in Africa; it had not got there then; so that I did not know really what had happened to me. But the good doctor on the steamer seemed to understand how to manage it, and with little things I knew to do for myself, I got relief in a few days. Then it seemed to turn again; and, oh! the pain I suffered. I told the Lord not to let me die and be buried at sea.

[...]

We got into Liverpool on Friday night. The stewardess said I could have lodgings with her. So she took me to her house. All night I suffered. On Saturday morning I felt a little rested; but the pains troubled me very much; so, as the evening drew near, I sent out and got some medicine, and thought I would go to bed early. But just about eight o'clock, my dear friend, Mrs. Stavely (whom I had written to say I had got in, but did not expect to see before Monday), and her husband came in. Dear souls, how very kind they were. They were delighted to see me, and said they thought I looked well to what they expected. I told them how miserable I had been, and had suffered. At once Mrs. Stavely said:

'Oh! why don't you trust the Lord to heal you?'

'Why,' I said, 'that is what I have been doing all along; and I believe if I had not done so I would have been dead long ago.'

She had often written me on the subject of faith healing, while in Africa, and had sent me numerous papers; then I knew dear Mrs. Baxter, and Mrs. Dr. Bordman, and many others of those choice spirits. But somehow I did not seem to be able to see the teaching as they did. They could not understand how anyone so strong in faith as I seemed to be, did not see it; and they knew, and I knew, that the Lord was with me, and did lead me, and bless me. But, like them, I did not understand it myself.

'However,' I said to Mrs. Stavely, 'if an effort on my part is necessary, I cannot make it, I am too weak. But like the man we read of in the Gospel, I am willing for anybody to do anything for me that he can.'

The man we read of in the Gospel was too weak to do anything himself, but was willing they should take the roof off the house and let him down before Jesus; and Jesus, seeing their faith, said to the sick of the palsy: 'Arise.' So I said, 'there is just where I am. I am willing, from the crown of my head to the soles of my feet.'

'Oh, well,' she said, 'if you are willing, the Lord can do it.'

'But, then,' I said, 'I have just swallowed a dose of castor oil and laudanum five minutes before you came in.'

'Well,' she laughingly said, 'you can trust the Lord.'

I knew how very conservative good Mr. Stavely was; that he

was not an enthusiast by any means, though one of the grandest
men I ever knew; and he spoke up:

'Yes, Sister Smith, why not trust the Lord to heal?'

'My,' I thought, 'if he has got to believing so, it is wonderful.'

After a pleasant chat they went home. All day Sunday I
suffered. There was a sick lady in the next room to me, and they
called in a doctor for her. He was a good Christian man. So, as
I was so very ill, my hostess said I had better have the doctor see
me. I agreed, and he came in. He was very pleasant, and I told
him I was just from Africa. He was much interested, and said that
they had a large mission on the Congo. He was delighted to see
little Bob, and said he would like me and Bob to come to Sabbath
School in their church.

He left me some medicine, which did me good, and relieved
the pain so that I was able to sleep a little on Sunday night. Then,
as he had to call on the other lady on Monday and Tuesday he
called each time to see me, also.

I took the medicine on Sunday and Monday, but did not take it
on Tuesday.

'Now, I ought to trust the Lord—now as I am willing,' I said,
'but the doctor is so kind, he may not like it if he knows I am
not taking the medicine; still, if he asks me, I will tell him I
am not taking it.' Then I prayed, 'Lord, do not let him ask me
anything about it.'

So sure enough he called in on Wednesday, had a nice chat,
and said, 'Well, Mrs. Smith, I see you are better.'

'Yes, Doctor,' I said, 'I am feeling much better. How much
shall I pay you?'

'Oh! nothing at all. I am very glad to do what I can for you.'

So I thanked him, and he left.

On Friday I heard that Bishop Taylor was in town, and would
leave on Saturday. So I went down to Mr. Stavely's office, the
Temple, Dale Street, Liverpool, and found that the office of
Anderson Fowler, Bishop Taylor's agent, was next to Mr. Stavely's.

This was the first time I ever saw a telephone work. It was a
new thing to me. But I soon heard from the Bishop. They said,
'Yes, he was there; had just gone out five minutes before.'

So I left my address, and asked the Bishop to call on me at my
lodgings. But, as the Bishop was poorly, with asthma, his son,
Mr. Ross Taylor, and Mr Welch, the former editor of the 'African
News,' called at my lodgings.

[...]

Again I turn to my story. Going out at that time gave me fresh cold; I had not got my winter clothes yet; so a dreadful cough set in, and rheumatism in my left arm; and what I suffered, God only knows. But I had quit taking any means. I was willing to trust the Lord.

'Lord,' I said, 'there are all the things I have been taking, and they have helped me up to a certain point, and then I had to trust you. So I will trust you and do without taking anything.'

Now this time the Lord did not seem to test me as before. I just wanted a little relief from pain, for I was going to die anyhow. So I went on.

One night about two o'clock, I had not slept a wink up to that time, I was sitting up in bed crying with pain in my arm. Dear little Bob was in bed beside me, sleeping away. Everybody in the house was asleep; my cough was terrible; and I said, 'Oh! Lord, help me. What shall I do?' and as though some one stood by me and spoke, I heard, 'Put cotton batting on your arm.'

'Thou knowest,' I replied, 'I have not got any; but in the morning I will ask the lady if she has any.'

So I did, and she gave me some. I got down before the fire on my knees, and put on the cotton batting. It did seem to relieve me, and the pain seemed to quiet down as I knelt down before the fire and it got warm, and I fell into a little doze of sleep. It was better next day, but, oh! so sore. I told my friends I believed it was the good Spirit that prompted me to put on the cotton batting. But they thought I should not have done it, but simply ignored the pain, and just trusted the Lord.

Well, I tried the best I could. They sent me books on the subject; but I said, 'I will not read anything but the Bible. I am going to take the Word of God, and ask help of the Spirit.'

All right. One night after this my cough troubled me so that I could not sleep. After a severe fit of coughing, I said, 'Oh! Lord, do help me. What must I do?' And in an instant a voice distinctly said to me. 'Beet root tea will allay the irritation.' And I said, 'Now, Lord, if that is Thy voice speaking to me, please keep it in my mind till morning and I will do it.'

I remembered that twenty years before I was told this thing, and did it for a friend who was ill with cold, and it helped her; but I didn't remember that I had ever thought of it from that time until it came to me that night.

This was between three and four o'clock in the morning. About day-break I got a little quiet; and at seven o'clock a servant came

in and made the fire, and it came to me about the beet root. I
said, 'Well, I am better now, and I needn't mind about it.'

I got up at eight, and it came again, 'Beet root tea.' But still I
did not heed. About nine o'clock the same whisper came to me
again:

'You said if the Lord would keep it in your mind till morning,
you would make the beet root tea.'

'So I did.'

And I called Bob and sent him downstairs to ask the lady if
she had any red beets. She sent me two small ones, but very nice
and red; I had a small sauce pan, and I put them in and boiled
them and made a strong cupful and drank it, and it did allay the
irritation so that I coughed but little after that to what I had done
before; and I shall ever believe that God was teaching me not to
ignore the use of all means in sickness.

I believe that God is honoured as much when He tells me to
do a thing and I obey, as when He says not to do it, and I obey.
'Thou shalt not covet.' 'Thou shalt love the Lord thy God with all
thy heart.' To me obedience in both cases is absolutely necessary
to honour God. I only receive blessings as I obey.
[…]
Christmas came. My dear friend, Mrs. Stavely, had invited me to
Seaforth. It was with great difficulty that I got there. When I did,
Oh! what a night of suffering. She prayed with me. Oh, how true
and kind she was. Her faith held on to God for me.

Next day another dear friend, Mrs. D., came; and they two
together prayed and encouraged me to still hold on; that all the
pain I suffered was simply a temptation; the Lord would heal me.
I made my will do the best it would; but I felt the pain just the
same.

About noon I got up, and they helped me to get my clothes on.
They were so anxious I should be down to Christmas dinner with
them. So I was, and as best I could, endured the pain through
dinner. When it was over I could not hold out any longer; I
went up to my room, and walked the floor in agony. I tried to
ignore the pain; but in spite of my will and faith, it would not be
ignored a bit!

About day-break I got a little quiet and slept a little; and while
the pain was not so bad as it had been, it was three weeks before
I was able to get my arm above my head. And when I would use
any means, or talk of it, my friends would feel so sorry for me,
and say that it was not honouring the Lord to do so.

But I had sincerely prayed for light. And I believe God has given it to me; if for no one else, He does to Amanda Smith, and I feel quite sure I am not mistaken in God's leading me. I think He has saved me from bondage on these points. Amen. Amen.

As one of the little incidents that reached its culmination after my return from Africa to England, I must here relate the story of my bonnet—not a very important story in itself, but, like most stories, it has its moral, also, if we choose to see it.

How I did hate to give up my nice Quaker bonnet! I had no special feeling about putting it on, so far as feathers and flowers were concerned. I settled that when I was converted. All of those things were surrendered, though the love of them was deep in my heart, so that when I sought the blessing of cleansing I had no difficulty on the dress question.

I always admired the Friends' dress, so this was at once my choice, and at that time many of the Christian sisters among all the coloured churches in Philadelphia, New York, and Baltimore, dressed like the Friends, and were generally called Band Sisters, and, as a rule, were noted for their deep piety and Christian character. I loved them for this, as well as admired their very plain dress, for the height of my ambition was to be a consistent, downright, outright Christian.

It was not a question of your belonging to the Society of Friends because you chose to dress like them. I remember that not only coloured Methodists dressed like them, but white Methodists as well, so that I never dreamed of anyone questioning me on my plain dress. When I got to England I found it was different, dressing like a Friend and not being a Friend, and none of my people being Friends. They did not understand it, so as I went about I was often questioned, though in a very nice way.

[Chapter 36] My first work in England, after my return from Africa, was at Gordon Hall, Mrs. Stephen Menzies', Liverpool, where I spoke at a large conference and sang, and the Lord blessed me greatly. My next work was at Freshfield, at Mr. Radcliff's. I began on Watch Night and spent a week. I was not well, but somehow the Lord helped me to speak to a large congregation in the little chapel. From there I went to Southport and assisted in some meetings held by Rev. D. F. Sanford, of Boston, U.S.A.

All this time I was miserable, but I would earnestly pray and ask the Lord to strengthen me, and He would always do it, but I see now the wise thing would have been for me to have rested entirely, for that was my real need, and the strength I used in praying I should have spent in resting, I believe this would have been pleasing to God. What a dull scholar I have been in His school and yet He has been so patient with me.

Then I held several meetings in Liverpool; then on to Doncaster, was entertained at the home of Miss Morris, Chequer House. I shall never forget her kindness to Bob and me. Here I had some rest, but held a number of meetings, some in the hall of the Y.M.C.A., and Mother's Meetings, and several drawing room meetings at Mrs. Richard Norris'; and various other meetings. From Doncaster we went to London on our way to Folkstone.

> Amanda Smith, *An Autobiography: The Story of the Lord's Dealings with Mrs. Amanda Smith, the Coloured Evangelist* (1893).

Dwight Lyman Moody (1837–99) continued the same line of evangelism as that practised by Amanda Smith, though more distanced from political and racial issues. In June 1873 he arrived in Liverpool after an invitation and began a tour throughout the United Kingdom with his partner **Ira B. Sankey**, who sang to complement Moody's preaching. The tour was very successful, drawing huge audiences and raising large sums of money for good causes. The following extract from one of Moody's sermons demonstrates his capacity to find lessons in everyday events.

A party of Americans a few years ago, on their way from London to Liverpool, decided that they would stop at the Northwestern Hotel, but when they arrived they found the place had been full for several days. Greatly disappointed, they took up their baggage and were about starting off, when they noticed a lady of the party preparing to remain.

"Are you not going, too?" they asked.

"Oh no," she said, "I have good rooms all ready."

"Why, how does that happen?"

"Oh," she said, "I telegraphed on ahead, a few days ago."

Now that is what the children of God are doing; they are sending their names on ahead; they are securing places in the mansions of Christ in time.

> Dwight L. Moody, *Heaven: Its Certainty* (1908).

An account of Moody in Liverpool was given by his compatriot and collaborator, the Presbyterian minister J. Wilbur Chapman. Sankey and Moody sailed home from Liverpool in August 1875.

Mr. Moody came to Liverpool as an old friend. As the city contained no hall large enough for his purposes, an immense temporary structure, called the Victoria Hall, had been erected. It held about 10,000 persons, and the expense of building it was met by voluntary contributions, no direct solicitation being made. This was the first hall erected during the campaign especially for revival services. At the first meeting two-thirds of the congregation were young men. The noon prayer meeting was sometimes attended by 5,000 or 6,000 persons. Eighteen services were held each week in the Victoria Hall, and the Gospel was also carried into the streets and byways, and missionary services were held in warerooms and in stables, as well as in the open.

It was during one of the Liverpool meetings, that Mr. Moody gave a remarkable exhibition of his organising abilities. A great meeting was being held and the theme for discussion was, 'How to reach the masses'. One the speakers expressed the opinion the chief want of the masses in Liverpool was the institution of cheap houses of refreshment to counteract the saloons. When he had finished, Mr. Moody asked him to continue speaking for ten minutes longer, and no sooner was this time up when Mr. Moody sprang to his feet and announced that a company had been formed to carry out the objects the speaker had advocated; that various gentlemen had taken 1,000 shares of £1 each, and the subscription list would be open until the end of the meeting. The capital was gathered before adjournment, and the company was soon floated, being known as the 'The British Workmen Company, Limited'. It has not only worked a revolution in Liverpool, but has paid a handsome dividend as well.

During the month at Liverpool, the number of persons converted, or awakened, ran into the thousands. The inquiry rooms were invariably crowded.

J. Wilbur Chapman, *The Life & Work of Dwight Lyman Moody* (1900).

Financial Reform Meeting 1889

Although slavery had been abolished, the political economist **Henry George** (1839–97), famous for his 1879 study *Progress and Poverty*, argued that it was far from a dead issue in industrial relations and land peonage. He first visited Britain in 1881 to study social conditions and he became particularly interested in the causes of Irish and Scottish Irish land reform. During his lecture tour he visited Liverpool a number of times. On 26 January 1884 the Liverpool *Daily Post* reported that even 'those who find themselves most opposed to Mr. George's theories will admit that he pleads his cause with eloquence and deep sympathy for the squalid classes in great cities' ('Mr. Henry George in Liverpool'). On 20 January 1885 the same newspaper gave an equally enthusiastic report of George's attack on the complicity of the Church in maintaining poverty (a common charge against slavery): 'The people had not merely been kept in ignorance, but they had been taught by their masters and pastors that this was a natural state of things; and the very name of the Deity – the name of religion itself – had been called on to compel men and induce men to quietly submit to this injustice' ('Mr. Henry George on the Crofters' Wrongs'). In 1889 he shared a platform in Liverpool with the son of the abolitionist William Lloyd Garrison. The occasion was a financial reform meeting held that August in the Rotunda Theatre, which stood at the junction of Scotland Road and Stanley Road and which had been rebuilt after a fire destroyed it in 1877. George's address attacks the USA for failing to live up to its stated ideals and uses abolitionist rhetoric to assert the continuing need to strive for freedom.

> It is a deep pleasure for me to be here tonight, the guest of the Liverpool Financial Reform Association, and to speak at my last meeting in England with my honoured countrymen, [including] William Lloyd Garrison of Massachusetts. (Cheers)
>
> You are right, Mr. Garrison. The true republic, the American Republic that we hope for and pray is not yet here. (Hear, hear) A poor thing is a republic where the tramp jostles the millionaire, where liberty is mocked by a paternal system of interference with human rights, where, under the pretext of protecting labour, labour is robbed! (Cheers) And here, in the motherland, in the United States, in Australia and New Zealand, we of the English tongue find the same difficulties confronting us. Liberty is not yet here; but, thank God, she is coming. (Cheers) Not merely the American Republic, not merely the Republic of the Southern

Cross, not merely the Republic of Great Britain and Ireland is it that we see in the future, but that great republic that some day is to confederate the English speaking people everywhere (loud cheers) that is to bring a grander "Roman peace" to the world. (A voice: More than that.) Aye, more than that — that is to bring civilization as much higher, as much better than what we call a Christian civilization, as this is higher and better than barbarism. And already, in meetings such as this, it seems to me that I feel an earnest [presentiment] of the coming time when we of one blood and one speech are also to be one. (Cheers) For the same principles, for the same great cause that we stand in the United States we stand here. And in a little over a week from now I will be standing on an American platform speaking to men whose hearts are beating in the same cause in which we are engaged here. (Cheers)

[Pays tribute to William Lloyd Garrison and argues that the cause of abolition is continuing in the present, though with a difference.]

Chattel slavery, thank God, is abolished at last. Nowhere, where the American flag flies, can one man be bought, or sold, or held by another. (Cheers) But a great struggle still lies before us now. Chattel slavery is gone; industrial slavery remains. The effort, the aim of the abolitionists of this time is to abolish industrial slavery. (Cheers)
[...]

The English Speaking People

Have you ever thought of the position that this English-speaking race of ours is going to hold in the next century? Here, the motherland — this little island. Put it alongside the United States, Canada, Australia, or South Africa; how small it is. Our outposts are now so planted, every sea knows so well our commerce, our millions are so many, that in the next century this English-speaking people will be to the world of that time a mightier power than Rome was to the civilized world of the past. (Cheers)

What is the cause of this, what is the reason of it? Why is it that English is spoken on the North American continent by so many millions of people, and not French or Spanish? Why is it that it is English that is being taught in the public schools of South Africa, of Australia, of New Zealand? (A voice: "They are

the public robbers of the world," and laughter) Robbers they have
been, but it is not by virtue of their robbery. Spain was even a
more unconscionable robber: No! I will tell you why. It is simply
because there has been more freedom; it is simply because the
English people have had less of a paternal government than the
people of the continent. (Cheers) It is not because her colonies
were fostered — it is because they were neglected, that they grew
up. (Laughter) That is today our strength, and that will give
us strength in the future. What we want today to bring us all
together is, not union under one government that shall assume
to govern, but that absolute freedom of intercourse that shall
entwine all interests, that absolute freedom of intercourse that shall
establish a daily ferry from this side of the Atlantic to the other
side of the Atlantic, that shall make everyone belonging to any of
these nations, wherever he may be on the territory of another, feel
as though he were at home: (Cheers)

That is what we strive for — for the freedom of all, for self-
government to all (hear, hear) — and for as little government as
possible: (Laughter and cheers) We don't believe that tyranny is a
thing alone of kings and monarchs; we know well that majorities
can be as tyrannous as aristocracies (hear, hear); we know that
mobs can persecute as well as crowned heads. (Hear, hear) What
we ask for is freedom — that in each locality, large or small, the
people of that locality shall be free to manage the affairs that
pertain only to that locality (hear, hear, and cheers); that each
individual shall be free to manage the affairs that relate to him;
that government shall not presume to say of whom he shall buy or
to whom he shall sell, shall not attempt to dictate to him in any
way, but shall confine itself to its proper function of preserving
the public peace, of preventing the strong from oppressing the
weak, of utilizing for the public good all the revenues that belong
of right to the public, and of managing those affairs that are best
managed by the whole. (Cheers) Our doctrine is the doctrine of
freedom, our gospel is the gospel of liberty, and we have faith in
it, why should we not? (Cheers)

Published in *The Standard*, 10 August 1889; from Kenneth C. Wenzer,
ed., *An Anthology of Henry George's Thought, Volume I of the Henry George
Centennial Trilogy* (Rochester, NY: University of Rochester Press, 1997).

8

Lecturers and Reformers

RALPH WALDO EMERSON (1803–82) was invited to lecture in England by Alexander Ireland, whom he knew from his 1833 visit to Britain. As he recalled in *English Traits* (1856), 'The occasion of my second visit to England was an invitation from some Mechanics' Institutes in Lancashire and Yorkshire, which separately are organized much in the same way as our New England Lyceums, but, in 1847, had been linked into a "Union," which embraced twenty or thirty towns and cities, and presently extended into the middle counties, and northward into Scotland. I was invited, on liberal terms, to read a series of lectures in them all.' In October 1847 he sailed on the packet ship *Washington Irving*, which docked on the 22nd. Initially he stayed at the Waterloo Hotel. The ground had already been prepared for him and even before he began his series of lectures the local press in Liverpool announced:

> Mr. Emerson, the distinguished American essayist and lecturer, will commence a series of six lectures ... on subjects which cannot fail to excite general interest, and which in the hands of such a profound scholar, deep thinker, and eloquent lecturer ... are sure to be treated with justice and power. Mr. Emerson has just arrived in our country from his native America. He comes to us as another of those great messengers, who are not only to encourage peace and good will between the nations on both sides of the Atlantic, but to give us the benefit of the thought and research of the American scholar and man of genius. As such we hope that the thoughtful and eloquent lecturer of New England will receive a right hearty welcome in the 'good old town'.

The *Liverpool Chronicle and General Advertiser*, 30 October 1847.

Apart from his lectures, Emerson used his 1847–48 visit as an opportunity to reflect on the nature of English culture and its relation to America. He made this clear in *English Traits*: 'The problem of the traveller landing at Liverpool is, Why England is England? What are the elements of that power which the English hold over other nations? If there be one test of national genius universally accepted, it is success; and if there be one successful country in the universe for the last millennium, that country is England' (Chapter 3: 'Land'). On 27 October 1847, he had already written to his wife: 'I am heartily tired of Liverpool', but from his Liverpool base he had begun recording national characteristics:

> Everything in England bespeaks an immense population. The buildings are on a scale of size and wealth out of all proportion to ours. The colossal masonry of the docks and of all the public buildings attests the multitudes of men who are to be accommodated by them, and to pay for them. So the manners of the people, the complete incuriosity and stony neglect of each other [...] They are physiognomically and constitutionally distinct from the Americans. They incline more to be large-bodied men; they are stocky, and especially the women seem to have that defect to their beauty; no tall slender girls of flowing shape, but stunted and stocky. The Englishman speaks with all his body; his elocution is stomachic; the American's is labial. The Englishman is very petulant and precise about his accommodation at inns and on the road; a quiddle about his toast and his chop, and every species of convenience, and loud and pungent in his expressions of impatience at any neglect.

[The following year, while staying in London, Emerson raised a subject that he does not discuss in *English Traits*: prostitution.]

> I talked with Forster, Dickens, and Carlyle, on the prostitution in the great towns, and said, that, when I came to Liverpool, I enquired whether it was always as gross in that city as it then appeared to me? For it looked to me as if such manners betokened a fatal rottenness in the state, and especially no boy could grow up safe: but that I had been told, that it was not worse nor better than it had been for years. C and D replied, that chastity in the male sex was as good as gone in our times; and in England was so very rare, that they could name all the exceptions. Carlyle evidently believed that the same thing was true in America. I assured them that it was not so with us: that, for the most part, young men of good standing and good education with us go virgin to their nuptial bed, as truly as their brides. Dickens replied that if incontinence is so much the rule with them that if his own

son were particularly chaste, he should be alarmed on his account, as if he could not be in good health.

Merton M. Sealts, ed., *The Journals and Miscellaneous Notebooks of Ralph Waldo Emerson Volume 10: 1847–1848* (Cambridge, MA: Harvard University Press, 1973).

Emerson's Lecture Schedule in Liverpool in 1847 was as follows:

3 November: 'Uses of Great Men'.
6 November: 'Swedenborg: The Mystic'.
10 November: 'Montaigne: The Sceptic'.
13 November: 'Shakespeare: The Poet'.
17 November: 'Napoleon: The Man of Action'.
20 November: 'Goethe: The Man of Letters'.
30 November: 'Reading'.

All lectures except the last were delivered in the Mechanics' Institution. 'Reading' was given at the inaugural meeting of the Essay and Discussion Society of the Roscoe Club. The Liverpool Mechanics' School of Arts was founded in 1825, its name being shortened in 1832 to the Liverpool Mechanics' Institution, and was roughly equivalent to the Lyceum in America. Emerson's demanding lecture tour took him to cities in the North of England, the Midlands and Scotland, in addition to visiting London. The lectures he gave in Liverpool were collected and published as *Representative Men* in 1850.

Harriet Beecher Stowe (1811–96), unlike Emerson, is primarily associated with one of the most controversial issues of the nineteenth century: slavery. Her visit to Liverpool took place in the wake of the publication of *Uncle Tom's Cabin* (1852), which was followed by a flurry of reviews, rejoinders, and even Uncle Tom artefacts. When Stowe landed she was met by crowds, invited to give addresses, and approached by autograph hunters, all reflecting her new status as a celebrity. After her return to America Stowe published an account of her European travels, *Sunny Memories of Foreign Lands*, which was explicitly rose-tinted and which combined family letters, travelogue and nature diary. It was something of a family production in that Stowe's son, Charles Edward, inserted the addresses that took place during her tour. He also went on to compile a life of Stowe from her papers, published in 1889.

The first letter in *Sunny Memories* is dated 11 April 1853 from Liverpool. Stowe and her family stayed at the home of James Cropper, a Quaker abolitionist who had made his money in shipping. Cropper bought part of the Dingle Estate in 1821, transforming it into the Dingle Bank Estate, which contained three houses and which became known as a local beauty spot. The 'summer house' Stowe mentions was probably an arbour facing the Mersey. The Croppers became known for their charitable activities and set up a 'ragged school' ('Croppers Old School') in Miles Street.

[Arrival.]

Before us lies the great city of Liverpool. No old Cathedral, no castles, a real New Yorkish place.

'There, that's the fort,' cries one. Bang, bang, go the two guns from our forward gangway.

'I wonder if they will fire from the fort,' says another.

'How green that grass looks!' says a third; 'and what pretty cottages!'

'All modern, though,' says somebody, in tones of disappointment. Now we are passing the Victoria Dock. Bang, bang, again. We are in a forest of ships of all nations; their masts bristling like the tall pines in Maine; their many coloured flags streaming like the forest leaves in autumn.

'Hark,' says one; 'there's a chime of bells from the city; how sweet! I had quite forgotten it was Sunday.'

Here we cast anchor, and the small steam tender comes puffing alongside. Now for the custom house officers. State rooms, holds, and cabins must all give up their trunks; a general muster among the baggage, and passenger after passenger comes forward as their names are called, much as follows: 'Snooks.' 'Here, sir.' 'Any thing contraband here, Mr. Snooks? Any cigars, tobacco, &c.?' 'Nothing, sir.'

A little unlocking, a little fumbling. 'Shut up; all right; ticket here.' And a little man pastes on each article a slip of paper, with the royal arms of England and the magical letters V.R., to remind all men that they have come into a country where a lady reigns, and of course must behave themselves as prettily as they can.

We were inquiring of some friends for the most convenient hotel, when we found the son of Mr. Cropper, of Dingle Bank, waiting in the cabin, to take us with him to their hospitable abode. In a few moments after the baggage had been examined,

we all bade adieu to the old ship, and went on board the little
steam tender, which carries passengers up to the city.

This Mersey River would be a very beautiful one, if it were
not so dingy and muddy. As we are sailing up in the tender
towards Liverpool, I deplore the circumstance feelingly. 'What
does make this river so muddy?'

'O,' says a bystander, 'don't you know that

'The quality of mercy is not strained'?'

And now we are fairly alongside the shore, and we are soon
going to set our foot on the land of Old England.

Say what we will, an American, particularly a New Englander,
can never approach the old country without a kind of thrill and
pulsation of kindred. Its history for two centuries was our history.
Its literature, laws, and language are our literature, laws, and
language. Spenser, Shakespeare, Bacon, Milton, were a glorious
inheritance, which we share in common. Our very life-blood is
English life-blood. It is Anglo-Saxon vigour that is spreading our
country from Atlantic to Pacific, and leading on a new era in
the world's development. America is a tall, sightly young shoot,
that has grown from the old royal oak of England; divided from
its parent root, it has shot up in new, rich soil, and under genial,
brilliant skies, and therefore takes on a new type of growth and
foliage, but the sap in it is the same.

I had an early opportunity of making acquaintance with my
English brethren; for, much to my astonishment, I found quite a
crowd on the wharf, and we walked up to our carriage through
a long lane of people, bowing, and looking very glad to see us.
When I came to get into the hack it was surrounded by more
faces than I could count. They stood very quietly, and looked
very kindly, though evidently very much determined to look.
Something prevented the hack from moving on; so the interview
was prolonged for some time. I therefore took occasion to remark
the very fair, pure complexions, the clear eyes, and the general air
of health and vigour, which seem to characterize our brethren and
sisters of the island. There seemed to be no occasion to ask them,
how they did, as they were evidently quite well. Indeed, this air
of health is one of the most striking things when one lands in
England.

They were not burly, red-faced, and stout, as I had sometimes
conceived of the English people, but just full enough to suggest
the idea of vigour and health. The presence of so many healthy,
rosy people looking at me, all reduced as I was, first by land and

then by sea sickness, made me feel myself more withered and forlorn than ever. But there was an earnestness and a depth of kind feeling in some of the faces, which I shall long remember. It seemed as if I had not only touched the English shore, but felt the English heart.

Our carriage at last drove on, taking us through Liverpool, and a mile or two out, and at length wound its way along the gravel paths of a beautiful little retreat, on the banks of the Mersey, called the 'Dingle.' It opened to my eyes like a paradise, all wearied as I was with the tossing of the sea. I have since become familiar with these beautiful little spots, which are so common in England; but now all was entirely new to me.

We rode by shining clumps of the Portugal laurel, a beautiful evergreen, much resembling our mountain rhododendron; then there was the prickly, polished, dark-green holly, which I had never seen before, but which is, certainly, one of the most perfect of shrubs. The turf was of that soft, dazzling green, and had that peculiar velvet-like smoothness, which seem characteristic of England. We stopped at last before the door of a cottage, whose porch was overgrown with ivy. From that moment I ceased to feel myself a stranger in England. I cannot tell you how delightful to me, dizzy and weary as I was, was the first sight of the chamber of reception which had been prepared for us. No item of cosy comfort that one could desire was omitted. The sofa and easy chair wheeled up before a cheerful coal fire, a bright little teakettle steaming in front of the grate, a table with a beautiful vase of flowers, books, and writing apparatus, and kind friends with words full of affectionate cheer,—all these made me feel at home in a moment.

The hospitality of England has become famous in the world, and, I think, with reason. I doubt not there is just as much hospitable feeling in other countries; but in England the matter of cosiness and home comfort has been so studied, and matured, and reduced to system, that they really have it in their power to effect more, towards making their guests comfortable, than perhaps any other people.

After a short season allotted to changing our ship garments and for rest, we found ourselves seated at the dinner table. While dining, the sister-in-law of our friends came in from the next door, to exchange a word or two of welcome, and invite us to breakfast with them the following morning.

Between all the excitements of landing, and meeting so many

new faces, and the remains of the dizzy motion of the ship, which still haunted me, I found it impossible to close my eyes to sleep that first night till the dim gray of dawn. I got up as soon as it was light, and looked out of the window; and as my eyes fell on the luxuriant, ivy-covered porch, the clumps of shining, dark-green holly bushes, I said to myself, 'Ah, really, this is England!'

[At her first breakfast Stowe was welcomed by Dr McNeile as the 'Honoured instrument of the noble impulse' to oppose slavery.]

We hurried to dress, remembering our engagements to breakfast this morning with a brother of our host, whose cottage stands on the same ground, within a few steps of our own. I had not the slightest idea of what the English mean by a breakfast, and therefore went in all innocence, supposing that I should see nobody but the family circle of my acquaintances. Quite to my astonishment, I found a party of between thirty and forty people. Ladies sitting with their bonnets on, as in a morning call. It was impossible, however, to feel more than a momentary embarrassment in the friendly warmth and cordiality of the circle by whom we were surrounded.

The English are called cold and stiff in their manners; I had always heard they were so, but I certainly saw nothing of it here. A circle of family relatives could not have received us with more warmth and kindness. The remark which I made mentally, as my eye passed around the circle, was—Why, these people are just like home; they look like us, and the tone of sentiment and feeling is precisely such as I have been accustomed to; I mean with the exception of the antislavery question.

That question has, from the very first, been, in England, a deeply religious movement. It was conceived and carried on by men of devotional habits, in the same spirit in which the work of foreign missions was undertaken in our own country; by just such earnest, self-denying, devout men as Samuel J. Mills [a pioneer of African missions] and Jeremiah Evarts [missionary campaigner against American Indian removal].

It was encountered by the same contempt and opposition, in the outset, from men of merely worldly habits and principles; and to this day it retains that hold on the devotional mind of the English nation that the foreign mission cause does in America.

Liverpool was at first to the antislavery cause nearly what New York has been with us. Its commercial interests were largely implicated in the slave trade, and the virulence of opposition towards the first movers of the antislavery reform in Liverpool was about as great as it is now against abolitionists in Charleston.

When Clarkson first came here to prosecute his inquiries into the subject, a mob collected around him, and endeavoured to throw him off the dock into the water; he was rescued by a gentleman, some of whose descendants I met on this occasion.

The father of our host, Mr. Cropper, was one of the first and most efficient supporters of the cause in Liverpool; and the whole circle was composed of those who had taken a deep interest in that struggle. The wife of our host was the daughter of the celebrated Lord Chief Justice Denman, a man who, for many years, stood unrivalled, at the head of the legal mind in England, and who, with a generous ardour seldom equalled, devoted all his energies to this sacred cause.

When the publication of *Uncle Tom's Cabin* turned the attention of the British public to the existing horrors of slavery in America, some palliations of the system appeared in English papers. Lord Denman, though then in delicate health and advanced years, wrote a series of letters upon the subject—an exertion which entirely prostrated his before feeble health. In one of the addresses made at table, a very feeling allusion was made to Lord Denman's labours, and also to those of the honoured father of the two Messrs. Cropper.

[Stowe wrote to Lord Thomas Denman on 20 January 1853 to explain why she had written *Uncle Tom's Cabin*. Denman was related to the Croppers by marriage.]

As breakfast parties are things which we do not have in America, perhaps mother would like to know just how they are managed. The hour is generally somewhere between nine and twelve, and the whole idea and spirit of the thing is that of an informal and social gathering. Ladies keep their bonnets on, and are not dressed in full toilet. On this occasion we sat and chatted together socially till the whole party was assembled in the drawing room, and then breakfast was announced. Each gentleman had a lady assigned him, and we walked into the dining room, where stood the tables tastefully adorned with flowers, and spread with an abundant cold collation, while tea and coffee were passed round by servants. In each plate was a card, containing the name of the person for whom it was designed. I took my place by the side of

the Rev. Dr. McNiel, one of the most celebrated clergymen of the
established church in Liverpool.

[...]

Several present spoke of the part which England originally had in
planting slavery in America, as placing English Christians under
a solemn responsibility to bring every possible moral influence to
bear for its extinction. Nevertheless, they seem to be the farthest
possible from an unkind or denunciatory spirit, even towards those
most deeply implicated. The remarks made by Dr. McNiel to me
were a fair sample of the spirit and attitude of all present.

'I have been trying, Mrs. S.,' he said, 'to bring my mind into
the attitude of those Christians at the south who defend the
institution of slavery. There are *real* Christians there who do
this—are there not?'

I replied, that undoubtedly there were some most amiable and
Christian people who defend slavery on principle, just as there had
been some to defend every form of despotism.

'Do give me some idea of the views they take; it is something
to me so inconceivable. I am utterly at a loss how it can be made
in any way plausible.'

I then stated that the most plausible view, and that which seemed
to have the most force with good men, was one which represented
the institution of slavery as a sort of wardship or guardian relation,
by which an inferior race were brought under the watch and care
of a superior race to be instructed in Christianity.

He then inquired if there was any system of religious
instruction actually pursued.

In reply to this, I gave him some sketch of the operations for
the religious instruction of the negroes, which had been carried
on by the Presbyterian and other denominations. I remarked that
many good people who do not take very extended views, fixing
their attention chiefly on the efforts which they are making for
the religious instruction of slaves, are blind to the sin and injustice
of allowing their legal position to remain what it is.

'But how do they shut their eyes to the various cruelties of the
system,—the separation of families—the domestic slave trade?'

I replied, 'In part, by not inquiring into them. The best kind
of people are, in general, those who *know* least of the cruelties of
the system; they never witness them. As in the city of London or
Liverpool there may be an amount of crime and suffering which
many residents may live years without seeing or knowing, so it is
in the slave states.'

Every person present appeared to be in that softened and charitable frame of mind which disposed them to make every allowance for the situation of Christians so peculiarly tempted, while, at the same time, there was the most earnest concern, in view of the dishonour brought upon Christianity by the defence of such a system.

One other thing I noticed, which was an agreeable disappointment to me.

I had been told that there was no social intercourse between the established church and dissenters. In this party, however, were people of many different denominations. Our host belongs to the established church; his brother, with whom we are visiting, is a Baptist, and their father was a Friend; and there appeared to be the utmost social cordiality. Whether I shall find this uniformly the case will appear in time.

After the breakfast party was over, I found at the door an array of children of the poor, belonging to a school kept under the superintendence of Mrs. E. Cropper, and called, as is customary here, a ragged school. The children, however, were any thing but ragged, being tidily dressed, remarkably clean, with glowing cheeks and bright eyes. I must say, so far as I have seen them, English children have a much healthier appearance than those of America. By the side of their bright bloom ours look pale and faded.

[Two young men take Stowe for a tour of the grounds of the Dingle, during which she notes many details of the local flora. Their arrival at the summer house occasions reflections on the difference between British permanence of residence and the relative mobility of Americans.]

After rambling a while, we came to a beautiful summer house, placed in a retired spot, so as to command a view of the Mersey River. I think they told me that it was Lord Denman's favourite seat. There we sat down, and in common with the young gentlemen and ladies of the family, had quite a pleasant talk together. Among other things we talked about the question which is now agitating the public mind a good deal,—Whether it is expedient to open the Crystal Palace to the people on Sunday. They said that this course was much urged by some philanthropists, on the ground that it was the only day when the working classes could find any leisure to visit it, and that it seemed hard to shut them out entirely from all the opportunities and advantages which they might thus derive; that to exclude the labourer from recreation on the Sabbath, was the same as saying that he should never have any recreation. I asked, why the philanthropists could not urge employers to give their workmen a part of Saturday for this purpose; as it seemed to me unchristian to drive trade so that the labouring man had no time but Sunday for intellectual and social recreation. We rather came to the conclusion that this was the right course; whether the people of England will, is quite another matter.

[Visit to Speke Hall, the half-timbered house whose construction started in 1490. At the time of Stowe's visit it was going through a series of tenancies. It boasted a haunted chamber in the Tapestry Room, hence her comments on its offering a possible subject for fiction.]

The next day at breakfast, it was arranged that we should take a drive out to Speke Hall, an old mansion, which is considered a fine specimen of ancient house architecture. So the carriage was at the door. It was a cool, breezy, April morning, but there was an abundance of wrappers and carriage blankets provided to keep us comfortable. I must say, by the by, that English housekeepers are bountiful in their provision for carriage comfort. Every household has a store of warm, loose over garments, which are offered, if needed, to the guests; and each carriage is provided with one or two blankets, manufactured and sold expressly for this use, to envelope one's feet and limbs; besides all which, should the weather be cold, comes out a long stone reservoir, made flat on both sides, and filled with hot water, for foot stools. This is an improvement on the primitive simplicity of hot bricks, and even on the tin foot stove, which has flourished in New England.

Being thus provided with all things necessary for comfort, we rattled merrily away, and I, remembering that I was in England, kept my eyes wide open to see what I could see. The hedges of the fields were just budding, and the green showed itself on them, like a thin gauze veil. These hedges are not all so well kept and trimmed as I expected to find them. Some, it is true, are cut very carefully; these are generally hedges to ornamental grounds; but many of those which separate the fields straggle and sprawl, and have some high bushes and some low ones, and, in short, are no more like a hedge than many rows of bushes that we have at home. But such as they are, they are the only dividing lines of the fields, and it is certainly a more picturesque

mode of division than our stone or worm fences. Outside of
every hedge, towards the street, there is generally a ditch, and
at the bottom of the hedge is the favourite nestling-place for
all sorts of wild flowers. I remember reading in stories about
children trying to crawl through a gap in the hedge to get at
flowers, and tumbling into a ditch on the other side, and I now
saw exactly how they could do it.

As we drive we pass by many beautiful establishments, about of
the quality of our handsomest country houses, but whose grounds
are kept with a precision and exactness rarely to be seen among
us. We cannot get the gardeners who are qualified to do it; and
if we could, the painstaking, slow way of proceeding, and the
habit of creeping thoroughness, which are necessary to accomplish
such results, die out in America. Nevertheless, such grounds are
exceedingly beautiful to look upon, and I was much obliged to
the owners of these places for keeping their gates hospitably open,
as seems to be the custom here.

After a drive of seven or eight miles, we alighted in front of
Speke Hall. This house is a specimen of the old fortified houses
of England, and was once fitted up with a moat and drawbridge,
all in approved feudal style. It was built somewhere about the year
1500. The sometime moat was now full of smooth, green grass,
and the drawbridge no longer remains.

This was the first really old thing that we had seen since our
arrival in England. We came up first to a low, arched, stone door,
and knocked with a great old-fashioned knocker; this brought
no answer but a treble and bass duet from a couple of dogs
inside; so we opened the door, and saw a square court, paved
with round stones, and a dark, solitary yew tree in the centre.
Here in England, I think, they have vegetable creations made on
purpose to go with old, dusky buildings; and this yew tree is one
of them. It has altogether a most goblin-like, bewitched air, with
its dusky black leaves and ragged branches, throwing themselves
straight out with odd twists and angular lines, and might put one
in mind of an old raven with some of his feathers pulled out, or
a black cat with her hair stroked the wrong way, or any other
strange, uncanny thing. Besides this they live almost forever; for
when they have grown so old that any respectable tree ought to
be thinking of dying, they only take another twist, and so live
on another hundred years. I saw some in England seven hundred
years old, and they had grown queerer every century. It is a
species of evergreen, and its leaf resembles our hemlock, only it

is longer. This sprig gives you some idea of its general form. It is always planted about churches and graveyards; a kind of dismal emblem of immortality. This sepulchral old tree and the bass and treble dogs were the only occupants of the court. One of these, a great surly mastiff, barked out of his kennel on one side, and the other, a little wiry terrier, out of his on the opposite side, and both strained on their chains, as if they would enjoy making even more decided demonstrations if they could.

There was an aged, mossy fountain for holy water by the side of the wall, in which some weeds were growing. A door in the house was soon opened by a decent-looking serving woman, to whom we communicated our desire to see the hall.

We were shown into a large dining hall with a stone floor, wainscoted with carved oak, almost as black as ebony. There were some pious sentences and moral reflections inscribed in old English text, carved over the doors, and like a cornice round the ceiling, which was also of carved oak. Their general drift was, to say that life is short, and to call for watchfulness and prayer. The fireplace of the hall yawned like a great cavern, and nothing else, one would think, than a cart load of western sycamores could have supplied an appropriate fire. A great two-handed sword of some ancestor hung over the fireplace. On taking it down it reached to C——'s shoulder, who, you know, is six feet high.

We went into a sort of sitting room, and looked out through a window, latticed with little diamond panes, upon a garden wildly beautiful. The lattice was all wreathed round with jessamines. The furniture of this room was modern, and it seemed the more unique from its contrast with the old architecture.

We went up stairs to see the chambers, and passed through a long, narrow, black oak corridor, whose slippery boards had the authentic ghostly squeak to them. There was a chamber, hung with old, faded tapestry of Scripture subjects. In this chamber there was behind the tapestry a door, which, being opened, displayed a staircase, that led delightfully off to nobody knows where. The furniture was black oak, carved, in the most elaborate manner, with cherubs' heads and other good and solemn subjects, calculated to produce a ghostly state of mind. And, to crown all, we heard that there was a haunted chamber, which was not to be opened, where a white lady appeared and walked at all approved hours.

Now, only think what a foundation for a story is here. If our Hawthorne could conjure up such a thing as the Seven Gables in one of our prosaic country towns, what would he have done if he had lived here? Now he is obliged to get his ghostly images by looking through smoked glass at our square, cold realities; but one such old place as this is a standing romance. Perhaps it may add to the effect to say, that the owner of the house is a bachelor, who lives there very retired, and employs himself much in reading.

The housekeeper, who showed us about, indulged us with a view of the kitchen, whose snowy, sanded floor and resplendent polished copper and tin, were sights for a housekeeper to take away in her heart of hearts. The good woman produced her copy of Uncle Tom, and begged the favour of my autograph, which I gave, thinking it quite a happy thing to be able to do a favour at so cheap a rate.

[...]

In the evening I went into Liverpool, to attend a party of friends of the antislavery cause. In the course of the evening, Mr. Stowe was requested to make some remarks. Among other things he spoke upon the support the free part of the world give to slavery, by the purchase of the produce of slave labour; and, in particular, on the great quantity of slave-grown cotton purchased by England; suggesting it as a subject for inquiry, whether this cannot be avoided.

One or two gentlemen, who are largely concerned in the manufacture and importation of cotton, spoke to him on the subject afterwards, and said it was a thing which ought to be very seriously considered. It is probable that the cotton trade of Great Britain is the great essential item which supports slavery, and such considerations ought not, therefore, to be without their results.

When I was going away, the lady of the house said that the servants were anxious to see me; so I came into the dressing room to give them an opportunity.

While at Mr. C.'s, also, I had once or twice been called out to see servants, who had come in to visit those of the family. All of them had read Uncle Tom's Cabin, and were full of sympathy. Generally speaking, the servants seem to me quite a superior class to what are employed in that capacity with us. They look very intelligent, are dressed with great neatness, and though their manners are very much more deferential than those of servants in our country, it appears to be a difference arising quite as much from self-respect and a sense of propriety as from servility. Every body's manners are more deferential in England than in America.

The next day was appointed to leave Liverpool. It had been

arranged that, before leaving, we should meet the ladies of the Negroes' Friend Society, an association formed at the time of the original antislavery agitation in England. We went in the carriage with our friends Mr. and Mrs. E. Cropper. On the way they were conversing upon the labours of Mrs. Chisholm, the celebrated female philanthropist, whose efforts for the benefit of emigrants are awakening a very general interest among all classes in England. They said there had been hesitation on the part of some good people, in regard to cooperating with her, because she is a Roman Catholic.

It was agreed among us, that the great humanities of the present day are a proper ground on which all sects can unite, and that if any feared the extension of wrong sentiments, they had only to supply emigrant ships more abundantly with the Bible. Mr. C. said that this is a movement exciting very extensive interest, and that they hoped Mrs. Chisholm would visit Liverpool before long.

The meeting was a very interesting one. The style of feeling expressed in all the remarks was tempered by a deep and earnest remembrance of the share which England originally had in planting the evil of slavery in the civilized world, and her consequent obligation, as a Christian nation, now not to cease her efforts until the evil is extirpated, not merely from her own soil, but from all lands.

The feeling towards America was respectful and friendly, and the utmost sympathy was expressed with her in the difficulties with which she is environed by this evil. The tone of the meeting was deeply earnest and religious. They presented us with a sum to be appropriated for the benefit of the slave, in any way we might think proper.

A great number of friends accompanied us to the cars, and a beautiful bouquet of flowers was sent, with a very affecting message from a sick gentleman, who, from the retirement of his chamber, felt a desire to testify his sympathy.

Harriet Beecher Stowe, *Sunny Memories of Foreign Lands* (1854), Vol. I, Letter II.

On 13 April 1853 a testimonial was given to Stowe with 21,953 signatures in recognition of her efforts in the cause of abolition. Her response was read by her husband:

It is impossible for me to express the feelings of my heart at the kind and generous manner in which I have been received upon English shores. Just when I had begun to realize that a whole wide ocean lay between me and all that is dearest to me, I found most unexpectedly a home and friends waiting to receive me here. I have had not an hour in which to know the heart of a stranger. I have been made to feel at home since the first moment of landing, and wherever I have looked I have seen only the faces of friends. It is with deep feeling that I have found myself on ground that has been consecrated and made holy by the prayers and efforts of those who first commenced the struggle for that sacred cause which has proved so successful in England, and which I have a solemn assurance will yet be successful in my own country. It is a touching thought that here so many have given all that they have, and are, in behalf of oppressed humanity. It is touching to remember that one of the noblest men which England has ever produced now lies stricken under the heavy hand of disease, through a last labour of love in this cause. May God grant us all to feel that nothing is too dear or precious to be given in a work for which such men have lived, and laboured, and suffered. No great good is ever wrought out for the human race without the suffering of great hearts. They who would serve their fellow-men are ever reminded that the Captain of their salvation was made perfect through suffering. I gratefully accept the offering confided to my care, and trust it may be so employed that the blessing of many "who are ready to perish" will return upon your heads. Let me ask those—those fathers and mothers in Israel—who have lived and prayed many years for this cause, that as they prayed for their own country in the hour of her struggle, so they will pray now for ours. Love and prayer can hurt no one, can offend no one, and prayer is a real power. If the hearts of all the real Christians of England are poured out in prayer, it will be felt through the heart of the whole American church. Let us all look upward, from our own feebleness and darkness, to Him of whom it is said, "He shall not fail nor be discouraged till he have set judgment in the earth." To him, the only wise God our Saviour, be glory and majesty, dominion and power, both now and ever. Amen.'—These are the words, my friends, which Mrs. Stowe has written, and I cannot

forbear to add a few words of my own. It was our intention, as
the invitation to visit Great Britain came from Glasgow, to make
our first landing there. But it was ordered by Providence that we
should land here; and surely there is no place in the kingdom
where a landing could be more appropriate, and where the
reception could have been more cordial. [Hear, hear!] It was
wholly unexpected by us, I can assure you. We know that there
were friendly hearts here, for we had received abundant
testimonials to that effect from letters which had come to us
across the Atlantic—letters wholly unexpected, and which filled
our souls with surprise; but we had no thought that there was
such a feeling throughout England, and we scarcely know how to
conduct ourselves under it, for we are not accustomed to this kind
of reception. In our own country, unhappily, we are very much
divided, and the preponderance of feeling expressed is in the other
direction, entirely in opposition, and not in favour. [Hear, hear!]
We knew that this city had been the scene of some of the
greatest, most disinterested, and most powerful efforts in behalf of
emancipation. The name of Clarkson was indissolubly associated
with this place, for here he came to make his investigations, and
here he was in danger of his life, and here he was protected by
friends who stood by him through the whole struggle. The names
of Cropper, and of Stephen, and of many others in this city, were
very familiar to us—[Hear, hear!]—and it was in connection with
this city that we received what to our feelings was a most effective
testimonial, an unexpected letter from Lord Denman, whom we
have always venerated. When I was in England in 1836, there
were no two persons whom I more desired to see than the Duke
of Wellington and Lord Denman; and soon I sought admission to
the House of Lords, where I had the pleasure both of seeing and
hearing England's great captain; and I found my way to the Court
of Queen's Bench, where I had the pleasure of seeing and hearing
England's great judge. But how unexpected was all this to us!
When that book was written, in sorrow, and in sadness, and in
obscurity, and with the heart almost broken in the view of the
sufferings which it described, and the still greater sufferings which
it dared not describe, there was no expectation of any thing but
the prayers of the sufferers and the blessing of God, who has said
that the seed which is buried in the earth shall spring up in his
own good time; and though it may be long buried, it will still at
length come forth and bear fruit. We never could believe that
slavery in our land would be a perpetual curse; but we felt, and

felt deeply, that there must be a terrible struggle before we could
be delivered from it, and that there must be suffering and
martyrdom in this cause, as in every other great cause; for a
struggle of eighteen years had taught us its strength. And, under
God, we rely very much on the Christian public of Great Britain;
for every expression of feeling from the wise and good of this
land, with whatever petulance it may be met by some, goes to the
heart of the American people. [Hear, hear!] You must not judge of
the American people by the expressions which have come across
the Atlantic in reference to the subject. Nine tenths of the
American people, I think, are, in opinion at least, with you on
this great subject; [Hear, hear!] but there is a tremendous pressure
brought to bear upon all who are in favour of emancipation. The
whole political power, the whole money power, almost the whole
ecclesiastical power is wielded in defence of slavery, protecting it
from all aggression; and it is as much as a man's reputation is
worth to utter a syllable boldly and openly on the other side. Let
me say to the ladies who have been active in getting up the
address on the subject of slavery, that you have been doing a great
and glorious work, and a work most appropriate for you to do; for
in slavery it is woman that suffers most intensely, and the suffering
woman has a claim upon the sympathy of her sisters in other
lands. This address will produce a powerful impression throughout
the country. There are ladies already of the highest character in
the nation pondering how they shall make a suitable response, and
what they shall do in reference to it that will be acceptable to the
ladies of the United Kingdom, or will be profitable to the slave;
and in due season you will see that the hearts of American
women are alive to this matter, as well as the hearts of the
women of this country. [Hear, hear!] Such was the mighty
influence brought to bear upon every thing that threatened
slavery, that had it not been for the decided expression on this side
of the Atlantic in reference to the work which has exerted, under
God, so much influence, there is every reason to fear that it
would have been crushed and put under foot, as many other
efforts for the overthrow of slavery have been in the United
States. But it is impossible; the unanimous voice of Christendom
prohibits it; and it shows that God has a work to accomplish, and
that he has just commenced it. There are social evils in England.
Undoubtedly there are; but the difference between the social evils
in England and this great evil of slavery in the United States is
just here: In England, the power of the government and the

power of Christian sympathy are exerted for the removal of those evils. Look at the committees of inquiry in Parliament, look at the amount of information collected with regard to the suffering poor in their reports, and see how ready the government of Great Britain is to enter into those inquiries, and to remove those evils. Look at the benevolent institutions of the United Kingdom, and see how active all these are in administering relief; and then see the condition of slavery in the United States, where the whole power of the government is used in the contrary direction, where every influence is brought to bear to prevent any mitigation of the evil, and where every voice that is lifted to plead for a mitigation is drowned in vituperation and abuse from those who are determined that the evil shall not be mitigated. This is the difference: England repents and reforms. America refuses to repent and reform. It is said, 'Let each country take care of itself, and let the ladies of England attend to their own business.' Now I have always found that those who labour at home are those who labour abroad; [Hear, hear!] and those who say, 'Let us do the work at home,' are those who do no work of good either at home or abroad. [Hear, hear!] It was just so when the great missionary effort came up in the United States. They said, 'We have a great territory here. Let us send missionaries to our own territories. Why should we send missionaries across the ocean?' But those who sent missionaries across the ocean were those who sent missionaries in the United States; and those who did not send missionaries across the ocean were those who sent missionaries nowhere. [Hear, hear!] They who say, 'Charity begins at home,' are generally those who have no charity; and when I see a lady whose name is signed to this address, I am sure to find a lady who is exercising her benevolence at home. Let me thank you for all the interest you have manifested and for all the kindness which we have received at your hands, which we shall ever remember, both with gratitude to you and to God our Father.

Sunny Memories of Foreign Lands, Vol. I, 'Introductory'.

Stowe went on to speak in cities in the north of England and Scotland, as well as in London.

Margaret Fuller (1810–45) was a leading American feminist, becoming widely known for her polemical volume *Woman in the Nineteenth Century* (1845). Horace Greeley offered her a post writing for the *New York Tribune* and in 1846 she sailed for Europe to act as his foreign correspondent. She agreed to contribute three articles a week on social and political topics and in October travelled to Liverpool with the New York cotton merchant Marcus Spring and his family. They sailed on the Cunard liner *Cambria*, whose captain C. H. E. Judkins the preceding year had made a point of treating Frederick Douglass with special consideration to counter the prejudice of the Southern passengers. Although Fuller's articles were pieces of reportage, she fed her social concerns into her accounts, as in the following ironic description of her landing at Liverpool.

> We had a foretaste of the delights of living under an aristocratical Government at the Custom-House, where our baggage was detained, and we waiting for it weary hours, because of the preference given to the mass of household stuff carried back by this same Lord and Lady Falkland.
>
> Captain Judkins of the *Cambria*, an able and prompt Commander, was the one who insisted upon Douglass being admitted to equal rights upon his deck with the insolent slaveholders, and assumed a tone toward their assumptions, which, if the Northern States had had the firmness, good sense and honour to use would have had the same effect, and put our country in a very different position from that she occupies at present. He mentioned with pride that he understood the *New York Herald* called him 'the Nigger Captain', and seemed as willing to accept the distinction as Colonel McKenney is to wear his last title that of 'the Indian's friend'. [Thomas Loraine McKenney was the US Superintendent of Indian Trade (1816–22) and Superintendent of Indian Affairs (1824–30), and wrote a number of studies on Indian subjects.]
>
> At the first sight of the famous Liverpool Docks, extending miles on each side of our landing, we felt ourselves in a slower, solider, and not on that account less truly active state of things than at home. That impression is confirmed. There is not as we travel that rushing, tearing and swearing, that snatching of baggage, that prodigality of shoe-leather and lungs that attend the course of the traveller in the United States; but we do not lose our 'goods', we do not miss our car. The dinner if ordered in time, is cooked properly and served punctually, and at the end of the day, more that is permanent seems to have come of it than on

the full-drive system. But more of that and with a better grace at
a later day.

The day after our arrival we went to Manchester. There we
went over the magnificent warehouse of —— Phillips, in itself a
Bazaar enough to furnish provision for all the wants and fancies
of thousands. In the evening we went to the Mechanics' Institute
and saw the boys and young men in their classes. I have since
visited the Mechanics' Institute at Liverpool, where more that
seventeen hundred pupils are received, and with more thorough
educational arrangements; but the excellent spirit, the desire for
growth in wisdom and enlightened benevolence is the same in
both. For a very small fee the mechanic, clerk, or apprentice,
and the women of their families can receive various good and
well-arranged instruction, not only in common branches of
English Education, but in mathematics, composition, the French
and German languages, the practice and theory of the Fine Arts,
and they are ardent in availing themselves of instruction in the
higher branches. I found large classes, not only in architectural
drawing, which may be supposed to be followed with a view to
professional objects, but landscape also, and as large in German
as in French. They can attend many good lectures and concerts
without additional charge, for a due place is here assigned to
Music as to its influence on the whole mind. The large and
well-furnished libraries are in constant requisition, and the books
in most constant demand are not those of amusement, but of a
solid and permanent interest and value. Only for the last year in
Manchester and for two in Liverpool, have these advantages been
extended to girls; but now that part of the subject is looked upon
as it ought to be, and begins to be treated more and more as it
must and will be wherever true civilization is making its way.
One of the handsomest houses in Liverpool has been purchased
for the girls' school, and room and good arrangement have been
afforded for their work and their play. Among other things they
are taught, as they ought to be in all American schools, to cut
out and make dresses.

[In keeping with her general emphasis on self-improvement, Fuller noted
with pleasure that the Director of the Liverpool Institute in one of his
addresses quoted from the Boston *Dial*, which Fuller had edited for a time,
on this very subject. The Liverpool Royal Institution for 'the Promotion of
Literature, Science, and the Arts' was founded by William Roscoe in 1817.
Its premises in Colquitt Street housed a number of art collections. Roscoe's

statue was by Sir Francis Legatt Chantrey. Fuller also visited the St James Cemetery, next to the Anglican Cathedral, which houses a memorial to William Huskisson, the Liverpool MP who suffered a fatal accident while officiating at the opening of the Liverpool and Manchester Railway in 1830. It contains a statue of Huskisson by John Gibson.]

Other things we saw in Liverpool – the Royal Institute, with the statue of Roscoe by Chantrey, and its collection from the works of the early Italian artists and otherwise, bearing traces of that liberality and culture by which the man, happy enough to possess them, and, at the same time engaged with his fellow-citizens in practical life, can do so much more to enlighten them and form them than Prince or Noble possibly can with far larger pecuniary means. We saw the statue of Huskisson in the Cemetery. It is fine as a Portrait Statue, but as a work of Art wants firmness and grandeur. I say it is fine as a portrait statue, though we are told it is not like the original; but it is a fine conception of an individuality which might exist, if it does not yet. It is by Gibson, who received his early education in Liverpool. I saw there, too, the body of an infant borne to the grave by women; for it is a beautiful custom here that those who have fulfilled all other tender offices to the little being, should hold to it the same relation to the very last.

Margaret Fuller, *'These Sad But Glorious Days': Dispatches from Europe, 1848–1850* (New Haven, CT: Yale University Press, 1991), Dispatch 1: 'First Impressions of England'.

While in Europe Fuller met and probably married Giovanni Ossoli, an Italian revolutionary. They were drowned with their son in 1850 while sailing to America. The following year **Horace Greeley** (1811–72) himself sailed to Europe on the *Baltic*, partly to see the Great Exhibition in London. He was evidently unimpressed by his landing at Liverpool.

We then ran up opposite the City, but there was no dock-room for the *Baltic*, and passengers and light luggage were ferried ashore in a 'steam-tug' which we in New York would deem unworthy to convey market garbage. At last, after infinite delay and vexation, caused in good part by the necessity of a custom-house scrutiny even of carpet-bags, because men *will* smuggle cigars ashore

here, even in their pockets, we were landed about 9 o'clock, and
tomorrow I set my watch by an English sun.

Once he had cleared these formalities, Greeley headed straight for London
and, like Margaret Fuller, used his letters to report on the state of society
in Britain and on the Continent. While waiting for his embarkation to
return to America from Liverpool, Greeley used his last letter to reflect on
English national character, like Hawthorne and other American travellers.
From the very outset, it is clear that Greeley is making a real effort to
overcome his many negative impressions.

> I do not wholly like these cold and stately English, yet I think I
> am not blind to their many sterling qualities [...] In the first place,
> they are eminently *industrious*. I have seen no country in which
> the proportion of idlers is smaller [...] The English are eminently
> devotees of *Method* and *Economy*. I never saw the rule, 'A place
> for everything and everything in its place', so well observed as
> here. The reckless and the prodigal are found here as everywhere
> else, but they are marked exceptions [...] *Gravity* is a prominent
> feature of the English character. A hundred Englishmen of any
> class, forgathered for any purpose of conference or recreation, will
> have less merriment in the course of their sitting than a score of
> Frenchmen or Americans would have in a similar time. Hence it
> is generally remarked that the English of almost any class show
> to least advantage when attempting to enjoy themselves. They
> are as awkward at a frolic as a bear at a dance. Their manner of
> expressing themselves is literal and prosaic; the American tendency
> to hyperbole and exaggeration grates harshly on their ears.

> Horace Greeley, *Glances at Europe: in a Series of Letters from
> Great Britain, France, Italy, Switzerland, etc. during the Summer
> of 1851* (Dewitt/Davenport, 1851), Chapters 1, 44.

Apart from speaking in Liverpool during the American Civil War (see
Chapter 9), the Congregationalist minister **Henry Ward Beecher** (1813–
87) made a lecture tour of Britain in 1876, a record of which was kept
by his manager James Burton Pond. On his arrival in Liverpool, Beecher
stayed an extra night to hear Gladstone speak – 'a stupendous argument
in favour of Home Rule', he commented. Beecher and his wife stayed
that night in the royal suite of the Northwestern Hotel. His tour then

included London, the Northern cities, Scotland and Ireland. Returning to Liverpool, Beecher spoke at the Kirkdale Wesleyan Chapel, then at Hengler's Circus (a regular feature in the city since 1857). The following day one news report described his delivery in the following terms:

> Last night, at Hengler's Circus, Mr. Beecher appeared as a platform orator. He was seen as it were in the open, with full license and freedom to roam, untrammelled by the surroundings of a Sunday congregation, and restricted by none of the sanctity of the pulpit. We are bound to confess that his style on the platform differed from his style in the pulpit only in proportion to the area of the buildings in which he spoke. Mr. Beecher is nothing if he is not natural, and he appears to be altogether too much a child of nature to be capable of any appreciable degree of alteration. His style is, as we said yesterday, essentially the style of the platform; and therefore, regarded as a pulpit orator, he must be viewed in a different aspect. In the latter, conventional restraint and common custom are potent factors. In the pulpit, a man must conform to the fashion of the country, or, even if he has the wisdom of Solon, he will come under the lash of criticism. No man without genius dare speak in the pulpit as Mr. Beecher does; but the very originality which might brand him in the pulpit may make his reputation on the platform. The latter is necessarily a far higher test than the former, as, in the pulpit, men of little brains and men of much meet on the common ground of conformity, accepted cadences of voice, gesture of limb, and almost of expression of countenance.

'Henry Ward Beecher on the Platform', *Liverpool Mercury* (17 August 1876).

Another report conveyed the size of the audience. 'The Reign of the Common People' was one of Beecher's most popular lectures:

> There were about three thousand people in Hengler's Circus last night to hear the Rev. Henry Ward Beecher's lecture on The Reign of the Common People. Councillor Warrington presided, and on the platform were a large number of ministers, the majority of whom belonged to the Nonconformist bodies in this city. The chairman judiciously confined his remarks to a few sentences, in which he spoke of the increasingly cordial relations between this country and America. It was with an endorsement of this remark that Mr. Beecher, whose reception must have

been very gratifying to him, began his lecture, and at once his characteristic style manifested itself in the statement that the relations between those two countries had not always been those of a child and her mother, but that it had seemed at times as if England had been a stepmother.

Liverpool Daily Courier (17 August 1876).

James Burton Pond, *A Summer in England with Henry Ward Beecher* (1887).

Charlotte Perkins Gilman (1860–1935) was a campaigner for women's rights and a social reformer. She passed through Liverpool as Californian delegate to the 1896 International Socialist and Labour Congress in London, representing a local Federation of Trades rather than as a Socialist, because she refused to join the party. Carrying her pamphlets in her trunk, she cleared Customs without being checked either on embarkation at Toronto or on landing at Liverpool.

My method of carrying my little paper books was of the crudest. I always carried some with me for the purpose, and I had quite a lot of the second edition in my trunk, which I hoped to dispose of in England. The trunk had not come when I reached the steamer, so I took a cab and brought it from the railroad, and it was hauled on board hurriedly at the last minute.

I spoke to one of the officers, regretting the haste, there had been no time for examination by the customs officers. He reassured me, 'There's nothing dutiable that you'd be likely to have, only tobacco and liquor – books.' 'Books!' I rather gasped. 'Oh, not such books as you'd take, Madam, only books to sell.' The trunk was in the hold. No use telling him about it now. I would explain when I got to England, and pay what I must.

But in all the bustle of arrival I could not find my keys. I searched and searched, called upon the stewards for help and got none – they seemed somehow amused! – landed, and was met by Alfred Hicks, an English friend I had known in America. To him I explained my predicament, we told the customs officers, and sent for the loose keys they keep for such emergencies; but they were in a hurry, judged us harmless, and I got into England with my contraband, untouched. Then I nobly gave them away, instead of selling!

Gilman spent her first night with one Mrs Worrall, the columnist 'Julia Dawson' of the *Clarion*, a Manchester Socialist newspaper. She left for London immediately to attend the Congress, subsequently returning to Liverpool at the end of August, staying in Rock Ferry. On 31 August she addressed a group of rope-makers in Old Swan 'in favour of Union' and on 2 September gave a talk at Seacombe Ferry on American Socialism. In her diary she recorded two other speaking events: 3 September to the Independent Labour Party in Liverpool on 'The New Morality', and 4 September, after tea with 'Julia Dawson', a talk to the Liverpool Fabian Society. On 19 November 1896 she sailed back to America. The only Liverpool memory she recorded in her autobiography concerned difficulties of communication with a greengrocer:

A more amusing memory is of staying with some pleasant people in Liverpool, my host a 'fruiterer' by trade. He was an intelligent, well-read man as far as I could see. In the course of conversation he remarked to me that we had no grapes in America. This I took calmly, only asking what he meant by 'no grapes'. 'Just what I say. You don't raise grapes in America'.

I thought of the wild grapes of New England – did not the exploring Norsemen call it 'Vineland'? – of the grape-arbour in every back yard, of the New York state crop, of the 'reeling, wheeling aisles of the vineyards, miles on miles' in California. But I merely asked, 'How do you know?' 'How do I know? Why we export grapes to America!'

Then I understood. Hot-house grapes. Cheap coal. Cheap labour. Supplying the steam-ships. 'But that's not *grapes!*' I said. Then I told him there was hardly a state in the union without them, of the workman taking home a basket for ten cents, and so on – but alas! He didn't believe me. American brag.

The Living of Charlotte Perkins Gilman (Madison, WI: University of Wisconsin Press, 1991), Chapter 14.

The American Civil War

Because of its dependence on transatlantic trade, especially in cotton, Liverpool was torn between rival allegiances during the American Civil War (1861–65). At the beginning of the war there was widespread support for the Confederacy in Liverpool. The American Consul in the city between 1861 and 1872 was **Thomas H. Dudley**, who stayed, like Hawthorne, at Mrs Blodget's boarding house on his arrival. Dudley's role was to rally the community of American loyalists and to report on pro-Confederacy activity like shipbuilding, and he created an intelligence network, which provided him with crucial information on Confederate shipping and shipbuilding. Soon after his arrival in Liverpool he addressed the Chamber of Commerce, stressing the special nature of the current conflict.

Rival Agencies

You must bear in mind that this rebellion is different in its character from any of those which history gives to us. Those rebellions were against oppression, it was the people rebelling against their oppressors – liberty against tyranny. This rebellion in the U.S. is not such, it is the reverse, it is the oppressors rebelling against liberty, it is a rebellion against liberty, it is a rebellion got up in favour of slavery against liberty, for the purpose of perpetuating human slavery.

David Hepburn Milton, *Lincoln's Spymaster: Thomas Dudley Haines and the Liverpool Network* (Mechanicsburg, PA: Stackpole Books, 2003), pp. 20–21.

Part of Dudley's role in the city was to rally support for the Northern cause. The lawyer William Everett recorded this atmosphere of embattlement in an address of 1887:

I was in England during the first two years of the war. I was one of that little company of Americans whose duty kept us in England, scattered, isolated, scantily informed, learning what was going on at home chiefly from garbled telegrams, not knowing what to believe, yet called to account for everything rash or foolish done or said to be done in North and South alike; sneered at, taunted and forced every hour to fight the battle of our country's honour as truly as you who were in the regiments at home.

American merchants forming the nucleus of the Liverpool community included Daniel James of the Phelps Dodge copper mining company, George Warren of the Warren Steamship Co., Stephen B. Guion the co-owner of the Black Star Line and a manager for Cunard, B. F. Babcock, William T. Whittimore, and Henry Nash. Dudley's dealings with Charles Francis Adams, the U.S. Ambassador from 1861 to 1868, have been described as follows:

Mr Dudley's relations with Mr Adams were constant and close. Surrounded by spies, a written correspondence was not always deemed safe, as every moment the Consul at Liverpool was watched and followed. For these reasons he often took the train for London from Edge Hill, having previously arranged to have his family take his valise in their carriage and meet him there. He had noticed that if he carried a handbag a spy was sure to follow and take the same train, surmising his destination. If without it, apparently he was free from this espionage. The numerous letters from his friend, Mr Benjamin Moran, the Secretary of Legation at London, were purposely written in such a vague way that if they were intercepted, they would be of no service to the rebel agents.
[...]
The Consul received numerous threatening letters warning him unless he ceased his opposition to those who gave substantial assistance to the Confederate government, his life would be taken, and if found in certain designated spots [the docks or shipyards] he would be shot on sight. These threats had little effect on his determination to do his duty.
[...]
Mr. Dudley was constantly subjected to insults and threatening letters, sneers, and social evidences with the plainest remarks of hatred for him as a representative of the United States. The flag at the consulate was often found with tin kettles and bricks tied to it as an object of contempt. On one occasion it is believed personal

violence was intended in an assault at his own house. Three men
apparently bent on mischief rang his door bell, and were so stern
in their demands to see Mr. Dudley, that the servant was in an
agony of fear, but taking in the situation at a glance the Consul,
with prompt presence of mind, quickly shut the door in their
faces and bolted it. It is believed they were armed and intended
assaulting him. His duties were therefore for the most part entirely
new and without precedent, requiring just such a man of more
than usual executive ability, promptness, and decision of character,
not open to blandishments or bribes.

William John Potts, 'Biographical Sketch of the Hon. Thomas H. Dudley',
Proceedings of the American Philosophical Society (January 1895), pp. 102–34.

Thomas Dudley's opposite number was **James Dunwoody Bulloch**, the
Confederate agent who was commissioned to have battleships built under
conditions of secrecy. Bulloch organized a rival network of informers and
arranged with Laird Brothers to have two ships built. These 'rams', as
they became known, were constructed in Lairds' Birkenhead shipyard,
which had opened in 1857. The *Florida* (originally called the *Oreto*) was
built by W. C. Miller, whose shipyard was adjacent to the Brunswick and
Toxteth docks, and was launched in 1862. It was eventually seized by the
Wassachusett in 1864 in the Bay of Bahia, Brazil. The engines of the *Florida*
and its successor were built by Fawcett, Preston at their Phoenix Foundry
in Liverpool. The *Alabama*, as it became, was known first as '290' in its
dockyard, then as the *Enrica*. Unionist spies were constantly active at Lairds'
looking out for any signs of the craft being a warship. As their suspicions
grew, Ambassador Adams and Dudley made repeated legal moves to have
the construction blocked. Bulloch was well aware, as he records below,
that he had to take great care not to compromise British neutrality by
falling foul of the Foreign Enlistment Act. When agreement finally came
through to make this move in 1862 it was too late, since the boat had
already sailed. Bulloch was well aware that the boat could not be built as
a gunboat, although it did have that design, and so he devised a scheme
whereby it would rendezvous in the Azores with another boat carrying
the guns that could then be fitted. The *Alabama* was eventually sunk in a
battle off Cherbourg in 1864.

At the time of the *Florida*'s departure from Liverpool, her still
more famous consort had not yet been dignified by any other
name or title than the dockyard number 290. Her comely frame
had been covered in by the binding grip of the outside planking,

which had developed the graceful curves of her counter and the delicate wave-lines of her bow; but, nevertheless, I was disappointed to find that she was hardly up to specified time.

The builders were determined to turn out a first-class ship, and feeling perhaps that their obligation to do so was, if possible, increased by my absence, and the fact that there was no one to look after the interests of the owner, they were especially critical and hard to please in the selection of the timber for the most important parts, and had discarded two or three stern-posts after they had been partly fitted and bored to take the screw shaft, because of some slight defect. This creditable, satisfactory, and punctilious care had caused some delay in completing the hull, but all the other work was in an advanced state, and the engines were ready to go into the ship as soon as she was off the ways.

The Birkenhead Ironworks lie some distance above the chief commercial parts of Liverpool, and being on the opposite side of the Mersey, they do not attract especial notice from persons engaged in business, or passing to and fro by the Woodside Ferry, and the boats plying to the loiter landings on the river. But the large number of people passing up river to Tranmere, Rock Ferry, and Eastham, would often pass along the dock-walls of Messrs. Laird's establishment, and they could not fail to observe the gradual development of the graceful craft that stood out in bold relief at the extreme south end of the yard, and to contrast her with the large iron structures they were accustomed to see upon the adjoining building slips and ways.

The departure of the *Florida* without being called upon to give a particular account of herself and her intentions had grieved and vexed the United States Consul, and his suspicions having been once aroused, his mind was kept in a wakeful and agitated condition during the remainder of the war. The voluminous correspondence submitted to the Geneva Arbitrators, and which appeared from time to time in the Parliamentary Blue-books, gives proof of his nervous activity and the irritable and sometimes irritating persistency with which he pressed the local authorities to seize, or at least to detain, ships which he affirmed it was quite notorious were intended to be armed and equipped as privateers for the 'so-called' which latter appellation came to be a common designation of the Confederate States among those United States officials who were sometimes willing to drop the still more common epithets of 'rebel' and 'insurgent' to which, however, the Liverpool Consul generally adhered.

The people who saw the '290' on the building-slip, and were attracted by her appearance, naturally talked about her, and no doubt remarks were often made in respect to her fitness for a cruiser, and it is not therefore surprising that she should have aroused the suspicions of those whose business it was to keep watch over the interests of the United States, I soon learned that spies were lurking about, and tampering with the workmen at Messrs. Laird's, and that a private detective named Maguire was taking a deep and abiding interest in my personal movements; but my solicitor assured me that there was nothing illegal in what I was doing, and there was nothing therefore to be done but to maintain a quiet reserve, to hasten the completion of the ship, and to get her away as soon as possible.

On the 15th of May '290' was launched, and as a matter of fact left that numerical title on the signboard at the top of the slip when she slid off into the Mersey, although it stuck to her some time, and continued to be the term used when mentioning her in the Consular affidavits, and in the diplomatic correspondence, until the frequent reports of her performances afloat gave greater notoriety and distinction to her now historical name of *Alabama*.

But this ship, like the *Florida*, bore more than one name in passing through the various phases of her life, from a mere entity in a dockyard to the position of a commissioned ship-of-war. It is one of the peculiar anomalies of our nautical English grammar that a man-of-war is feminine, and we should say of a frigate whose name was *Ajax*, or which bore the still more harsh and masculine appellation of *Polyphemus*, 'She is a fine sea-boat'. The office of christening a ship is almost invariably performed by a lady, which is an aggravation of the anomaly about the sex, because if custom justifies a sailor in calling his ship 'she', and if there is any propriety in his passionate affirmation, 'my barque is my bride' the function of handing her into her natural element would be more fittingly, though not so grace fully done, by one of the 'opposite sex'. I could not take the liberty of introducing the name of the lady who christened '290', into this narrative. She graciously consented to perform the office, and fulfilled it in a comely manner, little knowing that she was constructively taking part in a great Civil War, and wholly unconscious that she was helping to make work for five eminent statesmen at Geneva ten years after. I hope her conscience has never upbraided her since, and that she has not felt in any way responsible for the bill of 3,000,000, which her Most Gracious Majesty had to pay on account of the '*Alabama* Claims'.

When '290' was to be launched, it was necessary to provide an appellation for her. The Spanish language furnished a flexible and mellifluous equivalent for the Christian name of the lady who served the office, and when the ship got free of the blocks and glided down the ways, she had been christened *Enrica*. The Spanish name gave rise to another alleged mystery, and it was often asserted that there was a purpose to affect that the ship was intended for the Spanish Government, or at least for a Spanish firm in Spain; but I now state that there was no attempt to deceive anyone by any pretence whatever in the business of building and despatching the *Alabama* from Liverpool. I have already described the negotiations with Messrs. Laird for the building of the ship. There was no mystery or disguise about them, and it will be seen that all the further management of the transaction was conducted in the same ordinary commonplace way. A great effort was made by the United States Minister to induce her Majesty's Government to seize the ship, but no satisfactory evidence was produced that any violation of the Foreign Enlistment Act had been committed, and it appears from what is now known that the Government were not willing to 'strain the law' at that early date, or 'to seize a vessel which it would have been the duty of a court of law to restore'.

I have always attributed the success of getting *Alabama* finished as a sea-going ship, and then despatched, to the fact that no mystery or disguise was attempted. I was well advised as to the law, and had the means of knowing with well nigh absolute certainty what was the state of the negotiations between the United States Minister and her Majesty's Government. For the rest, I merely practised such ordinary business prudence and reserve as a man would be likely to follow in the management of his private affairs. I never told any *employé* more than was necessary for him to know, and never gave any reason for an order having reference to the outfit or movements of the ship. Everything was done quietly, without any excitement or appearance of haste. At the last moment she was hurried off with some precipitancy, but this will be explained in due course.

The Messrs. Laird, conscious of being somewhat behind time with the hull, appeared desirous to make up the loss by quick work in setting up the engines and completing the outfit. The ship was no sooner in the water than two tugs took her to the entrance of the graving-dock, and she was warped into it, and placed over the blocks at once. The engineer department at the

Messrs. Laird's is especially efficient. Before the *Enrica* was fully secured in her berth the great derrick was swinging over her decks, and the first heavy pieces of the machinery were going on board. The work was now rapidly pushed forward, and the progress was satisfactory. On about June 10th the ship was taken out for a trial trip, and was run over the usual course until all parties were satisfied.

As the ship approached completion, it was necessary to appoint a captain who held a Board of Trade certificate, to superintend the preparations for sea, to engage the crew, and transact all such business as by law and custom falls within the office of the commander of a vessel. The selection of the right man was a matter of grave consideration. The requirements were professional competency, prudence, control over the tongue, and absolute integrity. I consulted a friend, and he soon brought to me Captain Mathew J. Butcher, a gentleman who was then serving as first-officer in a Cunard steamship; but he held a master's certificate, and was therefore eligible.

It turned out that I had met Captain Butcher two or three years before in Havana, he being then chief-officer of the Cunard steamship *Kamak*, and thus he was not wholly unknown to me. A conversation of a half to three-quarters of an hour brought us to a satisfactory understanding, and we went across to Messrs. Laird's yard, and I introduced Captain Butcher as the commander of the *Enrica*, through whom I desired them to receive all further instructions with reference to the outfit of the ship. To prevent repetition hereafter, I will take this occasion to say that Captain Butcher fulfilled all the requirements of the offices he engaged to perform, not only with tact, judgment and discretion, but with that nice and discriminating fidelity which marks the man of true honesty. He was engaged merely to take the ship to an appointed place without the United Kingdom; and he was especially warned that no men must be engaged under any pretence whatever, except to navigate the ship to a port or ports in the West Indies, with the privilege of stopping at any intermediate port.

It may be stated here, once for all, that no men were hired or engaged for any other purpose than that of navigating an unarmed ship, and no man was enlisted to enter the Confederate service, nor was a word said to any man to induce him to enter that service, by anyone having the slightest authority to make any such proposition, until after the ship had passed far beyond British jurisdiction. It would have been quite easy to prove that the

affidavits obtained by the United States Consul at the time were
either the fictitious conceits of the men who made them, or else
that the men had been themselves deceived. But while Captain
Butcher was only engaged to take out an unarmed ship, and he
never did enter the Confederate Service, yet it was manifestly
necessary to confide to him more than what appeared on the
surface. He therefore knew enough before the arrival of the
ship at Terceira [in the Azores] to place the success of the whole
enterprise in his power. An indiscreet remark, or a hint from him
to a careless gossiping acquaintance, would have spoiled all of our
well-laid plans. I shrink from seeming to suggest that there might
have been a possibility of such a catastrophe; but there can be
no doubt that the United States would have given a considerable
sum to frustrate the departure of the ship, and a much larger
sum still to have got possession of her. There was a time when
the commander might have handed her over to an agent of the
United States, or for that matter he might have taken her to New
York, instead of to Terceira. I mention this to demonstrate the
prodigious trust it was necessary to repose in Captain Butcher.
But I never had the least uneasiness; men who have had much to
do with their fellows, if observant, learn to understand them, and
after our first interview I never hesitated to tell Captain Butcher
all that was necessary for him to fully comprehend the actual
state of affairs, although I never ceased to abide by the rule of
burdening no one with more of a secret than it seemed good for
him to know.
[…]
About the 1st of July the *Enrica* was so nearly ready for sea,
that I began to make preparations for my own departure in
her. Lieutenant J. R. Hamilton had arrived in England from the
Confederate States at the end of April, and reported to me for
duty as first-lieutenant of the *Alabama* (still *Enrica*). When I was in
Savannah with the *Fingal* in February, 1862, Lieutenant Hamilton
had expressed an earnest desire to get afloat, and asked if I could
bring it about that he should be detailed to serve with me. There
appeared to be some difficulty at the time, but the Secretary of
the Navy bore it in mind, and I was much gratified by Hamilton's
unexpected arrival. He entered with much spirit into the
arrangements for our cruise.
[…]
We knew that the American Minister was pressing the
Government to seize the ship; and the frequent inquiries addressed

to the builders by the Customs authorities at London, and the active watchfulness of the local officers of that department at Liverpool, warned me that the situation was critical.

Meanwhile the *Enrica* (*Alabama*) was taken into the Birkenhead Dock, where she was coaled and all her stores were put on board. Everything was kept in readiness for a start at short notice, but a full crew was not shipped, for fear that the men would be restive at the delay, and attract notice by their numbers and indiscreet talking.

In order to preserve due consistency in the order of events, it is now necessary to give an account of the arrangements for equipping the Alabama that is to say, the means adopted to supply that portion of her furniture which would complete her outfit as a vessel-of-war. It is not necessary to dwell long upon these arrangements. The battery was ordered very shortly after the contract for the ship was made, and all the ordnance supplies were put in train in good time; but such instructions were given as would ensure their being ready not much before the ship, although the parties contracted with were not informed for what purpose they were wanted, or even how they were to be shipped, until the time arrived for forwarding them. The necessary number of revolvers, short rifles with cutlass bayonets, ammunition, made-up clothing for 150 men, extra stores of all kinds, hammocks, and, in fact, everything required for the complete equipment of a man-of-war, were ordered, and instructions were given that the goods when ready should be packed, marked, and held for shipping orders.

About the end of May a suitable agent was instructed to look up a moderate-sized sailing-vessel in London, fit for a West Indian voyage, to carry heavy weights. She was to be staunch and in good condition; but high finish not wanted, and a clipper not required. We got just the craft – a barque of about 400 to 450 tons. Her recommendation was that she had lately brought home ordnance stores – old guns, shot, etc. – from Gibraltar on Government account. She was bought, and in due time was entered out from London to Demerara. The agent was ordered to put 350 tons of coal in her, and the necessary shipping orders were given to the parties holding the *Alabama*'s goods. Our barque was named *Agrippina*, and she attracted no especial notice and no suspicion while loading in the London Docks. It was easy to regulate the forwarding of the cargo and the lading, so as to fit in with the movements of the *Enrica* at Liverpool, without creating the suspicion that there was any connection between the two vessels.

I wished to know something definite as to the time of Captain Semmes's arrival, or at least that he had started from Nassau, before despatching the two ships, because it might be more dangerous to have them waiting at the rendezvous, where a pacing United States cruiser might by chance fall upon them, than for the *Enrica* to remain in Liverpool, where no foreign enemy could touch her. But there was a domestic enemy – the Foreign Enlistment Act – upon whom it was necessary to keep a watchful eye.

On Saturday, July 26th, 1862, I received information from a private but most reliable source, that it would not be safe to leave the ship in Liverpool another forty-eight hours. I went immediately to Messrs. Laird's office, and told them that I wished to have a thorough all day trial of the ship outside. Although the testing trial trip had already been made, and the delivery of the ship to me in accordance with the terms of the contract was complete, yet it had been verbally agreed that there should be another trial, when coals and stores were all on board, if I desired it. Captain Butcher was ordered to ship a few more hands, and to have every thing ready to come out of dock on Monday's tide.

None of the crew were given an inkling of the contemplated movement; but I informed Captain Butcher confidentially that the ship would not return, and directed him to get on board some extra tons of coal, and to complete his stores.

It was important to have as many trusty and intelligent men on board as possible, and I had already detailed Mr. John Low (now a master in the Confederate States Navy), who had rejoined me after going out to Nassau in the *Florida*, to be ready to accompany Captain Butcher.

On Monday the 28th the *Enrica*, came out of dock and anchored off Seacombe, and every preparation was made for going out of harbour the next day. A small party of guests were invited to go out for the trial trip, and the next morning – Tuesday, the 29th – the ship was partially dressed with flags, and at about 9 a.m. we got under weigh and steamed down the river with a number of guests on board, and a party of riggers and additional engineers men to assist if any help was needed. We had also in company the steam-tug *Hercules* as a tender.

James Dunwoody Bulloch, *The Secret Service of the Confederate States in Europe* (1884), Vol. 1, Chapter 5.

Deeming it unsafe to return to America after the Civil War, Bulloch spent the rest of his life in Liverpool. He took British citizenship and worked as a merchant, contributing to the Liverpool Nautical College and the Orphan Boys Asylum. He died in 1901 and was buried in Toxteth cemetery. His gravestone carries the legend 'an American by birth, an Englishman by choice'.

The Battle for British Minds

Henry Ward Beecher (1813–87) was the brother of Harriet Beecher Stowe and a minister in the Plymouth Church of Brooklyn, New York. The Fugitive Slave Act of 1850 helped shift his concerns from religion to abolition and that same year he made his first voyage to Europe, getting embroiled on his return trip with the Cunard Line authorities over what sort of religious observance was allowable on their ships. In 1863 he sailed for Liverpool on the *City of Baltimore* in the company of John Howard Raymond, a friend from his Brooklyn days. Raymond's record of their trip makes it clear how political an event Beecher's arrival was, despite the torrential rain. The following day he dined with the American Consul.

June 12, 1863

We had not landed, yesterday, before Mr. Beecher was boarded by deputations from Liverpool and from Manchester, and it was manifestly their purpose to use him as a new-come notoriety, in pulpit and on platform, for legitimate and for selfish objects, to their utmost possible extent. The Secession papers here announced that the Rev. Henry Ward Beecher had come over on a visit to England, 'ostensibly for the benefit of his health, but really (as was ascertained from the most trustworthy sources) as a secret agent for the Federal Government', and a series of public demonstrations and a free fight generally appears to have been expected, as a matter of course, by friends and foes. But that little game has been quietly blocked. Mr. Beecher informed the Liverpool deputation that he had come really for his health (which meant rest and not work); that as America understood her own interests best, and expected to take care of them without any foreign aid, so Englishmen were the proper parties to enlighten Englishmen, and to save their country from the unhappy results to which selfishness, prejudice, ignorance, and bad counsel were likely to lead her; that while he sympathized with the true Christians and enlightened friends of liberty among them, and would be glad to lend them any incidental aid in his power, his first duty was to husband and recruit his energies for his own country when and where he could labour for some object of real importance to her. The loyal Americans are tickled out of their boots at this decision, for they shared the common expectation; and though they all would be glad to hear Mr. Beecher speak, yet they believe that no eloquence, however splendid or persuasive, could have half the effect of this dignified silence, this practical proof that we really don't regard the destinies of America as dependent on the bray of great John Bull.

Harriet Raymond Lloyd, ed., *Life and Letters of John Howard Raymond* (1881).

Although sent abroad in 1863 to improve his health, Beecher used the occasion to enlist support for the Northern cause in the Civil War. That year British public opinion was turning in favour of the Union, thanks to Lincoln's Proclamation of Emancipation finally ending slavery and thanks to the Northern victories that summer at Gettysburg and Vicksburg. On his arrival in Liverpool Beecher stayed with his friend from the Plymouth church Charles C. Duncan. Despite threatening posters being put up around the city, on the evening of 16 October he gave an address in the Philharmonic Hall on Hope Street, which was sold out. The attempts to shout him down became notorious and were reported in the British and American press. On 30 October 1863, just before his return to the USA, Beecher was given a farewell breakfast by the Liverpool Emancipation Society in St James's Hall, Liverpool. The following report, which appeared in *The Century* magazine, gives us a good idea of the circumstances of the occasion.

'Beecher at Liverpool in 1863'

The year 1863 was an unpleasant time for a loyal American to be travelling abroad. The disloyal were in Europe in considerable numbers, and, wherever they could, they moulded public sentiment. Comparatively few had anything to say in defence of the Federal Government, and the hope that the Confederacy would prevail was freely expressed in conversation. Ignorant and insulting questions were propounded to all who declared themselves in favour of suppressing the rebellion. With one or two exceptions, the newspapers exaggerated the successes of the

South, spoke contemptuously of the achievements of the North of its generals, soldiers, and spirit. The average Englishman could not comprehend the right of the President to perform any act not specified in the Constitution. His powers as Commander-in-Chief of the Army and Navy of the United States they did not perceive or were unwilling to admit. At a dinner attended by avowed friends of the North, most of them noted ministers, only five appeared to know the ground upon which the President claimed the right to issue the Proclamation of Emancipation.

Here and there Americans travelling on business, clergymen in poor health, and those who were compelled to go abroad for domestic and other reasons met, and their universal testimony was that, while occasionally an intelligent sympathizer with the North could be found, the majority of those whom they encountered in England were either cold or openly antagonistic.

I met Mr. Beecher at the Charing Cross Hotel in London just before he went upon the Continent, and he said, 'What brings you over here?'

'Poor health,' was the reply. 'And what brings you? Surely you are not ill?'

No; but so worn with work that I need to freshen up and get away from excitement.'

Will you speak any in England?'

'Not much. I am so mad at the way they talk and act over here that I don't care to see an Englishman.'

On the 16th of October, four months after this conversation, I arrived in Liverpool to sail from that place for the United States the next day. Having come directly from Switzerland I knew nothing of Mr. Beecher's plans, but en route from London saw in the English papers that he had spoken once or twice. While riding from the station to the hotel in Liverpool I saw the following handbill:

TO THE INDEPENDENT AND INDUSTRIOUS CLASSES OF LIVERPOOL.

An individual of the name of Henry Ward Beecher, who, when at home, Brooklyn, N.Y., is called a Baptist minister, has come over to this country as a political emissary from Abraham Lincoln to stir up strife and ill-will among you, and for that purpose will hold a meeting at the Philharmonic Hall, Hope Street, this evening. This same Henry Ward Beecher it was who

recommended London to be sacked and this town destroyed
and this godly man, bear in mind, is a preacher of the Gospel
and good-will towards all men. As there will be an amendment
proposed at the meeting, you must attend and show by your hearts
and hands that the industrious classes in this town are opposed to
the bloody war which Abraham Lincoln is now waging against his
brother in the South, and the dastardly means he is resorting to
in employing such tools as Henry Ward Beecher, a minister of the
Gospel.

Friday, 16th October, 1863.

There were a half-dozen more, some of them much larger and
more conspicuously displayed.

The expression in the hill above quoted, 'As there will be
an amendment proposed at the meeting,' explains a peculiarity
of English customs with which we are not familiar in the
United States. When a public gathering of this kind is held, it
is considered proper for opponents to interrupt the proceedings,
and, when any motion is offered, to move an amendment, and, if
possible, to carry it; in which case the meeting will be made to
teach the very opposite of that which it was called to advocate. I
witnessed several such occurrences, and saw in one or two places
the friends of the North take a meeting out of the hands of the
South; and in Manchester a desperate attempt was made to capture
one called in the interest of the North which resulted in the
building being cleared by the police.

I determined, if possible, to hear Mr. Beecher. On inquiry it
was speedily ascertained that the bulk of the people of Liverpool
were not in sympathy with either Mr. Beecher or the cause he
advocated, that there would certainly be an attempt to break up
the meeting, and that tickets fully equal to the capacity of the
house had already been given out. I made every effort to obtain
tickets, but without success. No person who had one was willing
to sell it, ticket speculators could not be found, and it seemed as if
nothing could be done. But at half-past six a desperate expedient
occurred to me, and was tried. Ascertaining that Mr. Beecher
was the guest of Charles C. Duncan, I called at his residence and
sent in my card. Mr. Beecher was at tea, and came out into the
hall napkin in hand. I said, 'Mr. Beecher, I am going to sail to-
morrow to the United States. Your friends will wish to know all
about this address; and yet I cannot get in, and have called to ask

if I may accompany you when you enter. I will slip into some
obscure position in the rear of the platform; and even if I have
to stand the entire evening, it will be only what you will have to
do.'

'I would do it in a moment,' said he, 'but there have been three
hundred applications of that sort, and every square inch of the
platform is already bespoke.'

'Then there is no chance?'

'None, my dear fellow, that I can see – unless I give you my
place; and the Lord knows I would be glad enough to do that.'

With that he laughed and went back to his supper.

Just as I was reconciling myself to defeat, Mr. Duncan came
into the hall and said that a certain Baptist clergyman had
received two tickets and he had just heard of a death in his family.
'Would you call and ask him for those tickets? If you can get
them, you shall have one, and may return the other to me.'

The facts were as stated. The tickets were obtained, and
the result was that I sat within six feet of Mr. Beecher on the
platform during the evening. As he had said, every square inch
was spoken for. The crowd was immense, consisting almost
entirely of men. The few ladies to be seen here and there had
an appearance of trepidation, and every person seemed to be
apprehending a disturbance. The audience was comparatively quiet
during the preliminary exercises, which were exceedingly brief.

When Mr. Beecher was introduced there was faint applause
mingled with discordant sounds. The applause increased, and
so did the noise of the opponents. Neither class, so far as
demonstration was concerned, was very numerous. An English
is very different from an American mob; it is much more noisy,
but less vicious. It is accompanied by less bloodshed and violence,
but more yelling and pushing; it also has less humour and is more
persistent. Being able to see the entire building, I became aware
that men had been stationed in different parts expressly to act
in concert; and after a while I was able to identify two or three
who were obviously leaders. It was their policy not to make much
disturbance at first.

Mr. Beecher was in perfect health, but quite thin compared
with his condition before leaving home; still he appeared a
magnificent specimen of manhood, having just passed his fiftieth
birthday. He advanced and placed a manuscript upon the table,
and from it began to read a carefully prepared argument to
prove that, from a commercial point of view, Liverpool should

sympathize with the North rather than with the South. Slavery was a primitive institution, the South an agricultural region. Institutions built upon slavery would need comparatively little. What the slaves ate, they raised; they wore but scanty clothing, and the whole climate and mode of living favoured limited outside expenditures. It was not so with the North. He made various references to Liverpool – its business interests, its dependence upon American trade, the immense development that would certainly follow if slavery were abolished.

This line of thought failed to reach the high moral tone of the abolitionists who were present, though it did for a time interest the average citizen. So long as Mr. Beecher read, the audience was obviously greatly disappointed. The disturbers found little room to object, and his friends little or nothing to applaud. Mr. Beecher was never remarkable as a reader. On this occasion, as expectation was high, and the reports of his former oratorical performances had been heard, the impression was much less than it would have been under other circumstances. After he had read for fifteen or twenty minutes a loud roar was heard, 'Shut up that paper!' which was immediately responded to from the other side of the building, 'He can't get along without a book!' 'He don't know enough to speak!' 'He is a *coward!*' From another place came the question in a shrill, piercing voice, 'Where did you steal your sermon?'

In less than two minutes the whole audience appeared to be in motion. Men were pushing and elbowing, yelling and shrieking. One man in particular would jump up about two feet, howl, and then sink out of sight. The police began to move about with an expression of good humour upon their faces, pushing men with both hands extended. For the space of three or four minutes it was impossible for Mr. Beecher to be heard. He made several attempts to finish the manuscript, and practically did; and then began to handle questions with the incisiveness, wit, and occasional outbursts of eloquence for which he was famous. The disturbers had sense enough to see that they had aroused a lion, and that they must break him down or he would carry the great bulk of the audience with him. They resorted to every means imaginable, except actual violence, to accomplish this end.

Mr. Beecher's voice, when he was excited and spoke very loud, had a roaring sound. They would pitch their voices upon the same key, so that when he ended a paragraph in a clarion tone, taking the same pitch, they would bellow like a score of infuriated bulls, and continue sometimes five minutes at a stretch; for when some would be out of breath, others would take it up, and the first would come to their help again. Meanwhile Mr. Beecher would talk to the ministers on the platform, of whom there was a large number, and occasionally to the reporters. He would say to them, 'Gentlemen, I am talking to you and, through you, to all England. If I should not be heard at all by this audience, and you should take down my words, thirty millions of people would read them.' He was calm enough at one time when the roaring was going on to crack three or four jokes, as if he were conversing in a parlour; and the moment the rioters stopped, from sheer physical exhaustion, he screamed out, 'I have talked to these reporters. They have got down all I have said. There is another idea out, catch it if you can!'

It has been reported that Mr. Beecher's life was in danger on that occasion. The scene indeed was at times appalling. Mr. Beecher received anonymous letters warning him not to attend; but I saw no evidence that any person intended personal violence to him. He considered the opposition which he encountered at Liverpool 'worse than all the rest put together.'

When he was fully loose, he paced the platform like a lion about to spring upon the assembly. The crowd would hurl remarks at him which, if it were possible to turn, he would make such use of as to raise a laugh at the expense of the questioner. If they were embarrassing he would say, 'I will take that up when I come to it,' and in most cases he would prepare an effective way of answering it. He seemed to proceed upon the assumption that the friends of freedom were with him, and that his wisest course was to ignore both friends and foes.

[...]

He certainly acted upon this plan at Liverpool, and in doing so he lost for a considerable period the sympathy of those who in the beginning were prepared to applaud him.

But at last he struck the highest moral elevation, and no reporter, even though he took every word, could properly represent the majesty, the sublimity, the authoritative and electrical energy with which he spoke. A remarkable fact was, that after one of these outbursts he would catch up a question on a much lower plane, dispose of it with a witty turn, and converse with the assembly as though he were relating an anecdote to some gentlemen at a casual meeting. The policy of the factious element was to bawl the loudest after his finest passages.

[...]

There was one instant when Mr. Beecher seemed to be about
to break down. His voice cracked, and the crowd imitated the
cracked sound which it produced. He then turned to the platform
and said, 'Gentlemen, I take you to witness that I have controlled
this audience until my voice is gone. I can do nothing without a
voice.' And it seemed as if his nervous force as well as his voice
was failing. Had he stopped then, the assembly would have broken
up in confusion, the mob would have prevailed, no resolutions
would have been passed, and the meeting, though it would have
left an ineffaceable impression upon the minds of those who heard
him, would nevertheless have been considered unsuccessful.

But he gathered himself together once more, regained command
of the audience, and subsequently did some of the most effective
work of the evening. The hundreds of distinguished men who sat
upon the platform, most of them public speakers, at first wore the
aspect of men who were there to see what an American orator
would do and how he would do it; but long before the conclusion
their individuality was lost, and they were not only captivated,
but captured. For physical power, self-control, diversified forms of
public speaking, indomitable will without the loss of the power
to respond to the changing moods of the audience, and affability
essential to persuasion, I have never seen its equal and cannot
imagine its superior. A gentleman sitting near me, who appeared
to command universal respect from those upon the platform,
said at the close, giving a list of the famous men whom he had
heard on critical occasions: 'I was prepared to criticise and ready
to dislike, but I never heard anything equal to this.' Every loyal
American felt proud of his country, and proud of Henry Ward
Beecher as its representative.

After a stormy passage of fourteen days, two weeks from the
next Sabbath I had the pleasure of describing this scene to the
congregation of Plymouth Church, on which occasion resolutions
were passed commending the work of Mr. Beecher in England,
and extending his vacation for as long a time as he felt that he
could serve his country abroad.
[...]
He made the entire assembly feel the greatness of his country, the
justice of its cause, and the certainty of its triumph.

J. M. Buckley, 'Beecher at Liverpool in 1863',
The Century, 37.ii (December 1888).

Beecher's 1863 Speech

The following excerpts from Beecher's speech give an impression of the dialogue which he set up with his audience. He appeals to shared values of freedom and self-interest, and also to a common racial destiny shared by both nations.

For more than twenty-five years I have been made perfectly familiar with popular assemblies in all parts of my country except the extreme south. There has not for the whole of that time been a single day of my life when it would have been safe for me to go south of Mason and Dixon's line in my own country, and all for one reason: my solemn, earnest, persistent testimony against that which I consider to be the most atrocious thing under the sun—the system of American slavery in a great, free republic. [Cheers.] I have passed through that early period when right of free speech was denied to me. Again and again I have attempted to address audiences that, for no other crime than that of free speech, visited me with all manner of contumelious epithets; and now since I have been in England, although I have met with greater kindness and courtesy on the part of most than I deserved, yet, on the other hand, I perceive that the Southern influence prevails to some extent in England. [Applause and uproar.] It is my old acquaintance; I understand it perfectly—[laughter]—and I have always held it to be an unfailing truth that where a man had a cause that would bear examination he was perfectly willing to have it spoken about. [Applause.] Therefore, when I saw so much nervous apprehension that, if I were permitted to speak— [hisses and applause]—when I found they were afraid to have me speak—[hisses, laughter, and 'No, no!']—when I found that they considered my speaking damaging to their cause—[applause]— when I found that they appealed from facts and reasonings to mob law—[applause and uproar]—I said. No man need tell me what the heart and secret counsel of these men are. They tremble and are afraid. [Applause, laughter, hisses, 'No, no!' and a voice, 'New York mob.']

   Now, personally, it is a matter of very little consequence to me whether I speak here to-night or not. [Laughter and cheers.] But one thing is very certain—if you do permit me to speak here to-night you will hear very plain talking. [Applause and hisses.] You will not find a man,—you will not find me to be a man that dared to speak about Great Britain three thousand miles off, and then is afraid to speak to Great Britain when he stands on her shores. [Immense applause and hisses.] And if I do not mistake the tone and the temper of Englishmen, they had rather have a man who opposes them in a manly way—[applause from all parts of the hall]—than a sneak that agrees with them in an unmanly way. [Applause and 'Bravo!'] If I can carry you with me by sound convictions, I shall be immensely glad; but if I can not carry you with me by facts and sound arguments, I do not wish you to go with me at all; and all that I ask is simply *fair play*. [Applause and a voice, 'You shall have it, too.'] Those of you who are kind enough to wish to favour my speaking—and you will observe that my voice is slightly husky, from having spoken almost every night in succession for some time past—those who wish to hear me will do me the kindness simply to sit still and to keep still; and I and my friends the Secessionists will make all the noise. [Laughter.]

There are two dominant races in modern history: the Germanic and the Romanic races. The Germanic races tend to personal liberty, to a sturdy individualism, to civil and to political liberty. The Romanic race tends to absolutism in government; it is clannish; it loves chieftains; it develops a people that crave strong and showy governments to support and plan for them. The Anglo-Saxon race belongs to the great German family, and is a fair exponent of its peculiarities. The Anglo-Saxon carries self-government and self-development with him wherever he goes. He has popular GOVERNMENT and popular INDUSTRY; for the effects of a generous civil liberty are not seen a whit more plainly in the good order, in the intelligence, and in the virtue of a self-governing people, than in their amazing enterprise and the scope and power of their creative industry. The power to create riches is just as much a part of the Anglo-Saxon virtues as the power to create good order and social safety. The things required for prosperous labour, prosperous manufactures, and prosperous commerce are three: first, liberty; secondly, liberty; thirdly, liberty—but these are not merely the same liberty, as I shall show you.

First, there must be liberty to follow those laws of business which experience has developed, without imposts or restrictions, or governmental intrusions. Business simply wants to be let alone. ['Hear, hear!']

Then, secondly, there must be liberty to distribute and exchange products of industry in any market without burdensome tariffs, without imposts, and without vexatious regulations. There

must be these two liberties—liberty to create wealth, as the
makers of it think best according to the light and experience
which business has given them; and then liberty to distribute what
they have created without unnecessary vexatious burdens. The
comprehensive law of the ideal industrial condition of the world
is free manufacture and free trade. ['Hear, hear!' A voice, 'The
Murrill tariff.']

I have said there were three elements of liberty. The third is
the necessity of an intelligent and free race of customers. There
must be freedom among producers; there must be freedom among
the distributors; there must be freedom among the customers. It
may not have occurred to you that it makes any difference what
one's customers are; but it does, in all regular and prolonged
business. The condition of the customer determines how much he
will buy, determines of what sort he will buy. Poor and ignorant
people buy little and that of the poorest kind. The richest and
the intelligent, having the more means to buy, buy the most, and
always buy the best.

Here, then, are the three liberties: liberty of the producer,
liberty of the distributor, and liberty of the consumer. The first
two need no discussion—they have been long, thoroughly, and
brilliantly illustrated by the political economists of Great Britain,
and by her eminent statesmen; but it seems to me that enough
attention has not been directed to the third, and, with your
patience, I will dwell on that for a moment, before proceeding to
other topics.

It is a necessity of every manufacturing and commercial people
that their customers should be very wealthy and intelligent. Let us
put the subject before you in the familiar light of your own local
experience. To whom do the tradesmen of Liverpool sell the most
goods at the highest profit? To the ignorant and poor, or to the
educated and prosperous? [A voice, 'To the Southerner.' Laughter.]
The poor man buys simply for his body; he buys food, he buys
clothing, he buys fuel, he buys lodging. His rule is to buy the
least and the cheapest that he can. He goes to the store as seldom
as he can,—he brings away as little as he can—[much laughter]—
and he buys for the least he can. Poverty is not a misfortune to
the poor only who suffer it, but it is more or less a misfortune to
all with whom they deal.

On the other hand, a man well off—how is it with him? He
buys in far greater quantity. He can afford to do it; he has the
money to pay for it. He buys in far greater variety, because he

seeks to gratify not merely physical wants, but also mental wants. He buys for the satisfaction of sentiment and taste, as well as of sense. He buys silk, wool, flax, cotton; he buys all metals—iron, silver, gold, platinum; in short he buys for all necessities and of all substances. But that is not all. He buys a better quality of goods. He buys richer silks, finer cottons, higher grained wools. Now, a rich silk means so much skill and care of somebody's that has been expended upon it to make it finer and richer; and so of cotton, and so of wool. That is, the price of the finer goods runs back to the very beginning, and remunerates the workman as well as the merchant. Indeed, the whole labouring community is as much interested and profited as the mere merchant, in this buying and selling of the higher grades in the greater varieties and quantities.

The law of price is the skill; and the amount of skill expended in the work is as much for the market as are the goods. A man comes to the market and says, 'I have a pair of hands'; and he obtains the lowest wages. Another man comes and says, 'I have something more than a pair of hands—I have truth and fidelity'; he gets a higher price. Another man comes and says, 'I have something more; I have hands and strength, and fidelity, and skill.' He gets more than either of the others. The next man comes and says, 'I have got hands and strength, and skill, and fidelity; but my hands work more than that. They know how to create things for the fancy, for the affections, for the moral sentiments'; and he gets more than any of the others. The last man comes and says, 'I have all these qualities, and have them so highly that it is a peculiar genius'; and genius carries the whole market and gets the highest price. [Loud applause.] So that both the workman and the merchant are profited by having purchasers that demand quality, variety, and quantity.

Now, if this be so in the town or the city, it can only be so because it is a law. This is the specific development of a general or universal law, and therefore we should expect to find it as true of a nation as of a city like Liverpool. I know it is so, and you know that it is true of all the world; and it is just as important to have customers educated, intelligent, moral, and rich, out of Liverpool as it is in Liverpool. [Applause.] They are able to buy; they want variety, they want the very best; and those are the customers you want. That nation is the best customer that is freest, because freedom works prosperity, industry, and wealth. Great Britain, then, aside from moral considerations, has a direct commercial and

pecuniary interest in the liberty, civilization, and wealth of every
people and every nation on the globe. [Loud applause.]
[...]
Now, Great Britain's chief want is—what? They have said that
your chief want is cotton. I deny it. Your chief want is consumers.
[Applause and hisses.] You have got skill, you have got capital,
and you have got machinery enough to manufacture goods for
the whole population of the globe. You could turn out fourfold
as much as you do, if you only had the market to sell in. It is
not therefore so much the want of fabric, though there may be
a temporary obstruction of that; but the principal and increasing
want—increasing from year to year—is, where shall we find men
to buy what we can manufacture so fast? [Interruption over a
voice, 'The Murrill tariff.' Applause.]

   There is in this a great and sound principle of political
economy. If the South should be rendered independent——[At
this point mingled cheering and hisses interrupted the speaker
until 'half the audience rose to their feet, waving hats and
handkerchiefs, and in every part of the hall there was the greatest
commotion and uproar.' Mr. Beecher 'quietly and smilingly waited
until quiet was restored, and then proceeded.']

   Well, you have had your turn; now let me have mine again.
[Loud applause and laughter.] It is a little inconvenient to talk
against the wind; but, after all, if you will just keep good-
natured—I am not going to lose my temper; will you watch
yours? Besides all that, it rests me, and gives me a chance, you
know, to get my breath. [Applause and hisses.] And I think that
the bark of those men is worse than their bite. They do not mean
any harm; they do not know any better. [Loud applause, hisses
and continued uproar.]

   What will be the result if this present struggle shall eventuate
in the separation of America, and making the South—[loud
applause, hooting and cries of 'Bravo!']—a slave territory
exclusively—[cries of 'No, no!' and laughter]—and the North
a free territory; what will be the first result? You will lay the
foundation for carrying the slave population clear through to the
Pacific Ocean. That is the first step. There is not a man who has
been a leader of the South any time within these twenty years,
that has not had this for a plan. It was for this that Texas was
invaded, first by colonists, next by marauders, until it was wrested
from Mexico. It was for this that they engaged in the Mexican
War itself, by which the vast territory reaching to the Pacific was

added to the Union. Never have they for a moment given up the plan of spreading the American institution, as they call it, straight through toward the West, until the slave who has washed his feet in the Atlantic shall be carried to wash them in the Pacific. [Cries of 'Question' and uproar.] There! I have got that statement out, and you can not put it back. [Laughter and applause.]

[Beecher speculates on the Southern states achieving independence.]

My friends, I saw a man once, who was a little late at a railway station, chase an express train. He did not catch it. If you are going to stop this meeting, you have got to stop it before I speak; for after I have got the things out, you may chase as long as you please—you will not catch them. But there is luck in leisure; I'm going to take it easy. Two-thirds of the population of the Southern States to-day are non-purchasers of English goods. You must recollect another fact—namely, that this is going on clear through to the Pacific Ocean; and if by sympathy or help you establish a slave empire, you sagacious Britons—if you like it better, then, I will leave the adjective out—are busy in favouring the establishment of an empire from ocean to ocean that should have fewest customers and the largest non-buying population. ['No, no!' A voice, 'I thought it was a happy people that population parted.']
[...]
A great many men say to ministers of the Gospel: 'You pretend to be preaching and working for the love of the people. Why, you are all the time preaching for the sake of the Church.' What does the minister say? 'It is by means of the Church that we help the people,' and when men say that we are fighting for the Union, I, too, say that we are fighting for the Union. ['Hear, hear!' and a voice, 'That's right.'] But the motive determines the value; and why are we fighting for the Union? Because we never shall forget the testimony of our enemies. They have gone off declaring that the Union in the hands of the North was fatal to slavery. [Loud applause.] There is testimony in court for you. [A voice, 'See that!' and laughter.]
   In the first place I am ashamed to confess that such was the thoughtlessness—[interruption]—such was the stupor of the North—[renewed interruption]—you will get a word at a time; to-morrow will let folks see what it is you do not want to hear—that for a period of twenty-five years she went to sleep, and

permitted herself to be drugged and poisoned with the Southern prejudice against black men. [Applause and uproar.]

Now as to those States that had passed 'black' laws, as we call them; they are filled with Southern emigrants. The southern parts of Ohio, the southern part of Indiana, where I myself lived for years, and which I knew like a book, the southern part of Illinois, where Mr. Lincoln lives—[great uproar]—these parts are largely settled by emigrants from Kentucky, Tennessee, Georgia, Virginia, and North Carolina, and it was their vote, or the Northern votes pandering for political reasons to theirs, that passed in those States the infamous 'black' laws; and the Republicans in these States have a record, clean and white, as having opposed these laws in every instance as 'infamous.' Now as to the State of New York; it is asked whether a negro is not obliged to have a certain freehold property, or a certain amount of property, before he can vote. It is so still in North Carolina and Rhode Island for *white* folks—it is so in New York State. [Mr. Beecher's voice slightly failed him here, and he was interrupted by a person who tried to imitate him. Cries of 'Shame!' and 'Turn him out!']

No man can unveil the future; no man can tell what revolutions are about to break upon the world; no man can tell what destiny belongs to France, nor to any of the European powers; but one thing is certain, that in the exigencies of the future there will be combinations and recombinations, and that those nations that are of the same faith, the same blood, and the same substantial interests, ought not to be alienated from each other, but ought to stand together. [Immense cheering and hisses.] I do not say that you ought not to be in the most friendly alliance with France or with Germany; but I do say that your own children, the offspring of England, ought to be nearer to you than any people of strange tongue. [A voice, 'Degenerate sons,' applause and hisses; another voice, 'What about the *Trent?*'] If there had been any feelings of bitterness in America, let me tell you that they had been excited, rightly or wrongly, under the impression that Great Britain was going to intervene between us and our own lawful struggle. [A voice, 'No!' and applause.] With the evidence that there is no such intention all bitter feelings will pass away. [Applause.]

[...]

And now in the future it is the work of every good man and patriot not to create divisions, but to do the things that will make for peace. ['Oh, oh!' and laughter.] On our part it shall be done.

[Applause and hisses, and 'No, no!']

On your part it ought to be done; and when in any of the convulsions that come upon the world, Great Britain finds herself struggling single-handed against the gigantic powers that spread oppression and darkness—[applause, hisses, and uproar]—there ought to be such cordiality that she can turn and say to her first-born and most illustrious child, 'Come!' ['Hear, hear!' Applause, tremendous cheers, and uproar.] I will not say that England can not again, as hitherto, single-handed manage any power—[applause and uproar]—but I will say that England and America together for religion and liberty—[a voice, 'soap, soap,' uproar, and great applause]—are a match for the world. [Applause; a voice, 'They don't want any more soft soap.'] Now, gentlemen and ladies—[a voice, 'Sam Slick'; and another voice, 'Ladies and gentlemen, if you please!']—when I came I was asked whether I would answer questions, and I very readily consented to do so, as I had in other places; but I will tell you it was because I expected to have the opportunity of speaking with some sort of ease and quiet. [A voice, 'So you have.']

I have for an hour and a half spoken against a storm—['Hear, hear!']—and you yourselves are witnesses that, by the interruption, I have been obliged to strive with my voice, so that I no longer have the power to control this assembly. [Applause.] And although I am in spirit perfectly willing to answer any question, and more than glad of the chance, yet I am by this very unnecessary opposition to-night incapacitated physically from doing it. Ladies and gentlemen, I bid you good evening. [When Beecher had taken his seat there came another outburst of prolonged cheers mingled with hisses, groans and catcalls. From the gallery someone proposed three cheers for the lecturer, which were given with enthusiasm. A vote of thanks being then proposed, it was carried with prolonged cheers and waving of hats and handkerchiefs. Beecher afterward said of this experience, 'I got control of the meeting in an hour and a half, and then I had a clear road the rest of the way. But it required a three hours' use of my voice at its utmost strength.']

William Jennings Bryan, ed., *The World's Famous Orations: American Vol. 10* (New York, NY: Funk and Wagnalls, 1906). Debby Applegate's biography *The Most Famous Man in America* (London: Doubleday, 2006) is essential reading on Beecher's career.

Overviews of Liverpool and Public Events

W ALTER H. RIDEING's article of 1879, in its sheer detail, testifies
to readers' interest and demonstrates that Liverpool was far more
important to American travellers than a transit point. The essay is partly
factual, giving facts and figures about the commerce of the city, and
partly an urban tour highlighting many of the landmarks we have seen in
earlier chapters, although it finishes by admitting the poverty lying behind
Liverpool's prosperity. Scotland Road, to the north of the city centre, had
become a centre of immigrant and working-class communities in the city.
The Perch Rock Battery and Light were built at the mouth of the Mersey
in the 1820s and the lighthouse was completed in 1830. The explosion
Rideing mentions took place in the Wood Pit mine at Haydock in 1878
and resulted in around 200 deaths.

'England's Great Sea-Port'

There were over 170 cabin passengers on board our steamer as she
sailed up the Mersey, most of them being pleasure-seekers, and
some having much time at their disposal, with elaborate itineraries
that embraced pretty nearly every place on the continent from
Dieppe to Constantinople; but only two of the voyagers staid
in Liverpool; the others omitted the vast sea-port, and hurried
away to Chester or London by the first trains, content with the
superficial reconnaissance possible in the brief drive from the
landing to the railway. It is nearly always so with Americans.
Fully three-fifths of the whole number who go abroad embark
and disembark at Liverpool, and few devote more time to it than
that of the unavoidable delay between the arrival of the steamer
and the departures of the train. Many travellers have unfavourable
reminiscences of it.

[His arrival is marred by heavy rain, which does not prevent him from seeing the city.]

The chimneys are a feature of Liverpool. Every eminence reveals them bristling along the gable roofs of the cottages, and each pours out a heavy wreath of bituminous vapour, which drapes the handsomest buildings with intangible crape, and gives the streets an appearance of funereal mourning.

[Rideing then summarizes the history of Liverpool commerce.]

Passing Hilbre Island, which is insular at high tide only, and the Bell buoy, which peals out sadly at the rocking of the waves, the inward-bound ships enter the populous part of the river as they go by the Perch Rock Light—a circular tower of Anglesey granite in the same style as the celebrated Poldystone. On the western or Cheshire side there are the watering-place suburbs, New Brighton, Egremont, and Seacombe, the former two having ornamental iron promenades extending into the river, with landing-stages for steamboats at the ends. Near Seacombe a river wall of masonry begins, and continues as far south as Tranmere, passing along the borders of Woodside (the Brooklyn of Liverpool), Monk's Ferry, and the ship-building yards of the Lairds, who have launched scores of vessels that are celebrated, including the piratical *Alabama*. As far as the eye can reach on the Lancashire side there is a granite wall, like a splendid fortification, and behind this are the docks, with myriad masts rising from them, and a black net-work of rigging. The tide runs strong and fast, and difference between high tide and low tide is never less than fourteen feet; some times it is six feet more. When it is high, not more than eight or nine feet of the wall are seen; and when it is low, the whole height is visible, the lower part being green and brown with sea-weed and barnacles. Whatever its condition is, the shipping in the docks rides securely at an approximation to high-water mark, the water in them being kept at a uniform height by means of enormous flood-gates. The town is built upon a hill, but in ordinary weather the elevations are hidden in the smoke, and only the enormous rectangular warehouses, six or seven stories high—commercial fortresses, built of iron, brick and granite—can be discovered.

The scene of the river is active and exhilarating, and is particularly notable for the number of ocean-going steamers which it includes. Ten of the transatlantic lines, which have regular sailings, and employ the largest and best class of vessels, are established in Liverpool, some dispatching one and others two or three a week for New York, Quebec, Boston, Philadelphia, or New Orleans; and it is common to see a group formed of a representative vessel of each—one with the chaste white and black funnel of the Inman line, another with the startling red of the Cunard, another with the tasteful pink and white of the Allan line, another with the fashionable stocking-lie cardinal red and black of the Gnion line, another with the key-stone red and white design of the American line, another with the pure white of the National, and another with the creamy yellow of the White Star. There are other lines sailing to American ports at uncertain intervals, and a very extensive fleet of steamers is employed in the Mediterranean, Baltic, and coasting trades, most of them being of recent build, iron in material, and graceful in outlines. One is distinguished from the other by the colour of the funnel, and the same badge is used by the various tow-boats on the river. The tow-boats are broad-beamed side-wheelers, much larger and stauncher-looking than those in American harbours, the opposite being the case with the ferry-boats, which, excepting a few instances, are smaller and less commodious than those of New York, Boston, or San Francisco. The brilliancy of the funnels often relieves the dullness of the smoky pall upon the river, to which each one of the steamers, large and small, bound seawise or coastwise, contributes voluminously. Much have the Americans to be thankful for in the plenitude of anthracite, whose blue, spirit-like emanations do not cast upon their buildings a homogeneous gloom, nor seal the precious beauty of the sky. Soft bituminous coal is used in Liverpool, and the fairest days are choked by its contaminating, soot-distributing vapours.

Besides the steamers, a flotilla of sailing craft is constantly beating to and fro upon the river—handsome clippers which unite Occident and Orient, the pleasure yachts of the merchants, spry schooners, and bulky 'flats.' The latter are consummately ugly, lacking all the airiness that makes other vessels life-like and inspired. They are of great breadth, depth, and carrying capacity, but when they are loaded, only a few feet of their black and unornamental hulls are visible. A short thick mast gives them some resemblance to a sloop; their sails, like those of the fishing boats in the harbour and channel, are dyed to a copper bronze, and they drift inertly and ungracefully in the way of finer and larger vessels.

[Rideing describes the effects on Mersey shipping of stormy weather.]

Let us now glance at the arrangements for the landing and embarkation of passengers. The difference between high water and low water is so great that entrance to or from the docks can only be had when the tide is full, and for the same reason passengers can not be landed or taken on board vessels at the sea-wall except at certain hours. The passenger traffic, both on the numerous ferries and from ocean and coast wise steamers, is too large and important for restrictions, and the difficulty was met and removed by the construction of a floating landing-stage, placed at a central part of the river-front, and connected with the masonry sea-wall by hinged bridges. The stage rose and fell with the tide; when the tide was high, the bridges were level with the sea-wall, and when it was low, they formed an inclined plane, affording at all times a safe and commodious way to or from the vessels moored alongside the stage. The earliest structure being reserved for the ferry-boats, a second one was built a little to the south of the first for ocean and coastwise traffic, and after many years the two were united—an improvement which, with others in the approaches and docks, cost $20,000,000. The completion of the alterations was to have been celebrated in the autumn of 1874, and the Duke of Edinburgh had accepted an invitation to officiate, but an explosion of gas occurred, and the work was destroyed. As the disheartening news spread through the town, it was taken with ridicule and incredulity. 'Tell us that the deep and broad Mersey is ablaze!' said the confident citizen, with a pleasant touch of the Lancashire dialect in his voice, and he would not believe until the flames were reflected in the sky and still more positive ocular proof was given. The famous Brasseys [Thomas Brassey was a leading civil engineer of the period] were employed in March 1878, and it is the finest of the kind in the world. The new stage is 2052 feet in length, and from 80 to over 100 feet in width. The floating power is supplied by iron pontoons, upon which are placed five longitudinal iron kelsons twenty feet apart, and across the kelsons is a series of iron beams forming the support of the greenheart planking constituting the deck. The entire structure is kept in position by several heavy moving chains attached to the masonry of the sea-wall, and by four iron booms. It is approached by seven iron bridges for pedestrians, and a floating-bridge 300 feet long and 40 feet wide for vehicles. Nearly all the passenger traffic of the port is conducted by it, and not less than 50,000 persons use it daily, one ferry alone carrying 28,000 in every twenty-four hours, or 10,500,000 in a year. The passengers from the American and other foreign steamers are landed upon it by steam-tenders, which illustrate by their defective form the amazing conservatism and eyelessness to comfort of the English in their travelling arrangements. The only cabin is in the hold of the boat, and the seats on deck are insufficient and uncomfortable. When the passengers are disembarked upon the stage, however, the other provisions are found to be admirable. The baggage is carried by broad-backed licensed porters from the tender into a large well lighted and ventilated hall, the packages of each passenger are put together, an unusually courteous species of a customs officer examines them, and when they are passed, the porters shoulder them and carry them to the cabs, which are waiting at the head of the bridges, charging twenty-four cents for each trunk and twelve cents for each smaller package. These porters are under police supervision, and are uniformed, wearing a numbered brass badge on the right arm, and a peaked cap with a broad red band; they dress in white mole-skin, and though most of them are under-sized, the ease with which they seize a monstrous Saratoga, swing it upon their shoulders, and trot up hill with it is surprising.

In addition to the Customs Boarding Station the stage is provided with spacious sheds for the shelter of passengers, refreshment-rooms, a telegraph-office, post-office letter-boxes, and offices in which parcels may be left until called for or forwarded. It has the appearance of a great barge, and its ponderous bulk is unshaken in the heaviest gale. There is animation at all times, and life in many varieties is discovered upon it. A large proportion of the eager crowd is in a nervous hurry to catch a boat or train, and the anxiety about tickets or baggage removes the mask of self-consciousness from the throng—the man who struts when he feels that he is being looked at resumes his natural shambling and ungraceful gait; the fastidious young lady forgets her deportment, and gathers her skirts in her hands to dash for a departing steamer, her bland smile changing all unawares to an ominous and pink vexation—conceit, affectation, and all insincerities fall off like scales, to be renewed when the actors and actresses recover and find that they are observed. Should our gentle reader stand and watch near Simpson's Bowl, he could not wish for a more stirring sight than that which surrounds him. Parenthetically Simpson is a local oddity, mine host of the landing-stage refreshment-rooms, whose vagaries are mostly philanthropic, and the bowl is a wooden vessel for the reception of contributions to any charity that may be pressing in its necessities. Last June the bowl was out in behalf of the sufferers from the Haydock colliery explosion; day after day the passers-by filled it with coins varying in denominations from farthings to sovereigns, and an amount equivalent to $5000 was collected in this simple way in one month. Previously it had done service for the sufferers of the Indian famine; and because it is placed at a busy part of the stage, and is inclosed by the beneficent atmosphere of charity, it is a good point of view.

The sailor is omnipresent in Liverpool, and the landing-stage is a favourite haunt of his, where he may be seen coming ashore with the tan on his face and hands on the climes which Jean Ingelow prettily speaks of as

> 'that red land
> Where lovely mirage works a broidered hem
> To fringe with phantom palms a rule of sand.'

—coming home with his canvas bag thrown over his shoulder, his heart light, and the pent-up deviltry of a long voyage craving an escape. Ah! And Jack embarks again. It is the same old canvas bag that he carriers with him, but the dissipations of the shore have altered him; his big blue eyes are not quite clear, and his complexion is not so honestly brown. On a calm evening one can hear him and his mates singing as they chase one another around the capstan and drag the anchor up; and the same wind that floats this music brings to the ears the discord of the engine on the modern steamers, which with hissing and coughing puts up sails, works the cables, and does most of the things that belong to the crew on the older-fashioned ships. Now a grizzled veteran saunters past us with a clay pipe in his mouth and his hands in his pockets; he critically examines the various craft in the river, and turns a weather-wise eye up to the sky, shaking his head dubiously at the cumuli which are scudding in from the west. The sea and its messengers have still a charm for him, though they have twisted him with rheumatism and left his frame like a shattered hulk. But what a difference there is between the nautical life known to him, who now looks back upon the bitterest experiences with the tender regret into which memory betrays us, and the nautical life dreamed of and longed for by the school-boys who frequent the landing-stage and watch with ambitious desire the coming and going of the ships! What a difference indeed! and yet only that of the world untried and the aching disappointment of the world grown familiar. As if to broaden the shadow, two baneful touters of a sailors' boarding-house slouch by, uneasy under the gaze of a policeman, and their coarse faces make us think pityingly of the hapless prey that falls to them. Here is a string of emigrants bound for the Inman steamer that lies off the stage—Norsemen with knee-breeches, red or green vests, rows of buttons, and fresh, windy looking faces framed in yellow hair; chubby baby emigrants and withered old dames too frail for the severity of the passage; beetle-browed, iron-featured, bearded Muscovites, whose fur-trimmed, voluminous garments intimate how wild the climate of the steppes is; stolid peasants from Northern Germany; and overdressed Irish girls, who have been visiting the old country, and are returning to break the hearts of the unhappy house-keepers into whose service they enter. Mingling with these alien and yet familiar characters in the homogeneous Liverpool crowd of brisk commercial gentlemen, whose dress is the perfection of the tailor's art, their Albert coats fitting them like a glove, and the trousers idealizing their nether extremities; no matter what the weather is, these 'swells' wear the glossiest of 'top' hats, and a rose or a bunch of geranium adorns the silk lapels of their coats. Other constituents of the crowed are the clerks in suits of rough tweed, with low-crowned felt hats, and short brier pipes in their mouths; substantial girls and matrons with rosy cheeks and blue eyes, and dresses of quiet-coloured fabrics; tremendous market-women, with wicker baskets balanced upon their heads, and short petticoats expanded by the anachronistic crinoline; the dreadful little 'cad,' with loud-patterned clothing and murderous carelessness of the Queen's English; shoe-blacks in the red uniform of the brigade; river pilots with purple faces and voices that seem to come from the abdomen; pitiably ragged urchins, who offer fusees [matches] at two boxes for a penny; and yet more dilapidated mud-larks, who willingly scramble in the oozy mud along the river-wall for any copper thrown to them.

Considering how large the traffic is, the commotion is nothing to what it would be in America. The whistle of the steamers is not used as a signal, except during fogs, and only while the gangway is in position are passengers allowed to embark or disembark, any violation of the rule being attended by the arrest of the offender and his punishment with all the certainty that gives English law its reality and efficacy. The ferry to Woodside, a district of Birkenhead, is perfect in its equipment and management. The boats are similar to the American model; they are all built of iron, and have twin engines, which enable one paddle-wheel to be worked independently of the other; a telegraph communicates the captain's orders to the engineer; the steering is done by steam; smokers are strictly confined to the extreme ends of the deck; ladies have a separate cabin, and a spacious deck house and promenade is provided for both sexes. But the Woodside ferry is alone, and the others are very far behind it.

At the head of the bridges leading to and from the stage there is a carriage concourse, well paved and well lighted, and surrounded by an ornamental wall of brick with stone facings. This is the terminus of several omnibus lines; and at one side of it is a small building used for salt-water bathing, under the management of the corporation. The landing-stage and all the dock estate on both sides of the river are owned and administered by a body known as the Mersey Dock and Harbour Board [established in 1858], which also controls the pilots, and assesses and receives all dues of the port. It consists of twenty-four members, all of whom are honorary in their capacity; four are nominated by the Conservancy Commissioners of the Mersey, and the other twenty are elected by the dock rate-payers. Despite the variety of interests involved and the immensity of the trust, no scandalous charge has ever been brought against the administration, which is solely for the benefit of the port and the country. The value of the estate is about one hundred million dollars, and the income is about five million dollars annually. The docks extend for more than six miles in a continuous line, and comprise about four hundred and twenty acres—two hundred and fifty-five acres, with eighteen miles of quay margin, being on the Liverpool side, and one hundred and sixty-five acres, with nine miles of quay margin, on the Birkenhead side of the river. The total side of which ships can be moored is twenty-seven miles, and every quay is built of solid masonry, granite being the commonest material. The dry or 'graving' docks also are formed of masonry, and a large iron steamer inclosed in one, with her Titanic proportions fully revealed, is a sight to remember. The quays are all covered by substantial sheds or warehouses, those of the new corn dock being ten stories high, with a cellar below the water-level. The corn is conveyed from the vessel by hydraulic machinery into the cellar, which is rat-proof and water-tight, and thence it is raised by an elevator, at the rate of ten tons a minute,

to the parts of the building prepared for its storage, the capacity of
the warehouse being about one hundred and sixty-five thousand
quarters.

The Jack Tars are so numerous an element of the population,
and so inestimably valuable in contributing to the prosperity of
the port, that they are recognized in several institutions established
for their comfort and protection, one of the best being the Sailors'
Home, in Canning Place, a building which covers the whole of a
block.

[Rideing describes the method of paying sailors and the Sailors' Home.]

In the river there are four ships devoted to the education of
boys for the sea. The *Conway* trains the sons of gentlemen for
the position of officers, the *Indefatigable* is intended for poorer
boys, and the *Akbar* and *Clarence* are reformatories for Protestant
and Roman Catholic juvenile offenders respectively. On the
borders of Newsham Park, in a very pretty situation, is the
Seamen's Orphanage—a praiseworthy and extensive charity,
which is familiar by name, at least, to all who have travelled
on the Atlantic. Every ocean steamer collects contributions
from the passengers for it, and it is the beneficiary of those
mid-ocean entertainments which are a delightful feature of the
voyage 'across.' Sothern had played Lord Dundreary in a bleak
northwester for it, Albani has sung for it amid the bluster and
uneasiness of the 'roaring forties', and itinerant talent of all kinds,
from the low level of negro minstrelsy to the poetic and lyric
heights of Ristori, Nilsson, and Salvini, has been volunteered
aboard ship in its behalf. Here, again, the management is intrusted
to ship-owners, captains, and others connected with the interests
whose servants the institution is intended to benefit.

Though Liverpool has no cathedral of medieval splendour, and
few structures antedating the present century, it is a handsome
and substantially built town, with many irregular and precipitous
streets. The later erections indicate the art ambition which prevails
among English architects, and combine the utilitarian element
with the beauty of a correct and sincere style. The commonest
material is a soft yellow or gray sandstone, relieved by pilasters of
blue or red granite; the forms oftenest adopted are the Norman
Gothic and the Renaissance, with now and then an example
of that anthem in stone, the superb Corinthian. There are not
many buildings in the world so chaste, harmonious, massive, and

forcibly beautiful as St George's Hall, in Lime Street. It is 500
feet long, and the eastern façade forms a prostylar colonnade,
with sixteen fluted columns raised upon a wide sweep of steps
from a broad space in front, upon which are equestrian statues of
the Queen and her late consort. The southern portico surmounts
another pedestal of steps 150 feet wide, ending in a pediment,
the entablature of which is enriched by large sculptures executed
under the direction of Sir Charles Eastlake, the subjects being
allegorical of Britannia's reach and power. Within there is a great
hall 190 feet long and 80 feet wide. The ceiling is a continuous
arch 82 feet from the floor, elaborately decorated, and supported
by two rows of polished granite columns, with statuary in marble
panels between them; among others one figure, by Noble, of Sir
Robert Peel, another of Stephenson, by Gibson, and another of
the late Lord Derby. At the north end of the hall is the great
organ, which cost $50,000 and includes a pedal organ, solo organ,
swell organ and choir organ. It has four rows of keys, from GG
to A in altissimo, sixty-three notes, and two octaves and a half
in pedals, from CCC to F, thirty notes. There are 8000 pipes,
from thirty-two feet to three-eighths of an inch in length, and
108 stops, wind being supplied by a steam-engine six horse-
power. The grand hall is used for banqueting and other festivals.
The concert hall in another part of the building is an elliptical
apartment of very beautiful proportions, with about 1400 seats,
and elsewhere under the magnificent roof are the crown court,
the civil court, the sheriff's court, the library, the grand jury-room
and the court of the Duchy of Lancaster. The eastern façade is on
a spacious square at the father side of which is the new depot and
hotel of the London and Northwestern Railway—a building after
the French Renaissance, with a frontage of 317 feet and a height
of 81 feet.

To the north of this, upon a column 118 feet high, is a statue of
the Duke of Wellington, cast from cannon captured at Waterloo—
material poetically meet for the perpetuation of the outward form
of such a man—and behind the column are three light stone,
large, graceful structures, in which are consolidated the popular
agencies for the encouragement of art, science, and literature, that
have never lacked the most generous patronage in Liverpool. The
Free Library and Museum is the farthest west, and was given to
the town by the Anglo-American banker Sir William Brown, to
whom it cost $200,000. The library department has a reading-
room with 59,000 volumes and accommodations for 600 readers,

most of whom belong to the industrial classes. It has a free school of science connected with it, and the demands upon it have been so far in excess of its capacity that a new reading-room, doubling the accommodations, has been built in the form of a rotunda upon adjoining ground. The books are not allowed to be taken way, but there are branch lending libraries at the north and south ends of the town, where, upon the recommendation of two householders, volumes are gratuitously loaned for home reading. The museum is furnished with an aquarium, the extensive natural history collection made by the late Early of Derby, and the famous and priceless Mayor collection of Egyptian, Roman, and British antiquities. Next to the New Reading-room, which is a memorial to a useful member of the library committee, is the Art Gallery, the gift of Sir Andrew Barclay Walker, a local brewer and ex-mayor, which contains a permanent exhibition, including works by all the old Italian masters, Benjamin West, Armitage, David Roberts, Ansdell, Poynter, and Birket Foster.

About a mile way is the noble brown-stone building of the Liverpool College, on Shaw Street, which embodies in its design the hair-splitting but all-potent subdivisions of English society, and consists of three separate schools. The Upper School has two divisions, in which according to the catalogue, 'the pupils are on terms of perfect social equality,' one division preparing pupils for the universities, and the other for commercial pursuits; the Middle School gives 'a complete commercial education;' and the Lower School 'provides a practical education for the trading classes,' the distinction between a complete commercial education and a practical education not being very clear to us. Different charges are made for each grade, and allowances are made in favour of the sons of clergymen and younger sons. Thus the full fees for a boy in Upper School are twenty-two guineas per annum, but a third son is admitted for eighteen guineas, a fourth son for fourteen guineas.

The grandeur of the town is more apparent, however, in the commercial quarter—in the sumptuous offices and in the new Exchange—than in other directions, for Trade is enthroned, with Cotton for prime minister, in Liverpool, and art is pursued for diversion. The Exchange and the Town-hall form a hollow square, with a fine monument to Nelson in the centre, and the open space is called, from the character of its pavement, the Flags, whereon gather the spruce emissaries of the great mercantile houses to transact their business, with a quiet and earnest activity from which the stock-brokers of Wall Street might take a lesson. Between ten and three o'clock the scene is brilliant, and there is always behind it the satisfaction and dismay of those struggles with changing fortune which are hidden in the philosophic and well-bred placidity of the participants.

After the new public offices in Dale Street and St George's Hall, the Exchange Buildings are the handsomest in town. They cover two acres of land; their style is the recurrent French Renaissance, and the material a pale soft stone. The news-room is unusually splendid. It is seventy-five feet high, contains 1500 square yards, and is lighted by a central dome of stained glass, which sheds warm hues on the profuse decorations.

A prosperous multitude fills this neighbourhood. Castle Street, Lord Street, and Bold Street, in the vicinity, are bordered by tempting shops, and the sidewalks swarm with well-dressed pedestrians, but while no English crowd has the colour, vivacity, or dramatic impressiveness of the impatient stream on Broadway, that of Liverpool has less provincialism and more energy than any other north of the Strand. The town has lovely suburbs, among others, West Derby, Hoylake, Garston, Hale, Childwall, and Woolton, where the merchant princes live in houses set amid the umbrageous privacy of magnificent parks.

But Liverpool is iniquitous, and the phase of life revealed in Scotland Road is peculiarly revolting, not so much from its poverty and squalor, the sad attendants of all large cities, as from its utter and irremediable brutality. A journalistic friend of mine assures me that the leering, pallid, hollow-cheeked rough of New York is more offensive than his congener in Liverpool; that the former assumes the dress of a gentleman, and speaks of himself as one, while the latter has some sort of a frank recognition of his nature and position. If one is at all worse than the other, it appears to us to be the Liverpool species, however; and an amusement in which he develops himself and has the advantage of the American is wife-beating. A walk down Scotland Road on Monday mornings shows in extraordinary number of women bearing in bandaged heads and black eyes the testimony of the rough's Sunday recreation; and the women fight fiercely and frequently among themselves, no less than four combats of Amazons coming under our observation within half an hour one evening. At every street corner there is a flaring pubic-house or saloon, and strong drink is consumed in larger quantities than elsewhere in Great Britain. As a natural consequence of this drunkenness, the work-house, or paupers' retreat, is the most extensive in the kingdom; and Liverpool, despite her prosperity and grandeur, is afflicted with incomparable poverty.

William H. Rideing, 'England's Great Sea-Port', *Harper's New Monthly Magazine*, 344:58 (January 1879), pp. 161–75.

Chadwick and The Liverpool Exhibition of 1886

In December 1885 the American journal *The Manufacturer and Builder* announced the forthcoming International Exhibition of Navigation, Travelling, Commerce and Manufactures, which would take place in Liverpool the following year. A round letter was quoted as stating that 'the exhibition is intended to illustrate travelling by sea, land and air, and as allied to this subject, will also be shown exhibits representative of the manufactures and commerce of the world, bearing upon the means and methods of movement from place to place'. The exhibition consisted of special buildings erected for the occasion on a site bordered by Edge Lane. It was opened by Queen Victoria on 11 May 1886 and ran until 8 November. In the following extracts from an 1887 report on the exhibition, Commander F. E. Chadwick of the U.S. Navy concentrates on the rapid developments in technology and, not surprisingly, its military applications. Chadwick's compatriot Francis Barber Ogden, who served as American Consul in Liverpool from 1829 to 1840, had himself played a leading role in developing steam propulsion for boats. The first iron boat with a screw propeller to sail in American waters was built in Liverpool under Ogden's supervision.

It is a wonderful fact in the swift expansion of mechanical knowledge and appliances of the last hundred years that while for unknown ages the wind was the only propelling force used for purposes of navigation, apart from the rude application of power through oars worked by men, the whole scheme of steam transport has grown, practically, to its present wonderful perfection with the lifetime of men yet living.
[...]
A graphic history of the wonderful changes wrought in the great factor of the work's progress was set forth during the summer of 1886, at the International Exhibition at Liverpool, where by model and drawing, the various steps were made more completely visible and tangible than, perhaps, ever before. True, the relics of the earlier phases of the steamship age, when its believers were but

few and generally of small account, were sparse, but the exhibits of later models, from the date of the inception of transatlantic traffic, preparations for which were begun in earnest by laying down the steamship Great Western exactly fifty years ago, were frequent enough, and the whole of the steps in the development of the means of ocean traffic from then till now are sufficiently well shown.

The exhibition, of course, did not confine itself to the steam era alone. It even had a model of an Egyptian vessel, which was exhibited by the Liverpool Library Society, as taken from Thebes, and estimated to date about 1,500 years BC, and which Moses himself might thus have seen. It was long stretch, however, to the next in date, as no other antedated 1700 AD. There were many of the handsome and dignified eighteenth-century men-of-war, built at the time when men began to preserve a record of their work in the miniature shops which are now esteemed an essential addition to almost every vessel of importance put afloat. Firms now exist whose only business it is to make the various minute fittings—the ports, chains, anchors, blocks, etc.—of the Lilliputian craft, so that every detail of the original is given with an exact verisimilitude in very often most beautiful and elaborate work.

It would have been very interesting had the early struggles of the steamboat been this illustrated *in extensor*, but these is nothing of its concrete history earlier than a small model of the original Comet, built by Henry Bell, at Glasgow, in 1812, and so named because of the extraordinary comet of that year, and the engines of her successor, built in 1820. These recall, however, the vessel which was the first steamer engaged in passenger traffic in Europe, and thus worthy of honour.

In looking over the beautiful array of models which thus represented almost every stage of progress in British steamship building, from the Comet onward, one cannot help regretting that an effort had not been made by our Government to bring together models, of which there must be some, at least, available, illustrative of our earlier practice, particularly as there is much in it peculiar to us, and which would have been most interesting to the great public which visited the exhibition. Models of the Clermont; of the Stevens experimental screw boat; a later Mississippi steamer; the Savannah—the first vessel using steam which ever crossed the Atlantic; the Washington, the pioneer of regular transatlantic steam traffic under our flag; the Adriatic; the Hudson River and great

Sound steamers of today, would, apart from any warship models of interest which could have been sent, have made a most interesting and attractive collection. The only things, however, which were visible were the drawings of a New York ferry-boat (the type of which, by the way, we owe to Fulton), so placed as to be scarcely discoverable. These boats are so typical, so different from anything found in Europe, and so interesting to any student of steam ferriage, that a complete model of the boat and its ferry slip would have been a most satisfactory addition.

Ships, both for war and for peaceful pursuits, of almost every European type were present, with the exception of the great armour-clads of France; but the examples I have just mentioned were certainly needed to round out the exhibition to a complete show of varieties employed in passenger traffic. It must be remembered that the steamboat had in its earlier days a much greater extension in America than elsewhere. Our great rivers were an especially attractive field for is use. The Mississippi had but lately come under our control, and the beginning of the great tide of Western emigration and exploration was almost coincident with the steamboat's advent, so that through these favouring conditions it had a much more rapid growth among us than elsewhere.

The display, however, of British models was as complete as it could well be made. Private owners and builders, the Admiralty, and Lloyds' Registry, united to make the collection a very complete and perfect one. Of continental European exhibits, that of the Italian Government, which sent a very splendid collection of models of its great war-ships, was the most important. Associated with it was the exhibit of the Fratelli Orlando of Leghorn who have done much of both the public and private building of Italy. The only French exhibit was that of the Bureau Veritas, which followed the example of its English rival, Lloyds, in making a very striking and instructive show.

The only exhibits of modern war-ships were those of England and Italy, unless we except the numerous vessels built for foreign powers by English builders. The remainder of the display was chiefly connected with the strife of commerce, and in this it is likely to remain as complete and comprehensive as can be made in some time to come. It is one also in which Britain may well take pride, as however great we ourselves were as pioneers or as more than equals in the beginning of the race, we have long since been distanced by our kinsmen, and we must refer to Great Britain to study the principal changes in hull and machinery of the last half-century.

Commander F. E. Chadwick, 'The Development of the Steamship, and the Liverpool Exhibition of 1886', *Scribner's Magazine*, 1:5 (May 1887), pp. 515–43.

The novelist **Willa Cather** (1873–1947) made her first trip to Europe in 1902. She sailed with her companion Isabella McClung from Philadelphia on the *Noorland* and reached Liverpool in time to witness the coronation celebrations for Edward VII, who had acceded to the throne in 1901. His coronation was initially set for 26 June 1902 but it had to be postponed until 19 August because of the king's appendicitis. Cather stayed in the Northwestern Hotel, adjoining Lime Street Station, and she financed her trip by writing a series of travel sketches for the *Nebraska State Journal*. Her next stops after Liverpool were Chester, Shropshire, and London. Liverpool clearly impressed her as spectacle, but the impact on her of working-class dress and behaviour was clearly a shock, even more so when she reported on the East End of London. Cather is mainly remembered for her novels of Nebraska life, but she wrote her experience of transatlantic travel into her 1912 novel *Alexander's Bridge*, which revolves around cultural comparisons.

Liverpool, July 1, 1902

On the 26th of June Liverpool presented such an array of colour, flowers, and banners as very nearly disguised the grimness of the city itself. We arrived at about eight o'clock of the most radiant of June mornings, and our drive to the Northwestern Hotel was under canopies, arches, and flags. From pillar to pillar along the sidewalks ran chains of paper roses for miles. Everywhere hung pictures of the King and Queen. The shops were all closed, and workingmen were standing about the streets, yet there was a palpable shadow in the air that did not belong to a festival. Even had the news of the King's illness not reached us at Queenstown, we would certainly have recognized symptoms of discomfiture in the streets of Liverpool. Moreover, in hundreds of places the silk draperies which bore the inscription 'God Save the King' had been torn down and others substituted with the legend 'God Rise Our King.'

The Northwestern Hotel, at which my friend and I stopped, is

directly opposite the public square and St. George's Hall, which
is by far the finest building in Liverpool. The square was a sheet
of blazing sunshine that morning, and the Union Jack everywhere
fluttered and tugged in the wind. A blind man with a concertina
played national airs at the foot of a colossal statue of the Duke of
Wellington, that stands on a column 115 feet high. The 'bobbies'
were lined up on the steps of St. George's Hall, and a few redcoats,
with their caps perched at their favourite jaunty angle, and short
canes under their arms, came and went among the groups of people
who thronged the square. A group of girls with their hair hanging
loose over their shoulders, and the most strident voices imaginable,
sold flowers at the foot of an equestrian statue, done in bronze by
Thornycroft when the Empress was a young woman.

Although the whole effect was remarkably gay, there was
nothing of the smartness and neatness and trimness of an
American crowd. The square as a whole presented a beautiful
variation of line and colour, but the majority of the individuals
who made up these dark splotches on the yellow plane were far
from lovely. The dress of English women, and of English men
of the working class, is frankly a shock at first, no matter how
catholic one may be in such matters. I have been in England a
week now, and I have not seen one English girl or woman of
the middle class who is not stoop shouldered to a painful degree,
or who does not stand with her chest sunk in and the lower
part of the torso thrust forward. Even in the little, little girls
one sees the beginning of it—the topping of the shoulders and
contraction of the chest. This unfortunate carriage is so universal
that it amounts to a national disfigurement among the women.
Girls with the skin of a rose, and well-featured enough, have the
figures of riddled old dames. Their dress is almost as remarkable.
The American idea of neatness, of being genuine as far as you
go, of having little and having it good, which at home even the
shop girls imbibe more or less of, prevails not at all here. The
streets are always full of badly made, home-concocted silks and
satins and lawns and dimities. No shirtwaist is complete without a
daub of penny lace on it, no skirt is correct unless it trails in the
back, is too short in front, and is a cascade of draggled ruffles and
flounces. The railway trains are full of young women travelling
in white muslin, white stockings, and white shoes. Their hats
are something beyond belief. Hats have never at all been one of
the vexing problems of my life, but, indifferent as I am, these
render me speechless. I should think a well taught and tasteful

American milliner would go mad in England, and eventually hang herself with bolts of green and scarlet ribbon—the favourite colour combination in Liverpool. The flower girls have nothing in their trays half as brilliant as the blossoms on their bonnets. The English working girl, and especially the country girl, has a passion for cheap jewellery. She wears the most unblushing frauds of the sort, even to the extent of half a dozen breastpins at once. However, I am not at all sure that I would be willing to exchange the pretty voice. After hearing only English voices for a few days, the first American voice you hear in a boarding-house is very apt to suggest something of the nature of burrs or sandpaper.

On the afternoon of the 26th we went to see the poor of Liverpool fed at St. George's Hall, just across the street. The lord mayor and lord mayoress had arranged to dine all the worthy aged poor there, in honour of the new King's ascent to the throne; and in accordance to the King's wish that all the coronation festivities in which the poor were to receive gratuities should be carried out, the great dinner was given on the day set for it. There were over five hundred guests entertained in all, each of the guests being over sixty years old, and some upwards of ninety. The dinner consisted of roast beef, vegetables, plum pudding, beer. As the guests left the hall, they were each presented with packages of tea and sugar, and the men with plugs of tobacco. While the old folks were eating, Mr. Roberts, organist of St. Paul's, played the coronation march written by Mackenzie for the coronation of Edward VII, and afterward 'Zadock, the Priest,' one of the suite of four numbers written by Handel for the coronation of George II and Queen Caroline.

Constant comparisons are the stamp of the foreigner; one continually translates manners and customs of a new country into the terms of his own, before he can fully comprehend them. There are so many thoroughly engaging and attractive things about English life and people that it is not a little satisfaction to be able to say to oneself that in no American city could be nurtured such an array of poverty and decrepitude as filed into St. George's Hall on that holiday. They seemed worn to the bone, some of them, and all of them had had a sixty years' tussle with poverty in a land where the competition is exceedingly close. There was very little sullenness, however; they seemed as eager and pleased as children; and as the caterer's men, all in white duck, carried huge cauldrons up the street and into the side door, the long file of poor inhaled the savoury odour from the kettles with smiling satisfaction.

Every old dame who had a red rag of a flower in her black

bonnet was happy. The tickets which admitted guests to the hall had been distributed by the vestrymen and the guardians of the poor. Of course a great number of people arrived who had no tickets, hulks of drunken old sailors, whom you see everywhere in Liverpool, poor old women, who had, everyone, an excuse, but never a ticket when the cooks and the cauldrons arrived, and the odour of the food whetted their appetites. Some of them became quite desperate, and tried by every means to smuggle themselves into the happy ticket line, fairly clawing at the bobbies, who gently put them back. Some sat down on the steps and cried bitterly into their aprons; some railed upon the falseness and futility of human institutions in general. When we came out from the hall half an hour later, they were still there, held by the tantalizing odour; scolding, crying, sulking, so old and tired and poor that one's heart went out to them who had not on the wedding garment. The cause of their misfortune was not apparent; perhaps they were professional beggars; perhaps they had bad records behind them; but their age was evident enough, and their hunger, and when at last the bobbies drove them even from the steps, one could not help regretting their defeat.

The feeling of sympathy for the King seems to be a very genuine one. Most English people think he has not been altogether justly used. They believe Queen Victoria should have abdicated twenty years ago, when she retired to nurse her private sorrow [on the death of Prince Albert]. These twenty years, they say, Edward has been doing the sovereign's work, with none of the sovereign's perquisites. The evidence seems to be very much against the American notion that the King's life has been one rosy path of wine and song. A detailed account of the daily routine the King has gone through for the last twenty years rather staggers one. He embodies many of those qualities which the English people esteem most highly. He is a good sportsman, he can do a great deal of work without making any display, his personal courage is as unquestioned as his generosity. Even his extravagant taste for boxing and the turf endears him, not only to the smart world, but to the common people as well. His son, the present Prince of Wales, is the antithesis to his father, and is exceedingly unpopular. He is said to be foppish and effeminate to the last degree.

Willa Cather, 'Liverpool', *Nebraska State Journal* (1902);
collected in George N. Kates, ed., *Willa Cather in Europe*
(Lincoln, NB: University of Nebraska Press, 1988).

W. D. Howells (1837–1920), the prolific novelist and editor, first sailed to Liverpool in 1861 on his way to take up a consulship in Venice. Like Hawthorne, he was awarded this office in thanks for writing a campaign biography for President Lincoln. Howells had been reviewing travel books for years by the beginning of the twentieth century, when he published three books about Britain: *London Films* (1906), *Certain Delightful English Towns* (1906) and *Seven English Cities* (1909). In these volumes Howells casts himself as a typical traveller, shaping his impressions of places for the reader. *Seven English Cities* gives pride of place to Liverpool in its opening essay, reprinted here, and then surveys a number of other towns including Manchester, York and Doncaster. At the end of the volume, like Horace Greeley and other travellers, Howells tries to sum up his sense of the English, admitting that Emerson had already done a superlative job in his *English Traits*. He distinguishes his own approach to Liverpool from that of the Baedeker guidebook and towards the end of *Seven English Cities* declares his policy of making contact with the locals: 'I always talked with the lower classes when I could.' The Liverpool he describes below is a modern city with a well-developed transport system. The overhead railway had opened in 1893 and the tramway had become fully electrified by 1903. The latter's terminus in Crosby – Howells' destination – was at the junction of Cook Road and Victoria Road. He also refers to the Riverside Station of the London and Northwestern Railway, which had opened in 1895 specifically to serve the adjacent Ocean Liner Terminal at the Prince's landing stage.

'A Modest Liking for Liverpool'

Why should the proud stomach of American travel, much tossed in the transatlantic voyage, so instantly have itself carried from Liverpool to any point where trains will convey it? Liverpool is most worthy to be seen and known, and no one who looks up from the bacon and eggs of his first hotel breakfast after landing, and finds himself confronted by the coal-smoked Greek architecture of St. George's Hall, can deny that it is of a singularly noble presence. The city has moments of failing in the promise of this classic edifice, but every now and then it reverts to it, and reminds the traveller that he is in a great modern metropolis of commerce by many other noble edifices.

I

Liverpool does not remind him of this, so much as the good and true Baedeker professes, in the dockside run on the overhead railway (as the place unambitiously calls its elevated road); but then, as I noted in my account of Southampton, docks have a fancy of taking themselves in, and eluding the tourist eye, and even when they 'flank the Mersey for a distance of 6–7 M' they do not respond to American curiosity so frankly as could be wished. They are like other English things in that, however, and it must be said for them that when apparent they are sometimes unimpressive. From my own note-book, indeed, I find that I pretended to think them 'wonderful and almost endless,' and so I dare say they are. But they formed only a very perfunctory interest of our day at Liverpool, where we had come to meet, not to take, a steamer.

Our run from London, in the heart of June, was very quick and pleasant, through a neat country and many tidy towns. In the meadows the elms seemed to droop like our own rather than to hold themselves oakenly upright like the English; the cattle stood about in the yellow buttercups, knee – deep, white American daisies, and red clover, and among the sheep we had our choice of shorn and unshorn; they were equally abundant. Some of the blossomy May was left yet on the hawthorns, and over all the sky hovered, with pale – white clouds in pale – blue spaces of air like an inverted lake of bonnyclabber [thick soured milk eaten with a sweetener]. We stopped the night at Chester, and the next evening, in the full daylight of 7.40, we pushed on to Liverpool, over lovely levels, with a ground swell like that of Kansas plains, under a sunset drying its tears and at last radiantly smiling.

II

The hotel in Liverpool swarmed and buzzed with busy and murmurous American arrivals. One could hardly get at the office window, on account of them, to plead for a room. A dense group of our countrywomen were buying picture-postals of the rather suave office-ladies, and helplessly fawning on them in the inept confidences of American women with all persons in official or servile attendance. 'Let me stay here,' one of them entreated, 'because there's such a draught at the other window. May I?' She was a gentle child of forty-five or fifty; and I do not know whether she was allowed to stay in the sheltered nook or not, tender creature. As she was in everyone else's way there possibly she was harshly driven into the flaw at the other window.

The place was a little America which swelled into larger with the arrivals of the successive steamer, though the soft swift English trains bore our co-nationals away as rapidly as they could. Many familiar accents remained till the morning, and the breakfast-room was full of a nasal resonance which would have made one at home anywhere in our East or West. I, who was then vainly trying to be English, escaped to the congenial top of the farthest bound tram, and flew, at the rate of four miles an hour, to the uttermost suburbs of Liverpool, whither no rumour of my native speech could penetrate. It was some balm to my wounded pride of country to note how pale and small the average type of the local people was. The poorer classes swarmed along a great part of the tramline in side streets of a hard, stony look, and what characterized itself to me as a sort of iron squalor seemed to prevail. You cannot anywhere have great prosperity without great adversity, just as you cannot have day without night, and the more Liverpool evidently flourished the more it plainly languished. I found no pleasure in the paradox, and I was not overjoyed by the inevitable ugliness of the brick villas of the suburbs into which these obdurate streets decayed. But then, after divers tram changes, came the consolation of beautiful riverside beaches, thronged with people who looked gay at that distance, and beyond the Mersey rose the Welsh hills, blue, blue.

III

At the end of the tram-line, where we necessarily dismounted, we rejected a thatched cottage, offering us tea, because we thought it too thatched and too cottage to be quite true (though I do not now say that there were vermin in the straw roof), and accepted the hospitality of a pastry-cook's shop. We felt the more at home with the kind woman who kept it because she had a brother at Chicago in the employ of the Pinkerton Detective Agency, and had once been in Stratford-on-Avon; this doubly satisfied us as cultivated Americans. She had a Welsh name, and she testified to a great prevalence of Welsh and Irish in the population of Liverpool; besides, she sent us to a church of the Crusaders at Little Crosby, and it was no fault of hers that we did not find it. We found one of the many old crosses for which Little Crosby is named, and this was quite as much as we merited. It stood at the intersection of the streets in what seemed the fragment of a village, not yet lost in the vast maw of the city, and it calmed all the simple neighbourhood, so that we sat down at its foot and rested a long, long minute till the tram came by and took us back into the loud, hard heart of Liverpool.

I do not mean to blame it, for it was no louder or harder than the hearts of other big towns, and it had some alleviation from the many young couples who were out together half-holidaying in the unusually pleasant Saturday weather. I wish their complexions had been better, but you cannot have South-of-England colour if you live as far north as Liverpool, and all the world knows what the American colour is. The young couples abounded in the Gallery of Fine Arts, where they frankly looked at one another instead of the pictures. The pictures might have been better, but then they might have been worse (there being examples of Filippo Lippi, Memmi, Holbein, and, above all, the Dante's Dream of Rossetti); and in any case those couples could come and see them when they were old men and women; but now they had one another in a moment of half-holiday which could not last forever.

In the evening there were not so many lovers at the religious meetings before the classic edifice opposite the hotel, where the devotions were transacted with the help of a brass-band; but there were many youths smoking short pipes, and flitting from one preacher to another, in the half-dozen groups. Some preachers were nonconformist, but there was one perspiring Anglican priest who laboured earnestly with his hearers, and who had more of his aspirates in the right place. Many of his hearers were in the rags which seem a favourite wear in Liverpool, and I hope his words did their poor hearts good.

Slightly apart from the several congregations, I found myself with a fellow-foreigner of seafaring complexion who addressed me in an accent so unlike my own American that I ventured to answer him in Italian. He was indeed a Genoese, who had spent much time in Buenos Ayres and was presently thinking of New York; and we had some friendly discourse together concerning the English. His ideas of them were often so parallel with my own that I hardly know how to say he thought them an improvident people. I owned that they spent much more on state, or station, than the Americans; but we neither had any censure for them otherwise. He was of that philosophic mind which one is rather apt to encounter in the Latin races, and I could well wish for his

further acquaintance. His talk rapt me to far other and earlier
scenes, and I seemed to be conversing with him under a Venetian
heaven, among objects of art more convincing than the equestrian
statue of the late Queen, who had no special motive I could think
of for being shown to her rightly loving subjects on horseback.
We parted with the expressed hope of seeing each other again,
and if this should meet his eye and he can recall the pale young
man, with the dark full beard, who chatted with him between the
pillars of the Piazzetta, forty years before our actual encounter I
would be glad of his address.

IV

How strange are the uses of travel! There was a time when the
mention of Liverpool would have conjured up for me nothing
but the thought of Hawthorne, who spent divers dull consular
years there, and has left a record of them which I had read, with
the wish that it were cheerfuler. Yet, now, here on the ground
his foot might have trod, and in the very smoke he breathed, I
did not once think of him. I thought as little of that poor Felicia
Hemans [Liverpool-born poet of the early nineteenth century],
whose poetry filled my school-reading years with the roar of
the wintry sea breaking from the waveless Plymouth Bay on the
stern and rode-bound coast where the Pilgrim Fathers landed on
a boulder measuring eight by ten feet, now fenced in against the
predatory hammers and chisels of reverent visitors. I knew that
Gladstone was born at Liverpool, but not Mrs Oliphant, and the
only literary shade I could summon from a past vague enough to
my ignorance was William Roscoe, whose *Life of Leo X.*, in the
Bohn Library, had been too much for my young zeal when my
zeal was still young. My other memories of Liverpool have been
acquired since my visit, and I now recur fondly to the picturesque
times when King John founded a castle there, to the prouder
times when Sir Francis Bacon represented it in Parliament; or
again to the brave days when it resisted Prince Rupert for three
weeks, and the inglorious epoch when the new city (it was then
only some four or five hundred years old) began to flourish on the
trade in slaves with the colonies of the Spanish Main, and on the
conjoint and congenial traffic in rum, sugar, and tobacco.

It will be suspected from these reminiscences that I have been
studying a page of fine print in Baedeker, and I will not deceive
the reader. It is true; but it is also true that I had some wonder,

altogether my own, that so great a city should make so small an
appeal to the imagination. In this it outdoes almost any metropolis
of our own. Even in journalism, an intensely modern product,
it does not excel; Manchester has its able and well-written
Guardian, but what has Liverpool? Glasgow has its Glasgow
School of Painting, but again what has Liverpool? It is said that
not above a million of its people live in it; all the rest, who can,
escape to Chester, where they perhaps vainly hope to escape
the Americans. There, entrenched in charming villas behind
myrtle hedges, they measurably do so; but Americans are very
penetrating, and I would not be sure that the thickest and highest
hedge was invulnerable to them. As it is, they probably constitute
the best society of Liverpool, which the natives have abandoned
to them, though they do not constitute it permanently, but
consecutively. Every Cunarder, every White Star, pours out upon
a city abandoned by its own good society a flood of cultivated
Americans, who eddy into its hotels, and then rush out of them
by every train within twenty-four hours, and often within
twenty-five minutes. They understand that there are no objects of
interest in Liverpool; and they are not met at the Customs with
invitations to breakfast, luncheon, and dinner from the people
of rank and fashion with whom they have come to associate.
These have their stately seats in the lovely neighbouring country,
but they are not at the landing-stage, and even the uncultivated
American cannot stay for the vast bourgeoisie of which Liverpool,
like the cities of his own land, is composed. Our own cities have
a social consciousness, and are each sensible of being a centre,
with a metropolitan destiny; but the strange thing about Liverpool
and the like English towns is that they are without any social
consciousness. Their meek millions are socially unborn; they
can come into the world only in London, and in their prenatal
obscurity they remain folded in a dreamless silence, while all the
commercial and industrial energies rage round them in a gigantic
maturity.

The time was when Liverpool was practically the sole port
of entry for our human cargoes, indentured apprentices of the
beautiful, the historical. With the almost immediate transference
of the original transatlantic steamship interests from Bristol,
Liverpool became the only place where you could arrive.
American lines, long erased from the seas, and the Inman line,
the Cunard line, the White Star line, and the rest, would land
you nowhere else. Then heretical steamers began to land you at

Glasgow; worse schismatics carried you to Southampton; there were heterodox craft that touched at Plymouth, and now great swelling agnostics bring you to London itself. Still, Liverpool remains the greatest port of entry for our probationers, who are bound out to the hotels and railroad companies of all Europe till they have morally paid back their fare. The superstition that if you go in a Cunarder you can sleep on both ears is no longer so exclusive as it once was; yet the Cunarder continues an ark of safety for the timid and despairing, and the cooking is so much better than it used to be that if in contravention of the old Cunard rule against a passenger's being carried overboard you do go down, you may be reasonably sure of having eaten something that the wallowing sea-monsters will like in you.

I have tried to give some notion of the fond behaviour of the arriving Americans in the hotels; no art can give the impression of their exceeding multitude. Expresses, panting with as much impatience as the disciplined English expresses ever suffer themselves to show, await them in the stations, which are effectively parts of the great hotels, and whir away to London with them as soon as they can drive up from the steamer; but many remain to rest, to get the sea out of their heads and legs, and to prepare their spirits for adjustment to the novel conditions. These the successive trains carry into the heart of the land everywhere, these and their baggage, to which they continue attached by their very heart-strings, invisibly stretching from their first-class corridor compartments to the different luggage-vans. I must say they have very tenderly, very perfectly imagined us, all those hotel people and railroad folk, and fold us, anxious and bewildered exiles, in a reassuring and consoling embrace which leaves all their hands—they are Briarean [many-handed]—free for the acceptance of our wide, wild tips. You may trust yourself implicitly to their care, but if you are going to Oxford do not trust the head porter who tells you to take the London and Northwestern [Railway], for then you will have to change four times on the way and at every junction personally see that your baggage is unladen and started anew to its destination.

W. D. Howells, *Seven English Cities* (1909).

Further Reading

Buzard, James, *The Beaten Track: European Tourism, Literature, and the Ways to 'Culture'* (New York: Oxford University Press, 1993).

Caesar, Terry, *Forgiving the Boundaries: Home as Abroad in American Travel Writing* (Athens, GA: University of Georgia Press, 1995).

Chandler, George, *Liverpool and Literature* (Liverpool: Rondo Publications, 1974).

Coles, Gladys Mary, *Both Sides of the River: Merseyside in Poetry and Prose* (West Kirby: Headland, 1993).

Commager, Henry Steele, ed., *Britain Through American Eyes* (London: The Bodley Head, 1974).

Dulles, Foster Rhea, *Americans Abroad: Two Centuries of European Travel* (Ann Arbor: University of Michigan Press, 1964).

Fish, Audrey A., *American Slaves in Victorian England: Abolitionist Politics in Popular Literature and Culture* (Cambridge: Cambridge University Press, 2000).

Foster, Shirley, *Across New Worlds: Nineteenth-Century Women Travellers and their Writings* (Hemel Hempstead: Harvester Wheatsheaf, 1990).

——, *American Women Travellers to Europe in the Nineteenth and Early Twentieth Centuries* (British Association for American Studies, 1994) and at http://baas.ac.uk/resources/pamphlets/pamphdets.asp?id=27/

Gilman, William M., *Melville's Early Life and 'Redburn'* (New York: New York University Press, 1951).

Jones, Ron, *The American Connection* (Moreton: Ron Jones, 1986).

Kenin, Richard, *Return to Albion: Americans in England, 1760–1940* (New York: Holt, Rinehart & Winston, 1979).

Lawrence, Elwood P., *Henry George and the British Isles* (New York: Robert Schalkenbach Foundation, 1957).

Le Clair, Robert Charles, *Three American Travellers in England: James Russell Lowell, Henry Adams, Henry James* (Westport, CT: Greenwood Press, 1978).

Lockwood, Allison, *Passionate Pilgrims: The American Traveller in Great Britain, 1800–1914* (Madison, NJ: Fairleigh Dickinson University Press, 1981).

Mays, James O'Donald, *Mr. Hawthorne Goes to England: The Adventures of a Reluctant Consul* (Ringwood: New Forest Leaves, 1983).

Milton, David Hepburn, *Lincoln's Spymaster: Thomas Haines Dudley and the Liverpool Network* (Mechanicsburg, PA: Stackpole Books, 2003).

Mulhearn, Deborah, ed., *Mersey Minis. Volume 1: Landing* (Liverpool: Capsica, 2007).

Mulvey, Christopher, *Anglo-American Landscapes: A Study of Nineteenth-Century Anglo-American Travel Literature* (Cambridge: Cambridge University Press, 1983).

——, *Transatlantic Manners: Social Patterns in Nineteenth-Century Anglo-American Travel Literature* (Cambridge: Cambridge University Press, 1990).

Nash, Paul, 'Innocents Abroad: American Students at British Universities in the Early Nineteenth Century', *History of Education Quarterly*, 1 (1961), pp. 32–44, and at

http://www.jstor.org/view/00182680/ap020004/02a00050/0

Rennella, Mark, and Whitney Walton, 'Planned Serendipity: American Travellers and the Transatlantic Voyage in the Nineteenth and Twentieth Centuries', *Journal of Social History*, 38:ii (2004), pp. 365–83, and at

http://muse.jhu.edu/journals/journal_of_social_history/v038/38.2rennella.html

Schriber, Mary Suzanne, ed., *Telling Travel: Selected Writings by Nineteenth-Century American Women Abroad* (DeKalb, IL: Northern Illinois University Press, 1995).

Scudder, Townsend III, 'Emerson's British Lecture Tour, 1847–1848, Part I: The Preparations for the Tour, and the Nature of Emerson's Audiences', *American Literature*, 7:i (1935), pp. 15–36.

——, 'Emerson's British Lecture Tour, 1847–1848, Part II: Emerson as Lecturer in Britain and the Reception of the Lectures', *American Literature*, 7:ii (1935), pp. 166–80.

Smith, Harold F., *American Travellers Abroad: A Bibliography of Accounts Published Before 1900*, 2nd edition (Lanham, MD: Scarecrow Press, 1999).

Spiller, Robert E., *The American in Europe During the First Half Century of Independence* [1924] (Philadelphia: Porcupine Press, 1976).

Stowe, William W., *Going Abroad: European Travel in Nineteenth-Century American Culture* (Princeton: Princeton University Press, 1994).

Thorp, Willard, 'Redburn's Prosy Old Guidebook', *Publications of the Modern Language Association*, 53 (1938), pp. 1146–56, and at

http://www.jstor.org/view/00308129/ap020250/02a00160/0

Ziff, Larzer, *Return Passages: Great American Travel Writing, 1780–1910* (New Haven: Yale University Press, 2000).

Note: Most of the material reproduced in this volume is available on the Internet. One of the most useful sites devoted to Americans abroad in the nineteenth century can be found at

http://www.digitalbookindex.org/_SEARCH/search010histusamericans abroada.asp/